Congress Resurgent

Mershon Center Series on International Security and Foreign Policy

The Mershon Center of The Ohio State University develops and promotes a series of edited books to encourage original scholarship and vigorous exchanges among leading authorities on key issues in international security and foreign policy. Each book is edited by a Mershon Center faculty associate, sometimes in collaboration with another leading expert, who defines a perspective on a topic in international security or foreign policy. Leading authorities on the identified topic are invited to prepare draft essays, which are discussed at one or more conferences sponsored by the Center. Authors who make a significant contribution to the subject are invited to revise their essays for inclusion in an edited volume.

Located on The Ohio State University campus in Columbus, Ohio, the Mershon Center is a multidisciplinary facility seeking security and peace through innovative scholarship and education. Current titles in the book series are below:

Allan R. Millett and Williamson Murray, editors,
Military Effectiveness: The First World War

Allan R. Millett and Williamson Murray, editors,
Military Effectiveness: The Interwar Period

Allan R. Millett and Williamson Murray, editors,
Military Effectiveness: The Second World War

George E. Hudson, editor,
Soviet National Security Policy under Perestroika

Margaret P. Karns and Karen A. Mingst, editors,
The United States and Multilateral Institutions

Randall B. Ripley and James M. Lindsay, editors,
Congress Resurgent: Foreign and Defense Policy on Capitol Hill

Congress Resurgent

Foreign and Defense Policy on Capitol Hill

Edited by
Randall B. Ripley and James M. Lindsay

A book in the Mershon Center Series on
International Security and Foreign Policy

Ann Arbor

THE UNIVERSITY OF MICHIGAN PRESS

Library of Congress Cataloging-in-Publication Data

Congress resurgent : foreign and defense policy on Capitol Hill /
  edited by Randall B. Ripley and James M. Lindsay.
       p.   cm. — (Mershon Center series on international security
  and foreign policy.)
     Includes bibliographical references and index.
     ISBN 0-472-09533-1 (alk. paper). — ISBN 0-472-06533-5 (pbk. :
  alk. paper)
     1. United States. Congress—History—20th century.   2. United
  States—Foreign relations—1945–   3. United States—Military policy.
  I. Ripley, Randall B.   II. Lindsay, James M., 1959–   .
  III. Series.
  JK1081.C658   1993
  327.73'07658—dc20   93-16033
                                                               CIP

A CIP catalogue record for this book is available from the British Library.

Preface

The U.S. Congress has long played an important role in various aspects of foreign and defense policy. In the last several decades that role has grown. With the momentous changes in the world in the late 1980s and early 1990s, all the governing institutions of the nation are faced with major new challenges. Congress, newly self-confident in the foreign and defense arena after the Vietnam War, will—for good or for ill—play a major part in shaping the U.S. response to the new challenges. These facts of recent history and the short-range future helped stimulate this book.

A second stimulus is the fact that scholars from two major research communities within the discipline of political science—one focusing on Congress as an institution and the other focusing on the substance of foreign and defense policy—have not been in the habit of working together to pose questions that require research. They see even less of each other in the conduct of that research. This situation is understandable but, in our view, in need of change.

This book is a serious attempt to help change the situation. It did not come about by chance, but was the product of a project structured both to address interesting and important questions and to bring scholars from the two research communities together. A small steering committee composed of individuals from both communities discussed the design of the entire project in early 1990. Nearly thirty scholars participated in a conference in Columbus, Ohio, in September 1990. The purpose of the conference was to set an agenda for research and writing on the general topic of Congress and foreign and defense policy. Conferees focused on issues raised by seven discussion papers.

A subset of the first conferees, augmented by additional scholars, committed themselves to writing fully developed papers for a second conference convened to examine the topics treated in this volume. That conference was held in Columbus in September 1991. Each paper was presented and discussed by all of the authors. For a number of months after the second conference the volume editors worked with the individual authors to help them produce drafts that would stand as independent contributions but also would fit well together, allowing a genuine book to emerge.

The project was designed from the outset to produce an integrated book. We have included a diversity of authors in terms of their experience, the topics on which they have written, and the approaches they have used in dealing with those topics. But we have also sought to produce a volume with a discernible focus in which the whole is greater than the sum of the parts.

Two institutions have provided the resources for this project: the Mershon Center of Ohio State University and the Midwest Consortium for International Security Studies (MCISS). We are grateful to those institutions and especially to the director of the Mershon Center, Charles F. Hermann, and the executive associate of MCISS, Marian Rice.

We are also grateful to a variety of professional colleagues who have contributed to this project in many ways: the authors of the chapters; other participants in the two conferences; members of the MCISS Steering Committee; and colleagues who reviewed the entire manuscript.

Contents

Part 1.
The Research Challenge

CHAPTER 1

Foreign and Defense Policy in Congress:
An Overview and Preview

Randall B. Ripley and James M. Lindsay

Today the United States faces a watershed in its history. The collapse of the Soviet Union is forcing the first major rethinking in more than forty years of the premises of U.S. foreign policy. The choices that are made will determine what role the United States will play in world affairs as it heads into the twenty-first century. The outcome of the current debate over the future of U.S. foreign policy also will have major ramifications for defense policy. This, in turn, will influence the health of the American economy because the defense industry employs roughly one of every ten workers engaged in manufacturing and because resources saved by reductions in defense spending could be used to revitalize the American economy.

The demise of the Soviet Union made debate over the fundamental goals of U.S. foreign policy inevitable. But other events also are forcing a rethinking of U.S. foreign policy. China's continuing suppression of political dissent and its sale of ballistic missile technology to third world countries have put the future of amicable U.S. relations with the world's most populous country in doubt. The erosion in America's international economic competitiveness, the continued strength of the Japanese economy, and the economic unification of Europe all threaten America's position as the world's preeminent power. Environmental problems such as ozone depletion and global warming raise the potential for global catastrophe. Brutal civil wars—such as those in Afghanistan, Mozambique, Somalia, and the former Yugoslavia—provide severe tests of claims about a new world order.

Which institutions and individuals in the United States will shape America's response to its foreign policy challenges? The answer to this question matters because various institutions and individuals have different agendas and will work on behalf of very different policies.

An obvious answer to the question of who makes U.S. foreign policy is the president and the foreign policy bureaucracies. Whatever one's views of the person occupying the Oval Office at any given time, the president is the

3

one person to whom the entire nation looks for leadership on foreign and defense policy. As for the foreign policy bureaucracies, they do much more than simply implement programs. By virtue of their size, expertise, and control over information, the Department of Defense, the State Department, the National Security Council staff, and related federal agencies exercise tremendous influence over the course of American foreign and defense policy.

From the early 1950s until the mid-1970s, the list of who mattered in the realm of foreign and defense policy stopped with the president and the national security bureaucracy. In the era of the "imperial presidency," the executive branch was not only the center of the foreign policy universe but, for all intents and purposes, it was the universe. Presidential domination of foreign policy was reflected in the writing of political scientists. Most scholars interested in foreign policy-making studied the presidency and the executive branch more broadly. Other potential foreign policy actors, most notably Congress, drew scant attention (see, for example, Allison 1971; Halperin 1974; Huntington 1961; and Steinbruner 1974).

The scant attention paid to Congress by scholars in the foreign policy realm in the quarter century between 1950 and 1975 reflected the dramatic change that was then occurring in the congressional role in foreign policy. It had been important during much of our earlier history. For example, no major treaty passed the Senate between 1871 and 1898, which surely must have frustrated the administrations of the day. The failure of the Senate to ratify the Treaty of Versailles was literally a fatal blow to President Wilson. Franklin Roosevelt faced a series of neutrality acts that kept him from pursuing the policies he favored in Europe as Hitler became more and more powerful. In the years immediately following World War II, Congress played a key role in shaping the policy initiatives that led to the creation of the United Nations, the North Atlantic Treaty Organization (NATO), and the Marshall Plan for Europe (Cheever and Haviland 1952; Schlesinger 1973).

Yet, beginning in the early 1950s, members of Congress increasingly came to define their role in foreign policy as one of deferring to the wishes of the president. Although congressional deference to the executive branch was never complete—one need only recall the heated debates over the fall of Nationalist China, the Bricker Amendment, and the missile gap—on most foreign policy issues members of Congress eagerly followed the lead of the president (Carroll 1966; Kolodziej 1975; Manley 1971; Moe and Teel 1971; Robinson 1967). Congressional deference to executive authority was most vividly apparent when Congress passed resolutions in 1955, 1957, and 1964 authorizing the president to employ the armed forces of the United States as he deemed necessary to respond to crises in Formosa (Taiwan), Lebanon, and the Gulf of Tonkin. President Johnson used the much-reviled and later-repealed Gulf of Tonkin Resolution to expand the American military effort in Vietnam at a rapid pace and with minimal congressional involvement.

The debacle in Vietnam shattered the norm of congressional deference. In the two decades since U.S. troops left Saigon, members of Congress have fought to reclaim the powers they lost to the executive branch during the height of the imperial presidency. Three recent examples provide illustrative glimpses of the profound effect the resurgence of congressional activism is having on U.S. foreign policy.

A First Glimpse. On 4 November 1991 the *Wall Street Journal* reported the following: "Struggling to define the Pentagon's role in a rapidly changing world, House and Senate negotiators hammered out a $291 billion defense bill that rejects many of President Bush's long-standing military assumptions." The strategic disagreement between Congress and the president resulted in a halt to the acquisition of more B-2 Stealth bombers, cuts in research and development on a space-based missile-defense system, and the addition of funds to keep alive two aircraft programs, the F-117 Stealth fighter and the V-22 Osprey, which the Pentagon wanted to cancel. The president set the agenda debated in Congress but the final outcome for defense spending bore clear congressional footprints.

A Second Glimpse. In the fall of 1991, Congressman Les Aspin (D-Wis.) and Senator Sam Nunn (D-Ga.) proposed taking $1 billion from the defense budget to provide economic aid to the former Soviet Union. The effort initially collapsed when the White House shied away from the plan as part of its response to the politically telling charge that the president was paying too much attention to foreign affairs and not enough to domestic matters. Concerned that America's national security interests were being jeopardized by the vagaries of domestic politics, a bipartisan group of senators succeeded, in late November, in securing passage of a plan to provide $500 million in aid. Then, in January 1992, President Bush threw his support behind the idea of assisting the former Soviet republics and proposed an additional $645 million in aid.

A Third Glimpse. In January 1992, the government and rebels in El Salvador signed a peace treaty ending more than a decade of civil war. Congress played a pivotal role in making the treaty possible. Over the objections of the Bush administration, Congress in 1990 slashed U.S. military aid to El Salvador by 50 percent and linked future aid to progress in peace talks. Congress's action left the government of El Salvador with the choice of negotiating with the rebels or losing U.S. aid. The government chose to negotiate. At the same time, Congressman Joseph Moakley (D-Mass.), the chair of the House Rules Committee and a leader in the fight to terminate aid to El Salvador, helped to convince rebel leaders to take the peace talks seriously. In June 1991, Moakley and U.S. ambassador William Walker met with rebel leaders inside rebel-held territory. Rebel leaders later told U.S. officials that Moakley's trip marked the turning point in their approach to the peace talks (C. Madison 1992a).

The resurgence of congressional activism on foreign and defense policy attested to by these illustrative glimpses has elicited considerable popular and political comment. A few observers lament that Congress has not gone far enough. The bulk of the commentary, however, contends that Congress has gone too far. These critics worry that in an era of great flux in world affairs Congress has made it increasingly difficult for the president to chart a foreign policy course that serves the interests of the country. This charge, and the consequences that will follow from it, if true, make it imperative to understand Congress's role in foreign and defense policy-making.

The Research Challenge

The resurgence of congressional activism means that it is impossible to understand fully the foreign policy-making process in the United States today without accounting for Congress. Yet, despite abundant evidence of this resurgence, scholars interested in foreign and defense policy-making continue to pay relatively little attention to Congress (for a review of the literature see Lindsay and Ripley 1992). To be sure, some recent works have sought to catalogue and evaluate the consequences of increased congressional activism (e.g., Blechman 1990b; Lindsay 1991; Mann 1990a; Mayer 1991) but most of the books and articles published on the subject during the last two decades have explored the legal and normative aspects of Congress's role (e.g., Barnhart 1987; Crovitz and Rabkin 1989; Goldwin and Licht 1990; Jones and Marini 1988; Koh 1990). So, while we have had a rich debate over the constitutional and practical issues raised by a resurgent Congress, we have relatively little systematic knowledge about what that resurgent Congress does and to what effect.

Instead of being based on systematic knowledge, the literature on Congress and foreign policy subsists largely on anecdotes. For the most part these place Congress in an unfavorable light. Stories abound of hearings at which few members show up, of congressionally mandated reports that go unread, and of junkets to such international "flashpoints" as Barbados and Paris. No matter how popular and amusing these anecdotes may be, they reveal little about the quality of the policy that emerges from Congress or about how well members perform their duty to oversee the work of the executive branch. To conclude that members fail at their tasks of formulating and overseeing policy on the basis of some amusing anecdotes is both shortsighted and foolish.

To begin to develop systematic knowledge about the role Congress plays in foreign and defense policy, this volume addresses three broad questions.

What does the environment in which Congress operates in relation to foreign and defense policy look like? Congress does not make its decisions in a vacuum. The rules of the game laid down in the Constitution, the likes and dislikes of voters, budgetary constraints, and other external pressures work both to limit and to impel congressional activism. Any attempt to understand what Congress does in matters of foreign and defense policy needs to come to terms with the environment in which the institution operates. The chapters in part 2 of the book examine the constraints and pressures on congressional decision making.

How do the various groups in Congress operate in relation to foreign and defense policy? Although it is convenient to refer to Congress as an *it,* in reality the *it* is a *they.* The most important actors influencing foreign and defense policy in Congress are the relevant committees since these handle the details of legislation. Also important are the party leaders, whose institutional powers give them significant opportunities to influence the character and content of congressional decision making. An understanding of Congress and foreign policy requires an understanding of how decisions are made within the institution. The chapters in part 3 of the book go inside the institution in just this fashion.

Does congressional activism affect the substance of U.S. foreign policy? Attention paid to the context of congressional decision making and to what different actors in Congress do illuminates only part of Congress's role in foreign and defense policy. The question of whether Congress significantly affects the substance of foreign and defense policy remains. The answer requires an assessment of the impact Congress has in specific policy domains. The chapters in part 4 undertake this effort.

The chapters in this book, of course, do not exhaust the study of Congress and foreign policy. No single volume on such a vast subject can aspire to cover every aspect of the topic. One notable omission here is a chapter on the intelligence committees. Since their creation in the mid-1970s they have become major players in the U.S. intelligence community. Our decision not to seek a chapter on this topic was made easier by the recent publication of several excellent studies on the intelligence committees (Johnson 1989; Kaiser 1988; Smist 1990; Treverton 1990).

We also did not include a chapter on the general issue of war powers nor on the specific case of Operation Desert Storm. (Several chapters do discuss Congress's role in the events leading up to the Gulf war.) We made this decision partly because several recent works explore the war powers issue in great detail (e.g., Katzmann 1990; Smyrl 1988) and also because it reflects our belief that scholars devote too much attention to Congress's role in crisis policy. As we argue at greater length in chapter 2, institutional, political, and normative factors combine to deny Congress a meaningful role in the making of crisis policy. In the case of the Gulf war, the American commitment to use force was cemented once President Bush decided to double the size of U.S. forces in Saudi Arabia. (As chapter 11 discusses, members of Congress were shut out of the decisions that led to the shift from Operation Desert Shield to Operation Desert Storm.) The closeness of the vote in the Senate notwithstanding, it is very unlikely that Congress would have denied President Bush the authorization he requested. Even the Senate margin of five votes is misleading because a few senators probably would have changed their votes to support the president if that became necessary to avoid defeating him. Had Congress denied the authorization, Bush almost certainly could have found a pretext to justify the air and land offensive he was determined to launch, although a negative vote in Congress might have produced a constitutional crisis.

Finally, the chapters in part 4 by no means cover the entire array of foreign policy issues. Due to space limitations we had to leave some important topics unaddressed. Yet our aim was not to cover the universe of possible issues but to select a few important areas that would prove broadly illustrative. The chapters that examine national security, diplomacy, and trade each tell an interesting and important story with broad ramifications. We hope that the lessons these chapters suggest will stimulate research on Congress's involvement in other foreign policy issues.

Findings

The following eleven chapters examine the environment in which Congress operates, the nature of decision making in Congress, and the impact of activism in the institution. In this section we summarize briefly some of the most significant findings in each chapter. In the subsequent section, we will underline some common patterns that emerge from the chapters when they are considered together.

In chapter 2 we address the broad question of how Congress influences the substance of foreign and defense policy. We first argue that Congress's influence varies among different types of foreign policy, ranging from almost none in crisis policy, to a modest amount in strategic policy, to substantial influence in structural policy (the policy types are taken from Huntington 1961). We also discuss the four avenues by which Congress influences foreign and defense policy. In addition to the most obvious mode of influence—legislation—Congress shapes policy by provoking anticipated reactions on the part of the executive branch, by enacting procedural legislation that has substantive consequences, and by "framing" the terms of public debate on specific issues.

In chapter 3, Lance LeLoup lays out the broad budgetary constraints that

U.S. policymakers face. The shift toward "macrobudgeting"—that is, budgeting within giant categories with fixed limits on each—has changed the nature of the budget debate. The macrobudget categories agreed on by the Bush administration and Congress in 1990 pit domestic spending against defense spending and international spending. The international-spending category, which consists primarily of foreign aid programs, is much smaller in terms of absolute dollars than either the domestic or the defense spending categories, and, for reasons of size and political visibility, international spending almost surely will suffer the greatest cuts in percentage terms if the current macrobudgeting scheme persists. LeLoup concludes that, in a world of budget deficits and macrobudgeting, members of Congress will not find policy innovation to be easy.

In chapter 4, Eileen Burgin examines the link between the behavior of members of Congress with regard to foreign policy and their perceptions of the attitudes of their supporters. Whereas most studies of the link between constituents and legislators focus on roll call votes, Burgin uses original interview data to examine why and to what extent House members decide to become active participants in a legislative debate on foreign policy. She finds that members tend to avoid becoming active participants when they believe that their supporters oppose the policy in question. Once a member decides to participate, however, perceptions of constituent opinion matter far less in calculations about how extensively to participate. In short, members are both constrained by the preferences of key constituents and relatively free to act on the basis of their own judgments and preferences once they decide to get involved.

In chapter 5, the final chapter in part 2, John Tierney explores the role interest groups play in foreign policy. He argues that interest group activity varies both by type of group and by type of policy. He notes that, as in the domestic arena, interest groups have become more active in working on foreign and defense policy issues over time. Tierney also notes that, because of increased federal budgetary constraints, economic interest groups active in foreign and defense policy compete directly with each other, more so now than in the past.

Part 3 turns to the question of who makes decisions in Congress. In chapter 6, James McCormick examines the Senate Foreign Relations and the House Foreign Affairs Committees. He finds that Foreign Relations has declined in status and power in relation both to Foreign Affairs and to other Senate committees. Long gone are the days when Foreign Relations was one of the most prestigious and influential committees in the Senate. McCormick also charts the growing importance and competence of the House Foreign Affairs Committee. Despite its enhanced status, however, Foreign Affairs has found its ability to influence policy frustrated by the inability of the Senate

Foreign Relations Committee to reach agreement on the foreign aid bill in many years.

In chapter 7, Christopher Deering analyzes the work of the House and Senate Armed Services Committees. He shows that, despite a number of detailed changes in the two Armed Services Committees, there is a great deal of continuity in the way they have functioned since World War II. In his view, it is unclear whether they will help facilitate the policy shifts necessary for the United States to adjust to a post-Soviet world or whether they will be major impediments to such shifts. So far, no clear pattern has emerged. One feature of the committees is clear, however: they are players with major potential. Whether and how they realize that potential remain open questions.

In chapter 8, Joseph White explores the work of the Appropriations Committees. On the basis of extensive interviews with members of the defense and foreign operations subcommittees in both the House and the Senate, White describes "what the appropriators do." He argues that appropriators matter most when the issues on which they focus are concrete and small in scope. Above all, appropriators see themselves as "budgeteers" rather than as makers of grand policy. In general, the arena of structural policy offers the most opportunity for appropriators to matter. However, White points out that control of structural policy can, at least in part, turn out to be control of strategic policy.

In chapter 9, which concludes part 3, Barbara Sinclair reviews the role played by party leaders. She finds that, while House Republican leaders have retained their traditional role of serving as loyal lieutenants to a president of their own party, House Democratic leaders have become more active in foreign and defense policy matters *and* more likely to challenge the president (specifically, Republican presidents Reagan and Bush). House Democratic leaders have not adopted this stance out of mere whim or personal preference; they are responding to changing expectations on the part of rank-and-file members. (Whether House Democratic leaders will be equally willing to challenge President Clinton, a Democrat, will become clear in the next few years.) Senate party leaders, on the other hand, have been less visible in matters of foreign policy. Still, Democratic expectations may have begun to propel Majority Leader George Mitchell to greater activism, a position encouraged by the waning importance of the Foreign Relations Committee.

The chapters in part 4 address the question of Congress's impact on specific issue areas in foreign and defense policy. In chapter 10, Paul Stockton challenges conventional wisdom to argue that Congress is heavily involved in making fundamental national security policy. Using the evolution of the Bush administration's national security strategy to illustrate his argument, Stockton shows how Congress has used a combination of legislation and framing to push the White House to respond to the changes that swept the Soviet Union in 1990 and 1991. When members of Congress become involved in such "high policy" matters they are balancing concerns about good policy with the lure of providing (or protecting) tangible benefits to constituents.

In chapter 11, James Lindsay shows that Congress often involves itself in matters of diplomacy. The involvement is sporadic; on many issues Congress operates on the periphery of policy. On some occasions and on some issues, however, Congress participates in a sustained way with demonstrable influence. Lindsay also disputes the claim that Congress undermines the president's ability to negotiate when it intervenes in diplomatic matters. He shows that under some circumstances congressional activism actually strengthens the president's negotiating position, a lesson that several presidents have used to their advantage.

In chapter 12, Sharyn O'Halloran examines Congress's impact on trade policy. She challenges the conventional wisdom that Congress has all but handed trade policy formulation over to the White House. Using insights from the literature on the new institutionalism, O'Halloran argues that the fact that Congress delegates authority to the president does not warrant the conclusion that Congress has abdicated its power to set trade policy. Using the U.S.-Canada Free Trade Agreement to illustrate her argument, she shows how, in writing the Trade Reform Act of 1974, Congress fashioned a set of procedures that enable it to influence the substance of trade agreements while at the same time protecting itself from potentially destructive demands for protectionism.

Patterns

These eleven chapters, considered as a whole, reveal six broad patterns of congressional behavior in the realm of foreign and defense policy.

First, the role Congress chooses to play in foreign policy continually changes. Today members of Congress challenge the White House publicly and with a frequency they would not have dreamed possible in the two decades following World War II, an era characterized by deference to the president on many foreign policy matters, infrequent public challenges, and a fairly high incidence of bipartisanship. The chapters offer a variety of explanations for the changes in congressional behavior: a decline in external threats to American security; the arrival of new members of Congress with preferences and expectations different from those of departing members; shifting competence and policy initiatives on the part of presidents; and changes in the macrobudgetary context. To think of Congress in static terms misleads. There may be "constitutional verities," but the work of Congress is tempered constantly by the flux of events around the world, in American society, and in the institution itself.

Second, congressional activism on foreign policy is driven by more than the simple desire to win reelection. We all know that reelection matters. But, as the following chapters show, the electoral incentive is only part of the story. Fenno (1973) is correct in stating that personal policy preferences, the desire for prestige and influence inside the congressional institution, and reelection all drive member behavior.

When considering the motivations for congressional behavior it is important to recognize that constituents often do not follow foreign affairs (Almond 1950; Erskine 1963; Free and Cantril 1968; Simon 1974). It is also important not to assume, as many studies of Congress and foreign policy do, that electoral incentives inevitably run counter to members' policy preferences. Quite often members and their constituents prefer the same policies. The chief reason for overlapping preferences is simple: key aspects of the recruitment process for legislators—residence, coalition building, and elections—make it likely that members will share many policy attitudes with their constituents (Kingdon 1989; Poole 1988). Voter apathy and overlapping preferences mean that legislators have considerable freedom to act on foreign policy matters. Indeed, often they have electoral incentives to pursue their own preferences.

Third, the once-clear hierarchy and jurisdictions in Congress on foreign policy issues no longer exist. The days when foreign affairs were primarily the preserve of the Senate are gone. Despite the lack of some of the constitutional powers accorded the Senate, the House increasingly has made its voice heard on foreign policy issues. The increased struggle between the two chambers has been accompanied by an intensified competition for power among committees, both within and across chambers. The Senate Foreign Relations Committee has seen its prestige and influence eclipsed by both the House Foreign Affairs Committee and the Senate Armed Services Committee. For their part, the Armed Services Committees of both chambers have found themselves locked in a struggle with the Appropriations Committees over the shape of the defense budget. The collapse of hierarchy and the blurring of jurisdictional lines has had the dual effect of making it more difficult for Congress to pass legislation while making it possible for more members to participate in policy-making.

Fourth, substance cannot be separated from procedure when investigating the role of Congress in policy-making. As we argue at greater length in chapter 2, members of Congress recognize that their control over the policy process gives them influence over its substance. Unfortunately for scholars, much of the work on Congress and foreign policy ignores this insight. As a result such studies tend to treat procedural wrangles as mere nitpicking. But, as the discussions of macrobudgeting (chapter 3), party leaders (chapter 9), diplomacy (chapter 11), and trade (chapter 12) all show, the shape of the policy process influences policy outcomes.

Fifth, Congress's influence over the substance of foreign and defense policy varies in predictable ways across policy domains. The formulation we offer in chapter 2 (crisis, strategic, and structural policy) is surely not the only one (and may not even be the best one) but the chapters on the budget (chapter 3), on interest groups (chapter 5), on the appropriations subcommittees (chapter 8), and on the making of national security policy (chapter 10) all suggest that this formulation, or one relatively close to it, is helpful. Congress's influence varies because different policy domains involve different political actors and pressures as well as different allocations of authority and power. The variations in congressional influence and behavior in different types of foreign and defense policy mean that all-encompassing generalizations about Congress's role in the foreign policy realm are often misleading.

Finally, Congress's handling of foreign and defense policy is coming to resemble its handling of domestic policy. For many in Congress (and many outside it) the once clear line separating foreign and domestic policy is blurred. As Lance LeLoup argues in chapter 3, the shift toward macro-budgeting means that foreign and defense programs are subject to the same rules as are domestic programs. In chapter 5, John Tierney details the explosion in the number of interest groups working on foreign policy issues. Although many of these groups address standard economic concerns, albeit of an international character, many others address traditional high policy issues such as arms control. In chapter 9, Barbara Sinclair shows how party leaders have begun to assert themselves on foreign and defense issues as they have for many years on domestic issues.

Conclusion

We began this chapter by noting Congress's resurgent interest in foreign and defense policy. Several ongoing developments at home and abroad promise to fuel congressional activism further. The first is the end of the cold war. The dissolution of the Soviet Union opens the question of what will replace containment as the cornerstone of American foreign policy. Given that the United States lacks a foreign policy consensus, that debate is likely to be fractious. Moreover, as perceptions of the nature of external threats change, the public is much more likely to tolerate legislative dissent from the president's position on foreign affairs. Faced with fewer electoral costs in opposing the president, members of Congress are becoming more likely to deal the president public rebuffs.

A second reason why Congress is likely to become more influential is that global interdependence is blurring the line that once separated domestic from foreign policy. Global warming provides an example of such an "inter-mestic" issue (Manning 1977). The steps needed to curtail the emission of heat-trapping gases require both international cooperation and substantial changes in domestic policy, changes that will advantage some groups and disadvantage others. Acid rain, drugs, farm subsidies, and immigration are other salient issues that straddle the domestic and international spheres. Intermestic issues encourage congressional influence because they involve decisions traditionally considered part of domestic policy. Members of Congress, who can be counted on to protect their institutional prerogatives and their constituents, will feel increasingly comfortable rewriting presidential proposals on intermestic issues, regardless of the foreign policy implications.

The third development pushing Congress toward greater influence is the ever-widening gap between American commitments abroad and American resources. On the face of it, the collapse of the Soviet empire should have reduced foreign commitments by the United States and brought those commitments more in line with resources. To date, however, no sizable reduction in formal commitments has been made. Meanwhile, the United States operates under increasingly severe budget constraints as the deficit gobbles resources at a great rate. With the decreasing likelihood that the federal government can deal with the gap between commitments and resources simply by running larger deficits, Congress will have to make some hard choices between guns and butter. As the steady decline in real spending on defense illustrates, guns are likely to lose that showdown.

The last development fueling Congress's interest in foreign policy is the growing fear that the American economy is falling behind those of Germany and Japan. In the words of Congressman Aspin, today we are seeing "the emergence of an entirely new concept of national security. It embraces economics and competitive, commercial relations" (quoted in Greenwald 1989, 44). Former U.S. trade negotiator Clyde Prestowitz put the same point more bluntly: "Trade *is* defense. We must recognize the nature of the game" (quoted in ibid., 45). If the argument that economic vitality is national security continues to gain ground, Congress will become more involved in national-security policy for the same reasons it is more influential on intermestic issues. When issues are defined in terms of the domestic economy, Congress becomes less likely to defer to the president. In this respect the 1989 debate over the FSX fighter may be a harbinger of things to come (see Ortmayer 1990; and Stokes 1989).

The prospect of increased congressional activism makes it more imperative than ever to pursue rigorous study of the relationship between Congress and foreign policy. We know Congress matters, at least some of the time, but we know relatively little in a systematic sense about congressional behavior, its roots, forms, and impact. In the following chapters we and our colleagues attempt to fill some of the gaps in our store of systematic knowledge.

Part 2.
Context, Constraints, and Pressures

CHAPTER 2

How Congress Influences Foreign and Defense Policy

James M. Lindsay and Randall B. Ripley

Does Congress matter in the foreign and defense policy realm? If so, how? Skeptics answer the first question negatively. They argue that congressional activism is more smoke than fire, that Congress generally ratifies what the president proposes, and that the president leads in matters of defense and foreign policy. To be fair, the skeptics' charge has some merit. The president does have more influence over defense and foreign policy than does Congress, and the evidence does not support claims that defense and foreign policy is "co-determined" by the executive and the legislature (Franck and Weisband 1979). Simply put, the president enjoys substantial advantages in dealing with Congress.

But recognizing that the president is powerful does not mean that he is omnipotent. Congress has and does influence defense and foreign policy. Skeptics miss Congress's influence because they make two conceptual mistakes. One is the assumption that foreign and defense policy is a simple policy area without important internal distinctions. Therefore, they confuse the president's achievements in some highly visible areas with his success across the entire policy domain. In fact, defense and foreign policy encompasses a heterogeneous group of programs and policies. While the president exercises nearly sole control over decisions made during crises, precisely the situations skeptics focus on, he exercises considerably less influence over other defense and foreign policy matters. An error that often compounds this mistake is to think of the president and Congress as involved in a relatively simple, zero-sum game, in which one side must win, and the other must lose. The relationship is nowhere near that simple.

The second conceptual mistake typically made by skeptics is to assume that the best measure of congressional influence is the institution's success at generating and passing substantive policy legislation. Using legislative success, defined in this restrictive manner, as the benchmark, Congress does not appear to matter much. Despite the occurrence of more fractious policy debates than was the norm twenty-five years ago, Congress often approves presidential requests and fails to pass policies of its own. But fixating on substantive legislation obscures the fact that Congress influences policy by various indirect means: by setting up situations that generate desired reactions by the executive, by changing the way decisions are made in the executive branch, and by framing public and elite opinion about foreign policy. Indeed, the very factors that frustrate congressional attempts to lead on defense and foreign policy encourage legislators to use indirect means of influence.

Before turning to our discussion of the ways in which members of Congress influence foreign policy, a word of caution is in order. It is convenient when writing about Congress to treat the institution as a monolith. Yet Congress does not speak with a single voice, for its every action testifies to the ideological, partisan, regional, and personal divisions within it. Thus, while we (and others) often write about "Congress," rather than using more cumbersome constructions (for example, legislators in Congress who oppose the president's proposal), it is worth remembering that any significant foreign-policy debate on Capitol Hill features the clash of myriad ideas, interests, and perspectives. Congress truly is a *they* not an *it*.

In the remainder of this chapter we first sketch the general relative importance of the roles of Congress and the president in three types of foreign and defense policy. Then we examine the four main ways in which Congress influences foreign and defense policy: the familiar one of substantive legislation and the less familiar ones of anticipated reactions, procedural legislation, and framing opinion.

Types of Policy

Any study of the way foreign and defense policy is made in the United States must begin by recognizing that in this process the president is the most important actor and the executive is the most important branch of government. The Constitution creates the president's central role. Compared to Congress, he enjoys the inherent advantages of "decision, activity, secrecy, and dispatch" identified by Alexander Hamilton (1961, 424) more than two hundred years ago. Presidents have added institutional leverage by using the veto—Congress has overridden only one veto involving foreign policy since 1973—and by virtue of the partisan, regional, and organizational divisions in Congress. The constitutional, inherent, and institutional advantages of the presidency have been reinforced by the Supreme Court, which, by its rulings on the merits and its frequent invocation of the doctrine of political questions, has favored the president at the expense of Congress (Franck 1991; Koh 1990).

It goes too far, however, to argue that the executive branch is the only actor that matters in the realm of defense and foreign policy. Congress also matters. To understand the role Congress plays it must be recognized that defense and foreign policy is not a single, undifferentiated area. Defense and foreign policies fall into three general categories: crisis, strategic, and structural policy (Huntington 1961, 3–4; Lowi 1967, 324–25; Ripley and Franklin 1991, 23–24). The distinctive characteristic of crisis policy is the perception of an immediate threat to U.S. national interests, usually one involving the use or potential use of force. As such, crisis policy is the least common type of foreign policy. Strategic policy specifies the goals and tactics of defense and foreign policy. It encompasses much of what is commonly called foreign policy as well as those aspects of defense policy that specify the basic mix and mission of military forces. Structural policy governs how resources are used and most closely resembles decision making on domestic, distributive policies. In the defense realm, structural policy aims at procuring, deploying, and organizing military personnel and matériel. In foreign affairs, structural policy answers questions such as which countries will receive aid, what rules will govern immigration, and how much money will be given to international organizations.

The distinction among policy types is crucial, for each category involves different kinds of political actors and pressures, which in turn have important consequences for the ability of the president to achieve his goals. In crisis situations presidential power is at a maximum. Decisions are made by the president and those he chooses to consult. Congress tried to give itself a formal role in crisis decision-making with the passage of the War Powers Resolution, but that legislation has failed to have much effect in practice. In the months preceding the Gulf war, for example, both President Bush *and* Congress steadfastly refused to invoke the Resolution.

The president's domination of crisis policy stems first from the inherent and institutional advantages he has in dealing with Congress. Presidents also benefit from the fact that most legislators believe that the national interest is best served during a crisis by strong executive leadership. Electoral considerations reinforce the inclination on Capitol Hill to defer to the president. Members want to avoid stands that might leave them open to blame, and thus to punishment at the polls. They recognize that the public usually closes ranks behind the president when U.S. interests are threatened in a way that is dramatic (or at least can be portrayed as dramatic by the president). Because practical, normative, and electoral considerations all push in the direction of congressional passivity, crises generally reach Congress only when the president sees fit. Typically, then, Congress is limited in what it can or wants to do. As Senator Arthur Vandenberg (R-Mich.) once complained, crises "never reach Congress until they have developed to a point where Congressional discretion is pathetically restricted" (quoted in LaFeber 1972, 60).

The Gulf war illustrates the disadvantages members of Congress face during a crisis. In November 1990, President Bush, without consulting any members of Congress, unilaterally changed the mission of U.S. forces in the Persian Gulf from deterring an Iraqi invasion of Saudi Arabia to liberating Kuwait. The decision left legislators with few options. The unpredictability of the Iraqi government made it impossible to pass legislation that gave the president a detailed, but contingent, grant of authority to use force. As the January 1991 debate showed, members of Congress had but two options: to grant the president the authority he requested, and thereby risk a costly war, or to maintain the sanctions, thereby dealing a public rebuff to the president and perhaps making war more likely. In the end, practical, normative, electoral calculations led a majority of legislators to choose to grant the president the authority to wage war.

The president's power is less extensive on strategic policy, though it remains substantial. His greatest strength is that he initiates policy. Because the Constitution gives the president powers that it denies Congress, on some issues the ability to initiate policy is the ability to make policy. Recognizing the communist government in China, proposing deep cuts in nuclear weapons stockpiles, and maintaining relations with countries with abysmal records on human rights are all decisions that originate with the president.

This is not to say that presidential power over strategic policy is unchecked. On some foreign policy questions—treaties and trade policy are two obvious examples—the president needs the approval of Congress. At the same time, the farther removed a strategic policy decision is from a crisis situation the less inhibited legislators will be in challenging a president. As the sanctions imposed on South Africa in 1986 illustrate, Congress at times enacts its own strategic policy preferences into law in opposition to the president. Still, the president holds the upper hand because, as a general rule, in matters of strategic policy he benefits from a natural tendency toward inaction on Capitol Hill.

In structural policy, presidential power is at its weakest. Perhaps the most obvious example of this is military basing. Beginning in the 1970s the executive branch found its ability to close or realign military facilities essentially blocked by Congress (Twight 1989, 1990). Congress plays a similarly influential role in setting such policies as export subsidies and foreign aid. Substantial congressional influence even extends to high-profile programs that have clear links to strategic policy. President Carter, for example, found his efforts to kill the B-1 bomber frustrated when Congress appropriated enough funds to keep the program alive until the Reagan administration decided to resume production (Kotz 1988). Reagan experienced similar problems when Congress blocked his proposals for the antisatellite (ASAT) and MX missile programs (Lindsay 1991, 62–81).

Congress exercises greater influence over structural policy because in this realm decisions are dominated by subgovernments composed of bureaus, congressional committees, and other interested actors. Members of subgovernments cooperate to serve their clients and they make many decisions on the basis of mutual noninterference and logrolling. Members of subgovernments also are highly motivated to protect their domains from intrusions by an "outsider," whether it be the president, the secretary of defense, or a congressional leader (Ripley and Franklin 1991, 152–53). Congress also wields great influence over structural policy because in this case inertia usually works to its advantage. Structural policy requires appropriations, and if Congress fails to appropriate the funds the president requests, the policy ceases to exist, assuming, of course, that the administration obeys the law. To encourage compliant behavior on the part of the administration, for example, Congress passed the Budget and Impoundment Control Act of 1974 over a Nixon veto in part to limit the ability of the president to use his impoundment powers to block structural policies preferred by Congress.

In noting the differences among the types of defense and foreign policies, two caveats should be stressed. One is that many policies incorporate elements of each policy category. Trade policy, for example, involves both a strategic element (the preference for free trade over fair trade) and a structural element (the desire, for example, that quotas on peanuts and sugar be maintained). Defense policy is similar. Issues such as nuclear deterrence have both a strategic component (which is the more preferable targeting doctrine, counterforce, or countervalue?) and a structural component (should the United States procure another Trident submarine?). And, if future administrations choose to take a more aggressive stance in combating global warming, they will have to make both strategic decisions (should the policy emphasize reducing carbon dioxide emissions in the industrialized world or slowing their growth in the developing world?) and structural ones (should foreign aid be used to help Mexico develop cleaner smokestacks?).

The second caveat that needs to be stressed is that the policy categories are not hierarchical. Although, in theory, structural policy should flow from decisions made about strategic policy, in practice it often works the other way. Quite often in defense policy, for example, military doctrine is altered to justify the weapons programs that are already under development (Lindsay 1991, 164). In 1990, Congress's decision to mandate the phasing out of production of some ozone-depleting chemicals forced the Bush administration to revise a major component of its bargaining position at international talks on the threat to the ozone layer (Benedick 1991, 173–74).

The overlapping, nonhierarchical nature of the policy categories means that Congress's influence on defense and foreign policy is not somehow smaller merely because legislators have more say in structural than in strategic decisions. In making decisions on structural policy, Congress may deny the president the ability to carry out a strategic policy, as was the case when it refused to appropriate funds to aid the Nicaraguan Contras. Congress's decisions on structural policy may also push strategic policy in a direction opposed by the president, as happened when Congress directed the air force to develop the cruise and Midgetman missiles.

Our general point is that the relative power of Congress and the president in formulating defense and foreign policy varies with the type of policy at stake. In crisis policy Congress operates on the fringes of power. Legislators can suggest policies to the president, implore him to avoid others, and threaten him with political harm in the future but ultimately the president decides whom he will and will not consult. Congress has greater influence over strategic policy but even here the president's constitutional powers and the practical difficulties of overturning presidential initiatives hamper congressional influence. In dealing with structural policy the president is at his weakest in acting without congressional assent. By virtue of its control of the purse strings alone, Congress *must* be involved in such policy-making.

Substantive Legislation

How does Congress influence defense and foreign policy? The most obvious route is by enacting its policy preferences into law. Indeed, studies of the congressional role on defense and foreign policy typically judge the importance of the institution in terms of its ability to generate and enact its own substantive policy proposals (e.g., Crabb and Holt 1992; Destler, Gelb, and Lake 1984; Koh 1988, 1990; Purvis and Baker 1984; Robinson 1967). In the 1950s and 1960s, Congress appeared content to ratify presidential initiatives (Wildavsky 1966). After the turmoil caused by Vietnam and Watergate, however, congressional interest in substantive policy legislation grew and Congress enacted a variety of bills that contradicted the preferences of the White House.

The annual editions of *Legislation on Foreign Relations* give some indication of the growing congressional interest in defense and foreign policy legislation. The 1960 edition ran to 519 pages, the 1975 edition contained 1,856, and the 1990 edition had 5,483 pages in four volumes (Hastedt 1991, 129). Specific examples of successful congressionally initiated legislation come readily to mind. In the area of defense policy, Congress canceled plans by both the army and navy to develop a new generation of tactical nuclear missiles, blocked efforts to deploy an ASAT weapon, limited the deployment of the MX missile, and compelled the air force to develop the Midgetman missile (Blechman 1990a, 1990b; Lindsay 1991). In foreign policy, legislators blocked an attempt to reinterpret the ABM Treaty, overrode a presidential veto to impose sanctions on South Africa, and placed so many constraints on relations with El Salvador and Nicaragua that by the end of the Reagan presidency "U.S. policy toward Central America was effectively being set by Congress" (C. Madison 1991a, 104).

Despite the substantial increase in legislation, most observers contend that legislative victories on foreign policy remain the exception rather than the rule (e.g., Destler, Gelb, and Lake 1984, 129–62; Koh 1988, 1990; Rourke 1983). Many times Congress appears to do no more than ratify the president's proposals (witness President Bush's victory in the debate over most-favored-nation status for China). Congress may even fail to overrule the president when the circumstances seem favorable. Consider the Panama Canal treaties and the sale of AWACS aircraft to Saudi Arabia. In both instances substantial numbers of legislators opposed the president's preferred policy. They were highly motivated, enjoyed the support of well-heeled interest groups, and had public sentiment on their side. Congress seemed poised to overrule the White House. But in both cases the president prevailed.

Even when Congress succeeds in legislating foreign policy, the results may be less than what meets the eye. In passing legislation, Congress typically delegates tremendous power to the executive branch. Such discretion is justified on the grounds that the president needs flexibility when conducting foreign affairs. But discretion also gives the president the opportunity to subvert the intent of Congress. To take one of many possible examples, Congress appropriated military aid to El Salvador with the provision that President Reagan must

> certify every six months that the Salvadoran government was "achieving substantial control" of its armed forces . . . that it was "implementing essential economic and political reforms," . . . and that it was holding free elections and demonstrating a willingness to negotiate a political settlement. (Destler, Gelb, and Lake 1984, 158–59)

But the constraint was more apparent than real. Given President Reagan's ideological preferences, it is hard to imagine circumstances under which he would have withheld certification.

Efforts to explain Congress's lack of success in legislating the substance of defense and foreign policy usually cite the inherent and institutional advantages of the presidency. But secrecy and dispatch, veto threats, and legislators' fear of being held accountable tell only part of the story. An essential lesson of life on Capitol Hill is that members often have sound policy reasons for not wanting to defeat the president. Because congressional debate is public, the rejection of presidential requests may undermine the negotiating posture of the president or jeopardize U.S. relations with other countries.

Legislation, almost by necessity, is rigid but diplomacy frequently requires flexibility. Congress acts slowly but issues can change rapidly. In some cases, resorting to legislation may mean taking a sledgehammer to a problem that requires a scalpel. Legislation may even create perverse incentives: presidents may drag their feet implementing congressional directives because they believe any policy failure will be blamed on Congress. In short, legislators often do not want to win because they believe that legislated solutions will prove unwise or unworkable in practice.

Members often find themselves in situations in which their object is not to pass bills but to use the threat of legislation as a lever with which to pressure the president. Take, for example, the efforts of Congressman Les Aspin (D-Wis.) to save the MX missile. Like many of his fellow Democrats, Aspin doubted the strategic value of the MX. If stopping the MX were his sole concern, a no vote would have been in order. But Aspin concluded that killing the MX would undermine the higher policy goal of arms control. Keeping the missile alive would place pressure on the administration to negotiate an arms control treaty. Aspin articulated his strategy thus:

> It seemed to me that if Scowcroft came up with a bipartisan package and the President accepted that, the Democrats would not be in good shape if it was voted down. It was clear that most Democrats would vote against it. But if enough voted for it, and Reagan got it, the headline would say "Reagan Gets MX." If not, the headline would be "Democrats Block MX." Reagan could have used that as an excuse. Now that he has the tools he needs, the Administration is in a bit of a hot seat. It has to produce an agreement. (Quoted in Drew 1983, 75)

Similar concerns dominated the 1985 debate in the Senate Finance Committee over fast-track legislation for the U.S.-Canada free-trade negotiations. Angered by what they saw as an incoherent American trade policy, half the members of the committee voted against granting fast-track status to the negotiations. The opponents, however, also believed that the trade talks were necessary and that denying fast-track status would damage relations with Canada as well as future trade negotiations. The senators voted no anyway because they were "expecting to lose; theirs was to be a protest vote" (Tobin 1987, 8).

In recognizing that members of Congress sometimes do not want to win, it should be said that the incentive to seek legislative solutions varies with the type of policy at hand. As a general rule, members have a greater incentive to seek legislative solutions to structural policy problems than to those considered strategic. (Unless the president seriously misjudges public opinion, crisis policy is essentially impervious to legislation.) The reason is that, in structural issues, "dollars are policy" (Gordon 1961, 695) and dollars can't be spent unless Congress passes legislation appropriating the funds. So the member who wants to save the T-46 jet trainer or stop work on the MX missile must focus on legislation. In contrast, members working on a strategic policy often have less need for legislation, either because the issue lies largely beyond legislative impact or because legislators worry that legislation will be politically costly. For these members, indirect means of influence are far more appealing.

The desire of many legislators to change policy without passing legislation highlights the problem of using legislative success to measure congressional influence. Executive-legislative relations on defense and foreign policy are far more complicated than can be captured simply by examining which bills pass with what content. Congress often influences policy indirectly, a point to which we now turn by examining anticipated reactions, procedural innovations, and framing opinion.

Anticipated Reactions

The first indirect means by which Congress influences presidential behavior is by generating anticipated reactions in the executive branch. Just as a chess player considers an opponent's possible moves and plans several steps ahead, Congress and the executive branch anticipate one another's behavior and modify their own (Friedrich 1941, 589–91; for a qualified dissent, see Peterson 1990). The existence of such strategic behavior has important implications for the study of defense and foreign policy: the relative power of Congress and the president cannot be judged solely on the basis of observed behavior. The fact that Congress passes a presidential initiative reveals little about the relative power of the two institutions.

At the broadest level, the mood on Capitol Hill determines what policy options are politically feasible for the executive branch. This has long been true. Secretary of Defense Robert McNamara, for example, decided to deploy 950 Minuteman missiles rather than the 450 he preferred because he believed it was the smallest number Congress would accept (Halberstam 1983, 91). Lyndon Johnson agreed in 1967 to proceed with deployment of an anti-Chinese ABM system at least in part to placate conservative senators (Halperin 1972, 75). But the greater willingness in Congress after Vietnam to challenge the executive branch on defense and foreign policy increased the president's need to anticipate the mood in Congress. To take one prominent example, President Reagan's policy toward Central America no doubt would have been far more ambitious had Congress shared his policy preferences.

In addition to setting the boundaries around politically feasible policy options, anticipated reactions may also convince presidents to revise programs already unveiled. Nuclear weapons programs provide several relevant examples. In 1969, President Nixon replaced the Sentinel ABM program with the Safeguard system when it seemed unlikely that the Senate would approve further funding for Sentinel (Finney 1969; Frye 1975, 44; Yanarella 1977, 146–55). President Carter advanced several variants of the multiple protective-shelter-basing mode in order to contain opposition to the MX missile. Finally, President Reagan abandoned his October 1981 interim silo-basing plan for the MX, as well as several subsequent basing options, because of opposition on Capitol Hill (Holland and Hoover 1984; Lindsay 1991).

Arms sales provide another example of anticipated reactions at work. In the mid-1970s, Congress passed legislation giving itself the power to veto major arms sales. Although Congress has never vetoed an arms sale, the threat of a veto appears to have shaped many presidential proposals. On several occasions the Ford and Carter administrations modified their proposed arms packages to defuse congressional opposition (Gilmour and Craig 1984, 375–76). Three times between 1983 and 1985, the Reagan administration proposed selling arms to Jordan, and each time it withdrew the proposal because of the mood in Congress (Jentleson 1990, 161). Following the Iraqi invasion of Kuwait the Bush administration postponed its plans to ask Congress to approve the sale of $13 billion in weapons to Saudi Arabia in order to avoid antagonizing Israel's supporters on the Hill (Stanfield 1991).

To better anticipate the mood of Congress, and to make floor fights less likely, presidents increasingly are bringing members of Congress into the policy-making process. The history of arms control talks illustrates the point. In the 1960s, presidents typically ignored Congress on issues of arms control. During the first Strategic Arms Limitation Talks (SALT I), for example, the Nixon administration repeatedly rejected pleas that it include senators in the American delegation (Platt 1978, 19–20). Vietnam, Watergate, congressional activism, and the collapse of détente soon changed that. Jimmy Carter actively solicited congressional views, especially those of Senator Henry Jackson (Platt 1982, 169–70). Carter also approved the creation of a SALT advisers group in the Senate that attended delegation meetings and even read the joint draft text of the treaty. The Reagan administration initially tried to bar Congress from the arms talks but eventually it retreated in the face of concerted congressional pressure. A Senate Arms Control Observer Group was reestablished in 1985 with even greater access than its predecessor had enjoyed (Blechman 1990a, 122).

Just as the White House often brings members of Congress into the policy-making process, legislators work actively to influence executive branch perceptions of congressional attitudes and interests. A convenient vehicle for this is oversight hearings. Whether driven by "police-patrol" or "fire-alarm" considerations (Aberbach 1987; McCubbins and Schwartz 1984), oversight hearings can deter the executive branch from acting contrary to congressional preferences. The potential for detection and the political costs of exposure may be sufficient to convince the executive that compliance is preferable to noncompliance. Thus, even if hearings fail to generate remedial legislation, they may affect the behavior of the executive through the strategy of anticipated reactions.

Congressional opposition does not always force the executive branch to modify its programs. Often presidents will risk displeasing legislators to pursue programs they favor (Peterson 1990, 60–67). President Nixon remained committed to Safeguard even as the number of Senate opponents approached fifty. President Reagan never wavered in his commitment to deploy the Pershing II missile in Europe despite opposition in the House. Whether or not the executive branch redraws its proposals in the face of congressional opposition depends on several factors. One is the size of the opposition's coalition. Pershing II opponents were simply too few in number to threaten Reagan's policy. Another factor is whether the issue will be settled with a single vote or whether (as is the case with most structural policies) it will have to be revisited yearly. Repeated votes on contentious issues drain political capital and incline the executive branch to find some acceptable compromise. Finally, perseverance on the part of the administration is crucial. President Nixon never attempted to save the Sentinel program, even though he supported the concept of area defense. The Reagan administration, however, repeatedly submitted requests for MX missiles even when "informed opinion" on Capitol Hill held that the program was dead (Holland and Hoover 1984, 226).

As an influence on executive branch behavior, anticipated reactions function as a negative power (Friedrich 1941, 590–91). As presidents look to Capitol Hill, their reading of the congressional mood tells them what policies are not politically feasible. But the mood in Congress seldom compels the president to pursue specific policies. The one exception is the rare case in which consensus reigns on Capitol Hill on a particular issue. As U.S. policy toward China after Tiananmen Square attests, however, presidents can resist congressional attempts to push them in a specific policy direction even in the face of near unanimity.

Does the impact of anticipated reactions extend beyond the margins of policy? On a major policy issue a president may ignore congressional objections or sidestep the objections by changing the style but not the substance of policy (for examples, see Hertsgaard 1989; and Schell 1975). Refuting the claim of marginality is impossible at present, both because we lack systematic studies of anticipated reactions and because the claim inevitably involves counterfactuals (see Fearon 1991). Yet, even if anticipated reactions operate only at the margins, Congress's influence should not be dismissed as inconsequential. As the history of the U.S. involvement in Vietnam illustrates, incremental decision making can lead to major policy commitments.

Procedural Legislation

A second indirect means Congress uses to influence policy is procedural legislation. Unlike substantive policy legislation, which specifies what the content of policy should be, procedural legislation seeks to change the identity of those who participate in decision making and/or influence how decisions are made. The underlying premise is that changing the process changes the policy. Congressman Aspin (1975, 168) tells us that "often by establishing new procedures, which are, of course, ostensibly neutral, Congress is able to effect substantive changes."

Procedural legislation appeals to members of Congress for several reasons. One is that the "ostensibly neutral" character of procedure makes it easier to build a winning coalition around procedural changes than around substantive policy changes. Procedural legislation also appeals to members as a labor-saving device. Not only is "an ounce of prevention worth a pound of cure" but procedural changes can make it easier to identify executive-branch "transgressions" or even to shift the burden of monitoring executive behavior to other groups (McCubbins and Schwartz 1984). Procedural changes also may be electorally profitable. Legislators often change the decision-making process to give constituents a voice in policy formulation or to make it easier for them to seek remedies from an agency, the courts, or Congress itself (McCubbins, Noll, and Weingast 1987, 1989; McCubbins and Schwartz 1984).

Congress uses five major kinds of procedural legislation. One is to create institutions inside the executive branch that will be more sympathetic to the preferences of Congress. This tactic is not new. In 1961, for example, Congress created the Arms Control and Disarmament Agency (ACDA) in the hope of giving arms control issues greater prominence. In 1977, Congress created the Bureau of Human Rights and Humanitarian Affairs in the Department of State to ensure that greater emphasis would be given to human rights in the formulation of U.S. foreign policy (Forsythe 1988). In recent years, Congress has created the position of under secretary of defense for acquisition, the Office of Operational Test and Evaluation, and the Special Operations Command in the Department of Defense (DOD) to remedy perceived deficiencies in the Pentagon.

A second type of procedural change is the legislative veto, a procedure under which one or both Houses, or even one or two committees, have the authority to block proposed presidential actions. First used in 1932, the legislative veto became popular in the 1970s, its most visible use being in the War Powers Resolution. The Supreme Court's 1983 ruling in *I.N.S. v. Chadha* diminished the effectiveness of the legislative veto as a check on executive power (Franck and Bob 1985; Gilmour and Craig 1984). Still, the Court did not rule that all such vetoes are unconstitutional. As long as they affect congressional procedure rather than policy, legislative vetoes pass constitutional muster. For example, the Omnibus Trade and Competitiveness Act of 1988 allows the president to extend the fast-track procedure under which Congress debates proposed trade agreements unless both the House and Senate adopt a resolution of disapproval within 60 days of the request for an extension. President Bush invoked the procedure in March 1991 when he asked Congress to extend for two years the fast-track procedure for considering any agreement that emerged from the Uruguay Round of negotiations on the General Agreement on Tariffs and Trade.

A third type of procedural legislation enfranchises new groups in the decision-making process. Sometimes the newly enfranchised groups are existing agencies that share the preferences of Congress. In 1988, Congress required DOD to solicit recommendations from the Commerce Department when negotiating agreements with foreign governments on the production of defense equipment. At other times Congress incorporates nongovernmental groups into the decision-making process. The Trade Reform Act of 1974 created private-sector advisory groups representing labor, industry, agriculture, and consumers to provide advice during negotiations. Members also legislate themselves into the decision-making process. In the realm of drug policy, Congress has mandated a formal process of executive-legislative consultations (J. Meyer 1988) and it created the joint executive-legislative Commission on Security and Cooperation in Europe to monitor the Helsinki Accord (Galey 1985). Congress may even make a place for itself in international negotiations. The Trade Act of 1974 allows members to serve as official advisers in international trade negotiations. At a recent meeting of the Uruguay Round of trade talks, a dozen members of Congress and many more congressional aides participated (C. Farnsworth 1990).

A fourth type of procedural legislation stipulates conditions the executive must meet before it can proceed with a policy. This type has been popular in dealing with military basing issues. Congress reacted to extensive base closings during the Johnson and Nixon administrations by requiring DOD to conduct (among other things) detailed fiscal, environmental, and strategic studies before proposing any base for closure or reduction. For more than a decade these procedures effectively prevented the Pentagon from closing bases (Twight 1989, 1990). Stipulating conditions for executive action has also been popular in the formulation of human rights policy (Broder and Lambek 1988; Forsythe 1987, 1988). With the Jackson-Vanik amendment, for example, Congress barred the president from granting most-favored-nation status to nonmarket countries that deny their citizens the right to emigrate. Likewise, in 1981, Congress made approval of arms sales to Chile conditional, requiring presidential certification that Chile had taken steps to bring the murderers of Orlando Letelier to justice.

The last major type of procedural legislation is the reporting requirement. In 1991 the Pentagon was required to produce 676 reports and studies for Congress, and there were roughly an equal number of foreign policy reporting requirements (Fessler 1991, 2562). Many of these merely require the executive to inform Congress of agency decisions. Since the passage of the Hughes-Ryan amendment in 1974, for example, the Central Intelligence Agency (CIA) has been required to report each covert operation to the appropriate congressional committees. Other reporting requirements are designed to force the executive to assess the implications of its policies. For instance, Congress requires DOD to submit an arms control impact statement for every major weapons program. In addition to recurring requirements, Congress also directs agencies to undertake studies of specific issues. The topics covered in such one-time studies range from those of national interest (e.g., whether U.S. aid has been channeled to the Khmer Rouge) to those of only parochial concern (e.g., an evaluation of the environmental-restoration contract for the nuclear bomb plant in Fernald, Ohio).

Procedural changes influence policy in several ways: they keep Congress abreast of what the agency is doing; they discourage the agency from acting in ways that would be disapproved of by substantial numbers of legislators; they force the executive branch to consult with Congress or key legislators; and they ensure that someone in the executive branch is accountable. For instance, all efforts to create new agencies in the executive branch proceed from the assumption that policies are doomed unless they have champions in the bureaucracy. The sponsors of the arms control impact legislation believed that requiring the statements would force DOD to consider the arms control implications of the weapons it was developing, and, failing that, provide Congress with advance warning of the potential arms control ramifications of new weapons systems (Butterworth 1979). And the authors of the provision requiring DOD to consult with the Commerce Department when negotiating coproduction agreements believed that including the Commerce Department in the process would prevent DOD from negotiating agreements that hurt American commercial interests (Ortmayer 1990).

How successful is procedural legislation in shaping policy? Definitive answers are hard to come by because the subject is understudied. Even when scholars begin to address the question, anticipated reactions and counterfactuals make this a difficult question to answer. We have no way of knowing how many covert operations or arms sales packages were stillborn because administration officials knew the proposals would not pass muster in Congress. Nor is the absence of subsequent congressional activity evidence that a reform has failed. One of the purposes of procedural legislation is to push the executive branch to do the bidding of Congress. So a lack of legislative-executive conflict provides as much evidence that the president is complying with the wishes of Congress as it does that Congress is deferring to the president (Edwards 1986, 1989; Mann 1990b; Rockman 1987).

What conclusions can we reasonably draw? The least controversial one is that some procedural legislation fails. ACDA, the War Powers Resolution, and creation of the post of under secretary of defense for acquisition all failed to fulfill legislative expectations (Clarke 1979; Katzmann 1990; Morrison 1991a; Smyrl 1988). These examples notwithstanding, in many instances procedural legislation does affect policy. One example is Congress's success in limiting the ability of the Pentagon to close military bases (Twight 1989, 1990). Trade policy is another area in which Congress often tinkers with procedures to ensure executive compliance with legislative intent. The 1988 Trade Bill, for example, limited presidential discretion in several ways. Concerned that the president was unwilling to punish trading partners who engage in unfair practices, Congress transferred responsibility for retaliation from the president to the special trade representative. The 1988 Trade Bill also broadened the definition of unfair trade practices and terminated the International Trade Commission's discretion to investigate claims of dumping. Both changes were designed to make it easier for injured groups to claim relief (Nivola 1990; O'Halloran 1990).

In changing the rules of the game, the Omnibus Trade Bill of 1988 also changed behavior in the White House, which underscores the link between procedural skirmishes and anticipated reactions. When Congress began in the mid-1980s to debate proposals for restricting presidential discretion on trade, the Reagan administration suddenly made trade policy a priority (Koh 1986, 1223–25). Vice President George Bush spelled out the link between the new-found executive interest in trade and the mood on Capitol Hill:

Frankly, we are trying as hard as we can to derail the protectionist juggernaut now sweeping through the United States Congress. . . . That's one more reason why our recent actions have been necessary. If we don't demonstrate good faith in enforcing our existing trade laws, we risk inviting sterner medicine from the Congress. (Quoted in Boyd 1986)

When the Omnibus Trade Bill finally passed, after Bush's election as president, the administration initiated the Structural Impediments Initiative talks with Japan in an effort to avoid invoking the retaliatory provisions of the bill. The Omnibus Trade Bill also altered the behavior of several of America's trading partners. South Korea, for example, worked to increase imports of American-made goods in an effort to avoid becoming the target of the retaliatory provisions of the bill (Elving 1990, 969).

The success of procedural legislation on military basing and trade policy might not seem remarkable given Congress's historical and constitutional interest in both areas. But procedural change appears to work in other areas of foreign policy as well. Oversight of the CIA provides an example, one that challenges conventional wisdom. As a result of reforms implemented over the past fifteen years, virtually all CIA assessments go to the Intelligence Committees. The Appropriations, Armed Services, Foreign Affairs, and Foreign Relations Committees also receive CIA reports, and many individual members receive briefings (Gates 1987-88, 225; Johnson 1989, 97–99; Treverton 1990, 79). These reforms have made the CIA more attentive to the views of Congress. To quote Robert M. Gates (1987-88, 224–25), a former director of the agency,

> The result of these realities is that the CIA today finds itself in a remarkable position, involuntarily poised equidistant between the executive and legislative branches. The administration knows that the CIA is in no position to withhold much information from Congress and is extremely sensitive to congressional demands; the Congress has enormous influence and information yet remains suspicious and mistrustful.

Even the Iran-Contra affair supports Gates's conclusion about Congress's influence over the CIA. Former director William Casey tried to create an "off-the-shelf," covert-operations team precisely because he wanted to circumvent congressional oversight of covert operations (Woodward 1987).

Framing Opinion

A third way members of Congress influence foreign and defense policy is by changing the climate of opinion surrounding that policy. When the opinions of the public and of the political elite change, policies usually do too. Members use a host of techniques to influence opinion, including committee hearings, reports, speeches, and appearances on radio and television shows. As diverse as these activities may be, they share a common goal: to define the terms of debate on an issue in a way that will increase support for some policy options and decrease support for others.

That framing constitutes a strategy for influencing policy may come as a surprise. Because framing an issue usually involves efforts to attract media coverage, critics often dismiss it as mere "political grandstanding." (Note that Lindsay [1992–93] uses *grandstanding* in place of *framing;* here we adopt *framing* to underscore our intention to provide analysis, not pejorative judgment.) To be sure, members sometimes run to the media with an issue thinking more of their own electoral interest than the national good. Senator Frank Church (D-Idaho), for example, sounded the tocsin on the Soviet brigade stationed in Cuba in 1979 less to influence President Carter than to ingratiate himself with voters back home (Caldwell 1991, 159–69). Much the same situation occurred in 1977 during the neutron bomb controversy. Analysis of floor debates suggests that many legislators failed to understand the weapon they were discussing (Rubin 1978).

Still, complaints about political framing miss three important points. First, even when legislators seize on an issue for purely cynical reasons, their actions influence, for well or ill, the shape of U.S. foreign policy. Senator Church's actions complicated Carter's efforts to win Senate approval of the SALT II treaty, and the controversy over the neutron bomb eventually led to a major squabble in the Atlantic Alliance and the decision not to deploy the weapon in Europe. Even if one disapproves of the method, the reality of congressional influence remains.

Second, complaints that framing by members is mere self-aggrandizement rest on the erroneous assumption that the work of Congress should be an "eat your peas and spinach" endeavor. Many observers of Congress seem comfortable only when a member acts as a "lonely gnome who passes up news conferences, cocktail parties, sometimes even marriage in order to devote his time to legislative 'homework'" (Mayhew 1974, 147). For policy entrepreneurs, playing to the galleries is an essential tool for leveling the playing field with the White House (Cook 1989a). Legislators understand far better than their critics E. E. Schattschneider's point (1961, 1–3) that increasing the scope of the decision-making arena may change the ultimate decision. The media, especially television, give members the means to overcome the obstacles that block attempts to shape policy through substantive legislation. The glare of the spotlight is often the best weapon legislators have to dislodge a bill from a hostile committee, to force the administration to reverse a course of action, or to build public support for new policy initiatives.

Third, the fact that a member of Congress usually stands to benefit politically from efforts aimed at framing does not make these efforts any less useful in influencing policy. The American political system rests on the assumption that self-interest will motivate legislators to address pressing policy issues. As James Madison (1961a, 322) wrote, the best way to promote the public good is to create a system in which "the private interest of every individual may be a sentinel over the public rights." Framing, too, is no less useful because it invokes simple, if not simplistic, arguments. Not only do presidents themselves indulge in simple and dramatic appeals—recall President Reagan's Star Wars speech—such appeals are essential to winning public support. When issues are put in terms that anyone can understand, the burden of proof then rests with one's opponents (see Hilsman 1958, 737).

At the most general level, legislators try to frame issues in order to change public opinion. Warner Schilling (1962, 48) argued thirty years ago that legislators who want to influence defense policy should "change their policy target from the budget to the climate of opinion that shaped it." In the mid-1980s, Senator Charles Grassley (R-Iowa) showed the wisdom of Schilling's advice. Rather than attacking individual defense programs, Grassley released information that the air force had paid $916.55 to purchase a small plastic cap for the leg of a navigator's stool (Crackel 1985). The story captured national headlines and soon other stories of overcharging came to light. The resulting furor over waste, fraud, and abuse in the Pentagon dampened public enthusiasm for increased levels of defense spending (Barone and Ujifusa 1987, 424).

Legislators also try to frame issues in ways that directly pressure the administration to change its policies. When President Reagan disputed reports of massive fraud in the February 1986 elections in the Philippines, Senator Richard Lugar (R-Ind.), chair of the Senate Foreign Relations Committee, countered with a two-week media blitz.

> He appeared on all three network television interview shows (*Meet the Press, Face the Nation,* and *This Week with David Brinkley*). . . . From that television platform, Lugar called on Reagan to telephone Marcos to ask him to resign. (H. Smith 1988, 43–44)

Lugar's media campaign worked; within days Reagan withdrew his support from Marcos. In sending signals to the president, legislators also may act on behalf of mid-level officials in the executive branch who believe current policy is flawed. Senator Lugar, for example, was urged to call for Marcos's resignation by mid-level officials at the State Department, DOD, and the National Security Council. These officials saw congressional debate over the Philippines "as a way to persuade their bosses, not least the president, that Marcos might have to go" (Treverton 1990, 98).

Efforts at framing issues may even be aimed at other countries. Sometimes the administration encourages legislative framing as a means of strengthening its hand in negotiations. During the Nixon administration, for instance, Secretary of Commerce Maurice Stans asked Wilbur Mills (D-Ark.), chair of the Ways and Means Committee, to introduce a bill on textile quotas. Stans apparently hoped to create a good cop–bad cop scenario that would force Japan to make additional concessions in trade negotiations (Pastor 1980, 193). More often, however, members of Congress act on their own. Consider Operation Desert Shield. Germany and Japan initially balked at underwriting the costs of the allied military effort. In September 1990, a burden-sharing amendment to the House defense appropriations bill sparked "a storm of animosity, extraordinary in its extent and intensity," over the reluctance of Germany and Japan to help support the multinational force (Apple 1990). Within two days of the debate, Germany agreed to contribute to the Gulf effort and Japan quadrupled its aid offer (Tagliabue 1990; Weisman 1990).

A Concluding Note

Scholars debate whether Congress matters much in the development of the foreign and defense policy of the United States. Unfortunately, the debate usually proceeds without much thought being given to the tremendous differences among foreign and defense policies or to the means Congress uses to influence policy-making. This failing is damaging. Any understanding of the congressional role in the formulation of foreign policy requires careful examination of the ways in which Congress exercises its influence. Until scholars begin to deal with such fundamental conceptual issues, the potential for making further headway in the study of Congress and foreign and defense policy is remote.

In this chapter we make two points that we think will help those interested in paying more precise attention to the question of how much Congress matters. The first point is that the relative influence of Congress varies among three major types of foreign and defense policy: crisis, strategic, and structural. If that proposition is accepted, the discussion about Congress's influence on foreign policy can be refined. Expectations of the impact of Congress will differ depending on what is at stake.

The second point is that there are four principal ways in which Congress can influence foreign and defense policy. Only one of them—substantive legislation—is overt and obvious. The other three—anticipated reactions, procedural legislation, and the framing of opinion—are much less obvious but also important. In seeking to measure the influence of Congress anywhere along the spectrum from purely verbal to precisely quantitative it is important that observers record all relevant actions. We think some observers miss much of the action in Congress because they ignore events in some of the less visible categories we have discussed.

In short, although we have not generated precise measurements in this chapter, we hope that our development of categories and the rich array of examples we offer will help foster better attempts at measurement and more informed, empirically based discussion of the extent of congressional influence. It does not seem to us to be an open question *whether* Congress matters in foreign and defense policy. We are primarily concerned with *how, when, why,* and *under what conditions* Congress matters. We hope that our fellow social scientists share that focus, and we hope that this chapter has moved that kind of discourse incrementally forward.

CHAPTER 3

The Fiscal Straitjacket: Budgetary Constraints on Congressional Foreign and Defense Policy-Making

Lance T. LeLoup

In the transformed international arena of the 1990s, American policymakers face a host of new foreign policy challenges and problems. They do so, however, with the U.S. Treasury running on empty. The end of the cold war, the demise of communism in Central Europe, the Gulf war and its aftermath, the collapse of the Soviet Union, and ethnic fighting in the former Yugoslavia are among the dramatic changes that have taken place in recent years. But at home the budget deficits continue to set records and economic problems encourage members of Congress to put domestic concerns first. How confining is the fiscal straitjacket in which congressional policymakers find themselves? What will it mean for America's role in the world in the coming years and decades? In confronting a serious international military and economic threat such as the Gulf crisis, budgetary constraints are not decisive in shaping short-term national security calculations. But in the long run, budget deficits, soaring debt, and lagging economic growth will increasingly determine what the United States can do internationally.

The fiscal and budgetary context for congressional policy-making can be examined from several perspectives. Global shifts in economic balances, U.S. productivity, the national saving-rate, and competitiveness in world markets all influence U.S. foreign policy and national defense options in the long term. In the medium and short term, the performance of the U.S. economy, taxing and spending trends, extraordinary expenses such as the savings-and-loan bailout, and resulting budget deficits play a major role in shaping the policy environment. Budgetary stress and institutional combat with the presidency have also affected the performance of Congress as an institution. The previous decade witnessed dramatic alterations of the budget process, innovation in legislative rules and procedures, and changes in the distribution of power within Congress.

The analysis that follows focuses first on U.S. economic developments from a long-term international perspective. Although broad and somewhat

37

abstract, such a perspective is an essential backdrop to a discussion of the more immediate budgetary context. Second, Congress's response to the deficit crisis of the 1980s and 1990s is considered, including institutional changes, deficit reduction schemes, and their consequences for foreign affairs and defense spending. Third, the recent changes brought about by the Omnibus Budget Reconciliation Act of 1990 (OBRA) and the Budget Enforcement Act (BEA) are examined, including how foreign and defense policy options have been impacted. Fourth, the deficit problem is considered in more detail, comparing different measures and assessing the impact of deposit insurance and social security on the deficit. The final section measures the peace dividend, examines possible scenarios for the mid-1990s, and concludes with an assessment of how the budgetary context will affect Congress's capacity to meet new foreign and defense policy challenges.

The U.S. Budget and Economy in Global Perspective

Nearly a century ago, Walter Lippmann warned that insolvent economic policies would ultimately bankrupt the international power of a nation. Variations on that theme became popular in the last decade. Beginning as a few isolated voices, alarm over the possible economic and military decline of the United States grew to a chorus. In 1982, Mancur Olson contended in *The Rise and Decline of Nations* that interest group pressures, which inevitably expand the scope of government, lead to decline because of inefficient intrusions into the private economy that reduce productivity and growth. More commonly, warnings about American decline are based on overextension of international commitments and excessive military spending. The perspective was most persuasively argued in Paul Kennedy's *Rise and Fall of the Great Powers* (1987). His analysis of five hundred years of decline provoked widespread discussion—in congressional cloakrooms and the popular press—of the economic threat to the United States' position as a preeminent world power.

Kennedy (1987, 22) hypothesized that the process of growth and decline depends on "differentials in growth rates and technological change, leading to shifts in the global economic balances, which in turn gradually impinge on political and military balances." Expansive empires, from the Hapsburg empire five hundred years ago to the British empire in this century, committed themselves to massive amounts of military spending, which ultimately led to stagnation of their domestic economies. Measured by economic indices, Kennedy argues that a multipolar world exists today compared to 1950. However, a disjuncture between military and economic balances currently exists because of a time-lag between the trajectory of a nation's economic strength and its military and territorial influence. In declining states, pessimists speak of decline and patriots demand renewal: "Great powers in decline," he writes, "instinctively respond by spending more on 'security', and thereby divert potential resources from 'investment' and compound their long-term dilemma" (ibid., xxiii).

In its most general form, the decline thesis seems to fit a number of trends observed since World War II. The United States' share of the world's total output of goods and services has been reduced by nearly half since 1950, to below 20 percent. At the same time, Europe's share has grown and Japan has surpassed the states of the former Soviet Union with more than 10 percent of the world's total output. U.S. preeminence in manufacturing and unchallenged leadership in the development of new technology have disappeared. The Soviet Union's severe economic problems, followed by the rapid disintegration of its empire, appears to provide much stronger confirmation of the decline thesis. However, some conclude that, although it is occurring more gradually, the United States, too, may decline as a military and economic power. If this does occur, however influential the legislative branch, Congress will participate in making U.S. defense and foreign policy decisions increasingly restricted in their scope and influence.

The idea that the decline thesis should be applied to the United States, however, has not been widely embraced. Critics as diverse as Jeane Kirkpatrick, Daniel Patrick Moynihan, and James Schlesinger have resisted the notion that America is declining (Moynihan 1988; J. Schlesinger 1988). Politicians, eschewing gloom and doom, disavow declinism. George Bush specifically claimed in many speeches that America is not in decline. Some economists have used aggregate economic indicators to show that the United States' share of world output has changed little since the 1960s (McKenzie 1988). The rapid deployment of U.S. troops that led to the decisive military victory over Iraq was widely cited as disconfirming evidence of U.S. decline. The relatively minor role played by European nations, despite their robust economies and even heavier dependence on imported oil, has even led some to question the link between economic and military power.

Joseph Nye argues that the idea of decline is in itself a misleading metaphor and that historical comparisons are often inappropriate (1990, 86–94). In particular, Nye finds comparisons with Britain misleading because of greater U.S. predominance in the world, its continental-scale economy, and differences in the nature of the empires (ibid., 91–92). Samuel Huntington also disputes the decline thesis, particularly if it is based on the idea of military overextension. Despite the inconclusive academic and popular debate, the question of the long-term relationship between economic strength and international influence remains central to the topic at hand. Even Nye (ibid., 93) acknowledges legitimate causes for concern over the decline of U.S. productivity in the past decade. And Huntington (1988–89, 86) notes that "clearly the declinists are right in highlighting savings and investment as long-term systemic weaknesses that require correction if economic growth is to be maintained." Several developments seem particularly important to the prospects for the relative economic strength and budgetary capacity of the United States and its long-term international influence.[1]

Low productivity growth. Increases in output per worker in the United States have stagnated to an average of just over 1 percent per year. Despite the fact that its nearly $6 trillion economy remains the largest in the world, and U.S. workers still produce more than their German and Japanese counterparts, the rate of productivity growth has slowed to a crawl compared to other nations. Unless this is reversed, the U.S. economy will continue to shrink relative to the rest of the world and the standard of living in the United States will begin to lag.

Large trade deficits. The rapid reversal of the U.S. trading position in the world has created difficult times for U.S. export industries and left billions of dollars in the hands of overseas investors. From 1981 to 1987, the annual merchandise trade deficit swelled from $20 to $150 billion. With high real interest rates in the early 1980s, as a result of the anti-inflation policies pursued by the Federal Reserve, the value of the dollar soared (Congressional Budget Office 1988). The cost of American goods abroad skyrocketed while imported goods became cheaper. This put billions of dollars in the hands of foreign investors who used them to purchase U.S. assets but not necessarily goods and services. Although trade balances have showed marked improvement since 1989, the structural imbalance remains a concern.

Foreign debt. The trade and budget deficits have dramatically shifted international capital flows, transforming the United States' financial balances in a record period of time. After being a net world-creditor, owed $140 billion in 1981, the U.S. overseas debt reached $500 billion by the end of the decade, making the United States the world's largest debtor nation. Inflows of foreign capital were needed to finance a significant portion of the annual budget deficits, which added $1.5 trillion to the national debt during the 1980s (Helliwell 1991, 21–58). Foreign ownership of U.S. assets increased from 6.1 percent in 1980 to 12.7 percent in 1988. Foreign investment per se is not unhealthy but much of the foreign borrowing resulted in increased domestic consumption rather than net investment.

Low savings rate. The United States has one of the lowest savings rates in the world. Large foreign capital inflows were needed to finance the deficits because domestic savings provided insufficient capital. In effect, the United States consumed more than half a trillion dollars through borrowing and the

---

1. Figures in this section are derived from the World Bank, the Organization for Economic Cooperation and Development, the U.S. Council of Economic Advisors, the Office of Management and Budget, and the Department of Commerce. For a summary, see Passell (1990).

liquidation of assets in the 1980s. While the willingness of overseas financiers to invest in the U.S. economy is an indication of its continued strength and stability, it is widely agreed that low savings and high consumption based on borrowing is incompatible with strong economic growth in the long run.

Mainstream economists generally agree that low productivity growth, low domestic savings and investment rates, trade imbalances, and the rate of foreign-debt accumulation need to be reversed in the 1990s if the U.S. economy is to remain strong relative to the rest of the world. But the continuation of high budget deficits through the 1990s will make it extremely difficult to reverse these trends. The Office of Technology Assessment (1988) estimates that at its current pace the U.S. foreign debt could increase to $2 trillion by 1995, seriously lowering future living standards. This would represent one-fourth of the nation's gross domestic product (GDP) and cost billions annually to service.[2] If this level of foreign debt is reached, one-third of real growth in the economy would go to meet these obligations rather than increasing the standard of living of the next generation.

The potential long-term implications of these economic trends for Congress and for foreign and defense policy-making in the future are significant. The U.S. economy is not in an inevitable decline despite the shifts in global economic balances. However, a continuation of $300 to $400 billion deficits at 4 to 6 percent of GDP could lead to a slow, corrosive deterioration of the American economy (Barth et al. 1991, 69–130). In the long run, such a budgetary policy could gradually impinge upon the nation's ability to maintain a defense establishment capable of protecting multiple and widespread security interests throughout the world, even without the Soviet threat. Economic strength and budgetary integrity, in the long run, will affect how U.S. national security objectives can be defined in the twenty-first century.

More tangible and immediate are the effects of the budget deficit on foreign and defense policy options in the 1990s. Despite a hard-fought budget agreement reached after months of negotiation in 1990, the United States would set record deficits in fiscal 1991 and 1992 of $269 and $314 billion respectively (Congressional Budget Office 1992a, 28). The continued imbalance between federal revenues and expenditures constitutes the main budgetary constraint on defense and foreign policy decision making in Congress. To understand the context today, the budgetary developments of the 1980s and Congress's response to them must be examined.

---

2. In 1992, the federal government switched from gross national product (GNP) to gross domestic product (GDP) as the standard measure of national output. Although the two are very similar, GDP excludes some goods and services produced abroad and is more easily compared to measures used in other countries. Although some of the earlier figures refer to GNP, to avoid confusion, GDP has been used throughout in the text.

Congressional Responses to Budgetary Stress
in the 1980s

The chronic budget deficits of the 1980s emerged from the Reagan economic program of 1981, which rapidly increased defense spending while cutting taxes, neither of which were compensated through reductions in domestic spending (LeLoup 1982). The deficits were exacerbated by the recession of 1982. In broader historical perspective, underlying changes in the U.S. economy that eliminated the "fiscal dividend" of the 1960s and 1970s helped create the difficult budgetary environment of the 1980s (Schick 1990, 51–79; Stockman 1986, 57–66). The consequence was a massive increase in federal borrowing to meet the gap between revenues and spending. Table 1 examines outlays, revenues, and the deficit since 1970, and shows the deficit as a percentage of GDP. By 1983 the deficit had mushroomed to $208 billion, which constituted 6.3 percent of GDP. The political impasse between President Reagan, who refused to scale back his defense buildup or raise taxes, and

TABLE 1.   Revenues, Outlays, Deficits, and Deficits as a Percentage of GDP, 1971–90

Year	Revenues	Outlays	Deficit	Deficit as % GDP
1971	187.1	210.2	−23.0	2.2
1972	207.3	230.7	−23.4	2.0
1973	230.8	245.7	−14.9	1.2
1974	263.2	269.4	−6.1	0.4
1975	279.1	332.3	−53.2	3.5
1976	298.1	371.8	−73.7	4.3
1977	355.6	409.2	−53.6	2.8
1978	399.6	458.7	−59.2	2.7
1979	463.3	503.5	−40.2	1.6
1980	517.1	590.9	−73.8	2.8
1981	599.3	678.2	−78.9	2.6
1982	617.8	745.7	−127.9	4.1
1983	600.6	808.3	−207.8	6.3
1984	666.5	851.8	−185.3	5.0
1985	734.1	946.3	−212.3	5.4
1986	769.1	990.3	−221.2	5.3
1987	854.1	1,003.8	−149.7	3.4
1988	909.0	1,064.1	−155.1	3.2
1989	990.7	1,144.1	−153.4	3.0
1990	1,031.5	1,251.9	−220.4	4.1
1991	1,054.3	1,323.0	−268.7	4.8

Source: Congressional Budget Office 1992

House Democrats, who refused to cut domestic spending further, led to important institutional changes in Congress and radical changes in the budget process.

Institutional Changes

The budget crisis of the 1980s spawned a number of institutional responses: nearly constant revision of the budget process, adaptation of legislative rules and procedures, noticeable shifts in the distribution of power, and the utilization of new modes of negotiating with the president. Since 1981 the budget process has played a central role in the way Congress operates. The tentacles of the process reach into the far corners of the Capitol, from the timing of actions to the rules of floor consideration, while measures taken to avoid its strictures have revealed real ingenuity on the part of members. The process was unstable, however, and highly improvisational (Schick 1990, 159–96).

Deficits and budgetary stress in the 1980s led to a number of formal and informal changes in the legislative process. By the mid-1980s the legislative agenda came to be dominated by "must pass" money bills: budget resolutions, omnibus continuing resolutions, supplemental appropriations, reconciliation bills, and the statutory debt limitation. These bills often became catch-all legislative packages, enhancing the power of those who controlled them. One consequence was greater centralization of power in Congress, reversing many of the decentralizing trends of the 1970s (Reiselbach 1986). Dodd and Oppenheimer (1989, 48–49) call the beneficiaries of these changes "the new oligarchy," majority party leaders and chairs of the money committees who formulate legislative "packages" and negotiate directly with the White House. The emphasis in congressional budgeting in the 1980s shifted from micro-budgeting to macrobudgeting (LeLoup 1988).

The centralization of authority weakened subcommittees and most authorizing committees. The use of interbranch summits and high-level negotiation over budget totals reduced the influence of rank-and-file members in general. Tension increased between those responsible for the budget as a whole and those accountable for its many parts. The increased use of bills written by leadership task forces and other extracommittee forums heightened dissatisfaction. A growing number of bills taken up on the floor had not been reported by a standing committee. The proportion of legislation with open rules dropped from 85 percent in the Ninety-fourth Congress to 55 percent in the One-hundredth Congress (S. Smith 1989b, 339). Despite these changes, the new oligarchy proved somewhat fluid and centralization was far from complete. The leadership in both chambers, despite their growing budgetary clout, sometimes suffered humiliating defeats at the hands of various coalitions. Nonetheless, the budget process had clearly moved from a committee-centered to a floor-centered process (Gilmour 1990, 139–51).

The institutional changes and growing emphasis on top-down macro-budgeting in Congress had an impact on the congressional committees that deal with defense and foreign affairs. The House and Senate Armed Services Committees suffered somewhat from the changes in the budget process and shifts in institutional power. Because defense constitutes such a large proportion of discretionary spending, its aggregate levels were increasingly determined by other actors in Congress such as the Budget Committees, ad hoc leadership groups, or interbranch summits. Nonetheless, the Armed Services Committees remained influential in shaping programs and choosing among competing weapons systems within the aggregates.

The Appropriations Committees and their defense subcommittees were impacted more unevenly by the changes of the 1980s. On several occasions, Appropriations Committee leaders played a key role in macrobudgeting. In many other instances, however, they were not part of the critical decision-making group and found themselves highly constrained in their options. The Senate Foreign Relations Committee and the House Foreign Affairs Committee did not appear to suffer as greatly from the shifting power relationships simply because of the limited magnitude of the foreign aid budget and international programs. Like their defense counterparts, they continued to make important program decisions but largely within parameters determined by others.

The Balanced Budget Act (1985)

In 1985 Congress enacted the Balanced Budget and Emergency Deficit Control Act (better known as Gramm-Rudman-Hollings), which mandated deficit reduction and a balanced budget within five years (LeLoup, Graham, and Barwick 1987). A series of deficit targets for the next five years was enacted promising a balanced budget by 1991. Under the mandatory deficit reduction process, if Congress missed an annual deficit target by more than $10 billion, an across-the-board cut (sequester) would be levied on all eligible accounts to reach the target. Proponents claimed that they wanted to create an alternative so onerous that Congress would act responsibly to meet the targets on its own. Although largely a Republican initiative, a key provision was adopted that made Gramm-Rudman palatable to Democrats: any mandatory sequester would impose half its cuts on defense and half on domestic programs (Penner and Abramson 1988, 70–71). The Democrats reasoned that this provision would protect domestic spending by making mandatory cuts just as unacceptable to the administration as they were to Congress.

In the three fiscal years following the adoption of Gramm-Rudman, federal deficits declined from the range of 5 to 6 percent to around 3 percent of

GDP (see table 1). Still, the revised budget process could hardly be judged a success, creating incentives for members of Congress to use a host of gimmicks and tricks to avoid the discipline of the budget targets. Worse, the projected deficits often ballooned through no fault of Congress or the White House. Changes in economic assumptions and technical estimating errors often boosted the deficit by tens of billions of dollars in a matter of months. By 1987, after only two years, it was clear that the original path to a balanced budget would be impossible without a series of devastating sequesters. Spurred by the stock market crash in October 1987, a summit agreement between the two branches was reached. Congress revised the Balanced Budget Act and the annual deficit targets, delaying the goal of a balanced budget until 1993.

Consequences for Defense
and Foreign Affairs Spending

Foreign aid programs, although they felt the effects of budgetary austerity in the 1980s, were simply too small to have much influence on outlay and deficit totals. While they were not gutted as a result of the deficit crisis, they continued down a long path of real decline. In the late 1940s and early 1950s, when the United States played the leading role in postwar reconstruction, spending on foreign aid averaged around 2 percent of GDP, the equivalent of over $100 billion today (Doherty 1992c, 1356). Since 1960 spending has fallen from 1.3 percent of GDP to current levels of around $18 billion or 0.21 percent of GDP. Between 1984 and 1992, foreign aid fell 20 percent in real terms. Although still the largest supplier of total nonmilitary aid, according to 1990 data compiled by the Organization for Economic Cooperation and Development (OECD), the United States ranked seventeenth out of eighteen major nations in the proportion of GDP devoted to foreign aid, surpassing only Ireland (Doherty 1992c, 1356). Although technically "discretionary," foreign aid programs are highly inflexible because of previous treaties and "earmarking" agreements, and increases remain politically difficult when so many other programs are being reduced.

The effect on defense spending was more dramatic; the Balanced Budget Act marked an end to the rapid defense buildup of the early 1980s. Beginning in 1986 defense spending leveled out and began to decline slightly in real terms. During the 1980s defense spending was a dynamic component of a rapidly changing budget. In the first half of the decade, the United States engaged in the most rapid, peace-time, defense buildup in history. After 1985, as the deficits remained unresolved, a steady erosion of both budget authority and real outlays occurred. Figure 1 examines defense spending in current and constant dollars since 1946 (projected through 1993).

Equally interesting were the changes in the administration's five-year

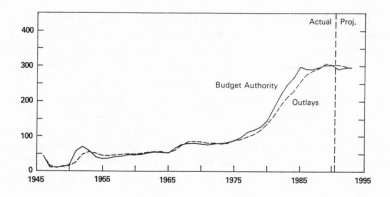

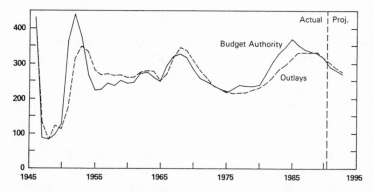

Fig. 1. Trends in defense spending, 1946–93, in billions of constant (1991) dollars. (*Source:* Congressional Budget Office 1991a.)

defense plans through the 1980s and 1990s in comparison to actual funding levels. Table 2 shows the annual five-year defense plans and actual budget authority enacted for that year. For example, actual budget authority in 1990 was $291 billion rather than the $478 billion Reagan had projected in his FY86 budget. Clearly, this reflects not only changing administration expectations but a Congress taking an active role in redefining the parameters of defense spending and planning.

The Effect on Supplemental Appropriations

Supplemental appropriations have traditionally provided important opportunities for Congress and the president to respond to urgent defense and foreign policy needs. In the austere fiscal environment of the 1980s, however, the use of supplementals declined noticeably. Supplemental appropriations averaged 4.6 percent of total budget authority approved by Congress in the 1970s, including a high of 7.8 percent in FY77 (Congressional Budget Office 1990a, x). Since 1985 they have averaged less than 0.5 percent of budget authority. Supplemental appropriations traditionally have been much more important to defense and international programs than other policy areas.

Foreign aid received $15.3 billion in supplemental appropriations in the 1980s, 19 percent of all discretionary supplementals (Congressional Budget Office 1990a, xii). This allowed the president and Congress to respond to a number of unforeseen events, allowing them, for example, to provide funds for African famine relief and payments to the International Monetary Fund (IMF). Defense supplementals in the 1980s amounted to $10 billion, 12.5 percent of discretionary supplementals, although most of those occurred in 1981 to spur the defense buildup. In addition, much of the $19 billion in supplemental appropriations for federal pay in the 1980s went to civilian employees of defense programs. Supplemental spending for veterans programs totaled nearly $6 billion or 7 percent. Although supplemental appropriations remain available, budgetary stringency, rules changes, and the Budget Enforcement Act have made them much more difficult to enact.

As a result of the budget summit agreement in late 1987, it was agreed that future supplemental appropriations could only be approved for "dire emergencies." Accordingly, only 0.1 percent of total budget authority approved by Congress in 1988 came through supplemental appropriations, the lowest proportion in recent history. Although the "dire emergencies" standard has not always been upheld (the $4 billion 1990 supplemental appropriation included funding for a fish farm in Arkansas), this avenue for adding monies to defense and foreign aid programs faces more procedural and political obstacles than in the past.

The Omnibus Budget Reconciliation Act of 1990

These institutional changes and spending trends provide important background for understanding the developments in 1990, when the 1974 Congressional Budget and Impoundment Control Act and the 1985 Balanced Budget Act were modified again. The path toward a balanced budget took a tortuous turn in 1990. In February 1990, President Bush submitted a budget projecting a deficit of only $64 billion, meeting the Gramm-Rudman target for FY91. But in a matter of months projected deficits ballooned by nearly $100 billion (Congressional Budget Office 1990b). It was revealed that the savings-and-loan bailout would cost billions more than expected. As the economy declined, revenue collections lagged behind estimates. By summer, estimates of the deficit approached $250 billion. A sequester to reach the Gramm-Rudman target of $64 billion for FY91 would plunge the economy into recession while gutting discretionary programs. The situation was complicated by Iraq's inva-

TABLE 2. Actual, Requested, and Projected Defense Budget Authority by Year of Submission, Fiscal Years 1981–96 (current dollars in billions)

Administration, Fiscal Year for Request, Date of Submission	81	82	83	84	85	86	87	88	89	90	91	92	93	94	95	96
Reagan FY82/Mar 81	178	[222	254	289	327	368]										
Reagan FY83/Feb 82		214	[258	285	332	368	400]									
Reagan FY84/Jan 83			241	[274	322	357	389	425]								
Reagan FY85/Feb 84				258	[305	350	379	412	446]							
Reagan FY86/Feb 85					287	[314	354	402	439	478]						

Reagan FY87/Feb 86	278	[312	332	354	375	396]				
Reagan FY88/Feb 87		282	[303	323	344	365	387]			
Reagan FY89/Feb 88			283	[291	307	324	342	360]		
Reagan FY90/Jan 89				290	[306	321	336	351	366]	
Bush Revision FY90/Apr 89				290	[296	311	322	336	350]	
Bush FY91/Jan 90					291	[295	300	304	308	312]
Bush FY92/Jan 91						292	[291	291	292	295	298]

Source: Library of Congress, Congressional Research Service
Note: The first figure in each row is actual budget authority; the figures in brackets are requested/projected.

sion of Kuwait, suggesting that earlier euphoria about a peace dividend may have been premature and that military action might cost billions. The Gulf crisis itself seemed to threaten the economy, temporarily increasing oil prices to over $30 a barrel. This is the situation that the budget summit negotiators faced in September 1990 as they attempted to fashion a meaningful deficit-reduction plan.

The Budget Summit

After five months without discernible progress, a small group of top congressional and administration negotiators agreed on a five-year, $500 billion deficit-reduction plan only hours before the beginning of the fiscal year. The administration and congressional leaders of both parties strongly supported the unpopular package but it was defeated by the restive rank and file of both parties in the House of Representatives. Despite this embarrassing defeat, and the subsequent modification of the plan, the summit agreement structured the settlement, including a major revision of Gramm-Rudman and the congressional budget process. The basic approach of the plan was to reach half a trillion dollars in deficit reduction over five years through equal parts of defense cuts, domestic cuts, and tax increases. These parameters represented compromise on both sides: President Bush abandoned his "no new taxes" pledge in agreeing to new revenues and congressional Democrats accepted sharp cuts in domestic programs such as Medicare. Despite the fact that defense was slated for cuts of some $130 billion below the Congressional Budget Office (CBO) baseline over five years, the cuts were less drastic than some had predicted or advocated before the Gulf war.

A number of important policy and budget process changes were embodied in the budget agreement. The most crucial was the suspension of Gramm-Rudman for three years and the simultaneous creation of separate caps for discretionary domestic, defense, and international program appropriations. One of the shortcomings of Gramm-Rudman was that Congress was held accountable for budget changes not of their own making. The revised process eliminated fixed deficit targets as meaningful goals and changed the nature of sequestration. Deficit targets became elastic, moving with economic and technical changes. The new budget process shifted the emphasis from deficit reduction to spending control; it focused on maintaining budgetary discipline in those areas in which Congress has direct control (Congressional Budget Office 1990c, 2).

Discretionary Spending Limits

The Budget Enforcement Act divided discretionary appropriations into three categories with separate outlay and budget authority limits for fiscal years

1991–93. For fiscal years 1994 and 1995, under the 1990 law, the three discretionary categories would again be merged and a single cap imposed on appropriations. Defense includes not only the activities of the Defense Department but other agencies' defense-related activities such as the Energy Department's nuclear weapons program. International programs include foreign economic and military aid, the State Department and other agencies, and international financial programs such as the Export-Import Bank.

The discretionary spending limits are adjusted twice each year based on changes in budgetary definitions under the act and the difference between estimated and actual inflation (Congressional Budget Office 1991b, 45). Table 3 examines the discretionary limits as originally specified in the budget summit agreement and the amount of savings over the previous baseline. Note that all the discretionary savings came from defense; international and domestic discretionary programs were allowed to grow to the baseline amount. Particularly in the domestic category, appropriators maintained some leeway to increase spending in certain programs. This resulted in part from the influence of Senator Robert Byrd (D-W.Va.), chair of the Senate Appropriations Committee, who wanted to ensure some spending increases on the domestic side. A number of items were exempted from the appropriations caps. The three discretionary totals were "held harmless" from additional outlays resulting from Operation Desert Shield (and Desert Storm), changes in economic assumptions or technical reestimates, costs associated with the savings-and-loan bailout, Egyptian debt forgiveness, and foreign contributions to the Department of Defense (DOD). Further, any spending determined to be an "emergency" by both the president (through the Office of Management and Budget [OMB]) and Congress was exempted from the caps.

The appropriations caps were enforced by a set of new congressional rules and procedures. Under the 1985 Balanced Budget Act, congressional budget resolutions covered the period of a single year, allowing spending increases and tax cuts to be shifted ahead to outyears. Under the new rules, budget resolutions and reconciliation bills covered five years, and limits in the act must be maintained for that period. If the spending caps are exceeded, excess spending is eliminated by a minisequester within the offending category. That is, if international programs spending exceeds allowable budget authority for a given fiscal year, across-the-board cuts will be assessed on all accounts within the category in order to reach the cap. For "cap-busting" bills enacted before 1 July, a "within session" sequester for that fiscal year is triggered fifteen days after enactment. Legislation enacted after 1 July causing the caps to be exceeded is subject to a "look back" sequester, which reduces the discretionary spending limits for that category in the next fiscal year by the amount of the spending breach (Omnibus Budget Reconciliation Act of 1990, sec. 253).

The development of appropriations caps represents an interesting devel-

TABLE 3. Discretionary Caps Agreed to in Budget Summit, October 1990

	1991		1992		1993		1994		1995		1991–95	
	BA	O	BA	O	BA	O	BA	O	BA	O	BA	O
Defense												
Baseline	313.6	306.2	326.0	316.9	338.3	326.1						
Savings	−25.1	−9.8	−35.1	−22.6	−47.2	−34.8						
Agreed level	288.5	296.4	290.9	294.3	291.1	291.3						
International												
Adjusted baseline	20.1	18.6	20.5	19.1	21.4	19.6						
Savings	—	—	—	—	—	—						
Agreed level	20.1	18.6	20.5	19.1	21.4	19.6						
Domestic												
Adjusted baseline	182.7	198.1	191.3	210.1	198.3	221.7						
Savings	—	—	—	—	—	—						
Agreed level	182.7	198.1	191.3	210.1	198.3	221.7						
Total Discretionary												
Adjusted baseline	516.4	522.9	537.8	546.1	558.0	567.4	570.1	588.0	588.0	602.8	2770.3	2827.2
Savings	−25.1	−9.8	−35.1	−22.6	−47.2	−34.8	−58.6	−53.2	−69.6	−62.0	−235.6	−182.4
Agreed level	491.3	513.1	502.7	523.5	510.8	532.6	511.5	534.8	518.4	540.8	2534.7	2644.8

Source: Unpublished staff document, U.S. Senate, 1990.
Note: BA = Budget Authority; O = Outlays.

opment in the evolution of congressional budgeting and attempts at spending control since the 1960s. As spending and deficits began to mount in the late 1960s, Congress experimented with different forms of overall spending caps five of the six years between 1967 and 1972 (Schick 1977, 49–50). The statutory limitations on expenditures failed, however, since no enforcement mechanisms existed. Power still rested with the authorizing and appropriating committees. Following the adoption of the Budget Act in 1974, functional categories in the budget resolutions (originally the second resolution) were to serve as caps of sorts. These functional subtotals failed to contain spending through the 1980s, however, since the figures were generally raised to accommodate the spending committees.

Shifts in influence toward more centralized control by the Budget Committees and party leaders did not occur until the 1980s in response to a confrontation with the White House. The adoption of Gramm-Rudman was in a sense another attempt to cap total spending by specifying a maximum deficit, knowing the target would not be met through tax increases. Even as budgeting shifted toward high-level, interbranch negotiations, an essential element of budgeting involved explicit trade-offs between defense and domestic spending. Despite the fact that Gramm-Rudman divided the sequester equally between defense and domestic programs, congressional Democrats could still shift money from defense to domestic programs in attempting to meet the target.

On one hand, the development of three separate appropriations caps in 1990 revealed the further strength of the leaders in their ability to negotiate with the president. On the other hand, they severely limited congressional discretion. This provided the administration with an insurance policy of sorts for defense and international spending through 1993 since it prevented raids for domestic programs. The budget process, relative power relationships, and policy consequences are much less certain for 1994 and 1995, if and when the three discretionary categories are collapsed and subject to a single cap. In early 1993, deficit targets, discretionary spending limits, and other totals in the budget will be renegotiated based on current economic conditions and technical reestimates. If the process is maintained as currently provided for in the law, Gramm-Rudman would return to enforce the totals in 1994 and 1995 and trade-offs between categories would be allowed. A sequester, falling equally on defense and domestic accounts, would be used to scale back discretionary spending to the statutory limit. Prospects for further changes in the budget process are discussed in a later section.

Pay-as-you-go Rules

Although several other elements of the revised budget process do not as directly affect defense and international programs, they have important consequences for Congress's overall performance and the larger budgetary context for decision making. The other major change in budget enforcement concerns the treatment of entitlements and revenues in the budget. Under the old system, a sequester of discretionary programs could be triggered by revenue shortfalls or increases in entitlement spending because of greater utilization or higher inflation. Under the Budget Enforcement Act, both revenues and entitlements were put on a pay-as-you-go basis. Any action to increase entitlement eligibility or reduce revenues must be offset by spending cuts or tax increases elsewhere in the budget. These provisions affect the total of all legislation in a given year, not individual measures.

Limits on the expansion of entitlements are enforced by a sequester across certain entitlement categories. Reconciliation procedures were extended to revenues for the first time to enforce the pay-as-you-go rules. The Budget Committees may issue reconciliation instructions to the Ways and Means or Finance Committees to mandate an offset for a revenue loss. Like discretionary spending, entitlement spending determined by both the president and Congress to be an emergency is exempted from the requirement. The impact of these rules is somewhat contrary to that of the spending caps in that it focuses on "deficit neutrality" rather than spending control since new entitlements can expand without limit if they are financed through new revenues.

Social Security was exempted from the pay-as-you-go requirement but was subjected to a series of special requirements. In particular, the act creates what is called a Social Security firewall to protect the trust fund from legislation that would expand benefits or reduce payroll taxes (Omnibus Budget Reconciliation Act 1990, sec. 13133). Social Security trust fund surpluses were excluded from the deficit, resulting in much larger on-budget deficit numbers. Credit reform was included in the new budget process, bringing direct loans and loan guarantees under the scope of discretionary spending caps and pay-as-you-go rules.

In general, OBRA represents a radical departure from past methods of dealing with chronic deficits. On the surface it appears to retreat from the priority of deficit reduction and the achievement of a balanced budget since deficit targets are no longer binding. The deficit can increase for any number of reasons—changing economic conditions, technical reestimates, emergencies, or additional deposit insurance costs—without triggering any spending reductions. But the revised process is both more realistic and more flexible. It asserts discipline over decisions that Congress actually controls—discretionary spending, entitlement expansion, and revenue reduction—and provides much stronger enforcement procedures. It helps avoid the frustration of fixed deficit targets, which inevitably are missed because of unforeseen developments. With a five-year framework for budget resolutions and reconciliation and credit reforms, the opportunity for budget highjinks and gimmicks has been reduced (but not eliminated).

Assessing the Deficit Problem

Despite the fact that unexpected increases in the budget deficit no longer trigger across-the-board cuts, the deficit continues to be the most important budgetary constraint on policy options in the 1990s. In 1991, less than a year after the enactment of OBRA, projections that had showed a balanced budget by 1996 were revised to forecast deficits remaining in the $200 billion range through the decade (Office of Management and Budget 1991, 1–10). Despite the intense criticism aimed at the 1990 budget deal, the annual deficits in the 1990s would have been as much as $80 billion greater per year without OBRA, as is shown in figure 2. To understand the potential impact of deficits on defense and international programs, a number of issues should be addressed. First, why are deficit projections so notoriously inaccurate, and why did the projections for the 1992–97 period increase so dramatically? Second, how is the deficit measured and what measures are most meaningful? Specifically, what are the consequences of the savings-and-loan crisis and the budgetary treatment of Social Security? Third, what are the long-term chances that the deficit problem will continue?

Forecasting the Deficit

For twelve consecutive years the actual deficit has exceeded the deficit specified in the congressional budget resolution. In FY90, the actual deficit was a record $119 billion above the level specified by Congress. Understanding the source of error in forecasting deficits is important for interpreting projections through the 1990s and for estimating the potential effects on defense and international programs. Reported deficits are highly sensitive to changes in the economy and also vary with changes in technical estimates of revenues, entitlements, and other outlay categories. Deficits also expand because of policy changes—additional spending and reductions in revenues.

Deficit projections are highly dependent upon the economic assumptions on which they are based. Increases in interest rates, unemployment, and reduced economic growth all increase the size of the deficit. Higher inflation used to reduce the deficit but, since tax rates were indexed in the early 1980s, inflation has relatively little effect on the annual deficit. For example, a rate of economic growth one percentage point lower than expected increases the deficit by $26 billion in the first year and increases the annual deficit in five years by $130 billion (Congressional Budget Office 1991b, 76). A one-percent increase in unemployment adds $33 billion to the deficit; a

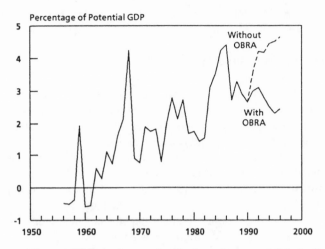

Fig. 2. Effect of OBRA on the standardized employment deficit, by fiscal year. (*Source:* Congressional Budget Office 1991.)

one-percent increase in interest rates adds $15 billion to the deficit. Whatever budget agreements or statutory requirements exist, unexpected changes in the economy are reflected directly in deficits.

Technical estimating errors can compound the problem as well. The budget is based on forecasts of revenues and outlays based on such factors as new tax provisions, price increases for medical care, changing eligibility and utilization rates, and other variables. Technical errors, particularly with regard to Medicare and Medicaid, were primarily responsible for the reestimates of the deficit in 1992 and beyond. A serious error was made by the Treasury in estimating revenue under OBRA's new tax provisions (Hager 1991). Revised figures showed that revenues would be $132.9 billion less over the five-year period, almost equal to the total new revenue of $137 billion generated by the summit agreement. Added to higher than anticipated spending for health care and other programs, a total of $216 billion had been returned to the projected deficits through 1996. Estimates for the 1991 deficit were actually reduced downward because of the one-time-only contributions for the costs of Desert Storm and slower than planned resolution of insolvent thrifts. As a result, because much of the spending was deferred until later years, the projection for the deficits in the 1990s soared.

Rapid changes in the deficit also may reflect policy choices. On numerous occasions Congress and the administration have approved measures that either lowered revenues or increased outlays, independent of economic or technical changes. Table 4 compares the sources of difference between the deficit specified in the congressional budget resolution and the actual deficit. Between 1980 and 1990, the actual deficit exceeded the forecast deficit by an

TABLE 4.   Sources of Differences between the Congressional Budget Resolution and the Actual Deficit, 1980–90, in Billions of Dollars

Year	Policy Changes	Economic Assumptions	Technical Reestimates	Total
1980	13.4	4.0	19.1	36.6
1981	28.2	1.4	28.6	58.1
1982	−11.8	76.0	8.8	73.0
1983	22.2	58.5	10.8	91.5
1984	15.2	2.7	−14.1	3.7
1985	23.0	14.8	−16.2	21.6
1986	15.7	10.9	22.2	48.8
1987	−15.3	15.1	6.3	6.2
1988	8.9	8.1	28.5	45.5
1989	16.8	−19.7	19.6	16.8
1990	20.0	49.5	49.6	119.1
Average difference	12.4	20.1	14.8	47.3
Average absolute difference	17.3	23.7	20.4	47.3

Source: Congressional Budget Office 1991.

average of $47 billion. In general, the reasons for differences between predicted and actual amounts are fairly well balanced between economic, technical, and policy factors, with economic factors accounting for the most variation, and policy changes the least. Economic changes were particularly dramatic in 1982, 1983, and 1990, and technical errors were worst in 1990. Despite this flawed record, forecasts of outlays and revenues remain essential to budgeting. Although multiyear deficit-forecasts have proven unreliable, they provide the best estimate of the consequences of current policy and a base upon which to judge the potential effects of policy changes.

Assessing the policy-making constraints imposed by the deficit also depends on interpreting different measures of the deficit and recognizing political decisions about how to account for different kinds of federal borrowing. Much of the surge in the deficit was due to the cost of deposit insurance to bail out insolvent savings and loans and other financial institutions. Second, budgetary treatment of the Social Security trust fund has been changed several times in recent years reflecting political disagreements over how best to measure the deficit and what the nation's "real" deficit is. Table 5 examines several measures of the deficits projected through 1996. The first row presents the August 1992 projection of the deficits through 1997.

Deposit Insurance and Desert Storm Contributions

Several components of the on-budget deficit reflect transitory factors that do not represent long-term deficit trends. Much of the recent uncertainty in fore-

TABLE 5. Deficit Projections Using Alternative Measures, in Billions of Dollars

	Actual 1991	1992	1993	1994	1995	1996	1997
Total deficit assuming discretionary caps	269	314	331	268	244	254	290
Deficit excluding deposit insurance and Desert Storm contributions	246	306	282	251	239	261	307
Standardized-employment deficit[a]	190	232	223	214	212	240	291
On-budget deficit (excluding Social Security and Postal Service)	321	364	388	336	322	340	383

Source: Congressional Budget Office, 1992a.
[a]Excludes deposit insurance and Desert Storm contributions.

casting outlays, revenues, and the deficit stems from the deposit insurance debacle. There are two main components to the costs associated with the bailout: insurance losses that represent permanent outlays, and working capital needed to resolve insolvent thrifts and banks.[3] Significant amounts of working capital can be recovered later when the government disposes of assets it has acquired. In 1989, Congress enacted the Financial Institutions Reform, Recovery, and Enforcement Act (FIRREA) to deal with the nearly one thousand insolvent thrifts across the country and created the Resolution Trust Corporation (RTC) to resolve insolvent savings-and-loan institutions. The total costs for insurance losses covered by the RTC are now estimated to total $150 billion, three times the original authorization. Congressional reluctance to fund the bailout sufficiently has further skewed deficit projections. By not authorizing additional sums in 1992, the deficit was lowered by some $50 billion but outlays were simply transferred to later years.

Despite the scope of the deposit insurance losses and the resulting increases in the deficit, borrowing for working capital does not have the same economic effects as other borrowing. The money borrowed to resolve insolvent thrifts and banks is returned to the financial markets and hence does not create upward pressure on interest rates. And, although spending increased in the early 1990s, it will decline more quickly in subsequent years. Contributions from allies to finance Operation Desert Storm also distort the deficit. The

---

3. Insolvent thrifts are defined as those having a capital-to-assets ratio of less than 3 percent on a book value basis and are insolvent on a market value basis. In addition, a number of thrifts with a capital-to-assets ratio greater than 3 percent on a book value basis are nonetheless insolvent on a market value basis.

contributions of $42 billion in 1991 and $5 billion in 1992 had the one-time-only effect of lowering the deficit. Therefore, the second row in table 5 provides a more accurate measure of the deficit than one including deposit insurance and Desert Storm contributions.

Social Security and the Deficit

The other major issue in assessing the size and impact of the federal deficit concerns treatment of Social Security trust fund surpluses in the totals. Under the Balanced Budget Act, Social Security was shown as off-budget, although it was included for purposes of calculating annual deficits. In 1990 a number of politicians in both parties claimed that the large Social Security surpluses were masking the "true" size of the budget deficit and should not be included in calculations of the government's deficit. This was accomplished through the enactment of OBRA: the government's official "on budget" deficit (table 5, row 4) does not include the trust fund surpluses or the Postal Service. The surpluses grew from $63 billion in FY92 to a projected $90 billion in FY97. This raises the official deficit to nearly $400 billion in 1993. As disturbing as this may appear, it is not a very meaningful number.

Dropping trust fund surpluses from deficit totals does not result in a better measure of the "true" deficit, particularly in terms of economic effects. Trust funds are no less an integral part of taxing and spending decisions than are transactions in general funds.[4] The trust fund surpluses result from inter-budgetary transfers that increase the apparent size of the deficit but have no effect on the government's borrowing requirements. The trust fund surpluses directly reduce the Treasury's need to borrow from the public and overseas investors.

The treatment of deposit insurance and Social Security in deficit calculations tends to overemphasize the size and fiscal consequences of the deficit. Nonetheless, under current policy, the deficits remain high and continue to grow. The standardized employment deficit, a measure used by economists to indicate the approximate size of the deficit if the economy were operating at full capacity, is also headed upward. As shown in row 3 of table 5, even when the cyclical factors are removed, the structural gap between revenues and outlay commitments continues in the 1990s with recurring deficits in the range of $300 billion, or around 4 percent of GDP. Based on the forecasting record of the past decade, one can expect them to be significantly greater than now predicted. This means that foreign aid and defense programs will be under

---

4. Trust fund surpluses are exchanged with the Treasury for securities; much of the future surplus results from interest on these securities, which are merely intragovernmental transfers.

tremendous budgetary constraints in the mid- and late 1990s. Congress and the president will continue to be under pressure to produce another major deficit reduction package, and will likely again revise the budget process, allowing trade-offs between defense and domestic programs.

Life under the Budget Enforcement Act: Congressional Influence on Defense and International Programs

Implementation of OBRA, with its new budget process, provided a new set of challenges for members of Congress who wished to press competing foreign and defense policies with the administration. The new requirements constrained the president as well. In general, during both 1991 and 1992, both branches followed the strictures of the Budget Enforcement Act with few exceptions, to the surprise of many observers. The Bush administration's supplemental requests reflected the restrictions of the BEA. In 1991, the administration proposed increases in housing projects, additional money for nuclear weapons cleanup, and additional funds for Radio Free Europe. However, so as not to violate the caps, these supplemental appropriations requests were accompanied by rescission requests in each of the three categories to offset the spending increases. Under pay-as-you-go rules, three separate extensions of unemployment benefits were financed through rescissions or revenue increases, rather than by exceeding the caps. Despite some grumbling, Congress retained the caps. When forecasts revealed that the U.S. economy would decline for two successive quarters, allowing Congress to vacate the caps, on several occasions both the House and the Senate voted overwhelmingly to retain the spending limits and enforcement rules.

Issues surrounding score keeping occasionally proved contentious. The Budget Enforcement Act designated OMB as the official scorekeeper of the process: it alone makes the determination about violations of the pay-as-you-go rules. OMB had an opportunity to flex its new-found muscle only weeks after OBRA was signed. Because of a drafting error in the foreign aid bill, the international program appropriations cap for 1991 was exceeded by $395 million (Doherty 1990d). As a result, OMB director Richard Darman ordered a minisequester of 1.9 percent across all international affairs programs, including State Department salaries and aid to Israel. OMB continued to take a hard line on score keeping as much out of principle as for policy reasons. In April 1991 a seemingly trivial transfer of $7 million from a defense to a discretionary account was met with a promise of a mid-session sequester by OMB. An even smaller sequester was ordered after OMB determined that the 1991 supplemental appropriation violated the discretionary domestic cap by $2.4 million. Congressional Democrats remained unhappy that OMB rather than CBO had the ability to judge cost overruns.

A number of conflicts between the administration and the Democratic Congress emerged over the designation of certain kinds of spending as "emergency," thereby avoiding the discretionary spending caps. In March of 1991, Congress enacted two supplemental appropriations bills. The first included $42.6 billion for the Gulf war. Under OBRA, these costs were excluded from spending caps or pay-as-you-go rules. The second supplemental, which included $5.4 billion justified under the "dire emergency" provision, included both emergency and nonemergency provisions. Negotiations between branches on this bill were shaped by the new budget rules. OMB refused to accept the House's assertion that additional funds for the United States Information Agency or veterans' health programs constituted emergency spending. Congress then turned the tables on the administration by refusing to agree that increased military fuel costs not associated with Desert Shield constituted an emergency. OMB quashed three funding requests from the Commerce Department related to Gulf war costs by ruling that they did not constitute an emergency and threatened a minisequester. However, OMB backed down on a much higher profile issue, $850 million in emergency aid to Turkey and Israel. In most cases, however, the Bush administration used the budget rules to prevent congressional additions. Even some seemingly irresistible bills failed to get an emergency designation. Legislation introduced to aid U.S. troops in the Persian Gulf included plans to increase life insurance, to expand education benefits, and to offer grants to communities hard hit by the deployment. The administration, backed by some key congressional Democrats, resisted giving these "motherhood" bills an emergency exemption.

The greatest challenge to the caps was mounted in 1992 following the collapse of the Soviet Union. Many Democrats, including the leadership, felt that in a less threatening world and in the midst of a domestic recession the spending caps for defense were too high and the caps for domestic programs too low. Legislation was introduced to tear down the "budget walls" between the three caps. The House enacted an unusual, two-track, budget resolution, one maintaining the discretionary caps, the other allowing significant transfer from defense to domestic programs. Republicans and the Bush administration strongly opposed the so-called walls bill. Conservative Democrats—"deficit hawks" such as Charles Stenholm (D-Tex.)—proved decisive in defeating the plan to allow trade-offs between categories. They supported applying any discretionary savings from defense or international programs to the deficit rather than to new domestic spending. The best way to accomplish that was to maintain the separate caps. In a small concession to the post–Soviet Union era, both branches agreed to classify as discretionary spending for defense a billion dollars worth of projects generally considered domestic, among them job retraining and aid to school districts with military dependents.

In 1992, Congress approved spending significantly below the original caps for both defense and international discretionary programs. The FY93 budget resolution permitted defense appropriations of $278 billion, $11 billion below the 1993 cap and $4 billion below President Bush's request. Congress also cut the president's foreign aid requests with the House slicing $1.3 billion from the $13.8 billion package.

Despite the fiscal straitjacket, President Bush convinced Congress to adopt a bill to aid the states of the former Soviet Union. Bush submitted a plan in April of 1992 after he was criticized for acting too slowly by Democratic presidential candidate Bill Clinton, former President Richard Nixon, and a number of congressional leaders. With the economy still mired in a recession, it was a hard sell. Passage was most difficult in the House where members, facing reelection in the fall, feared voting for a massive increase in overseas aid when so many Americans were still suffering. The administration won support from the Democratic leaders by promising to accelerate public works spending and loan guarantees to localities by as much as $2 billion (Fessler 1992). The House approved an increase of $12.3 billion in the U.S. commitment to the IMF and $1.2 billion in direct aid. The package avoided the budget rules, however, since the IMF commitment did not result in direct outlays and the $1.2 billion came from foreign aid, existing defense, and security assistance funds.

Congress was not without influence over defense and foreign affairs programs under the Budget Enforcement Act, but it was clearly at the level of microbudgeting rather than macrobudgeting. Within the confines of the spending caps, the authorizing committees and Appropriations subcommittees debated a host of issues and competing priorities ranging from changing patterns of foreign aid to the Strategic Defense Initiative and the B-2 bomber. Several weapons systems that the administration wanted canceled were saved. In general, however, Congress has found itself at a slight disadvantage in dealing with the administration compared to the budget process before OBRA. That fact would be on members' minds when the budget deal was renegotiated in 1993.

The Peace Dividend and Prospects for the Mid-1990s

Since the fall of communism and the collapse of the Soviet Union, many have looked to savings in defense spending—the peace dividend—to help solve the nation's budget woes. In the 1990s, the peace dividend and defense and international programs will be shaped by four factors: the continuation of severe deficits, the maintenance of relative world stability, the outcome of the 1992 presidential election, and revision of the budget agreement in 1993. Given the budget projections shown earlier, continued pressure for cuts in defense and foreign aid because of the deficit seems certain. Only some

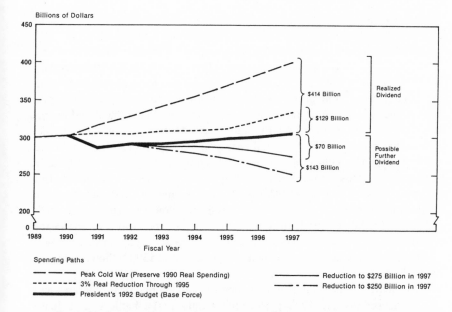

Fig. 3. Measuring the peace dividend: potential savings. This assessment excludes budget authority for Operations Desert Shield and Desert Storm. The peace dividend is measured as cumulative savings through 1997. (*Source:* Congressional Budget Office 1992b.)

dramatic and dangerous international development such as a successful coup or a renewed military threat from the former Soviet Union could seriously derail the defense buildddown. Assuming that will not happen, can drastic cuts in the defense budget provide enough additional money to meet growing demands for more domestic spending to create jobs, rebuild the infrastructure, and provide assistance to localities?

Figure 3 shows CBO estimates of alternative defense spending paths through 1997 and measures the peace dividend as cumulative savings. As the figure shows, much of the peace dividend has already been counted in current estimates. Assuming that defense spending had remained at real 1990 levels, a savings of $414 billion has already been realized; assuming a 3 percent real reduction in defense spending since 1990, the peace dividend is closer to $130 billion. In either case, the deficit projections shown in table 5 already have factored in those savings. Just to preserve real spending levels in domestic discretionary programs in 1994 and 1995, something close to the lowest path, representing $20 and $30 billion defense cuts, respectively, would have to be chosen.

The question of how much defense can be cut while adequately protecting the United States' international commitments and interests will continue to be debated through the mid-1990s. A Brookings Institution study in 1991 concluded that U.S. defense spending could be reduced by one-third in real terms throughout the decade (Tyler 1991). The study challenged the necessity of the administration's defense path. To achieve this level, defense spending would decline at a rate of 6.5 percent annually over the next decade. This rate of decline would require rapid and massive cuts in procurement and operations, including personnel. A CBO study showed serious technical constraints associated with such rapid demilitarization (Congressional Budget Office 1991b, 61). The cuts proposed in the Brookings study were significantly greater than those advocated by Democratic presidential candidate Bill Clinton. However, by mid-1992, even the Pentagon began planning for future cuts as much below the Bush baseline as $20 billion per year through 1997 (Schmitt 1992a). In short, those who place high expectations on the peace dividend will be disappointed. Even with the steepest decline, the savings will do little to satisfy domestic claimants, to put a dent in $300 billion deficits, or provide meaningful middle class tax relief.

Congressional policy-making in defense and international programs will be influenced by the 1992 presidential election. The battle over defense spending is likely to be fierce throughout the 1990s but, as the previous analysis suggests, the outcome is likely to vary only by a few percentage points regardless of which party is in the White House. The election of Bill Clinton and retention of Democratic control of both houses of Congress will not make the budget choices much easier. A more important consequence of Clinton's election will be the nature of a multiyear budget agreement and new rules of the budget game negotiated in 1993. This agreement will set the ground rules under which critical choices between defense, foreign aid, and domestic needs will be made.

What are some of the possible scenarios for the budget process? One is that the 1990 rules will be maintained through 1995 under the single cap. Not surprisingly, negotiators in 1990 postponed the largest cuts in discretionary spending as long as possible. The spending caps for 1994–95 are extremely stringent compared to 1991–93 and will require real cuts in both budget authority and outlays. Another option, of course, is to expand the caps to allow greater spending. Given the hefty increases in deficit projections for 1993–97, however, there will be enormous political pressure to keep the deficit from rising. If the single discretionary spending cap is retained, domestic, international, and defense programs will engage in a brutal competition to avoid deep cuts.

Another scenario, perhaps more likely had Bush won re-election, is another agreement with separate caps, once again erecting budget walls protecting defense and international programs from domestic claimants. Given the high level of dissatisfaction among many congressional Democrats with the walls enacted in 1991–92, this may be a hard sell on Capitol Hill. However, support from Democratic "deficit-hawks" could make something like this possible. Separate caps do not protect programs from cuts, as we saw with defense spending reductions in 1992, but they do ensure that cuts are applied to deficit reduction rather than domestic needs.

A more likely scenario is a budget process and deficit reduction plan along the lines of those proposed by then House Budget Committee chairman, Leon Panetta (D-Calif.) in 1992 (Hager 1992a). The House Democrats' plan would partially revive the Gramm-Rudman process. Instead of deficit limits, it would set deficit-reduction targets to be met through discretionary spending cuts, entitlement cuts, and tax increases. A single cap would restrict all discretionary appropriations. Entitlement cuts and tax increases would be included in a separate "spin-off" bill. If targets are not met, an across-the-board freeze on spending and tax indexing would occur with a temporary tax increase levied on upper-income Americans. Unlike the original Gramm-Rudman bill, all spending, including that for Social Security, would be included. Some variant of this plan would likely help discretionary defense and international programs since it would cast a much wider net in the process of deficit reduction. Congress will play a major role in shaping the priorities between defense, international, and domestic programs. But, given the budgetary context, these promise to be extremely difficult choices rather than opportunities to engage in policy innovation.

Conclusion

Continued big deficits have placed U.S. foreign and defense policymakers under tremendous constraints. While America's role as a military superpower remains unchallenged, its leadership has been undermined in other areas. Spending on foreign aid continues to decline and the United States has played a secondary role in helping the nations of Central Europe. Despite the approval of an aid package for the former Soviet Union in 1992, it was a struggle for Bush and congressional leaders of both parties because of the deficit and domestic problems. The Earth Summit in Rio in 1992 demonstrated the effects of economic problems on U.S. policy options. The other industrialized democracies attending that meeting continued to accept a twenty-year-old commitment to raise economic aid to 0.7 percent of GDP; the United States refused (Lewis 1992). As one observer noted,

Financially, the administration believes that it cannot afford to sign on to the most dramatic proposals at Rio even if it wanted to. The multibillion-dollar infusions demanded to address poor nations' environmental problems, and which Germany, Japan, and some Western nations are touting, neither exist in America's strapped treasury nor could pass political muster if they did. (Wines 1992, A6)

Despite these obvious constraints, Congress will not be without influence in the funding of foreign and international programs. First, as suggested above, budgetary constraints diminish or temporarily disappear in the face of a crisis such as the Gulf war. Second, Congress can have significant policy influence even under conditions of budget stringency. Members often are extremely passionate about defense and international issues that have little or no budgetary consequence such as a 1990 filibuster over a seemingly innocuous Senate resolution to create a national day of remembrance for the Armenian genocide. Third, once major decisions have been made, such as the 1990 summit agreement, fiscal constraints usually affect Congress and the presidency similarly and simultaneously. Hence, purely budgetary considerations cannot explain legislative-executive conflict. Fourth, whatever the budgetary context, Congress's performance in foreign and defense policy-making will not be the same across all dimensions of policy. It will vary depending on whether one is considering base closings, force levels and deployment, procurement, research and development, military or nonmilitary aid, trade, third world debt, immigration, or energy policy.

Despite these caveats, the budgetary context will continue to affect the ways in which Congress makes policy. In the long term, the underlying strength of the U.S. economy will set parameters for national security strategies and options. In the next few years, continued budgetary stringency related to the deficits will affect both the content of defense and foreign-policy decisions and the processes in Congress by which they are made.

CHAPTER 4

The Influence of Constituents: Congressional Decision Making on Issues of Foreign and Defense Policy

Eileen Burgin

More than five hundred legislators, confronting and perceiving somewhat unique pressures in their roles as foreign and defense policy participants, constitute the United States Congress. Despite differences among the individual members and the pressures affecting them, almost all sense the influence of constituency when making decisions. Obviously, since a legislator's survival in office hinges on adequate district support, a member will try to respond to perceived constituent pressures. "Even those congressmen genuinely concerned with good public policy must achieve reelection in order to continue their work" (Fiorina 1989, 37).[1]

In this chapter I examine one piece of the constituency influence story in the area of foreign and defense policy. I focus on the critically important matter of a representative's decisions on involvement. More specifically, I explore how, when, why, and to what extent the pervasive constituency influence sways a representative's decisions on participation. The approach includes examining actions taken by both committee and noncommittee members in a variety of decision-making venues. I also look briefly at some normative issues raised by empirical evidence on constituency influence.

The impact of constituents on a member's involvement in foreign and defense policy issues has received little scholarly attention. Analysts have addressed various aspects of this topic but not the topic as a whole. The most relevant literature falls into four broad clusters. First, many observers, assum-

Morris Fiorina, James Lindsay, Patrick Neal, Mark Peterson, Tom Rice, Randall Ripley, and George Young offered valuable guidance or suggestions at various stages of this project. I greatly appreciate their comments. This work was supported, in part, by an award from the University Committee on Research and Scholarship, University of Vermont.

1. Members do not have to be "single-minded seekers of reelection" (Mayhew 1974, 5) to grasp the electoral imperative.

ing that a member chooses rationally and behaves purposefully, have examined motives and the significance of constituents without concentrating on foreign policy (for two classic studies of this type, see Fiorina 1989 and Mayhew 1974). The second cluster includes general works on Congress's involvement in foreign and defense policy-making. Literature in this area focuses on Congress (the institution), however, and not on individual members and constituency influence (see, e.g., Burgin 1993; Crabb and Holt 1992; Franck and Weisband 1979; Kegley and Wittkopf 1992). Third, political scientists have begun exploring influences affecting member's committee involvement (Evans 1989; Hall 1987). Although such research highlights the significance of participation, it centers on domestic issues exclusively at the committee level. Studies of roll-call votes, the fourth grouping of works, discuss individual members, constituency influence, and occasionally also specific substantive areas such as foreign and defense policy (see, e.g., Clausen 1973; Kingdon 1989; Miller and Stokes 1963). Yet these analyses emphasize decisions regarding floor votes, and thus neglect determinations about participation and the pivotal period in the legislative process before possible floor action.

Notwithstanding the importance of roll-call votes, the contributions of research analyzing voting decisions, and the prevalence of this scholarly approach, my concentration here on decisions regarding involvement is logical for two reasons. First, a member's participation in Congress in issues of foreign and defense policy is of consequence. Who in Congress participates and the extent of that participation, along with the number of involved people, will help determine the course of the legislative process and the policy outcome. A legislator who is quite involved in an issue may assist in shaping the substance of legislation as well as in prompting House action. A less involved member also may help influence the House agenda, for without sufficient member interest the House may not even act on a subject and a floor vote may not occur. In addition, congressional involvement in issues of foreign and defense policy affects the executive branch agenda. A member may cause the executive to alter a policy, priority, or action through informal advising and prodding, through anticipated reactions, or through more formal action, that is, engaging in oversight or introducing and promoting legislation (see chapter 2). Second, conclusions drawn from roll-call data may not always be accurate. Recently, VanDoren (1990) has underscored the problems with using roll-call data to ascertain the effects of various influences on a member's decisions, and Overby (1991) has explored the problems by using these data to study constituency influence. Thus, considering the significance of congressional activity and the controversy over roll-call data, it is reasonable to look at a member's decision making mainly through choices on involvement.

Supportive Constituents: A Representative's Lifeblood

Before one can begin to explore constituency influence, however, one must decide which constituents to study. I refer to a member's constituents (as consistently as possible) as those people a member calls supportive constituents, or, in Fenno's words, the reelection constituency (1978, 8–18). In addition to responding to this cue in the literature, I concentrate on supporters because this is the group about which a member is most concerned.[2] A member's distinction between supporters and nonsupporters, and hence between all constituents and supportive constituents, became clear in interviews with about one hundred representatives and staff on the factors affecting members' foreign and defense policy activities. In virtually all of the questions concerning the district I asked about constituents generally but interviewees consistently and independently focused on supporters. Congressional actors themselves thus raised and highlighted the distinction.

Differentiating the segment of constituents to which a member looks, moreover, is essential for understanding the causal linkages between the district and a member's actions. As an example will illustrate, a member does not perceive the district as monolithic. Referring to constituents generically may therefore result in misleading findings. In the Ninety-eighth Congress, the funding debate over the MX missile presented Massachusetts representatives with some interesting choices. A widely distributed report documented that the state would benefit from MX production, receiving $2.7 billion and more than nine thousand new jobs (Anderson 1982, 3; Vogler and Waldman 1985, 2). In addition, most districts in Massachusetts would benefit directly (ICBM Associates 1983). Despite these potential economic gains, nuclear freeze and other local groups actively opposed the MX. Thus, on the one hand, money and jobs were at stake; on the other hand, the anti-MX forces were resolute. Under these circumstances observers might assume that most delegation members would vote for the MX, for, as Kingdon (1989, 36–37) explains, "If there is a piece of legislation pending that would help a district industry in a direct way, or especially one that would hurt it, nearly all congressmen defend

---

2. Certainly the debate rages on about which constituency actually merits attention. Over the years such scholars as Bullock and Brady (1983), Fenno (1978), Fiorina (1974), Kingdon (1989), Miller (1970), Shapiro et al. (1990), Weissberg (1979), and G. Wright (1989) have all entered the fray. Nonetheless, despite the lack of complete consensus, it is fair to say that observers have demonstrated the significance of the supporting coalition, variously defined. Along these lines, it should be noted that members can, and in many cases may, redefine the reelection constituency during a congressional career. It is intuitively logical, moreover, that senators have more flexibility than representatives in shifting their base of support over time because of their longer terms and typically larger geographical constituency. Hence, senators are probably more apt than representatives to redefine the supportive constituency while in office.

that industry's interests." But, in fact, every member opposed the MX, and some even helped orchestrate the battle (*Congress and the Nation* 1981–84, 924–25, 940–41). In discussing why the conventional wisdom was incorrect in this case, Vogler and Waldman (1985, 2–3) suggest that altruistic global concerns prevailed over parochial interests. Yet fears of nuclear disaster did not inspire the entire group of members. In fact, most members reacted to a local constituency; perceptions of anti-MX supporters' desires affected their actions. People I interviewed from the Massachusetts delegation explained that most supporters were not employed in MX-related plants or principally concerned about its economic effects. As Lindsay (1990b, 956) observes, "doves who represent constituencies that benefit from weapons production may . . . [find that] opposition to a weapons system may actually *help.*" The MX example thus demonstrates the importance of focusing on supportive constituents.

More specifically, I focus on a member's *perceptions* of supporters' opinions, desires, and potential reactions. Because a member reacts to his or her own view of reality, not to a force that is objectively measured and evaluated, understanding a member's sense of supporters is key (Fenno 1978; Miller and Stokes 1963). My concern in this work is not to test whether a member's perceptions correspond with what some might deem an objective view of reality (Clausen 1977). Consequently, questions of policy congruence are outside the scope of this study (see Eulau and Karps 1977). Also beyond the chapter's boundaries is the actual level of constituent information. While extensive supporter knowledge is not a prerequisite for supporter influence (since a member's perceptions are paramount), it should be noted that recent work paints a more positive picture of the electorate, particularly in the aggregate (Carmines and Kuklinski 1990; Converse 1990; Ferejohn 1990; Iyengar 1990; McKelvey and Ordeshook 1990; Stimson 1990; G. Wright 1978).[3]

Research Design

My observations on constituency influence are based on data gathered from approximately one hundred semistructured interviews with staffers and mem-

---

3. A caveat to this approach, explicitly examining supporters, is necessary. It is possible that a member may be able to create a supportive constituency that reflects personal views, hence somewhat blurring the causal linkages between constituents and a member's actions (Poole 1988). In other words, supporters may naturally reflect a legislator's opinions instead of providing an influence to which the member responds. This concern, while possibly valid for roll-call works not based on interview data, is less relevant in this research. As I explain in the text, the supporter influence on involvement is complex; it is composed of many factors besides supporter views on an issue. In addition, in this research, because interviewees discussed whether, how, and why supporters affected participation, the direction of the causal relationship is also fairly clear.

bers in the U.S. House of Representatives. These interviews concerned seventy representatives' activities concerning four diverse issues that faced the Ninety-eighth Congress: aid to the Nicaraguan Contras, the International Monetary Fund (IMF) quota increase, funding for the MX missile, and the deployment of marines in Lebanon.[4] In conversations I asked respondents about 11 possible influences on involvement, one of which was constituents. Interviewees had at least two opportunities to discuss the impact of each pressure. Upon completion of the interviews, I coded each variable for each of the 280 cases (70 members on 4 issues) as a primary incentive ($+2$), secondary incentive ($+1$), insignificant influence (0), secondary disincentive (-1), or primary disincentive (-2). The substance of comments regarding each consideration determined my scoring (see appendix A for examples of how I operationalized the variable).

The sample of seventy members includes representatives with varying degrees of participation in the four issues, from little involvement to the most active involvement.[5] To assemble such a sample of members I designed a scale to measure involvement (see appendix B). The scale captures the range and diversity of action on foreign and defense policy matters in which a representative may or may not have been inspired to take part. The classification scheme, as seen in appendix B, is subdivided into four levels: leaders (actively involved), activists (moderately involved), position takers (slightly involved), and voters (minimally involved). Completely uninvolved members (i.e., nonvoters) were almost nonexistent in these four issues. (For further information about the sample, interview process, participation scale, and the four levels of involvement, see Burgin 1988, chap. 2; 1991a, 523–24, 538–41).

The Nature of Supporter Influence on Decisions Regarding Involvement

In this section I examine the nature of supportive constituency influence on a member's decisions regarding participation in foreign and defense policy issues. I describe and explore three facets of this topic: (1) the modes of

---

4. This sample includes four diverse issues in four distinct, substantive areas. As I have demonstrated elsewhere, the similarities in the impact of constituents among these different issues indicate that generalizations about the constituency influence can be made based on this model (Burgin 1991b). Moreover, the similarities across diverse issues show that the results here probably are not simply produced by the specific topics I chose to study.

5. The sample includes 38 Democrats and 32 Republicans. In 66 percent of the 280 sample cases the member sits on a committee with jurisdiction over an issue; in 34 percent the member has noncommittee status.

TABLE 1.   The Influence of Supporters on Involvement in Four Foreign and Defense Policy Issues

Supporter Influence	Number of Cases	Percentage of Cases
Disincentive		
Primary disincentive	66	24
Secondary disincentive	64	23
Subtotal	130	46[a]
Incentive		
Secondary incentive	86	31
Primary incentive	31	11
Subtotal	117	42
Insignificant influence	33	12
Total (all cases)	280	100

[a]Subtotal varies due to rounding.

supporter influence including why backers affect activity, (2) the impact of supporter pressure, and (3) minor issue-related variations in the influence.

Table 1 presents a simple overview of supporter influence in the 280 sample cases. The table shows the frequency with which backers affected involvement and what pressure was exerted. (When supporter influence was inconsequential, it is identified as an insignificant influence.) As seen in table 1, the importance of supporters is undeniable. Backers were a significant (i.e., primary or secondary) determinant of participation in almost 90 percent of the cases.[6] This far surpassed the importance of any other factor, as I discuss below.

Modes of Supporter Influence

The significance of constituents has been widely recognized in the literature on Congress. Mayhew (1974), for instance, sees constituency influence as a positive guide to action, encouraging a member to undertake three kinds of activities: advertising, credit claiming, and position taking. These activities are perceived as helpful to a member's reelection effort. And Kingdon (1989, 27–71) stresses that constituents impose constraints on a member in the area of voting. These constraints on voting behavior, although typically rather vague in nature, are present "most of the time" (ibid., 68). In contrast to both Mayhew and Kingdon, I demonstrate that, regarding participation on foreign and defense policy issues, constituency influence serves as *both* a positive

---

6. These figures may even slightly understate the impact of supporters, for some respondents may have been reticent to expose extensive reliance on backers. Several staffers, for instance, stressed that their straightforward replies were exceptional. "Others may try to downplay the importance of constituents, but don't let them fool you," one administrative assistant commented.

guide to action *and* a constraint. More specifically, supportive constituents may directly and indirectly inhibit and motivate involvement.[7]

Supporters as Disincentives to Involvement
As seen in table 1, in slightly more than half of the sample cases in which supporters influenced a member's involvement, they inhibited participation. Of these disincentives, four issue-specific deterrents stand out.[8] A common thread tying these disincentives together is anticipated reactions: a member is constrained by perceptions of how supporters might respond to involvement instead of by direct pressure not to act.

The most typical issue-specific constraint is a low level of supporter interest. A member considers backers to be lacking interest when a "significant bloc of supporters"—as subjectively determined by the member—is not pushing for a distinct result. The absence of concerned reelection constituents inhibits a legislator for one of two reasons. Infrequently lack of supporter interest curtails activities because of a member's vague notions of an officeholder's duties, that is, participating only when supporters evince interest regardless of a member's personal concerns. One staffer discussed why her boss remained only slightly involved in the IMF debate despite his interest and his subcommittee seat:

[His supporters] just weren't interested. And he places a heavy emphasis on what they want in deciding what he'll get involved in. . . . If his constituents had been more concerned, he'd have gotten more involved.

More often, minimal supporter interest inhibits activities regarding a foreign or defense policy issue because of the belief that involvement would trigger adverse political consequences. A representative anticipates supporter reactions. For example, constituents could accuse the member of being detached from the district or political opponents could highlight the activities in conjunction with oversight on other, more parochial issues. Obviously, this would cost votes. An aide of a member who often served as an activist or leader on foreign policy issues said that her boss decided to participate only on issues for which strong supporter interest existed. He was "worried about the perception in the district that he cared more about foreign policy issues than

---

7. Supportive constituents affect involvement as either general influences, with an impact on all legislative activities, or as issue-specific influences (Burgin 1988, chap. 4). This paper concentrates on issue-specific factors.
8. Some all-embracing supporter restraints also delimit a member's opportunities to engage in a range of activities, including foreign and defense policy activities. These deterrents, such as performing constituent work and traveling home, stem from a member's inevitable balancing of limited time and diverse responsibilities (see ibid.).

local issues." This characterization had hurt him in a previous race and he thought he could not supply his next opponent with such powerful ammunition and survive.

The second constraint is political caution. Even when supportive constituents exhibit interest in an issue in agreement with a member's stand, a member may fear that participation is politically detrimental if the issue is controversial—and on seemingly noncontroversial topics a legislator may be anxious about the issue becoming a policy disaster. Either way, the risk of being associated with a controversial or potentially controversial subject is that people may harp on the involvement. When supporters lack interest in an issue already perceived as being laden with controversy or having the potential to bring on a catastrophe, a member will be even more circumspect about participation.

Perceived cross-pressures—a member's opinion differing from supporters' opinions—presents the third issue-specific disincentive. (This deterrent also emerges when supporters are split, for then a member clearly disagrees with some of the reelection constituency.) The reasons cross-pressures limit activity vary by how a representative decides to vote. A member's vote may reflect perceived supporter preferences; while following backers' desires when voting, however, the member will not alter a personal position. Thus, a legislator does not participate in support of his or her vote because it would require lobbying against a personal stand. As an aide explained,

He would have voted for aid to the Contras if his supporters hadn't opposed it so strongly. He probably even would have been a little involved. But the political reality forced him to go with a position he wasn't comfortable with. So he was completely uninvolved.

This member did not participate behind the scenes in support of his own views, for that would require inconsistency, and inconsistency may be discovered and then highlighted in a campaign.

Alternatively, a legislator may vote in accordance with his or her own views rather than following supporters. Yet here, too, cross-pressures present a powerful constraint—anticipated reactions again are critical. A member sees publicizing opposition to supporters' opinions, and thereby "rubbing it in peoples' faces," as tantamount to political suicide. One representative's survival instinct on the issue of marines in Lebanon was clear:

He had a strong base of support in the Jewish community, and most of those people wanted the marines there. But [he] thought the whole thing was handled poorly. . . . So he voted against the eighteen-month extension, and wanted to speak out about it. But he . . . didn't want to alienate his Jewish supporters. . . . So he just kept quiet. . . .

Rather than trying to "educate" supporters about the merits of his position, so that he might participate, this member (as is typical) chose to remain silent (on members as educators, see Fulbright 1979).

The final disincentive occurs when a member, participating because of an issue's district connection, is constrained by the very district link that is inspiring involvement. A member may believe that supporters expect devotion solely to one aspect of an issue—the local angle. Participating in other aspects of the issue would consume time, and thus perhaps decrease district-related work. In other words, the lack of backer interest in all facets of a subject may inhibit activity. As one aide noted, "She didn't offer other amendments because it would take away from her efforts on ____. . . . This went to the core of the district's interests. And her involvement was dictated by the needs of the district."

Supporters as Incentives to Involvement
Supportive constituents, as seen in table 1, also frequently motivate foreign and defense policy activity. Supporter incentives are usually issue-specific influences, for backers tend not to invite willy-nilly involvement in all foreign and defense policy matters. The issue-specific stimuli may be direct or indirect. As with supporter disincentives, anticipated reactions are key: a representative spurred to action by a direct or indirect incentive generally expects electoral benefits from involvement, and a member sensing a direct incentive also may participate because of the fear that inactivity will incur retribution at the polls.

Reelection constituencies may directly motivate involvement when they express or exhibit interest in an issue in agreement with a member's substantive views. In rare instances, supporter concern engenders activity because a member believes it is a representative's responsibility to respond to constituent interest through participation. As one aide noted,

Even Jack and Jill six-pack were really interested in [the marines in Lebanon]. This affected his involvement. He thought he should reflect peoples' concerns. So he spoke out about it several times, even though he would have been more comfortable remaining silent.

More often, supporter interest inspires activity because of the perception that action is politically wise. A member may think that involvement demonstrates responsiveness, and responsiveness provides electoral payoffs. Thus, at a minimum, a legislator will try to cultivate the appearance of responsiveness through participation, however peripheral.

A significant bloc of supporters showing interest in an issue or encouraging activity, though, is not a prerequisite for a member to perceive supporter incentives. The most common indirect incentive (i.e., an incentive that operates despite no perceived supporter interest) is based on expected reactions and consequent political gains. When a representative can stress concrete district hooks to a foreign or defense policy question, for instance, the member may participate, thinking that such activity will prompt positive backer responses. A member assumes that local links help arouse interest, and that the legislator wins political points for district-related involvement.[9] One interviewee explained how a local angle inspired his boss on the IMF debate:

> His supporters weren't interested in the issue but they were very interested in how the banking system works and how rural economies fare with the banking community. So he tied the issue to their interests. . . . He thought that politically it would be a good issue for him because of these things. And boy did it play well with the folks back home.

Similarly, a member from a southern district discussed how local links indirectly encouraged him on the Contra controversy: "This was a foreign policy issue I could sell at home. It was easy to go back and expound on the issue, showing the importance of it, since Nicaragua is so close to ____. And people liked that I got involved here." Although supporters did not push this member to participate, he accurately gauged their reactions and the electoral payoffs.

Indirect incentives, in addition to being based on expected supporter reactions, may flow from the anticipated need to explain a vote to the reelection constituency (Fenno 1978, 141–46). Preparing an interpretation or justification of a vote may prompt a member to participate. For example, to explain a vote a member may find that self-education is necessary, and that the education process entails some participation. An aide described this phenomenon as follows.

> People asked him about [the MX vote] when he went back to the district. And he didn't want to appear dumb. So he had to get himself conversant in the issue. . . . So he went to meetings, talked to his colleagues, read articles, and even asked me to put statements in the *Congressional Record*. . . .

---

9. Clearly, district links and supporter interest are often related; backers may discover a local link independently and develop interest in an issue. In cases in which supporter interest inspires a member's involvement, the effect on activity is covered in the preceding section on direct incentives.

The need to explain also may prompt floor statements simply to supply a member with handy *Congressional Record* mailers for interested supporters.

The Modes of Influence and Voting Decisions
Obviously, the modes of constituency influence in decisions regarding participation will, to some degree, resemble the modes of influence in voting decisions. In terms of involvement, we have seen the importance of anticipated reactions or electoral consequences, supporter desires or interests, and the need to explain. Kingdon (1989, 47–67) discusses factors such as these as mechanisms of constituency influence in the voting arena as well. Considering the necessity of reelection, the concern over appearing responsive to supporters' preferences, and the expectation that explanations may be requested, similarities in the modes or mechanisms of influence are not surprising.

The Influence of Supporters on Whether and to What Extent a Member Participates

The discussion thus far has shown that perceived supporter influences may involve easy judgments of supporter interest or lack of interest in an issue and a topic's relevance to the district and supporters, or the pressures may be more indirect. Constituency influence, though often identified otherwise, is complex and varied. Yet the question remains: to what extent do reelection constituency incentives and disincentives actually affect a member's involvement?

Supporter influence may sway a member's decision to participate on two separate occasions: first, when a legislator considers whether to participate; and, second, when a member considers how extensively to participate. Thus, to grasp fully the impact of supporters it is essential to explore the possible effect of backers on both aspects of involvement and to compare the effect with that of other considerations (Burgin 1991a, 530–31).

The Influence of Supporters on the Fact of Involvement
In table 2, I use a regression equation to examine the influence of eleven independent variables (including supportive constituents) in the decision on the fact of involvement. The coding for the eleven independent variables ranges from a primary incentive at +2 to a primary disincentive at −2 (as described above). The dependent variable distinguishes between taking no action other than voting and engaging in some substantive activity beyond voting. For this binary variable a member is either a voter (minimally involved) or a participant: voters are coded 1 and position takers, activists, and leaders are coded 2. Table 2 presents an OLS regression equation for this dichotomous dependent variable to provide a means of comparison with an OLS regression equation employed in a subsequent table, discussed below.

Nonetheless, I also performed a logit analysis, and the relative order of the independent variables in terms of significance remained essentially the same for the more important factors.

As seen in table 2, the influence of supportive constituents presents the principal determinant of whether a member participates, with a t-score of 20.87 and a standardized coefficient of .63, both clearly dwarfing all the others. When a representative determines whether to participate in a foreign or defense policy issue, supportive constituency influence is pivotal. To understand why this is so, it is helpful to recall the discussion about the modes of supporter influence.

A supporter disincentive exerts an overwhelming constraint, and this constraint accounts in part for the influence's importance in the decision of whether to participate. The correlation between a primary supporter disincentive and the fact-of-involvement dependent variable is striking—in no case did a sample member viewing supporters as a primary disincentive do more than vote. (And, as shown in table 1, backers served as a primary deterrent in almost one-quarter of the sample cases.) Whether due to a lack of supporter interest, political caution, perceived cross-pressures between the member's

TABLE 2.   Foreign Policy Participation in the House:
Regression Analysis of a Member's Decision about Whether to Participate

Independent Variables	Unstandardized Coefficient	Standardized Coefficient	t-score
Constant	1.54		57.48
Substantive independent variables			
Supportive constituents	.23*	.63	20.87
Personal policy interests	.10*	.24	7.92
Committee or leadership assignment	.08*	.15	4.71
Desire for influence	−.01	−.01	−.26
Personal style	.09	.10	3.48
Junior status	.06*	.07	2.86
Party, including leadership and administration influences	.07	.03	1.29
Press of other legislative business	.03*	.06	2.17
Colleagues	.04*	.11	3.73
Staff	.06*	.05	1.84
Interest groups	.02	.02	.60
Control independent variables			
Party affiliation	.03	.03	1.16
Committee status	.07*	.07	1.98
$N = 280$	$R^2 = .82$		$df = 267$

Source: Burgin (1991a).
*Indicates that relationships are significant at the .05 level.

own opinion and supporters' views, or a limiting district angle, a primary supporter constraint is heeded. The fear of electoral consequences or antici-pated reactions deters even a member prone to action.

In the absence of apprehensions about retribution at the polls, however, a member is less inhibited by a supporter disincentive. When a supporter con-straint exerts a secondary disincentive and lacks electoral implications, there-fore, it does not always prevent involvement. For instance, when perceived supporter lack of interest begets a secondary deterrent because of a member's sense of duty, the constraint tends not to preclude activity.

The correlation between a supporter incentive and the fact-of-involvement variable is even more pronounced. A member virtually always responds to a supporter incentive: in only 1 case (out of 117) did a legislator do no more than vote when perceiving reelection constituents as a stimulus. As previously discussed, a member responds to a perceived supporter incen-tive because activity may provide electoral benefits and inactivity may create electoral problems. And responding to a supporter incentive generally re-quires little effort. A representative often can satisfy supporters without be-coming deeply involved; making a few one-minute speeches, participating briefly in floor debates, or inserting a couple of statements in the Extension of Remarks is usually deemed sufficient. Supportive constituency influence thus tends not to tax severely a member's most precious resource—time (Fenno 1978, 34; U.S. Congress House Commission on Administrative Review [Obey Commission] 1977, 875–76).

One sample member's response to perceived supporter interest in the Contra issue exemplifies how most members react to most supporter incen-tives. This member took to heart Mayhew's (1974) suggestion that respon-siveness may be merely symbolic in nature and still reap political gains; a legislator need not actually achieve supporters' policy goals. The member engaged in high-visibility, superficial actions, and to insure that his activity was noticed he sent copies of his *Congressional Record* statements to con-cerned supporters. In his aide's words,

> His supporters were quite interested. . . . So he wanted to make sure that . . . he would do things in Congress to show them that he was interested and involved. Therefore, he did a lot of things that didn't require a lot of time or effort but looked impressive.

The Influence of Supporters on the Level of Involvement
In table 3, I present an OLS regression equation to examine the influence of eleven independent variables in the decision on the level of involvement or on how extensively a member participates. The coding for the eleven indepen-dent variables, ranging from +2 to −2, is the same as that used in table 2.

The dependent variable in table 3 addresses why some participants become more involved than others by differentiating degrees of activity or how much effort a member expends. Three tiers of substantive participation are identified: a member may be a leader (coded 4), activist (3), or position taker (2). Minimally involved members are not included here, as depth of activity is irrelevant for a legislator who has decided to do no more than vote.

The picture painted of supporter pressure in table 3 is quite different from that in table 2. Supportive constituency influence is most critical in a member's decision about whether to participate, as the foregoing indicates. Yet, in the determination of how extensively to participate, as seen in table 3, supporter influence does not stand out. Although the influence is still statistically significant, it is much less critical in decision making; more than half of the other independent variables have higher standardized coefficients. In particular, three other pressures are pivotal: (1) personal policy interests, encompassing a legislator's interest in, familiarity with, or knowledge about a topic; related personal experiences, ideological views, or religious beliefs; and individual and subjective assessments of a matter's importance and complexity;

TABLE 3. Foreign Policy Participation in the House:
Regression Analysis of a Member's Decision about How Extensively to Participate

Independent Variables	Unstandardized Coefficient	Standardized Coefficient	t-score
Constant	2.04		20.25
Substantive independent variables			
Supportive constituents	.16*	.11	2.44
Personal policy interests	.23*	.34	5.73
Committee or leadership assignment	.27*	.42	5.83
Desire for influence	.38*	.40	6.56
Personal style	.27*	.24	4.02
Junior status	.19*	.17	2.80
Party, including leadership and administration influences	.09*	.11	1.85
Press of other legislative business	.22*	.17	2.98
Colleagues	.09*	.11	1.87
Staff	.12*	.09	1.68
Interest groups	−.16*	−.11	−2.09
Control independent variables			
Party affiliation	−.01	−.01	−.11
Committee status	−.02	−.02	−.28
$N = 159$	$R^2 = .57$		$df = 146$

Source: Burgin (1991a).
*Indicates that relationships are significant at the .05 level.

(2) committee or leadership assignment, which may pertain to opportunity, perceived responsibility, or the intercommittee reciprocity norm; and (3) the desire for influence, referring to a member's goals or aspirations in committee, the House, the Washington community, or the nation at large (Burgin 1988, chap. 5; 1991a, 535–36).

Notwithstanding the importance of personal policy interests, committee or leadership assignment, and the desire for influence on how extensively a member participates, supporter influence also exerts a statistically significant pressure in the decision. A perceived supporter stimulus may help encourage a member to become a leader or an activist in several instances. First, the direct incentive of supporter interest may motivate deeper involvement if interested supporters include knowledgeable "primary constituents," that is, a member's "strongest supporters" who "display an intensity capable of producing additional political activity" (Fenno 1978, 18–24). A member may consider the mere appearance of responsiveness, without genuine attempts to influence a policy, unacceptable in such a case. It is logical, moreover, for a member to devote extra effort to pleasing primary (versus supportive) constituents. Mayhew (1974, 40) notes that "an incumbent has to be concerned . . . especially about actors who can marshal resources other than their own votes." One staff person described the impact of primary constituents' campaign contributions as follows:

> The copper industry was concerned about the [IMF] issue. . . . He got money from [them]. . . . The interest encouraged him to get involved. . . . His people were so enraged about the whole thing that he had to *really* do something.

Second, infrequently a member stimulated by a sense of duty may also participate more actively. The member may think that he or she should serve as a seismograph, with activity level reflecting the intensity of supporter interest. As an aide explained it,

> He felt that he was the voice of his people in Washington, and that he should speak out and work on their behalf. So he got pretty involved. If more of his people had been more interested, he would have gotten even more involved.

Third, a member may attempt to profit politically from a leadership role by participating extensively in an issue in which supporters are interested or from which positive supporter reactions to activity are anticipated. A legislator recognizes that being in the forefront establishes the member's power within Congress: "Members explain their use of power . . . because they believe it will help them win" (Fenno 1978, 139).[10]

The Influence of Supporters on Voting
Extrapolating from the impact of supportive constituents in decisions regarding involvement, it seems logical that a member would also think about supporters when casting votes on issues of foreign and defense policy. In fact, in a perusal of the debate prior to the vote on the authorization to use force in the Persian Gulf (January 1991), the relevance of constituency influence was clear. Senator Donald Riegle (D-Mich.), who opposed the authorization to use force, expressed a common refrain: "I have been hearing from the people of Michigan about this because they care very deeply about it. . . . The messages I am getting . . . are running 9 to 1 against going to war at this time" (*Congressional Record,* 1991, S216). While not a scientifically valid measure of the impact of various influences, floor statements are at least somewhat reflective of a member's thinking. And, of the over 425 legislators who made floor remarks during the Persian Gulf debates from 9 January 1991 through 12 January 1991, more than a quarter—and a larger percentage of senators than representatives—mentioned the importance of constituents in the voting decision (*Congressional Record* 1991). These numbers are not inconsequential, even if some members raised constituency preferences simply to appease or please backers at home.[11]

Many studies examining voting decisions on foreign and defense policy issues also confirm the importance of constituency influence. From Miller and Stokes (1963) and Clausen (1973) to more current analyses by Bartels (1991) and Overby (1991), the significance of constituents emerges. Considering my findings on supporter influence in decisions on involvement, this is not unexpected. It should be noted, though, that some observers disagree, highlighting instead the limitations of constituency pressure (Fleisher 1985; Lindsay 1990a; McCormick and Black 1983; Russett 1970).

The Influence of Supporters and Issue-specific Variations

The influence of supporters—while pivotal in the decision about whether to participate and statistically significant in the decision of how extensively to participate—is not exactly uniform across various issues of foreign and de-

---

10. Although to some observers the claim that supporter influence affected a member's extensive involvement in the last two instances may appear to be a justification for activities, interviewees clearly viewed the influence as an incentive, albeit a secondary one.

11. Personal views or ideology and the president were cited slightly more often as determinants in the vote.

fense policy. Certain issue-related factors may heighten the influence's importance whereas others may have the reverse effect.

A foreign or defense policy issue with salience and longevity produces more supporter awareness, attentiveness, and interest; this, in turn, strengthens the relationship between supporter pressure and the fact of involvement. People are more apt to be watching on a salient and long-lived subject. Such an issue, moreover, may attract and focus national organizations with branches across the country. This occurred in the MX case, when groups nationwide adopted opposition to the MX missile as their cause (Pressman 1983, 1984), and these anti-MX forces affected many members' involvement.

Conversely, on an issue lacking salience and longevity the specific supporter influences that predominate may be relatively indirect and soft in nature, and thus easier to ignore. Backers are more likely to view a less-prominent issue as "boring" or as a "nonissue." A member perceiving this apathy and ignorance may sense a secondary disincentive to involvement because of lack of supporter interest. Yet a representative may participate despite the secondary supporter constraint, for the debate's low salience marginally decreases the typical fear that activity will trigger adverse political consequences. On the issue of the IMF quota increase, a short-lived subject without national visibility, the supporter constraint was not omnipotent for the reasons just outlined.

Controversy at the national level (often arising on issues of high salience) also may affect supportive constituency influence—heightening it—on the decision about whether to participate. A national controversy is frequently mirrored in clashes among a member's supporters, and supporter disagreements present cross-pressures, an overwhelming disincentive to involvement. As alluded to above, a member will act cautiously when supporters are divided, for if action is taken some supporters may be critical or they may even become nonsupporters. An aide's remarks on the MX issue illustrate this phenomenon.

> Her supporters and advisers were interested and split [on it]. . . . The split was probably 50–50. . . . She knew that if she got involved, she would lose either way politically. So the idea was not to heighten the issue. . . . The political situation at home kept her from getting involved.

The existence of local economic links about which supporters are concerned is another key element shaping supporter pressure on an issue. Economic connections in the home district may generate backer interest and provide a strong, direct incentive to involvement. Local angles also engender indirect incentives because of likely supporter responses to actions on behalf of a regional industry: a member expects political points for district-related work benefiting supporters. Hence, a member cannot disregard such possible "goodies" as jobs and money, be they from the Pentagon or from a trade-related issue, if the reelection constituency will be helped. Supporters employed in industries profiting from MX production, for example, often inspired activity, as one staff person noted, "People in ____ build the MX. It is a clear, direct, district issue. . . . Even though the plant isn't in the district, his supporters work in it. He [participated] because of this." The reactions of this member and many others differed from that of the Massachusetts members because of the origin of the perceived influence. The Massachusetts members did not respond to *nonsupporters'* concerns about MX production.

The IMF issue stands in contrast to issues with extensive local economic links. Consequently, unlike other foreign economic policy issues— particularly trade issues—on which district hooks engender supporter concern and thus inspire involvement (Crabb and Holt 1989, 193; Nivola 1990), on the IMF issue such backer pressure was rarely present. Where district economic angles did emerge, however, supporter influence had the expected impact.

Finally, the nature of supporter influence may be affected by an issue involving the use of troops (crisis policy, according to chapter 2). Issues of troop involvement with human lives at risk are particularly emotional subjects as well as being extremely salient. A representative thus may perceive that supportive constituents want more than nominal participation, and he or she may either feel a duty to reflect the intensity of interest through activity or simply see political benefits in responding. In addition, if the issue has a perceived Israeli connection, as in the issue of marines in Lebanon, backer influence may be further reinforced. Some sample members who identified Jewish supporters as influences on involvement in the Lebanon case viewed these backers as knowledgeable, primary constituents, looking for active support of Israel; substantive involvement consequently was deemed a politically wise action. According to one aide, "The Jewish [supporters provide] his largest source of contributions. . . . This affected his involvement. As a matter of fact, on any Middle East issue there would be interest, and so he'd get real involved."

In sum, this research highlights the impact of several issue-related characteristics on the influence of supportive constituents. On a subject with salience and longevity the relationship between supporter pressure and the fact of involvement is likely to be particularly strong. An issue with such features, moreover, is more apt to be controversial, another factor that may heighten the impact of supporter influence in the decision about whether to participate. The existence or absence of local economic links, most relevant to issues of foreign economic policy and military and defense strategy, will also affect the significance of supporter influence. Finally, in the decision of how extensively to participate, such factors as troop involvement and an Israeli connection may increase the importance of supporters (see Burgin 1991b for more detail).

Implications of the Influence
of Supportive Constituents

As Fiorina (1974, 121) so aptly wrote,

> Those who study the American voter or his representatives seldom can resist the temptation to utter some purportedly profound thoughts on the great normative questions of democratic theory—thoughts inspired by their research, of course.

At the encouragement of the editors of this book I will follow tradition, though my remarks are limited and claims of profundity are certainly absent. Before proceeding it should be underscored that this analysis has confirmed that constituency influence matters. The nature and implications of the pressure, however, deserve further discussion. In particular, two subjects pertaining to constituency influence in foreign and defense policy-making merit some attention here.

It may appear at first blush that the influence of constituents discussed in this essay indicates that members are truly responsive to constituent pressures in the area of foreign and defense policy (see Eulau and Karps 1977 for a thorough discussion of responsiveness). Yet on closer reflection of the empirical evidence there are signs that some caveats are in order. The responsiveness I have described, not surprisingly, lacks three elements: it is not complete, it is not always or necessarily meaningful, and it is not exactly uniform. First, a member is responsive to only a segment of the constituency—the supportive constituency. This selective attentiveness was clearly demonstrated in interviews with both members and staffers. Although responsiveness can never be absolutely complete, it is noteworthy that the respondents themselves stressed its selective nature. Second, the member's responsiveness in terms of involvement tends to be primarily symbolic in nature (Mayhew 1974); backers affect *whether* a member participates much more than *how extensively* the member participates. Perceptions of supporters' preferences generally do not lead a member to engage in the forms of involvement likely to affect a debate's outcome, instead prompting activities that may simply help electorally. This is not to imply, however, that symbolic responsiveness is meaningless in terms of representation and (indirectly) of policy formation. Third, the effect of constituency influence may not be perfectly uniform across various foreign and defense policy topics with particular issue-related features such as salience, longevity, and troop involvement. Some observers may argue that an expectation of uniformity is unrealistic. Nonetheless, this disparity in the influence's effect may be symptomatic of minor, issue-related distortions in a member's responsiveness.

On another level, defenders of a powerful executive in the realm of foreign and defense policy might assume that the analysis here, stressing the importance of constituency influence, confirms that legislators are parochial and reelection-oriented, and hence unable to see beyond selfish interests to support policies in the "national interest." Again, such an assumption is inappropriate, primarily for two reasons. First, parochial and reelection considerations generally are not the primary incentives encouraging a member to become a leader or activist. The members most actively engaging in agenda setting and helping to determine and mold the foreign and defense policy legislation that Congress votes on, therefore, are not driven by constituency influence. Regarding participation, we saw that supporter influence has its greatest impact on the fact, not the level, of involvement. Second, even if supporter influence affects a member's votes or decisions regarding whether to participate, it is not axiomatic that the consequent actions will promote policies that are ineffective or contrary to the good of the nation (Burgin 1993; Lindsay 1990a). Thus, the implications of this work should not serve as ammunition for opponents of congressional activism in foreign and defense policy-making who fear the decisions or actions of electorally obsessed legislators.

APPENDIX A

From Interviews to the Five-Point Coding System

Several examples will illustrate how I translated material from interviews into the five-point coding system. On the subject of a primary incentive or disincentive, the conversation might begin as follows.

> Author: "Did your boss's constituents affect her involvement (or lack of involvement) on the MX?"
> Interviewee: "Of course they did. If it hadn't been for them, she wouldn't have done anything."

Later in the interview the following exchange might occur.

> Author: "What do you think affected Rep. ____'s activity (or lack of activity) on the MX?" [Note that in every case I asked the respondent a broad question in order to offer him or her another opportunity to raise the key influences.]

This appendix is reprinted, in slightly different form, from Burgin 1991a, 540–41.

Interviewee: "Without a doubt, it was her constituents, her supporters. She knew that she had to speak out because they were so into the issue. And so she got involved. . . . It was by far the most important factor."

For a secondary incentive or disincentive, the discussion might proceed as follows.

Author: "Did Congressman _____'s personal policy interests influence his participation in the debate over the marines in Lebanon?"

Interviewee: "He was quite interested in the issue. He had traveled to the Middle East, and he thought he was knowledgeable about the area."

And later in the interview:

Author: "What, then, do you think were the most important factors helping to determine why your boss became slightly involved but not more than slightly involved?"

[In response, the interviewee discussed one incentive and one disincentive with no mention of personal policy interests.]

For an insignificant influence, the following exchange might occur.

Author: "People often claim that involvement is influenced by staff. Did you or any other person on Representative _____'s staff affect his participation on the IMF debate?"

Interviewee: "No, not at all. He had decided what he was going to do, and then he did it. I didn't want him to do anything because I thought it was a bad issue to get involved in, but he didn't listen to me."

Later in the interview the respondent made no mention of staff when summarizing the key influences.

Clearly, not every independent variable for every case emerged as clearly as those in the above examples. But there were fewer than a half-dozen instances in which I had any question about how to code a variable.

APPENDIX B

The Scale of Involvement

The leaders, actively involved:

1. played a significant sponsoring role (or a facilitating role by performing key behind-the-scenes work) in legislation that moved through the legislative process;[12] or

---

This appendix is reprinted with minor changes from Burgin 1991a, 538.

12. A "significant sponsoring role" is only one of the subjective phrases I use in the scale. For further clarification, see Burgin 1988, appendix A.

2. introduced a major piece of legislation or offered a major amendment in subcommittee, in full committee, or on the floor for which the member cultivated support.

The activists, moderately involved:

1. actively participated in subcommittee, full committee, or floor debates;
2. introduced a minor piece of legislation or offered a minor amendment in subcommittee, in full committee, or on the floor for which the member cultivated support;
3. initiated and circulated a "Dear Colleague" letter soliciting cosponsors of legislation, seeking support for a position before a floor vote, or soliciting cosignatories to a letter for a conference committee or for the administration; or
4. performed miscellaneous activities such as engaging in major behind-the-scenes work, testifying on the relevant legislation, publishing an editorial piece in a national newspaper, or filing an amendment in the *Congressional Record* that the member did not offer but for which he or she cultivated support.

The position takers, slightly involved:[13]

1. made substantive remarks during hearings, markups, floor debates, one-minute speeches, or special orders;
2. sponsored legislation or offered a subcommittee, full committee, or floor amendment for which the member did not cultivate support;
3. inserted a statement into the *Congressional Record* (e.g., during floor debate, in Extension of Remarks, or as a special order);
4. cosponsored legislation or cosigned a "Dear Colleague" letter (applies if, and only if, the member cultivated support for the measure); or
5. performed miscellaneous activities such as engaging in minor behind-the-scenes work, publishing an editorial piece in a local newspaper, writing additional or dissenting views in a committee report, traveling abroad on a fact-finding mission, serving as a conferee, or filing an amendment in the *Congressional Record* that the member did not offer and for which he or she did not cultivate support.

The voters, minimally involved:

1. attended some hearings or markups; or
2. voted in markups or voted on the floor.

---

13. To be classified as actively or moderately involved, a member must undertake one of the activities falling under the appropriate category. To be classified as slightly involved, a member must engage in more than one of the activities listed under this tier.

CHAPTER 5

Interest Group Involvement in Congressional Foreign and Defense Policy

John T. Tierney

To observers of the politics of American foreign and defense policy, one of the noticeable developments over the past couple of decades has been the increase in the number and involvement of organized interests intent on influencing the direction of policy decisions. The reasons for the increased presence of organized interests are numerous. Some have to do with unfolding events and changing conditions such as the globalization of the American economy, changes in the strategic security interests of the United States, and the growing federal budget deficit.

Other reasons have to do with the changing mix of groups in society having concerns that are touched by foreign and defense policy. For example, there are the traditional interests—corporations, trade associations, labor unions, ethnic lobbies, etc.—that mobilize politically around an economic interest such as a trade agreement, a foreign aid appropriation, or a weapons contract. But recent years also have seen the emergence of many new groups (such as nuclear freeze and human rights organizations) contending over nonmaterial interests and values.

Still other reasons for the greater visibility of organized interests in foreign and defense policy have to do with the changing structure of power and decision making on these issues. When foreign policy was controlled primarily by the president and an exclusive foreign policy elite, the number of access points open to organized interests was small. But by the mid-1970s the institutional and political environments within which foreign and defense policy is made were changing dramatically, offering organized interests new opportunities to participate in policy deliberations and encouraging their active involvement. The attentive public was becoming more polarized ideologically on foreign policy issues and the mass public was becoming more active, more distrustful, and more volatile and unpredictable as it hankered simultaneously for peace and strength (Mann 1990b). Moreover, the press was newly aggressive and skeptical in its coverage of foreign and defense policy and thus became a potential new ally for those on the outside eager to shape policy agendas.

Finally, Congress was carving out a formidable institutional presence for itself in the development of foreign and defense policy. The national legislature was becoming more assertive, more resourceful, more decentralized— and more permeable to those eager to have some influence in policy-making processes.

For all these reasons, then, both the number of organized interests and the level of involvement of these groups in the congressional politics of foreign and defense issues have increased. Because it is now a larger phenomenon both in reality and in terms of visibility, it is easy to forget that lobbying on foreign policy questions is not a new feature of our political process. Even the currently maligned practice of former legislators hiring themselves out as agents for foreign governments (see Choate 1990) has roots reaching far into our past. Daniel Webster was retained by a wealthy British aristocrat, Lord Ashburton, with whom he later negotiated a treaty roundly criticized for the concessions it made to the British. Ashburton even provided Webster with British "secret service" funds to help shape American public opinion on the treaty (Baxter 1984; Knott 1990).

For many years sugar-producing countries made sure they had a presence on Capitol Hill—often by hiring former members of Congress or staff people—to influence the amount of above-market-price sugar purchased by the U.S. government. And, from the 1940s through the 1960s, the "China Lobby"—consisting of the Committee of One Million and other groups— worked persistently on the Hill to keep the United States from "betraying" Taiwan and Chiang Kai-shek (Ornstein 1984, 51).

Though this is not a new phenomenon, the interaction between organized interests and Congress in areas of foreign and defense policy has become so conspicuous and ubiquitous as to merit more examination. As the old, executive-centered, foreign policy elite is weakened by the inroads of a more dynamic and inclusive mix of policy actors, those who wish to understand the politics of foreign and defense policy need to have a better handle on the ways in which Congress and organized interests are linked on these issues. In thinking about the role organized interests play, it makes sense to pay attention first to the kinds of interests that are attentive to and active on these issues. These, of course, have changed over time as new groups emerge to express preferences on foreign and defense policy issues and as extant organizations (some environmental and civil rights groups, for example) expand their agendas to include issues of foreign policy.

The Interests: Who Is Involved?

The organized interests engaged in trying to influence congressional decisions on issues of foreign and defense policy are neither as numerous nor as wide in scope as one finds in the broader arenas of domestic politics wherein both the number and diversity of interests represented in the political process are truly striking. Still, foreign and defense policy engages hundreds of organizations that represent American economic interests, a variety of specific "causes," ethnic issues, and issues important to foreign governments and overseas economic interests.

American Economic Interests

It is not surprising that in a capitalistic economy such as ours the overwhelming majority of organizations actively engaged in representing their interests to the government are economic organizations of one sort or another—labor unions, corporations, trade associations, business alliances, and the like. The ways these organizations behave with respect to issues of foreign and defense policy are no different from the ways they behave on other issues, nor are the ways in which they divide the political tasks among themselves. Peak business associations such as the National Association of Manufacturers, the Chamber of Commerce, and the Business Roundtable tend to be involved primarily in issues on which they can work to advance the general interests of business and industry, for example, general promotion of the foreign aid program and policies aimed at trade expansion. But these general purpose, industry organizations sometimes thrash around ineffectively (as they did with regard to trade issues in the mid-1980s) as they become subject to cross-pressures within their broad memberships. Sometimes special industry-backed organizations or ad hoc coalitions are able to act on the broadest issues with greater effect. For example, in recent years the Emergency Committee for American Trade, an industry-backed organization pushing for general trade expansion, has worked effectively behind the scenes, cultivating key legislators and staffers, supplying needed analysis and argumentation, and remaining alert to the timing of policy-making processes in a way that their opponents have not (Destler 1986a, 161).

Trade associations are typically involved when issues affect particular industries such as oil, sugar, or semiconductors. But, like the peak business associations, trade groups also can be rendered politically inert when proposed policies would affect their members dissimilarly. For these and other reasons, individual corporations increasingly represent their own interests in Washington. This is clearly evident in the realm of trade policy as well as in program areas related to the arms industry, which is so concentrated and competitive that firms depend on industry association groups for lobbying for only the most universal of causes (Franck and Weisband 1979).

Labor unions also get involved in a wide variety of foreign policy issues. In the early 1980s, for example, the United Auto Workers was at the center of the struggle over proposed domestic content legislation. Labor's shift in the past couple of decades from its long-standing tradition of trade liberalism to a trade-restrictive stance may be one of the major developments in the interest group politics of trade policy but, as Destler (1986a, 160–61) has noted, labor's protectionist efforts have had little direct impact on trade legislation.

Labor's involvement is not limited to policies in which the labor movement has a direct economic stake. In addition to its "worker's ally" hat, organized labor often dons a "social justice" hat, lobbying on issues ranging from the interests of Jews seeking to emigrate from Russia to human rights (the AFL-CIO was instrumental in securing Senate approval in 1987 of two treaties protecting international labor rights [Forsythe 1989]).

Advocacy and Cause Groups

There is nothing new about the presence in foreign and defense politics of "public interest" citizens groups organized around common concerns or political causes of a noneconomic or nonoccupational nature. Such groups have been around for decades. For example, the Women's International League for Peace and Freedom has been lobbying in Washington for eighty years on issues ranging from the prevention of war to cutbacks in military spending to the treatment of political prisoners (Berry 1977). What is new, however, is that the number of such organizations politically active on foreign and defense issues is much greater than ever before, and their interests range far beyond war-and-peace issues to include such matters as global environmental degradation and human rights.

Some of these citizens groups are organizations of persons who care intensely about a single issue or a small group of issues having to do quite directly with foreign and defense policy. For example, a constellation of organizations has been active in recent years on issues relating to arms control, disarmament, and a nuclear freeze—the Council for a Livable World, Physicians for Social Responsibility, the Committee for a Sane Nuclear Policy, the Union of Concerned Scientists, and a host of others. Some broad ideological citizens organizations such as the Americans for Democratic Action and the American Conservative Union are continually alert to, and prepared to weigh in on, a wider variety of foreign policy issues. The same is true of such veterans organizations as the American Legion and the Veterans of Foreign Wars.

Some citizens groups that get involved in foreign policy ordinarily have domestic policy as their primary focus but are induced by circumstance or opportunity to broaden their perspectives. This is the case, for example, with respect to many environmental groups that have become involved in foreign policy as global environmental issues have loomed.

Other citizens groups active on foreign policy issues are advocacy organizations that seek selective benefits on behalf of persons who are in some way politically incapacitated or are otherwise unable to represent their own interests effectively. Among these are Amnesty International, the Friends Committee on National Legislation (the Quaker lobby), the United Church of Christ, and the International League for Human Rights—all organizations that lobby in Washington on human rights issues, pressing the United States to help persons suffering from conditions that range from torture in Paraguay, to slavery in Mauritania, to starvation and malnutrition in East Africa and Southeast Asia (Forsythe 1989, 4).

Ethnic Groups

Ethnic groups are among the most noticeable of the private organizations active on issues of foreign and defense policy. More has been written about ethnic lobbying groups than about any other kind of organized interest in the foreign policy arena (see, for example, Ahrari 1987; Bard 1991; Garret 1978; Goldberg 1990; Ogene 1983; Said 1977; Tivnan 1988; Uslaner 1991; and Watanabe 1984).

Ethnic lobbies get involved in foreign policy issues on behalf of many different racial, cultural, and religious subgroups in the American population. There are sizable and active organizations representing Irish-, Italian-, Polish-, African-, and Asian-Americans, to name a few. The phalanx of organizations active in Washington on behalf of particular ethnic interests is growing, now including such organizations as the Cuban American Foundation, the Ukrainian National Association, the Polish American Congress, and the Armenian Assembly of America. Some of these have been influential at various points in time. A prominent example is the Greek-American community's response to the Turkish invasion of Cyprus in 1974. The American Hellenic Institute Public Affairs Committee mobilized to coordinate the activities of various Greek-American groups and succeeded, despite strong resistance from the Ford Administration, in persuading Congress in 1975 to impose an embargo of American arms shipments to Turkey.[1]

But, of all the ethnic groups, the so-called Jewish lobby is widely regarded as having been the most important and powerful throughout most of the past forty years and especially in recent years. With support for Israel at the heart of American Jews' foreign policy concerns, the political influence of the Jewish lobby seems to stem chiefly from two factors: (1) the extraordinary issue attentiveness and high voting participation rates of American Jews, and

---

1. Indeed, an imposed 7-to-10 ratio of Greek to Turkish military aid (Greece is guaranteed $7 of military aid for every $10 that Turkey gets) still persists. This is, from a policy standpoint, quite bizarre (even if understandable politically as a reflection of Greek-American's political power) since, by any measure, Turkey has been a far better American security partner than Greece, both before the Cyprus incident and afterward.

(2) skillful assemblage in Washington of several Jewish-American organizations that lobby on issues affecting Israel, the best known of which is the American Israel Public Affairs Committee (AIPAC). Since its founding, in the early 1950s, AIPAC has built itself into one of the most formidable lobbying organizations in the United States. While other major organizations (such as the American Jewish Congress and the American Jewish Committee) focus on alternative ways to influence American foreign policy, AIPAC's focus is on Capitol Hill, where it works its will by orchestrating aggressive, grassroots, pressure campaigns, cultivating key members and staffers in the House and the Senate who become strategic allies and sources of timely political intelligence, and showing its muscle often enough to reinforce its image as a heavyweight (as when AIPAC successfully targeted Senator Charles Percy [R-Ill.] for defeat in 1984).

Over time the Jewish lobby has enjoyed a variety of successes, especially in persuading Congress to appropriate huge amounts of foreign economic and military aid to Israel, which now receives far more aid from the United States than does any other country. Indeed, AIPAC's only real political "losses" over the past forty years have been its occasional failures to block the sale of military aircraft and arms to Arab states in the Middle East. But even on those occasions AIPAC was able to secure modifications of various sorts that made the arms transfers less threatening to Israel.

Generally speaking, however, when one moves away from AIPAC and the politically active constituency of American Jews, the record of ethnic group lobbying success is far less imposing. In fact, most analysts seem to agree that the impact of such groups on American foreign policy is minimal (Horowitz 1977). Mohammed Ahrari (1987) points to two primary characteristics that seem to increase an ethnic lobbying group's influence or (as he calls it) "power quotient" in Washington. First, and most importantly, the policy the group is promoting must be congruent with the strategic interests of the United States. As much as anything else, the similarity of interest between Israel and the United States has provided the Jewish lobby with the sort of political advantage that has contributed to its long-standing policy effectiveness. (This point is reinforced by a contrasting example: it is worth recalling how difficult it was for the Baltic states' lobby to persuade the United States to extend diplomatic recognition to their homelands, in spite of heavy domestic pressure in support of their proposal, until Washington policymakers were certain that this recognition would not disrupt emerging ties with the Soviet Union.)

Second, to be politically effective an ethnic group must have reached a finely balanced point in the process of assimilation into American society: the ethnics must be part of the mainstream of American life but still identify strongly enough with their "homeland" to be willing to take political action on its behalf. Irish-Americans are an example of a group so thoroughly assimilated that it has lost the impulse to mobilize around issues relating to Ireland. Arab-Americans, on the other hand, may be seen as a group whose effectiveness is hindered by many factors, not the least of which is the fact that it largely remains on the perimeters of American life. By contrast, the Jewish lobby benefits from the fact that American Jews have somehow retained what Ahrari (1987, 156) calls their "paradoxical ability to assimilate enough yet still retain ample ethnic identification to pursue foreign policy goals affecting Israel."

Foreign Governments and Foreign Economic Interests

One of the more conspicuous developments on the landscape of interest group politics in recent years is the increased presence in Washington of foreign governments and foreign businesses lobbying on behalf of their own interests or hiring American lobbyists to do it for them. There is nothing surprising or unnatural about this. After all, the American government adopts many policies—on defense arrangements, arms sales, foreign aid, immigration, import restrictions and other trade practices, and so on—that affect the economic strength, political stability, and national security of other countries.

Most foreign governments get involved in congressional politics directly through their embassies. Embassy personnel monitor unfolding events on the Hill with an eye toward protecting their national interests. Visits to the Hill by embassy staff are now so commonplace that members of Congress consider foreign emissaries a staple part of the retinue of lobbyists trooping through the corridors each week. Foreign governments also approach Congress by means of direct communication from their leaders, as Jordan did in 1975 when King Hussein sent personal letters to every senator and fifty important members of the House in an effort to persuade them to vote for the proposed sale to Jordan of Hawk missiles. Whereas before that time it was unheard of for a foreign head of state to communicate directly with members of Congress (formal communications were with the president and his foreign affairs officers), the practice has become commonplace in the past fifteen years.

Many foreign governments also try to shape congressional dispositions toward them by hiring public relations firms that use the mass media to fashion a politically acceptable public image for the client country (Albritton and Manheim 1983; Manheim and Albritton 1984). Still more indirectly, some foreign governments have taken to investing in academia, endowing professorships and creating research centers at prestigious universities, increasing the likelihood that prominent American academics, available to testify before congressional committees, will be sympathetic to the views of the patron country (Franck and Weisband 1979, 182).

By far the most conspicuous way that foreign governments now seek to influence congressional decision making is by retaining highly regarded Americans to be their lobbyists in Washington. Many former cabinet secretaries, House members and senators, White House staffers, and trade officials, once out of office, are hired as foreign agents, representing the interests of other nations on Capitol Hill. The long roster of those employed in this way (now and recently), which reads like a *Who's Who* of the modern American political elite, includes Clark Clifford, Lloyd Cutler, William Rogers, William Ruckelshaus, Stuart Eizenstat, and Paul Laxalt.

Although foreign governments are maintaining an ever-higher profile in Washington, their political activities have been eclipsed in recent years by those of foreign businesses, which play the American lobbying game with even more vigor (and often with more at stake). Many foreign companies establish lobbying offices in Washington to monitor American political developments and to represent their interests in Congress and before executive agencies, believing that their interests are best advanced by their own employees who know their businesses well.

But by far the most prevalent pattern is for foreign companies to follow their governments' lead in retaining high-priced Washington lobbyists to represent their interests. These agents represent their clients' interests just as they would those of domestic clients. They forge links with legislators from districts in which their clients have facilities. They help their clients create and manage political action committees (PACs).[2] In short, they use the legislative and political networks they have nurtured for years and make the most of their access, political skills, and credibility.

While many observers of Washington politics remain sanguine about lobbying by foreign-owned corporations (seeing it, for example, as supportive in the fight against protectionism), many others are now arguing that foreign-owned corporations are becoming too influential as they penetrate the American political system in ways that may not be in U.S. national interest. Part of the concern undoubtedly stems from the transformation of the United States in the past decade from a nation of exporters to a nation of importers—the trade imbalance between the United States and Japan is especially severe—and the attendant increase in political tensions over loss of American jobs and earning

---

2. It is illegal for foreign nationals to make campaign contributions in the United States but the Federal Election Commission has ruled that a U.S. subsidiary of a foreign corporation may sponsor a PAC so long as U.S. citizens provide the money and decide how it is spent. A Congressional Research Service study in 1989 found that such PACs made contributions totaling $2.8 million in the 1987–88 election cycle ("Lobbying" 1990).

power. Foreign investment also has become a hot issue, with many observers warning of the cumulative long-term effect of the nation's growing dependence on foreign money (see, for example, Tolchin and Tolchin 1987).

Although foreign economic interests with real clout in Washington hail from points all around the globe (from Britain, Canada, Switzerland, Germany, the Netherlands, South Korea, and countless other countries), in the view of many observers the most disturbing specter of foreign political power has Japanese features. Critics of "the Japan lobby" assert that Japanese companies (and the Japanese government) spend tens of millions of dollars each year on Washington lobbyists, consultants, and public-relations firms, infiltrating Washington's fragmented decision-making apparatus to such an extent that the Japanese hold considerable sway, especially over American trade policy (Choate 1990).

Defenders of Japan's involvement in Washington politics argue that the case against the Japan lobby is vastly overstated, that Japanese lobbying differs little from other such activities on Capitol Hill (where competing interests often cancel each other out and have only a marginal impact on policy), and that much Japanese lobbying actually has been counterproductive because of the negative publicity it has generated (Fessler 1990b).

While scholars disagree about the importance of foreign economic lobbying efforts, it is sufficient for our purposes to note that the Japanese and others have established in Washington vast and formidable networks of highly regarded American advocates who have the kinds of skills, insider knowledge, strategically placed contacts, and far-reaching financial resources that typically spell access and influence in American politics.

The Vexing Question of Influence

Although it is instructive to note the growing number and changing mix of organized interests mobilized around foreign policy issues, it obviously would be much more helpful to be able to gauge how much *influence* organized interests have over congressional action on foreign and defense policy matters. Unfortunately, making such assertions is fraught with difficulty. The outcomes of political processes are decided by a multiplicity of factors, only one of which is the preferences of organized interests. Although organized interests often are important elements in the coalitions that emerge on Capitol Hill around issues, they are only a part of the larger mix of actors who may have an important say in policy decisions: the president and his advisers; political executives, program administrators, and policy analysts in executive agencies; the legislative leadership and congressional staffers; and the broad public. Specifying how influential organized interests are in shaping policy decisions is thus extremely difficult.[3] It is seldom clear (even to insiders) who among all these diverse actors has wielded power or influence—that is, who has made a difference in the outcome—in a particular case and how.

Moreover, the appropriate standard for assessing a particular interest group's policy impact is difficult to specify, since what is important is not merely whether the organization did or did not get what it wanted, but *what difference* its efforts made. Sometimes organized interests are able to ameliorate the extent of a defeat; thus an apparent loss masks the degree to which the outcome would have been worse had the organization not become involved. On the other hand, apparent victories for an interest group may be false evidence of organizational effectiveness since the outcome might have been determined by other factors (such as the efforts or intervention of other policy actors) rather than by the interest group's activities.

Despite these difficulties, we can generalize about the circumstances under which organized interests are likely to be influential on Capitol Hill on foreign and defense matters. One thing that we know matters is the type of policy being influenced. Just as Congress's role (vis-à-vis that of the president) increases as one moves along the spectrum from crisis policies, to strategic policies, to structural policies (see chapter 2), so does the role of organized interests. Generally speaking, organized interests do not have much say in decision-making processes surrounding crises. But, as presidential dominance and "national interest" considerations decline in intensity with movement away from crises along the policy spectrum, the potential for interest group influence presumably increases. (Some readers may prefer another, parallel distinction, often made in the literature on foreign policy, between "high politics" [consisting chiefly of peace and security issues over which executive officials are dominant] and "low politics" [consisting chiefly of distributive issues such as trade and aid that involve a wider mix of political actors].)

The nature of the issue also matters in another way. Organized interests are less likely to be influential both on highly visible issues that engage widespread, contrary public passions or media coverage and on issues in which there are strong, competing ideological, partisan, or constituency pressures. Conversely, organized interests are more likely to be able to affect outcomes on issues that are shielded from public or media scrutiny and do not conflict with legislators' deeply felt convictions, lines of party cleavage, or particularistic constituency needs. Organized interests also are more likely to have some influence on the outcome of policy issues when they are resisting a

---

3. For a more elaborate discussion of the obstacles to assessing the influence of organized interests (overall or in particular policy areas), see Tierney (1987, 96–100). And, for a useful discussion of the problem in foreign policy, see Forsythe (1989, 140–59).

proposed change in policy rather than trying to alter the status quo, when they focus on affecting the details of a policy rather than its broad outlines, and when their lobbying efforts are not met by opposing pressure from other organized interests (Schlozman and Tierney 1986, 310–17).

Finally, it is surely true that the ability of organized interests to influence outcomes on Capitol Hill depends upon their resources and their skill in applying them. Especially important are the possession of substantive information and defensible policy rationales but also crucial are resources such as money, an appealing cause, a skillful staff, an attentive membership widely dispersed across many congressional districts, and strategically placed allies among policymakers in government.

To some extent, of course, the influence of interest groups hinges on what they *do*—that is, what sorts of political activities they pursue and how they marshal and allocate their resources to advance their policy preferences. In their efforts to influence congressional decisions, the organized interests engaged on issues of foreign and defense policy rely on much the same arsenal of established political strategies and tactics employed by organized interests trying to shape domestic policy. Some of their techniques are direct, such as testifying at congressional hearings or establishing personal contacts with legislators and staffers. Others are more indirect and include mobilizing organization members or the broader public, organizing protests and demonstrations, and trying to affect electoral results.

But, like other political actors, organized interests do not necessarily have to *do* anything to be effective. In other words, just as the "law of anticipated reactions" (see chapter 2) enables Congress to influence executive branch behavior indirectly, congressional behavior is surely governed on occasion by legislators' anticipation of the reactions of organized interests and, presumably, by an impulse to behave in ways that garner credit and avoid blame or political costs.

Organized Interests and Public Policy

In order to acquire a clear sense of the role organized interests play in congressional deliberation and decisions on foreign and defense policy issues, and how much influence they have, the ideal approach would be to examine a wide assortment of issue areas within the large realm of foreign and defense policy, complete with detailed case studies, from which we could draw sensible inferences about the extent of organized interest influence. After all, the activities and influence of organized interests vary across policy and issue areas, and, of course, over time, with changing circumstances and conditions. A systematic examination of that sort is far beyond the scope of this short chapter. Included in its place is a brief look at organized interest involvement in two broad areas—trade policy and national security policy (specifically arms control and defense spending). While neither systematic nor exhaustive, these commentaries are meant to illustrate both the variety of organized interests and the extent to which their role is affected by changing events and political circumstances (which further exacerbates the difficulty of achieving a firm assessment of their influence).

Trade

Trade is historically a policy preoccupation of Congress, and over the years the setting of trade policy has given rise to spasms of concern about the influence of pressure groups on legislators. Recognizing that they were pathologically incapable of resisting the importuning of special interests on trade legislation, members of Congress in 1934 passed the Reciprocal Trade Agreements Act, delegating to the executive branch the authority to negotiate tariff levels. (The legislators' own base instincts on such matters had led them four years earlier to enact the disastrous Smoot-Hawley tariff, which raised tariff levels to their highest point in American history and was widely perceived to have aggravated the Depression.) Turning over this power to the executive branch relieved legislators of routine responsibility for making such politically charged decisions. It also left them in the politically appealing position of being able to respond sympathetically to their constituents' complaints about unfair competition by castigating and haranguing the executive branch. Less open to, or affected by, interest group blandishments, executive branch officials generally paid rhetorical notice to domestic demands but bridled any impulse to provide policy relief. For the most part, this shift in the institutional arrangements for making trade policy proved mutually acceptable to Congress and the executive, and the United States settled into a long period of consensual fidelity to liberal, open trade policy (Destler 1986a).

In the period following World War II, the prevailing pattern of interest group involvement on the issue saw a small number of industries seeking protection, each essentially watching out for itself. Smaller industries were encouraged by congressional leaders to use the quasi-judicial trade remedy procedures of the Tariff Commission, later renamed the International Trade Commission (ITC). But, as Destler (1986a, 158–59) has noted, larger industries such as textiles sometimes managed to negotiate separate deals for themselves—deals that usually involved promises not to stand in the way of broader trade-liberalizing initiatives. No significant groups were staking out a broad protectionist position nor were those groups that stood to benefit from open trade (such as consumers) active on the issue.

By the mid-1980s, however, the confluence of important economic developments around the world gave the politics of trade some new twists. Trade began to attract anew the attention of Congress. Among the more salient economic developments were the dramatic worsening of the U.S. trade deficit (from $22.3 billion in 1981 to just over $150 billion in 1987), the looming emergence in 1992 of the European Community as an economic giant whose movements would send shock waves around the world; the emergence of Canada and Mexico as more important trading partners of the United States, and the economic awakening of new entities on the Pacific Rim.

In addition to changes affecting the politics of interest groups, there were changes in the politics of symbols and ideas. In the slogan of "fair trade," protectionists finally found an effective symbolic counterweight to the "free trade" theme that for so long had played so well for their opponents. Moreover, economic nationalism was again becoming a potent political force in American politics, and especially on Capitol Hill, as more citizens and political leaders came to perceive that it was not the Soviet "evil empire" of Reagan's legendary rhetoric that the United States had fallen behind, but Japan and the capitalist powers of the West. Many members of Congress found themselves drawn to trade policy as they saw more evidence for the proposition that the United States had been fighting in the wrong trenches for thirty-five years. Noting the general changes in the political and intellectual climate on the trade issue, Destler (1986a, 163) concluded:

> Trade politics has become more partisan. The elite has grown less committed to liberal trade. Intellectual challenges to open-market policies have grown. Patterns of trade politics have become more complex. All these changes have weakened the old system for diverting and managing trade policy pressures, and most have increased the political weight of those backing trade restrictions.

The growing number and range of U.S. industries seeking trade protection (or at least a government-secured "level playing field") have now come to include not just mature, relatively low-tech industries whose manufacturing processes can be readily duplicated in other countries but also the high-tech makers of such products as semiconductors and telecommunications equipment.

Thus, the pressure on members of Congress to legislate trade relief for pet industries is great and growing. Members of Congress who try to obtain new legislated constraints on imports that compete with industries in their districts face a difficult task, as Pietro Nivola (1990) has pointed out, because the politics of legislative coalition-building on new protectionist measures leads to a broadening of the number of industries covered by it and then to opposition from legislators whose constituents depend on crucial imports. Thus, legislators and lobbyists seeking protection for a particular industry find that they are likely to fare better by quietly amending existing laws, especially such arcane ones as the antidumping statutes. The appeal of this approach is clear, as Nivola (1990, 227) notes:

> The amendments are often visible only to cognoscenti, and sometimes even they do not appreciate the full implications until later. If the sleepers are spotted, their proponents cloak a particularistic intent in the language of a collective good (ridding the marketplace of discriminatory pricing, fixing distortions caused by subsidies, and so on).

Persuading Congress to amend a law that is proving troublesome in its administration is, of course, a cherished practice of organized interests in the American system of fragmented political authority. And it is increasingly common in trade politics for a firm or industry that loses on a technicality in its initial suit before the ITC to lobby Congress to enact small, technical amendments to existing legislation, allowing them to win later. Many changes in the laws governing such matters as antidumping duties can be traced to pressures from industries that earlier had failed to obtain satisfactory judgments in the executive branch (Yoffie 1989, 124). In short, when Congress tinkers with general trade statutes—as it did in 1988 with passage of the Omnibus Trade and Competitiveness Act—it jiggles the regulatory and administrative remedies in ways guaranteed to be politically profitable to special claimants.

None of this means, of course, that narrow interests looking for protection always win. Sometimes organized interests (such as the steel industry in the mid-1980s) are unsuccessful in pushing their parochial trade demands, even when countervailing societal pressures are weak, because government policymakers (or "state actors," as statist theorists would say) resist those demands out of regard for the proposal's widespread political and economic implications (Stritch 1991). Sometimes organized interests will fail even in a vigorous bid to win a protectionist measure such as an import quota if legislators fear the effects of retrospective voting by a public that is generally inattentive but capable of reacting to large and immediate costs that are traceable to legislative actions (Arnold 1990, 240).

But frequently legislators do choose to serve attentive and organized interests on trade matters. In some instances doing so poses no readily discernible costs to domestic interests and is thus quite easy. In the late 1980s legislators and staffers persistently pushed the Japanese on behalf of American chocolate manufacturers who wanted help in reducing excessive Japanese tariffs that inhibited the export of their candies (and who provided legislative offices with unending supplies of one-pound bags of M&Ms as a constant reminder of the issue) (Bisnow 1990, 308). Organized interests attract legislative support by virtue of their presence on the Hill every day, providing tangible reminders of their interests (such as M&Ms), other attractive incentives (such as lunch for staffers at the Monocle or La Colline), or—more to the point—substantive information and defensible policy rationales, which are the real political currencies on the Hill.

Legislative instincts toward trade protection are especially understandable in instances in which legislative activity benefits concentrated, attentive interests but imposes costs on broad, less attentive publics (Arnold 1990; J. Wilson 1973). Explaining the political link between legislators' interests and those of lobbying groups on trade issues, Mark Bisnow (1990, 282–84), a former aide to Senator Robert Dole (R-Kans.) writes:

> It is not difficult to see why Congress would approach matters narrowly. Wherever a powerful industry lost ground to foreign imports, offices could expect to hear from managers, unions, and lobbyists urging solutions, most of which, no matter how disguised, had as their obvious object the curtailment of foreign imports. . . .
>
> Congress, of course, is oriented not to academic theory but to constituencies—whose voices, financial contributions, and votes carry decisive weight in elections. In trade matters, as a result, it tends to listen to well-organized groups that have a clear focus of concern, strong local support, and a situation susceptible to ready emotional understanding: the loss of jobs of autoworkers in Detroit or steelworkers in Pennsylvania or garment and apparel workers in North Carolina. . . .
>
> In contrast, economics professors or consumer advocates, who might be counted on to expound the virtues of free trade or at least to counsel patience, are not renowned for their ability to raise campaign funds or to get out the vote for their friends. . . . Politicians can be forgiven if they are not particularly receptive to the argument that painful economic adjustment—the rise and fall of different industries, possibly in their states—is the natural and desirable result of shifting advantages among nations in technology, capital, and human resources. Congress knows that if the causes of a problem are "economic," it can do little and therefore it often prefers diagnoses for which it can write prescriptions. It wants to see problems as amenable to new laws.

National Security

When it comes to decisions about spending money on weapons—on what kinds, in what amounts, for what purposes—or about the extent to which our reliance on arms ought to be harnessed, the roles and activities of organized interests are heavily influenced by unfolding events and by the changing political climate. Not surprisingly, at the broadest level, the policy posture on such matters is set by perceptions of threats to national security and calculations of the most appropriate strategic response. To a great extent, then, the involvement of organized interests and their influence in these areas tend to be highly mercurial and variable. But one constant of the past quarter century is that organized interests are much more heavily involved than earlier in trying to influence Congress on such issues for the simple reason that Congress is more engaged in these policy decisions than it was in the past. Although the issues of arms control and defense spending obviously are connected in countless ways, the politics of these issues can be seen more clearly if they are discussed separately.

Arms Control
The volatility of mass (and even elite) opinion on arms control was fully evident as the 1970s gave way to the 1980s. By the end of 1979, Washington and much of the rest of the nation were gripped by an anti-Soviet fervor occasioned by evident growth in Soviet military power and increasing military activism, especially the invasion of Afghanistan. Within two years the nation's mood had changed noticeably (even if that of official Washington had not). As Barry Blechman (1990b, 117) has noted, the collapse of arms control negotiations, the withdrawal of the SALT II treaty from the Senate before ratification, and the immoderate rhetoric of the new Reagan administration about the winnability of a nuclear war fueled widespread public alarm about the growing dangers of nuclear conflict and energized a constellation of interest groups to push for an end to the development and procurement of all nuclear weapons systems—in short, for a "nuclear freeze."

The nuclear freeze movement of the early 1980s was organized around the existing political foundations of previous disarmament and peace movements, which had left behind an organizational infrastructure that could support a new mobilization (D. Meyer 1990). Among these were groups that had constituted the core of movements that in the 1950s and 1960s had pushed for a nuclear test ban treaty and in the 1960s and 1970s had agitated against the development of antiballistic missiles. Some were arms control groups such as the Committee for a Sane Nuclear Policy, the Union of Concerned Scientists, and the Council for a Livable World. Others were traditional pacifist or peace organizations such as the American Friends Service Committee, the Women's International League for Peace and Freedom, and the War Resister's League. In 1979, Helen Caldicott, concerned initially about nuclear power, began to revive Physicians for Social Responsibility, which had been founded in 1960 to push for a nuclear test ban. But the immediate organizational impetus for the freeze movement came from Mobilization for Survival, a loose coalition of more than two-hundred groups and forty national organizations intent on raising awareness of the threat of nuclear holocaust. Later it was joined by the

Nuclear Weapons Freeze Campaign, which essentially became the organizational core of the freeze movement.

In their effort to halt the production of nuclear weapons systems, freeze lobbyists used every weapon in the political arsenal. Between 1981 and 1983 there were massive demonstrations and teach-ins; widespread grass-roots mobilization that activated doctors, lawyers, and clergy, as well as antinuclear extremists; PAC contributions to freeze candidates for Congress; skillful manipulation of media attention; and strategically useful alliances with eager policy entrepreneurs such as Congressman Edward J. Markey (D-Mass.) and Senator Edward Kennedy (D-Mass.).[4] By mid-1982 the efforts of freeze activists had elevated the issue to the top of the foreign policy agenda. Freeze resolutions had been introduced in both houses of Congress and almost three-quarters of a million people demonstrated for the freeze in New York City in June of that year, indicating its popular appeal.

The movement had considerable impact on the 1982 elections. In part because the freeze resolution itself had lost by only two votes on the floor of the House in August, freeze activists worked hard throughout the fall to influence the outcome of elections. The movement's electoral battle cry was "Change one vote and pass the freeze" (Waller 1987, 158). On election day, voters supported the freeze by wide margins in eight of the nine states in which it was a referendum item (it lost in Arizona) and in thirty-six of the thirty-eight cities and counties with freeze referendums. And, although the freeze's effect was more difficult, of course, to gauge in the congressional races, supporters won thirty-eight of the forty-seven races in which the freeze had become a campaign issue, and freeze activists calculated a net gain in the House of twenty to thirty supporters (Waller 1987, 165).

The following spring, a carefully orchestrated lobbying campaign by profreeze interest groups led to the passage of the freeze resolution by the House. But the struggle for victory was not easy, and the resolution made no headway in the Republican-controlled Senate. Moreover, within a month of voting for the freeze resolution, the House approved funding for procurement of the MX missile, leading to crushing disillusionment on the part of many of the disarmament activists. Growing internal tension among the different organizations in the freeze coalition also contributed to a gradual weakening of the movement.

By 1985 the freeze movement had almost completely dropped out of sight but its lasting political effects in Congress were apparent. Legislators had come to see that political benefits could be reaped by taking a stand on

---

4. Among the good available accounts of the political strategies and tactics—and the successes and failures—of the freeze movement are Waller (1987) and D. Meyer (1990).

arms control issues. And members of Congress, newly enlightened by this experience of the political implications of defense issues generally, were also emboldened to use Congress's constitutional power of the purse as a means of influencing executive branch decisions on weapons systems and defense structures (Blechman 1990b).

Defense Spending

Of course, Congress had been taking a more active role in defense budget-making for years, especially since the 1970s, primarily because of the critical posture toward defense and the military that many members had adopted following the Vietnam War. Congressional budget-making became somewhat more rational (if not always more politically appealing) with the advent in 1974 of changes in the congressional budget process that required Congress for the first time to consider the effect of individual spending decisions on overall expenditures and to evaluate the cumulative implications for revenue needs. The new budget process served to highlight two trade-offs, both of which are difficult to negotiate: the trade-off between expenditures for defense and expenditures for domestic programs, and between total expenditures and new revenue needs. Members were made to see clearly the consequences for other priorities of spending money on defense. Even so, defense contractors continued to do well, slicing out a considerable portion of the federal budget as they worked with legislators from across the ideological spectrum, some-times (just how often is debated) trying to spread the spending for defense projects and weapons systems over many of the country's congressional dis-tricts in the hope of maximizing the coalition of support on the Hill. This was clearly the case, for example, with the B-1 bomber. Rockwell lobbyists and the air force prepared detailed "lists of every B-1 subcontract location, cross-referenced by state, town and congressional district," allowing the lobbyists to "show members of Congress, down to the last dollar, how their constituents benefitted from the B-1" (Kotz 1988, 129). The actual geographical dispersion of defense money to contractors even on large projects is not as great as is often suggested. For example, the Defense Department is alleged to have made contracts that parceled out B-1 money to forty-eight states and more than four hundred congressional districts. That figure is probably true in one sense. On the other hand, 95 percent of the money went to fifteen states and more than 70 percent went to just five states (Lindsay 1991, 97). In addition to providing jobs for legislators' constituents, defense contractors solidified con-gressional support for new or continued contracts through the liberal use of campaign contributions and honoraria. Contributions to political action com-mittees from defense contractors more than doubled in the first four years of the Reagan administration, and the top twenty defense firms poured $3.6 million into the 1984 campaigns (Parry1985).

But by 1986 the congressional politics of defense spending began to change rapidly in response to two circumstances, each of them leading to declines in congressional support and thus to declines in the complacency of most defense contractors. First, the skyrocketing federal deficit dictated that high levels of defense spending, sacred earlier in the decade, must be scaled back along with spending on domestic programs. Second, defense contractors had become popular symbols of "waste, fraud, and abuse" in the wake of a series of highly publicized defense-related scandals. Headlines told of defense firms selling equipment and spare parts to the government at what appeared to be recklessly inflated prices—seven thousand dollar coffeemakers and six hundred dollar toilet seats. The American people also were treated to the news that federal prosecutors had uncovered widespread improprieties in the relationships between military contractors and procurement officials at the Pentagon.

Congress responded not only by embracing more ardently its plans to cut defense spending but by enacting a variety of measures under the rubric of "procurement reform." These include numerous technical modifications in the procedures by which the government pays defense contractors. Among the changes are cost-sharing provisions requiring a company to pay for research and development on a weapons project even though there is no guarantee that the company will be chosen to produce it or that the weapon will be developed. There is a reduction, from 90 to 75 percent, in "progress payments," which provide interest-free financing for work under way, and a lowering of profit margins to about 10 percent.

One of the political consequences of this has been alteration in contractors' political behavior. For one thing, defense budget politics has become more of a zero-sum game as military spending declines. Contractors are chasing fewer dollars, and programs are competing not only to perform the same military mission but simply to secure a niche in a stripped-down budget. The consequence is a cutthroat climate in which lobbyists are more inclined than before to criticize each other's products. While Sikorsky Aircraft circulates a report to key Washington decision makers deriding Boeing's Osprey "tiltrotor" transport, Northrop lobbyists sneer at Martin Marietta's Midgetman missile, claiming that it is unnecessary given Northrop's stealth bomber. Although this kind of sniping has always been part of the warfare among defense contractors, it is now far more open and intense (Morrison 1990).

It is not just their own competitors that concern the contractors. As Lindsay (1991, 139) points out, citizens groups often rise up to lobby against controversial weapons programs, especially nuclear weapons. This was true, for example, of the anti–MX missile coalition, which mobilized a wide array of lobbying groups from Americans for Democratic Action to the United Church of Christ. The planned deployment in the mid-1980s of the antisatellite (ASAT) weapon system gave rise to active opposition by the Union of Concerned Scientists and the Federation of American Scientists, two groups working for arms control. The scientists' lobby worked on the issue for several years, using its credibility and its persuasive command of the technical issues to obtain bipartisan backing for a moratorium on ASAT testing (Blechman 1990b).

Finally, lobbyists on defense-spending issues now must deal with the dramatically altered strategic environment stemming from the collapse of the Soviet Union and its aftermath—including a joint declaration early in 1992 by presidents George Bush and Boris Yeltsin that their countries will no longer regard each other as adversaries but as partners in promoting democracy. This not only ends the arms race and makes obsolete the rationale for feverish spending on weapons but it gives fresh impetus to those who wish to see defense dollars diverted to domestic needs. Weapons producers, and their patrons in the Pentagon, will counter that reasoned policy calls for continued spending in the face of new scenarios involving low-intensity conflict, third world crises, and the like. But the policy rationales and many of the lopsided political considerations that undergirded defense contractors' long-time bonanza no longer exist.

A Concluding Note

What are we to make of this? Several points merit attention by way of conclusion. First, the interactions between Congress and organized interests on foreign and defense issues furnish substantial confirmation for one of the central axioms of interest group politics: that the pathways connecting interest groups to Congress bear two-way traffic. To be more precise, the role organized interests play not only *affects* policy outcomes, but is in turn *affected by* the larger institutional and political settings. This is clear, for example, with respect to changing global political conditions and consequent changes in foreign and defense policy priorities. The sweeping political changes in Russia and Eastern Europe obviously have had significant effects on the politics of American defense budgeting and on the fortunes of organizations such as the Committee on the Present Danger, which argued that U.S. policy had to take more account of the threat to world peace and American security posed by the Soviet arms buildup. Furthermore, it is clear that the globalization of the American economy and the transformation of the United States from an exporting to an importing nation have contributed to fundamental alterations in domestic political beliefs about the wisdom of free trade, thus changing the political dynamics of trade policy-making. In addition, changing fiscal conditions in the United States have had significant impacts, lending a zero-sum character to the politics of defense budgeting, pitting various claimants against each other in the struggle for dollars, and making our politics more bitter and strident.

Moreover, a number of institutional changes on Capitol Hill over the past two decades have rendered Congress more open and accessible to organized interests while at the same time recasting the institutional character of Congress, making it more individualistic and unpredictable than in the past. The decentralization of congressional power has opened up some new avenues for potential influence but it has also multiplied the number of people on the Hill who may have a say on matters of foreign policy and defense. Gone are the days when a defense lobbyist could clinch the financing for a cherished program by forging a back-room deal with the almighty chairs of the Armed Services Committees. Today's committee chairs have enough trouble persuading their own panel members to hold ranks, much less being able to sway other members of this highly individualistic Congress. In trade policy, too, gone are the days when control over the contents of trade bills was in the hands of the chairs of the Senate Finance and House Ways and Means Committees. With the changed opportunity structure in Congress, participation in trade policy-making has spread to include the House Energy and Commerce Committee, the Armed Services Committees, the Banking Committees, and the Judiciary Committees (Nivola 1990, 233). Just as it has in other policy arenas, this fragmentation of power has markedly changed the political dynamic in foreign and defense policy. Policy entrepreneurialism abounds as members ride their own hobbyhorses in pursuit of reelection or personal aggrandizement. In sum, institutional changes on the Hill constitute yet another important factor affecting the way organized interests interact with Congress on defense and foreign policy issues.

Organized interests are more involved in the congressional politics of foreign and defense policy than they were in the past, in large part because Congress has become more central to deliberation about these matters. Moreover, these interests have found in the contemporary Congress a highly permeable and open institutional setting that is generally hospitable to their efforts to influence policy decisions.

In the future there is likely to be even more organized interest activity on Capitol Hill on foreign and defense issues. One reason for this is the increasing number of policy issues being internationalized such as civil rights and the environment. As the "global community" continues to shrink, more and more issues that once were confined primarily to the domestic agenda will spill over into foreign policy, bringing with them more groups intent on shaping decisions. Another factor that will give rise to more organized interest activity on foreign policy and security issues is the end of the cold war, which gives many groups in American society cause to contend for the dollars that will be diverted from the machinery of the warfare state.

One likely consequence of this is that the politics of foreign and defense policy will become not just more contentious but more polarized, shrill, and unruly. As organized interests push more cross-cutting issues onto the agenda, the varied clashes over material and nonmaterial interests and values are likely to become fierce and malignant. The symbol manipulators and blame allocators who know so well how to mobilize mass bias (whether it takes the form of Japan-bashing or the America First movement) will stir public emotions up and steer public discourse down. Moreover, the sort of uncertainty that is likely to pervade politics in the shakedown period of the "new world order" will exacerbate fears and increase conflicts. For the many members of Congress already thinking about leaving politics because the constant importunings of strident interests have robbed political life of much of its pleasure, the continuing changes in the role of organized interests in foreign and defense policy may make them long, if not for retirement, then at least for a return to the days of the imperial presidency.

Members of Congress are likely to face more of the same, and they will find themselves even more often in the position of having to divine the delicate balance between short-run political exigencies and long-run policy consequences, or between acquiescence to the clearly expressed wishes of narrow groups that care intensely and respect for the frequently unexpressed needs of larger publics.

This is, of course, an old concern. Observers of American democracy long have been concerned that among our representative institutions Congress is especially vulnerable to the potentially pernicious influences of organized interests. It is an institution pervasively open to importuning by such interests, rendered so both by original design and by the forces of gradual institutional development. That openness is worrisome to many people. Lobbyists representing organized interests operate in the thick of the legislative process, forging mutually beneficial relationships with legislators and their staffs. Each participant has resources that the others need—information, access to scarce dollars, strategically placed allies, political support, and the like. And the revolving door that has put a large number of former members of Congress into the employ of foreign businesses and governments ushers in the same malodorous whiffs of ethical misconduct that we find offensive in defense procurement or any other policy area in which the door is left spinning.

Observers are understandably nervous about circumstances that seem to render the public interest vulnerable to subjugation by special interests. Many thoughtful observers believe that deference to particularistic interests is encouraged when we let former top American officials, who gained their inside knowledge at the taxpayers' expense and have unparalleled access to decision makers, represent special interests (including foreign corporations and governments) in the halls of Congress. Perhaps such senior officials, who were granted high public trust, should be held to a loftier standard (see the proposals in Choate 1990; Levy 1987).

But, if we are to heed James Madison's warning that the cure may be more pernicious than the disease, it may be that the price we must pay to remain a free and open society is allowing former government officials to represent foreign entities or special domestic interests, the advancement of whose goals could adversely affect the best interests of the American public. After all, as we have seen, such practices go back at least to the days of Daniel Webster, who hired himself out as an agent of the British.

Some historical perspective is important in thinking through these matters since, as Lawrence Brown (1983, 5) has noted, political scientists—like journalists and other professional, political observers—tend to be "carried away by a public-spirited desire to be the first authority on the block to identify the latest threat to American democracy." In the process, we may be led to "decry each development as a grave threat to the roles and functions of time-tested institutions," and to be overly impressed with the fragility of what in fact are very durable processes and institutions. There are, after all, beneficial consequences to the continuing internationalization of organized interest politics. Most important is that more widespread involvement by organized interests in foreign policy questions means that foreign policy decisions will be tested in the political process and shaped and tempered through consensus-forming procedures, all of which makes for policies that take into account competing values and interests and so are more likely to enjoy popular legitimacy.

Part 3.
Inside the Congressional Institution

CHAPTER 6

Decision Making in the Foreign Affairs
and Foreign Relations Committees

James M. McCormick

Both the House Committee on Foreign Affairs and the Senate Committee on Foreign Relations have long and rich histories. Foreign Affairs dates its lineage to 1775 and its existence as a standing committee in the House of Representatives to 1822, while Foreign Relations dates its lineage to 1816 when standing committees were first established in the Senate. Indeed, the Senate Foreign Relations Committee has been identified as the "ranking" committee in the Senate and the Congress because it was the first committee identified in the resolution establishing standing committees (U.S. Congress House Committee on Foreign Affairs 1985, 9; U.S. Congress Senate Committee on Foreign Relations 1986, 2).

Despite their longevity, the two foreign policy committees have had historically different roles and reputations within Congress. The Senate Foreign Relations Committee is generally portrayed as the premier committee in Congress because of its dual involvement in both executive and legislative affairs (U.S. Congress Senate Committee on Foreign Relations 1986, 12; D. Farnsworth 1961). The committee, of course, has primary responsibility for reviewing all treaties and foreign policy nominations, and thus has the ability to affect policy beyond the normal legislative and oversight functions of most other committees. As a consequence, the conventional view has been

The qualitative assessments and unattributed quotations are based upon a series of anonymous interviews conducted over a number of years with individuals knowledgeable about the House Foreign Affairs and Senate Foreign Relations Committees. Interview trips were generously supported by the Dirksen Congressional Center and the College of Liberal Arts and Sciences and the Graduate College of Iowa State University. I am most grateful for such support and for the kind cooperation and assistance of the interviewees. Thanks are also due to Ronna Eley and Jenifer Baker for assistance with data collection, to Chris Deering and Roger Davidson for some helpful information on this line of research, and to Ellen Collier, James Lindsay, Jorgen Rasmussen, Eugene Wittkopf, and anonymous reviewers for several helpful suggestions on earlier drafts.

that the Senate Foreign Relations Committee has taken a more activist decision-making role in affecting U.S. foreign policy, especially in the post–World War II period.

By contrast, the House Foreign Affairs Committee traditionally is portrayed as operating in the shadows of its Senate counterpart with a limited agenda and responsibility. The committee is perceived to pass few pieces of legislation (principally the foreign aid bill) and take few foreign policy initiatives. When the committee does act, it is seen primarily as taking voting cues from a leadership that is responding to executive preferences (Fenno 1973). Indeed, one prominent study has described the committee as declining in importance in the post–World War II years, even as U.S. global foreign policy responsibilities and involvements were increasing, and as having lost ground on foreign policy matters to a series of other congressional panels—the Appropriations, Armed Services, Agriculture, Banking and Currency Committees (Carroll 1966).

Within the past two decades, and due to changing conditions within Congress and the world at large, these depictions of the two committees have come under some challenge (see, for example, Henderson 1979; Kaiser 1977a, 1977b; McCormick 1985; C. Madison 1987b, 1991c; Ornstein and Rohde 1977; Stanfield 1990). Some have criticized both committees for their ineffectiveness in the foreign policy process. As a former official of the Reagan administration noted, "One has died on the vine; the other has fragmented into little empires" (quoted in Stanfield 1990, 2916; see also C. Madison 1987b). Others have viewed Foreign Affairs as more active than its Senate counterpart (e.g., Henderson 1979) and still others have disparagingly characterized Foreign Relations as a "backwater" committee of Congress (*Congressional Quarterly Almanac 1989*, 510).

In this chapter, I analyze the decision making of these two foreign policy committees since the 1970s and seek to account for the differences in activity levels between them. I begin by describing the principal decision-making activities of the committees and the ways in which these activities have changed over the past twenty years. Then I discuss several internal committee factors and several external ones that seem to account for the relative differences in the activities of the foreign policy committees in the two chambers. The internal committee factors that I analyze are the structure and operation of the committees (and subcommittees), the composition of the memberships of each committee, and the role that the leadership has played within each one. The factors external to the committees that seem to explain the changes in decision-making activities are the role of other committees with foreign policy interests, the impact of the appropriations process, and the increasing centralization of policy-making within Congress. Finally, I conclude by identifying several new and challenging issues that the committees will face in the 1990s and suggesting several modest reforms that may enhance the role of the House Committee on Foreign Affairs and Senate Committee on Foreign Relations in the foreign policy process.

Decision-making Involvement by the Committees

The House Foreign Affairs and Senate Foreign Relations Committees have two important *legislative* responsibilities: the foreign aid and the foreign relations (State Department) authorization bills.[1] These pieces of legislation allow the committees to set important U.S. strategic policy by authorizing how much economic or military aid will be provided to other countries and how much funding will be provided to the executive branch to conduct relations abroad. But these measures can do more than that; they can be important vehicles for the committees to affect U.S. foreign policy across a broad spectrum of issues. In the last twenty years, moreover, the committees have attempted to use both measures to serve just that role. As the foreign aid bill has had more and more difficulty in clearing legislative hurdles and being enacted into law, increasingly the foreign relations authorization bill has assumed this role.

The Issue Context

While the rest of the chapter discusses the procedural and structural problems that have affected the foreign policy committees in debating these two pieces of legislation (and in dealing with their other decision-making responsibilities), the political context in which these committees operate ought to be kept in mind. The committees face a political environment in which more and more issues have important foreign policy dimensions (e.g., global ecology), in which more and more issues are politically divisive (e.g., Contra aid), and in which popular presidents (e.g., Reagan and Bush) often oppose their policy efforts.

In the 1970s, however, Congress was still using the authorization bills to address a number of important and divisive political issues even in the face of presidential opposition: the war in Vietnam, Turkey's invasion of Cyprus, and aid to rebels in Angola. These two measures went beyond the realm of general policy guidance, seeking—at least in the view of the executive—to "micro-

---

1. Both committees share virtually the same legislative jurisdiction. There are two exceptions, however. On the one hand, the House Foreign Affairs Committee has some jurisdiction over trade policy (although Ways and Means has primary responsibility); in the Senate, trade jurisdiction has been given to the Senate Finance Committee. On the other hand, the Senate Foreign Relations Committee has jurisdiction over the international financial institutions; in the House, this jurisdiction has been given to the Banking, Finance, and Urban Affairs Committee.

manage" foreign affairs. Restrictions imposed upon the executive included earmarking roughly two-thirds of all aid to only a handful of countries, limiting the activities of the CIA in particular countries and regions, attempting to set procedures for making international agreements with other states, and enacting extensive reporting requirements on the executive branch on a wide array of foreign policy activities.

In the 1980s the political issues played out in the debates of the foreign aid and foreign relations authorization bills proved perhaps even more divisive and often met with even greater administration opposition. Throughout the Reagan administration, and during the early part of the Bush administration, Republican and Democratic members on each committee were at odds with one another and with the executive over the size and composition of the foreign aid bill. The Reagan administration, for example, generally wanted the bill tilted toward military and Economic Support Fund (ESF) assistance, while the committee membership generally wanted a greater balance between these two items and development assistance.

Within these categories of assistance, differences arose over funding levels for particular countries. Throughout the 1980s, for instance, dispute over the level of assistance to El Salvador was common. The administration, and its Republican allies in Congress, generally wanted more assistance, and especially military assistance, while the Democrats on the foreign policy committees did not. Similar disputes arose again and again over the earmarking of funds (and the amounts) for Israel and Egypt, Greece and Turkey, and other "base rights" countries such as the Philippines. Political disputes also arose over providing assistance to several countries because of some internal, political questions—to Guatemala and Chile over the issue of human rights, and to Pakistan over that country's possible development of nuclear weapons. Finally, the foreign aid bill also has become a vehicle for debating one of the most divisive domestic policy issues, abortion. During the 1980s, for instance, a dispute arose over incorporating a provision to restrict funding to the United Nations Population Program because China, a recipient of such funds, used abortion as a means of population control.

Foreign Aid and State Department Authorizations

The enactment into law of these authorizations has been used as an important barometer of the relative success and influence of these two committees within Congress (tables 1 and 2 summarize the legislative record on the two bills since 1971). While both bills were almost always passed in the 1970s, the passage of the foreign aid bill has become more difficult in the 1980s and early 1990s. In fact, only two were enacted into law in the 1980s (in 1981 and 1985).

The two committees have differed, however, in their success in passing foreign aid measures. While both Foreign Affairs and Foreign Relations had difficulty getting floor action in the early 1980s, the House committee was generally able to get an authorization bill passed in the House every two years in the late 1980s. The Senate committee had greater difficulty in getting floor action on its bills. Between 1985 and 1991, in fact, no reported foreign aid authorization bill was brought to the Senate floor by the leadership (Collier 1990, 7; Nowels 1989, 129). Several explanations have been offered for this: a crowded floor schedule, fear of extended debate and endless amendments to the foreign aid bill, uncertainty over the committee leadership's ability to manage the bill on the floor, and even possible defeat of the bill.

By the summer of 1991, the situation in the Senate had changed, however. The committee reported out a foreign aid authorization bill in June, and it passed the full Senate in late July. In early October, the Senate passed the conference report but, in a stunning reversal of its usual support for the

TABLE 1. The Fate of Foreign Aid Authorizing Legislation, 1971–91

Year	House Action	Senate Action	Law Enacted
1971	Passed	Passed	Yes, one-year bill, passed in early 1972
1972	Passed	Passed	Failed in conference
1973	Passed	Passed	Yes, two-year bill
1974	Passed	Passed	Yes, one-year bill
1975	Passed	Passed	Yes, two-year bill[a]
1976	Passed	Passed	Yes, one-year bill[b]
1977	Passed	Passed	Yes, one-year bill[c]
1978	Passed	Passed	Yes, one-year bill[c]
1979	Passed	Passed	Yes, one-year bill[c]
1980	Passed	Passed	Yes, one-year bill
1981	Passed	Passed	Yes, two-year bill
1982	Did not reach floor	Did not reach floor	No
1983	Did not reach floor	Did not reach floor	No
1984	Passed	Did not reach floor	No, used continuing resolution
1985	Passed	Passed	Yes, two-year bill
1987	Passed	Did not reach floor	No
1989	Passed	Did not reach floor	No
1991	Passed	Passed	No, conference report defeated in House

Sources: Congressional Quarterly Almanac (various years); U.S. Congress, Senate Committee on Foreign Relations, *Legislative Activities Report of the Committee on Foreign Relations* (various years); and U.S. Congress, House Committee on Foreign Affairs, *Survey of Activities* (various years).

[a]Economic aid only.
[b]Military aid only.
[c]Separate bills for economic and military aid.

foreign aid bill, the House rejected it by a margin of 262 to 159. While a provision on funding a United Nations program that allowed abortions had drawn the threat of a presidential veto and precipitated congressional opposition, the domestic climate discouraged support for foreign aid during a time of economic troubles and ultimately doomed a measure that had proceeded farther than any other bill since 1985 (Doherty 1991a; Nowels and Collier 1992, 13).

As table 2 suggests, both Foreign Relations and Foreign Affairs have had more success in enacting their other major piece of legislation, the foreign relations authorization bill. Before 1972 the Department of State and the United States Information Agency (USIA) had operated under a permanent authorization but since then authorizations have been required periodically. The committees have been able to report out a bill every year (or every other year in the case of two-year authorizations) and have generally been successful in getting such a bill passed on the floor. Recently, though, passage of the authorization bill for FY90 and FY91 was delayed into early 1990 over a dispute with Senator Ernest Hollings (D-S.C.) over language in the bill limiting appropriations (Collier 1990, 9–10). As a result, it was not enacted into

TABLE 2.   The Fate of Foreign Relations (State Department)
Authorizing Legislation, 1972–91

Year	House Action	Senate Action	Law Enacted
1972	Passed	Passed	Yes, one-year bill
1973	Passed	Passed	Yes, one-year bill
1974	Passed	Passed	Yes, one-year bill
1975	Passed	Passed	Yes, one-year bill
1976	Passed	Passed	Yes, one-year bill
1977	Passed	Passed	Yes, one-year bill
1978	Passed	Passed	Yes, one-year bill
1979	Passed	Passed	Yes, two-year bill
1981	Not passed	Passed	No
1982	Passed	Passed	Yes, two-year bill
1983	Passed	Passed	Yes, two-year bill
1985	Passed	Passed	Yes, two-year bill
1987	Passed	Passed	Yes, two-year bill
1989	Passed	Not passed initially	Passed two-year bill in Jan. 1990
1991	Passed	Passed	Yes, two-year bill

Sources: *Congressional Quarterly Almanac* (various years); U.S. Congress, Senate Committee on Foreign Relations, *Legislative Activities Report of the Committee on Foreign Relations* (various years); and U.S. Congress, House Committee on Foreign Affairs, *Survey of Activities* (various years).

law until February 1990. Nonetheless, the foreign aid bill—more than the State Department bill—has been the stumbling block for both committees and has affected their reputations within Congress.

An important factor in understanding why these two pieces of legislations have had difficulty in gaining passage is that they also serve as vehicles for congressional initiatives on foreign policy. Several of the items included in the FY92–93 Foreign Relations Authorization Act, which became law in October 1991, illustrate how this legislation is used as a broader foreign policy vehicle.[2] Title III of this law, which consisted of twenty-three sections and was appropriately entitled "Miscellaneous Foreign Policy Provisions," asked for reports on various foreign policy actions from the executive (e.g., human rights conditions, trade restrictions, and weapons proliferation on the part of the People's Republic of China), outlined congressional views on arms sales to the Middle East, imposed limits on lifting arms sales restrictions to terrorist countries, and made several declarations on policy toward Hong Kong, Taiwan, East Timor, and Tibet, among other actions. Title IV instructed the president to develop an arms transfer policy toward the Middle East and the Persian Gulf and to report periodically to Congress on it. Finally, Title V set out guidelines for the control of chemical and biological weapons, including a requirement for sanctions against offending countries. Thus the foreign relations bill goes far beyond authorizing the activities of the State Department and USIA and has become a potpourri of congressional statements and requirements on foreign policy. Indeed, in the estimation of one observer in the Senate, roughly 70 percent of the bill is now "nongermane."

Other Legislative Decision Making by the Committees

If the foreign aid and foreign relations authorization bills are the principal measures for identifying the decision-making activities of the committees, two other measures also provide some indication of the changes in the committees' decision making since the 1970s: their total legislative output, and the enactment of significant legislation passed by a committee or promoted by its members.[3] By these standards, too, the foreign policy committees have changed in the past twenty years but once again the committees differ from one another.

For the Senate committee, fewer significant bills and joint resolutions referred to it have become law in the 1980s than in the 1970s. In the five most recent Congresses (97th through 101st), for example, only between fifteen

---

2. The legislation referred to here is Public Law 102-138 of 28 October 1991.

3. While legislative productivity cannot stand alone as a measure of effectiveness (since some activity may be intended to prevent what is viewed as bad legislation), the failure of the committees to get their measures enacted into law does reflect upon their work.

and twenty-two significant measures became law in each Congress, while from the 93d to the 96th Congress about twenty-five measures per Congress became law. Each committee also passes a number of minor resolutions—recognizing a particular individual, commemorating a particular day, or making a minor policy recommendation. In large measure, though, these resolutions are pro forma and ordinarily pass without controversy. While the changes over the years are not dramatic, they do indicate the shift in legislative direction that the Foreign Relations Committee has taken.

The House committee has done a bit better, enacting into law more bills referred to it than has its Senate counterpart. On average, about twenty-seven bills reviewed by the committee were enacted into law during each Congress since the Ninety-third.[4] Before that, and extending back to the Eighty-fourth Congress, the number of bills enacted into law ranged widely (from thirteen to thirty-five in a particular Congress) but the average is slightly greater in recent Congresses.

The House committee also has produced more significant legislation than the Senate committee of the type that Lindsay and Ripley (in chapter 2) label as "procedural legislation." Unlike the early 1970s, when the Senate Foreign Relations Committee took the lead in developing several procedural reforms and placing conditions on the conduct of foreign policy, neither the committee nor its key members has been particularly visible on significant legislation in the last decade. In the 1970s, for instance, Senator Jacob Javits (R-N.Y.) was pivotal in initiating and passing war powers legislation; Senator Clifford Case (R-N.Y.) enacted notification procedures on commitments abroad; and senators Frank Church (D-Idaho) and John Sherman Cooper (R-Ky.) sought to end funding for military activities in Vietnam. In the 1980s, few such examples stand out. During his tenure as chair, Senator Richard Lugar (R-Ind.) took the lead in anti-apartheid legislation against South Africa and in efforts to remove Ferdinand Marcos from the Philippines, and Senator Claiborne Pell (D-R.I.) explored the possibility of sanctions against Iraq even before it became popular. Beyond those isolated actions, however, the committee and its members have not been very prominent in the foreign policy arena in the 1980s and early 1990s.

The House committee remained relatively involved in this kind of legislation during both decades. In the 1970s, the committee and its members were involved in developing war powers legislation (e.g., Thomas Morgan [D-Pa.] and Clement Zablocki [D-Wis.]); in requiring reports on arms sales, including a legislative veto provision (e.g., Jonathan Bingham [D-N.Y.], and in condi-

---

4. The data for the House draw upon those reported by McCormick (1985) and incorporate updates from committee sources. Data for the earlier Congresses (Eighty-fourth to Eighty-ninth) come from Fenno (1973).

tioning foreign assistance on human rights compliance (e.g., Donald Fraser [D-Minn.]). Unlike the Senate committee, though, the House committee and its members have continued such involvements in the 1980s and early 1990s, usually by means of promoting a policy position opposed by the White House. Congressman Stephen Solarz (D-N.Y.) took the lead in providing covert aid to the Cambodian opposition in the mid-1980s, Michael Barnes (D-Md.) was prominent in Central American policy, and Howard Wolpe (D-Mich.) worked for years to impose sanctions on South Africa over apartheid and also sought to end aid to Kenya over human rights violations (*Congressional Quarterly Almanac 1990*, 790).

Treaties, Nominations, and the Senate Foreign Relations Committee

While Foreign Affairs has been more active than Foreign Relations in several areas, the Senate committee has an area of responsibility from which the House is excluded: presidential nominations and treaties. Foreign Relations considered between 2,000 to 3,100 presidential nominations during each Congress from the 91st through the 101st. Most of these nominations are routine (McCormick and Wittkopf 1992). Roughly 90 percent, for example, involve promotions for foreign service personnel and receive approval without formal hearings. The number of disapprovals or nominations returned to the executive (indicators of controversy) are quite small, ranging from only seven (in the 95th Congress) to thirty-six (in the 96th).

Still, some nominations can stir controversy. Senator Jesse Helms (R-N.C.) gained a reputation during the 1980s for holding up a number of presidential nominations for ideological reasons. In 1989 and 1990, however, some Democratic senators (such as Alan Cranston [D-Calif.] and Paul Sarbanes [D-Md.]) occasionally held hostage some presidential appointments because the nominees allegedly lacked foreign policy experience or appeared to be only large financial contributors to a presidential campaign (see *Congressional Quarterly Almanac 1989; Congressional Quarterly Almanac 1990*). Other nominations spark policy debate. The extended debate over the appointment of Donald Gregg as ambassador to South Korea is a case in point. His appointment was held up for a considerable length of time because of his alleged involvement with the Iran-Contra affair beyond what he publicly acknowledged (*Congressional Quarterly Almanac 1989*).

Committee activity on treaties is less routine, perhaps, than in the nomination process but it actually has diminished over the last twenty years. From the 91st to the 100th Congresses, for instance, the committee acted on only about 45 percent of the treaties submitted for consideration. In the 101st Congress, however, it acted on only about 35 percent. The percentage reported to the floor was typically above these figures when the committee was chaired by J. William Fulbright (D-Ark.) (the 91st through the 93d Congress) and has typically been below that figure for the Congresses since then. While the number of treaties reviewed is not an unquestioned measure of committee activity (after all, greater committee diligence in examining and stopping troublesome treaties by inaction may explain some of these changes in output), the failure of the committee to complete more work on treaties, especially in combination with its other inactivity, does not reflect well on its decision-making capacity.[5]

Oversight Activities and the Foreign Policy Committees

In the area of oversight, the House committee has been more active than the Senate committee. Reforms in the House have made oversight activities in Foreign Affairs routine, with much of the work done by subcommittees. In a real sense, this monitoring of the policy behavior of the executive branch comports well with the "police-patrol" model of systematic proactive oversight (McCubbins and Schwartz 1984). In the Senate Foreign Relations Committee, on the other hand, oversight activities remain haphazard and episodic. The Senate Committee has no regular procedures for oversight. To the extent that monitoring of the executive branch takes place at all, it is largely consistent with the reactive, "fire-alarm" model of oversight. In differing ways, moreover, both approaches provide some mechanisms by which Congress can affect the policy position of the executive. In this sense, oversight assists in making the "anticipated reaction" process operate between the two branches, as Lindsay and Ripley have discussed (chapter 2).

In the House committee, for instance, each of the regional subcommittees has developed a pattern of reviewing its area of responsibility on a regular basis, annually or even quarterly. The Subcommittee on Europe and the Middle East serves as the model for the rest of the subcommittees. On a regular basis, usually every three months or so, the assistant secretary of state for either European affairs or Middle Eastern affairs, is asked to testify before the subcommittee. A review of "developments in the region" is the goal of these hearings, although specific topics will undoubtedly be highlighted. Over the years, the other regional subcommittees have adopted a similar course in their hearings.

The functional subcommittees also have increased the number of hearings, but they demonstrate more of a mixture of the police-patrol and the fire-

---

5. The data on the nominations, treaties, and laws enacted by the Committee on Foreign Relations are derived from information provided in the *Legislative Activities Report of the Committee on Foreign Relations*, issued after every Congress.

alarm approaches to oversight. The Subcommittee on Human Rights and International Organizations, for instance, tends to hold hearings and elicit inquiries on current topics as well as reviewing global human rights. Similarly, the Subcommittee on Arms Control, International Security and Science reviews arms control policy but it also has highlighted current issues (e.g., U.S. policy toward the Persian Gulf).

One important aggregate indicator of the increased activity of these subcommittees is the number of hearings they convene. Since the 1970s the number of hearings held by all the House Foreign Affairs subcommittees has grown dramatically. In the Ninety-first Congress, for example, Foreign Affairs held 267 subcommittee meetings. In the Ninety-fifth Congress, the number of meetings increased to 560 and settled back to 398 during the Ninety-eighth Congress.

In the Senate committee, oversight hearings usually are convened by the full committee in the context of reviewing legislation. Even with this irregular process, though, the number of hearings has increased in recent years. Foreign Relations subcommittees, by contrast, have generally not engaged in oversight. Important exceptions, however, were the ad hoc oversight subcommittees of the early and middle 1970s—the Symington Subcommittee on U.S. Security Agreements and Commitments Abroad, the Church Subcommittee on Multinational Corporations, and a Subcommittee on Foreign Assistance.[6] More recently, the Subcommittee on Terrorism, Narcotics, and International Operations chaired by Senator John Kerry (D-Mass.) achieved some measure of success in investigating international drug trafficking and uncovering the illegal activities of the Bank of Credit and Commerce International (BCCI). Yet such subcommittee oversight is frowned upon by the full committee staff, particularly its chair, and occurred more by happenstance than in the course of regular oversight activities (M. Tolchin 1991).

Perhaps more indicative of the committee's approach to oversight were the fire-alarm inquiries into what former ambassador April Glaspie said, and how she said it, to Iraq's Saddam Hussein in July 1990. Testifying before the committee in March 1991, she claimed that she had informed Hussein that the United States would defend its interests in the Gulf. Yet, when her Department of State cables from Iraq finally were made available in July 1991, it appeared that the committee had been misled. Those cables suggested that Glaspie had not been nearly as staunch in her approach to Hussein as her earlier testimony had suggested. Still, the committee was left to pursue this matter more or less after the events, and without many options at its disposal. In short, when the fire alarm over the Persian Gulf went off the committee

---

6. For some mention and discussion of these committees, see especially Henderson (1979) but also U.S. Congress Senate Committee on Foreign Relations (1986).

reacted but its reaction was relatively slow and remained rather muted. Even if the committee had wanted to pursue a different oversight approach, though, there appear to be few mechanisms in place for regular police patrols.

What, then, accounts for these different levels of decision-making activities by the two committees? Why has the House committee been more successful in passing the foreign aid bill and initiating foreign policy legislation recently? Why has the Senate committee experienced some controversy in fulfilling some of its executive-related (e.g., treaty) functions? Why have there been differences in oversight activities by the two committees? I shall first examine several internal committee factors for possible answers.

Structure and Operation of the Committees

The structure and operation of the House and the Senate and of the committees themselves are appropriate places to begin to explain the differences in the activism of Foreign Affairs and Foreign Relations. In the House, for example, the changes in the rules of operation in that chamber and in the committee, the increased powers of the subcommittees and the subcommittee chairs, and the growth of staff at both the committee and subcommittee levels are important factors in accounting for increased foreign policy involvement. In the Senate, more modest changes in rules and procedures, combined with several other factors, have hindered the ability of Foreign Relations Committee to play a larger role in foreign policy or even to maintain its former role. In 1991, however, some informal committee changes may have set into motion an effort by the committee to recapture some lost ground.

The Structure and Operation of Foreign Affairs

The basic structure of the House Foreign Affairs Committee has remained relatively stable since 1945 when it was first established. The subcommittees have generally consisted of four or five regional bodies—currently designated as Europe and the Middle East, Asia and Pacific Affairs, Western Hemisphere Affairs, and Africa—and four functional subcommittees—most recently International Operations, International Economic Policy and Trade, Human Rights and International Organizations, and Arms Control, International Security and Science. (The only exception to this format was in the Ninety-fourth Congress when all subcommittees were designated as functional in nature.) Before the congressional reforms of the 1970s (Smith and Deering 1990) these subcommittees had few delegated responsibilities, had no independent staff, and were largely used at the discretion of the committee chair. They held few meetings and most important measures were retained by the chair for full committee consideration only (see U.S. Congress House Committee on Foreign Affairs 1971, 5). On occasion, the head of the committee established a special subcommittee on foreign assistance, which he chaired. This device was less a measure intended to empower the subcommittee than it was a mechanism by means of which the chair could dominate the committee.

The reforms of the 1970s altered the procedural arrangements within the House Committee on Foreign Affairs and substantially reduced the formal powers of the committee chair (see U.S. Congress House Committee on Foreign Affairs 1973; U.S. Congress House Committee on Foreign Affairs 1991). Subcommittees were now specified as having particular jurisdictional responsibilities within the committee and also were authorized to review foreign assistance and other legislative programs within their jurisdiction. With such clear specificity of jurisdiction, the role of subcommittees clearly had been enhanced. The chair of the committee now must refer all legislation to the appropriate subcommittee within two weeks. The subcommittee chair, in turn, is allowed the discretion to set hearing dates for these legislative questions. While the subcommittee meeting dates should be set in consultation with the committee chair and other subcommittee chairs, the subcommittee chair obviously has gained considerable leverage in setting the agenda of his or her group.

In practice the subcommittee chair actually has even wider discretion, especially under the leadership style of recent committee chair Dante Fascell (D-Fla.). The subcommittee chair may take up issues within the subcommittee's jurisdiction, according to his or her own discretion and timetable. Although the usual procedure has been to check with the committee chair and committee staff before initiating such an independent course, the wishes of the subcommittee chair have generally been honored. The process also can work in the other direction. The chair of the committee may suggest an area of subcommittee inquiry. While the subcommittee chair theoretically could refuse such a request, once again the congressional norm has been to follow the lead of the committee chair.

Another procedural change has enhanced the power of the subcommittee chairs. Under the current rules, the subcommittee chairs meet periodically (at least once a month under the rules for the 102d Congress) to coordinate activities and discuss current legislation. Although these meetings include the committee chair and carry an invitation to majority party members, they again reflect the enhanced role of subcommittee chairs in the foreign policy process in the House and indicate yet another avenue of influence in shaping policy.

A final important structural and procedural change has been the ability of subcommittee chairs to appoint their own staff. Such independent assistance has given the subcommittees an important research power base within the committee. Perhaps no better indicator of the growth in the power of such staff is the occasional grumbling heard at the level of the full committee staff over the difficulty of dealing with the staff of the subcommittees. While such complaints are relatively rare and should not be exaggerated (most subcommittee and full committee staff describe their relationship as close and cordial), the fact that any tension exists is an important barometer of the enhanced independence of the subcommittees and their staffs. Finally, the size of these subcommittee staffs has continued to grow since the initial reforms in the 1970s. In 1971, the year before subcommittee staff was introduced, the professional staff of Foreign Affairs numbered eleven. By 1991, the total staff size was eighty-five, with forty-five professionals assigned to the full committee and forty assigned to the subcommittees.

The Structure and Operation of Foreign Relations

During most of the period since World War II, the Senate Foreign Relations Committee had a hierarchical and centralized structure and operation.[7] The full committee was the place where virtually all decision making was done. The committee chair and the ranking minority member acted as the major shapers of policy. The subcommittees had no legislative power, and the subcommittee chairs (and other members) were at best entrepreneurs in undertaking any foreign policy initiatives. With a few exceptions, such individual initiatives were largely ineffective.

The subcommittees of the Senate Foreign Relations Committee were originally set up as consultative committees to work with the Department of State. These subcommittees could not hold public hearings or consider any legislation without the permission of the full committee and the committee chair. Notable exceptions occurred, of course. In the 1960s and early 1970s, the Symington Subcommittee on Commitments Abroad and the Church Subcommittee on Multinational Corporations launched important inquiries. In 1975, a Subcommittee on Foreign Assistance was established and given legislative jurisdiction over foreign aid for a time. More recently, Senator Kerry's subcommittee investigation of BCCI proved to be important. In general, though, subcommittees rarely have been given much responsibility and seldom accomplish much.

Until very recently, the staff of the Senate Foreign Relations Committee was small, bipartisan, and answered only to the full committee. Subcommittee needs were met by assigning full committee staff to them as part of their regular duties. In 1971, for example, the total professional staff for the Senate Foreign Relations Committee numbered thirteen. Beginning in 1979, the staff

---

7. A summary of the Committee's procedure over time and most recently can be found in ibid. (1986, 1991b). The committee rules outlined in the latter reference do not include the subsequent *informal* changes outlined below.

was categorized as majority or minority, and the number then totaled about twenty-five. By 1991, it had been enlarged further, reaching thirty-seven full-time, professional staff and roughly thirty support staff for the committee.

In January 1991, however, two important informal changes took place in the distribution of power and in the operation of the full committee and the subcommittees of the Senate Foreign Relations Committee. The first change was that the subcommittees, in particular the two functional subcommittees, were given legislative responsibility. The Subcommittee on International Economic Policy, Trade, Oceans, and Environment was given legislative responsibility to develop the foreign assistance authorization bill for the committee. The Subcommittee on Terrorism, Narcotics, and International Operations was given legislative responsibility for the foreign relations authorization bill. Each subcommittee chair was authorized further to develop a "subcommittee chair's mark" on the delegated piece of legislation and to bring the finished product to the full committee for approval. The other five subcommittees were slated to take future pieces of legislation, albeit on a case-by-case basis. Informally, for example, agreement was reached to provide the Subcommittee on European Affairs with responsibility for handling the U.S.-Soviet maritime boundary dispute over Alaska and Siberia and Conventional Forces in Europe (CFE) Treaty. Still, some measures (e.g., the START treaties and the 1992 Russian aid bill) were reserved by the chairman for full committee consideration, emphasizing the ad hoc nature of this devolution of responsibility.

The second major change in committee arrangements was the decision to provide separate staff to the subcommittees. This was accomplished in two ways: the subcommittees now are provided funds for hiring new staff, and five of the seven subcommittees are permanently assigned a member of the full committee staff. Both the majority and the minority on the subcommittees were offered the opportunity to hire staff, but the minority, led by Senator Helms, declined to do so.

In January 1992, however, Helms did undertake a major overhaul of the minority staff that appears to have important consequences for committee operations. He fired nine aides, including his long-time staff director, and he appointed a new one committed to a more orderly, less confrontational process (C. Madison 1992b, 752). So far the new staff and its approach have won praise from both the majority (which characterized them as a "big improvement") and the minority (which characterized their approach as "pragmatic").

There were several reasons for the changes in the organization of Foreign Relations. The first was to ensure that the committee would complete its work on the foreign aid and foreign relations authorization bills. The second was to build a consensus among subcommittee members in order to facilitate action at the full committee level. In the past, full committee action often had been stymied by one or two members. A third reason simply was to challenge a weak chair and give greater responsibility to more active and effective members. Because the committee chair had been viewed as ineffective, members hoped that the new arrangement would help Foreign Relations complete its legislative agenda and thereby regain some of its previous stature.[8]

Membership on the Foreign Policy Committees

A second major factor that explains the changed activism of the Foreign Affairs and Foreign Relations Committees is the changing composition of committee membership. Both committees have had difficulty attracting and retaining new members (although a core group has remained on Foreign Affairs over time), and both have witnessed a shift toward greater partisan and ideological membership. When these compositional changes are combined with the alteration in the structure and operation of the committees, they help us to understand why Foreign Relations has struggled to maintain its prominence, while Foreign Affairs has fared better.

The Changing Composition of Foreign Relations

Attracting and keeping members has been a perennial problem for Foreign Affairs but it is a newer problem for Foreign Relations. The Senate committee's reputation as the most prestigious in the Congress presumably would ensure it an active and stable membership. In reality, though, the committee has begun to experience substantial turnover. From the Ninety-second Congress (1971–72) to the present, for instance, roughly 25 percent of the committee membership changed from one Congress to the next. In other words, an average of four new members joined the committee every two years over the last two decades. In the 1950s and the 1960s only about two or three new members joined the committee during each Congress.

Several reasons exist for such turnover. Some senators have left for other, more important, committee assignments. Others have lost reelection or retired—hurt in some instances by their service on Foreign Relations. Senator Church, for example, suffered electorally in 1980 because of his foreign policy stances on such issues as arms control and the Panama Canal treaties. Senator Charles Percy (R-Ill.) incurred strong opposition from the Israeli lobby over his "even-handed" approach to the Middle East. The two electoral changes in the control of the Senate—one in 1980, the other in 1986—also resulted in committee turnover. Even discounting this electoral change,

---

8. For an initial assessment of the impact of these changes on the committee after one year, see C. Madison (1992b).

though, the rapid turnover in committee membership has contributed to the problems of the Senate Foreign Relations Committee.

Most troubling has been the number of voluntary departures to other committees. Such departures rarely occurred in earlier decades. In the 1970s and 1980s, however, the departures quickened.[9] Changes in Senate rules in 1977 that limited service to two committees may partially explain some of these departures. Yet the fact that members relinquished their assignment on Foreign Relations is a significant measure of the committee's standing in the chamber as a whole.

The turnover in membership means that Foreign Relations now tends to be composed of members with more limited service and less political influence within the institution. This contrasts sharply with its make-up two decades ago. In the late 1960s and early 1970s, the committee consisted of the most senior members of the Senate. In the Ninety-first Congress, for example, the committee membership had such long-serving Senate members as Fulbright, Sparkman, Mansfield, Gore, Church, and Symington on the majority side and Aiken, Mundt, and Case on the minority side. By the Ninety-seventh Congress, by contrast, only Pell had served for more than a decade and less than half of the committee members has served that long in the Senate. In the space of ten years, then, the membership had almost completely turned over.

The political and ideological complexion of the members serving on Foreign Relations has also changed. While senators from eastern and midwestern states continue to dominate committee membership, they are more deeply divided than in earlier decades. Ideologically, for instance, the divisions have increased dramatically within the committee. In the Ninety-first Congress, for example, the average score assigned to committee members by the Americans for Democratic Action (ADA) was fifty-three for Democrats, while it was forty-eight for Republicans. By the Ninety-fourth Congress, just after Watergate and the resignation of President Nixon, the ideological gulf increased sharply within the committee. The ADA scores among Republicans then averaged about forty-five, while they averaged seventy among Democrats. By the 100th Congress, and the beginning of Claiborne Pell's committee chairmanship, the ideological chasm was wide indeed. The average ADA score among Republicans was now seventeen, while it was eighty-one among Democrats.

---

9. In the 1970s, Russell Long (D-La.) left to assume the chairmanship of the Finance Committee, Eugene McCarthy (D-Minn.) left the committee shortly before leaving the Senate, and Muriel Humphrey (D-Minn.) served out her late husband's session on Foreign Relations but then went to Armed Services. In the 1980s, the departures were John Glenn (D-Ohio) and Connie Mack (R-Fla.), who joined Armed Services, and Brock Adams (D-Wash.), who went to Appropriations. In June 1991, Orrin Hatch (R-Utah) left the committee after serving only briefly to take a seat on Finance.

TABLE 3.   Average ADA Scores for Members of the House Foreign Affairs and Senate Foreign Relations Committees, by Party and Congress, 1969-90

Congress	House Foreign Affairs		Senate Foreign Relations	
	Democrat	Republican	Democrat	Republican
91 (1969–70)	66 (48)[a]	23 (20)	53 (53)	48 (29)
92 (1971–72)	59 (50)	26 (18)	59 (56)	44 (23)
93 (1973–74)	62 (55)	33 (20)	66 (62)	52 (29)
94 (1975–76)	67 (59)	31 (18)	70 (58)	45 (29)
95 (1977–78)	63 (50)	23 (19)	66 (56)	46 (26)
96 (1979–80)	66 (57)	27 (18)	54 (54)	27 (26)
97 (1981–82)	68 (60)	31 (18)	80 (67)	24 (21)
98 (1983–84)	79 (70)	21 (15)	77 (71)	28 (23)
99 (1985–86)	80 (68)	18 (15)	80 (69)	21 (18)
100 (1987–88)	84 (76)	25 (19)	81 (74)	17 (23)
101 (1989–90)	84 (72)	23 (18)	81 (71)	36 (18)

[a]The average ADA scores for all members of the House or the Senate belonging to each party are given in parentheses.

As table 3 also shows, the increasing ideological divisions within the committee generally parallel the increasing divisions within the Senate, albeit with a notable difference. Before the Ninety-sixth Congress, the ideological differences between members tended to be narrower than in the Senate as a whole. Since then, however, that gap has widened for committee members even more than for the Senate as a whole. On an ideological level, then, the possibility of accommodation has become more and more of a challenge.

Politically the picture is much the same. Scores rating the support members of the committee give the president on foreign policy votes show generally the same pattern as do the ADA scores—increasing divisions between Democrats and Republicans over the last two decades (see table 4).[10] In the Ninety-first Congress, for instance, the gap between committee Republicans and committee Democrats in their support of President Nixon's foreign policy was relatively narrow. Committee Republicans supported him 72 percent of the time, while committee Democrats supported him 66 percent of the time. The gap between committee partisans began to widen in the succeeding Congresses, reaching a gap of 27 percent in the Ninety-seventh Congress (70

10. The foreign policy support scores were computed by identifying all foreign policy votes on which the president took a position in a particular Congress and calculating the degree of agreement between the executive branch and the member of Congress. These scores range from 0 to 100; with the higher the score, the greater the agreement between the president and the member of Congress. A detailed description of the methodology used to create this measure can be found in McCormick and Wittkopf (1990).

percent support for President Reagan by committee Republicans, 43 percent by committee Democrats). By the Ninety-ninth Congress, the gap had almost doubled, to 50 percentage points, although it fell back slightly to 42 percent in the One-hundredth Congress.

As table 4 also shows, these growing gaps among committee members also reflect the widening divisions on foreign affairs support within the Senate as a whole. Like the increasing ideological gulf reported in table 3, committee members are more deeply divided on foreign policy than is the Senate as a whole. Similarly, the more recent Congresses, during the last years of the Reagan administration, particularly reflect this trend.

The implication of these compositional changes is that the Senate Foreign Relations Committee currently is more sharply divided than in the early 1970s. Such increased politicization within the committee reduces the prospect for compromise, and hence for effective decision making. Indeed, the decline in the legislative record of the committee bears this out.

TABLE 4. Average Presidential Foreign Policy Support Scores of Members of the House Foreign Affairs and Senate Foreign Relations Committees, by Party and Congress, 1969–88

President/Congress	House Foreign Affairs		Senate Foreign Relations	
	Democrat	Republican	Democrat	Republican
Nixon				
91 (1969–70)	73[a] (63)[b]	68 (61)	66 (64)	72 (78)
92 (1971–72)	50 (50)	77 (73)	43 (46)	59 (73)
Nixon/Ford				
93 (1973–74) Nixon	37 (38)	57 (60)	49 (53)	71 (74)
Ford	37 (33)	53 (44)	42 (43)	78 (64)
Ford				
94 (1975–76)	50 (47)	68 (66)	55 (62)	77 (79)
Carter				
95 (1977–78)	64 (58)	41 (36)	82 (71)	71 (45)
96 (1979–80)	74 (66)	50 (34)	74 (70)	60 (53)
Reagan				
97 (1981–82)	44 (46)	66 (71)	43 (44)	70 (72)
98 (1983–84)	37 (40)	77 (78)	42 (46)	76 (77)
99 (1985–86)	17 (26)	75 (76)	30 (39)	84 (82)
100 (1987–88)	25 (33)	74 (79)	41 (50)	84 (77)

[a]The presidential foreign policy support scores were calculated by identifying all foreign policy votes on which the president took a position in a particular Congress and calculating the degree of agreement between the executive branch and the member of Congress. These scores range from 0 to 100; the higher the score, the greater the agreement between the president and the member of Congress. A detailed description of the methodology used to create these scores can be found in McCormick and Wittkopf (1990).

[b]The presidential foreign policy support scores for members in each party in the entire House and Senate are given in parentheses.

The Changing Composition of Foreign Affairs

The composition of the House Foreign Affairs Committee shares many of the same changing characteristics as Foreign Relations. First, it has experienced considerable membership turnover, and that turnover has increased lately. Since the Ninety-first Congress, the turnover on the committee from one Congress to the next has averaged between 13 and 38 percent. On average, eight new members joined the committee from the Ninety-first through the Ninety-fourth Congresses. Since the Ninety-fifth Congress, however, ten new members joined the committee with each new Congress. The exception was the 102d Congress, during which only six new members joined, but at least four members from the previous Congress stayed on as temporaries. Indeed, the committee has had trouble filling vacancies and has had to rely increasingly upon temporary and freshman appointments.[11]

Part of the reason for high committee turnover relates to the limited attractiveness of serving on Foreign Affairs. Unlike Foreign Relations, which usually ranks at or near the top in attractiveness, Foreign Affairs usually ranks in the middle or slightly below the middle (see Smith and Deering 1984, 280–81).[12] The reason that Foreign Affairs is only modestly attractive is because foreign policy issues are unlikely to further a member's reelection efforts and may hurt them. Only in limited cases can Foreign Affairs service help a member at home.[13] For members from heavily urban and ethnic districts serving on the committee may be viewed as advancing constituency interests, as in the cases of Stephen Solarz, Edward Feighan (D-Ohio), Howard Berman (D-Calif.), and Mel Levine (D-Calif.). Some members even may be able to translate their Foreign Affairs assignment into constituency service. When Don Bonker (D-Wash.) served as chair of the Subcommittee on International Economic Policy and Trade, for example, he argued that this assignment

---

11. Before the Ninety-second Congress, and going back to the Eighty-fifth, appointments of new and continuing members to the House Foreign Affairs Committee were about equally divided for the majority and rarely occurred for the minority. Since then, new members of Congress have been appointed at a rate of about 2 to 1 over continuing members to fill openings on the committee. For the minority, it continues to be the case that continuing members are more likely to receive such an appointment.

12. The limited attractiveness of Foreign Affairs is even more evident for new members of Congress. See Smith and Deering (1990, 87) for a listing of committee preferences by new members to the 101st Congress. None mentioned Foreign Affairs as a preferred committee. For the 102d Congress, see R. Cohen (1991).

13. Service on Foreign Affairs also may affect the raising of campaign funds or political action committee (PAC) monies since domestic interests seemingly are not directly served by this committee. This explanation for avoiding Foreign Affairs, however, should not be pushed too far since funds from ethnic interest groups or military lobbying groups might well still be available to committee members.

benefited his Washington district with its heavy lumbering interests and its need for international trade. Douglas Bereuter (R-Nebr.) could make a similar argument that his service on this subcommittee served as a mechanism to enhance agricultural trade. Most members serve on Foreign Affairs, however, because of their personal policy interests, even though such service may not be to their immediate political advantage.

The number of transfers from Foreign Affairs to other committees also attests to its decline in attractiveness. From the Eighty-fourth through the Ninety-second Congresses, for instance, only five continuing members transferred from the committee, while from the Ninety-third to the 102d Congress, twenty-two members gave up their Foreign Affairs assignment. Thirteen members gave up their seats on Foreign Affairs for the most prestigious and powerful committees in the House—Appropriations, Rules, and Ways and Means.[14] Nine members, however, left Foreign Affairs for committee assignments that might be viewed as only comparable in stature to Foreign Affairs (e.g., Armed Services and Energy and Commerce). Such assignments may have appeared more compatible with the serving of constituent needs. Yet, transfer totals do not wholly portray the membership problems on Foreign Affairs since some long-serving members have now decided to leave or have assumed other roles on the committee. At the start of the 102d Congress, for example, Gerry Studds (D-Mass.) and Peter Kostmayer (D-Pa.) left Foreign Affairs to take seats on other committees, although they agreed to continue as temporary members. And Howard Wolpe—after facing a series of close elections—gave up his chairmanship of the Africa Subcommittee to accept a similar position on a Science, Space, and Technology subcommittee (R. Cohen 1991).

Despite these membership changes, the basic regional composition of the panel has not changed appreciably over the past four decades. Its membership, like that of the Senate Foreign Relations Committee, is drawn from the East and the Midwest. Since the Ninety-first Congress, about 70 percent of the membership has come from these two regions, and those percentages have remained relatively stable over the years. Such percentages are 10 to 15 percent higher than what might be expected based upon the regional composition of the Congress. The percentage of legislators from the other regions has changed very little over the years. The only exception is the West, which has begun to pick up some additional representation, to the point at which its committee participation actually surpasses its representational size in the most

---

14. Four left before the Ninety-third Congress (Battin and Burleson to Ways and Means; Roybal to Appropriations; and Murphy to Rules), but nine have left since (Vander Jagt and Pease to Ways and Means; Wilson, Gray, Atkins, and Smith to Appropriations; and Beilenson, Hall, and Solomon to Rules).

recent Congresses. The South, by contrast, continues to be underrepresented.[15]

The greatest change in the composition of the House Foreign Affairs Committee has been in the political characteristics of the members serving on that panel. Paralleling what has occurred on Foreign Relations, the membership on Foreign Affairs has become increasingly divided ideologically (see table 3). Although Foreign Affairs has always been more divided than Foreign Relations, ideological divisions widened in the 1980s (see also Noble 1990). By the time of the 100th Congress, for instance, some of the most liberal members (Studds, Wolpe, Gejdenson, Ackerman, Feighan, and Levine) and some of the most conservative (Dornan, Burton, Mack, Solomon, Hyde, and Dewine) were serving on Foreign Affairs. Like Foreign Relations, the increasing ideological differences between committee members on Foreign Affairs parallel what has occurred in the House as a whole. That comparison has remained relatively stable over time, with committee members generally more divided ideologically than the entire House.

These ideological divisions, as one would expect, have been translated into policy divisions that become apparent in members' voting records on foreign policy issues (see table 4). The ideological gulf between the two parties has made it increasingly difficult to effect policy compromise, and the average gap in foreign policy support scores for the president has appreciably widened as well. In the Ninety-first Congress, committee Democrats actually had a higher average of foreign policy support for President Nixon than did Republicans. While these support scores reverted to more familiar partisan patterns for the rest of the Nixon administration and during succeeding presidencies, the gap between the parties widened dramatically. The gaps for the Reagan presidency (and especially during the Ninety-eighth Congress and later) were especially pronounced. Finally, when the support-score gaps for committee members are compared to the scores for the House as a whole, the partisan gaps between committee members often were wider than those between all members of the House on foreign policy voting—a pattern paralleling what is occurring in the Senate (see table 4).

In light of these sharp political differences, it is surprising that the committee has been able to accomplish as much as it has. Unlike the Senate Foreign Relations Committee, though, the House committee has developed an effective subcommittee system for channeling some of these political divi-

15. Representational size is based upon my calculation of the proportional total membership from each of four regions (East, Midwest, South, and West) and then by comparing those percentages with the regional percentages of membership on the Foreign Affairs Committee. The database for the House and the Senate is drawn from that reported in McCormick and Wittkopf (1990).

sions. As a result, not all political battles have had to be waged in the full committee. Unlike its Senate counterpart, too, the House committee has maintained a core set of moderate to liberal members who more often have been willing to compromise in an effort to make certain that the committee's main legislative responsibilities are fulfilled. Further, and again unlike its Senate counterpart, the quality of committee and subcommittee leadership— even minority leadership—has assisted the House Foreign Affairs Committee in completing its work. A closer look at the leadership dimension will demonstrate this point.

Leadership of the Committees

By virtually all analyses, the quality of the leadership of the Senate Foreign Relations Committee has suffered since the early 1970s while the quality of the leadership on the House Foreign Affairs Committees has been enhanced. The leadership question, of course, focuses largely on the committee chairs in each chamber but it also focuses on the relationship between the committee chair and the ranking minority members. Because of the decentralized structure of the House committee, the role of subcommittee leadership also must be included in the discussion.

Committee Chairs of Foreign Affairs

Since 1959, Foreign Affairs has had four chairs, each of whom adopted a different approach to leading the committee. The first two chairs found it difficult to operate the committee effectively and yielded more power to the subcommittees than perhaps even the reformers of the 1970s intended. In this sense, the role of the subcommittees was especially pronounced during their tenure. For the recently retired chair, Dante Fascell, that conclusion is less accurate. While Fascell certainly did not repudiate any of the reforms of the 1970s, he was able to exercise more centralized authority than did the first two chairs. The differences among Fascell and his predecessors in their degree of committee control largely turned on their personalities, styles of legislative leadership, and ability to adjust to, and use, the changing subcommittee arrangements. The approach of the new chair, Lee Hamilton (D-Ind.), is not yet fully evident, but I can suggest some elements of it.

Thomas (Doc) Morgan chaired the committee from 1959 to 1977. His tenure encompassed a period both before and after reform in the House. Before reform, the committee seemingly was run from the top down, while after reform it was more open and diffuse. The adjustment to this more open system proved less difficult for Morgan than might be imagined for at least two reasons: his leadership style and his involvement on foreign policy issues.

His style mainly was to delegate authority, and thus the dispersion of power that the reforms encouraged was compatible with his modus operandi. Morgan's involvement on foreign policy issues was equally detached, which encouraged others to take the lead. In fact, Morgan saw his role mainly as one of shepherding the president's foreign policy agenda through the committee, regardless of which party was in the White House, and not to promote a separate legislative position. If challenges to the executive were to come, they would come from others. As the agonies of Watergate and Vietnam mounted, however, even Morgan became disenchanted with the limited congressional role in the policy process and increasingly he was willing to allow subcommittee activities that challenged the executive. In most of these instances, however, he was reluctant to lead the charge.[16]

Clement Zablocki served as committee chair from January 1977 until his death in December 1983. Like Morgan, he encountered great difficulty in running the committee effectively. While he did not necessarily support the decentralization of authority that had taken place in Congress, he had very little choice but to adjust to it. In fact, he may have gone too far in that regard. He delegated much of his authority to his staff and allowed the subcommittees a great deal of flexibility. In the opinion of one close observer, he was "far too free and open" in the way he ran the committee, and he allowed the subcommittee chairs "a way to flex their muscles more than others would have. . . . " In effect, he "tolerated" the committee and its procedures, rather than trying to manage them (Felton 1983, 2622–23). Unlike Morgan, Zablocki had been deeply involved in some areas of committee activism before his chairmanship—his work on executive agreements and war-powers legislation is well documented—but he proved to be much less policy driven during his chairmanship. Although he attempted to lead the committee on some issues (e.g., the Taiwan Relations Act and arms control measures), he was susceptible to cajoling from the subcommittees and their chairs, and supported measures to which he was not wholly committed (Felton 1983, 2622; Smith and Deering 1984, 135). His support for the nuclear freeze resolution and for attempts to end aid to the Nicaraguan Contras are notable examples. The failure to get those measures passed may be attributed in part to the degree of his own resolve on these issues.[17] Perhaps his greatest leadership challenge, however, occurred in the realm of foreign aid legislation. While he was successful in getting a foreign aid bill passed in 1981, the committee failed even to get the 1982 and 1983 bills discussed on the floor of the House.

---

16. Congressman Morgan did show a bit of activism through his sponsorship of the Executive Agreements Review Act of 1975, a measure to allow the use of the congressional veto for international agreements made by the executive involving a "national commitment" by the United States. The measure, however, was not enacted into law.

17. This analysis is based upon anonymous interviews with committee staffers.

Although Morgan and Zablocki generally provided weak legislative leadership and were greatly affected by the congressional reforms of the 1970s, the next chair, Dante Fascell, proved to be different (McCormick 1985, 17–18; P. Cohen 1985; see also Noble 1991). No longer was the committee chair largely a captive of the subcommittee chairs; now the committee and subcommittee chairs began to play a more equal role (for an alternate view, see C. Madison 1991b). In effect, while subcommittee leadership remained important, committee leadership was restored.

The key factor in the resurgence of the committee chair was the development of an effective leadership style by Fascell. He was willing to allow considerable subcommittee autonomy because he believed that the process within the committee ought to be democratic and that the subcommittees ought to make legislative recommendations. Yet Fascell also wanted the subcommittees and their chairs to work with him in accomplishing these legislative goals. To make this relationship work, he relied upon his considerable legislative and political skills. He was a "legislative tactician" and a consummate "results-oriented" politician, in the words of those who worked with him. Unlike his predecessors, he enjoyed the confidence of the majority of his own party and was closer to them ideologically than were the more conservative Morgan and Zablocki. He also had the respect of the Republican minority on the committee and maintained a good working relationship with its leaders. In short, Dante Fascell positioned himself in such a way that he was able to "manage" the committee more effectively than had his two predecessors.

Three specific traits assisted Fascell in operating the committee. First, he ran "a tighter ship" than Morgan and Zablocki had, and he took a more decided interest in the issues facing the committee. That is, he was more conscious of the need for organizational coordination between the committee and its subcommittees and took an abiding interest in the issues active within the subcommittees. On the organizational side, for instance, he tended to leave fewer of these tasks to his staff. Fascell also made more frequent contacts with subcommittee chairs and with minority members through an informal network that he developed. In this way, he had a better sense of subcommittee activities and the problems he was likely to face at the full committee level, and he worked to head off problems by raising questions with the subcommittee chairs. Second, he was both knowledgeable about and interested in issues. One observer could not recall an issue that failed to interest Fascell. While that comment is undoubtedly hyperbole, it conveys the general interest that he showed in all phases of committee operations. Furthermore, Fascell was acknowledged to be extremely bright ("bright as the sun," as one admirer put it) and a quick study on issues of the committee. He knew the key issues and the arguments associated with them, or he quickly learned them. In addition, he possessed an important political quality, the knowledge of what was "doable" in the committee and the House. In this connection, he was probably more committed to accomplishing something than to winning an ideological argument. Finally, Fascell (and the committee) benefited from the assistance of a number of excellent subcommittee chairs (C. Madison 1987a, 1271), among them Lee Hamilton, Stephen Solarz, Michael Barnes, and Howard Wolpe. The full committee depended on the subcommittees to complete its own legislative work since most policy initiatives started within the subcommittees. By one estimate, 90 percent of the subcommittees' recommendations were approved by the full committee.[18]

Effective decentralization seemingly worked for Fascell and the committee as a whole, yet it also caused tension (see C. Madison 1991b). In his effort to allow the subcommittees autonomy, Fascell permitted the process to go on at considerable length. His reluctance to rein in subcommittees or their chairs led to the view that the committee had become too differentiated and less effective than it might be. While this criticism seems overdrawn, the issue of subcommittee autonomy was a continuing source of disagreement within the committee.

On balance, though, there is no better indicator of Fascell's effectiveness as a leader of the committee than his initial efforts at passing the 1984 and 1985 foreign aid bills. In 1984 he was able to get a measure through the committee and through the House. In 1985 he was even more successful. With that 1985 bill he was able to mark up the measure quickly and without major controversy, to win approval on the House floor, and to complete the conference on the bill with the Senate in essentially one day of meetings. Similar successes were registered in 1987, 1989, and 1991. In each of those years, he was able to guide a two-year, foreign aid authorization bill through the House, though in 1987 and 1989 he was stymied by inaction on the part of the Senate and in 1991 by the response of the whole House to the conference report.[19] In no small degree, this legislation was the hallmark of his tenure as chair and, by all accounts, reflected his effort to restore committee leadership to Foreign Affairs.

Fascell's successor, Lee Hamilton, will probably continue the approach of combining elements of centralization and decentralization in the operation of Foreign Affairs, with a greater emphasis on the former than on the latter. Hamilton will seek to use some talented subcommittee chairs to develop legislative initiatives but, in contrast to Fascell, he will exercise stronger central guidance to bring that legislation to the full House. He likely will employ this approach for several reasons. First, it fits his style of leadership.

---

18. Interview with committee staffer.

19. The foreign aid authorization conference report was defeated in the House in October 1991 (see Doherty 1991a).

While extraordinarily respectful of his colleagues' views, he is also determined to achieve results. He can, and will, be forceful if necessary. Second, he has the benefit of working with a new ranking minority member with whom he has had a long association. Hamilton and Benjamin Gilman (R-N.Y.) served for four Congresses as the chair and ranking minority member of the Subcommittee on Europe and the Middle East before moving to their present positions. In addition, they jointly led a House task force on reforming foreign assistance in 1988. Finally, Hamilton will be aided by a stronger and more assertive Foreign Affairs Committee staff. After recent changes in its composition, the staff will have a new look and a new vigor.

Also, Hamilton likely will have a broader issue agenda than Fascell or his predecessors. Two reasons suggest this prospect. First, on a personal level, Hamilton's interests are diverse. While he has focused on European and Middle East issues with his subcommittee assignment, he has also been involved in a wide-ranging set of issues throughout his twenty-eight-year career. Second, before his chairmanship Hamilton had already begun to think and write about the issues facing the United States in the post–cold war era. The issue agenda that he has recently identified (L. Hamilton 1992) includes such traditional concerns as conventional and nuclear proliferation, foreign aid, and regional instability but it also incorporates the more recently recognized (if not new) issues of the global economy and environment. By expanding the committee's agenda and achieving some initial results, Hamilton will be in a position to make Foreign Affairs a more central participant within the House and in the Congress as a whole.[20]

Committee Chairs of Foreign Relations

Since the chairmanship of Senator Fulbright, the quality of leadership on Senate Foreign Relations Committee has waned. This lack of effective leadership has been identified as the central reason for the decline in the effectiveness of the committee. Part of the leadership problem has been the frequent turnover in committee chairs over the last two decades. Five chairs have served in about the same length of time that Fulbright did. Party control of the committee also switched twice during the same amount of time. A second and more central reason for the decline in the quality of leadership is that most of these individuals were not forceful leaders.

In the 1970s, two Democratic chairs of Foreign Relations had differing approaches but neither succeeded in continuing the preeminence experienced under Fulbright. John Sparkman (D-Ala.), Fulbright's immediate successor,

---

20. For a more cautious assessment of Hamilton's likely impact on the committee, see C. Madison (1992c, 1469).

who served as chair from 1975 to 1978, faced a committee membership that was beginning to divide ideologically. Sparkman, a conservative himself, was not inclined to challenge presidential leadership, and in one estimate was often "asleep at the wheel." His successor, Frank Church, who chaired Foreign Relations from 1978 to 1980, had the potential to become an effective leader but his tenure proved to be too short. During his time in office, though, he reinvigorated the staff (ultimately dividing it into a minority and a majority) and undertook a relatively large policy agenda, ranging from further inquiries into intelligence matters to changes in the Soviet Union (Henderson 1979). Ultimately, though, his efforts were overshadowed by his domestic political concerns. Increasingly he turned his attention to his reelection efforts, a task at which he failed in 1980.

The 1980 election resulted in Republican control of the Senate and ushered in two Republican chairs of Foreign Relations, Charles Percy, from 1981 to 1985, and Richard Lugar from 1985 to 1987. Percy came to office determined to return the committee to its former stature (Whittle 1981) but he was largely unsuccessful. He sought to initiate an overall review of American policy but he was confronted by an administration, albeit of his own party, that was determined to adopt a hard-line approach to foreign policy in general and to the Soviet Union in particular. Further, his style of leadership became a problem within the committee. His penchant for compromise and his "middle-of-the-road" approach did not work well in an increasingly divided committee, and he satisfied "neither the conservatives of his own party nor the more forceful members of the opposition" (McPherson 1981, 19). In the words of one staffer, he was "too accommodating" on policy and the "process went on and on." No policy closure occurred, only one foreign aid bill was passed in Congress during his tenure, and the ineffectiveness of Foreign Relations continued. His successor, Richard Lugar, indicated his basic support for the Reagan administration's policy (Gwertzman 1984, 20) but he still initiated a review of policy around the world and sought a more activist role for the committee. Indeed, Lugar was credited with leading the committee effectively "by charting a course and sticking with it, working behind the scenes to build consensus through compromise and patient prodding" (Dewar 1989). More than that, he was viewed as successful in bringing the moderates in the committee together and isolating the extremes of left and right. His efforts, however, much as those of Church, fell victim to electoral politics when the Democrats regained control of the Senate in 1986.

Claiborne Pell, who moved up to the chairmanship in 1987, has not been able to arrest the decline in the fortunes of Foreign Relations. Indeed, he may have accelerated it. Although a respected member of the Senate, he has not proved to be an effective chair and the stature of the committee may have reached a new low during his tenure. His difficulties center on his personal style and his inability to lead the committee on important policy questions. (see, for example, Blumenthal 1991).

Pell does not enjoy the leadership position and he has not been able to use it effectively. He is probably more of a "pack man" than a "point man," in one characterization. While he is eminently fair and very accommodating to all members (and perhaps too much so), Pell is unwilling to extract retribution from those who take advantage of his good will. In a deeply divided committee, this style has become a prescription for stalemate. For example, the ranking minority member, Jesse Helms, has been able to "exploit" their good relationship, and as a result Helms has been able to exercise considerable and undue influence within the committee. On policy questions, Pell has few legislative priorities on which he seeks to lead the committee. His policy interests are more in the "capillaries" of foreign policy than in its "arteries," according to one who has worked with him. For instance, he has an abiding interest in the United Nations Environmental Program and has worked assiduously to ensure that it receives regular funding. He also has an interest in arms control and has retained consideration of the START treaties at the full committee level, even as some policy responsibilities have been transferred to the subcommittees. Nonetheless, Pell does not have the kind of broad foreign policy agenda necessary to restore the influential role of Foreign Relations.

The result of Pell's style and policy positions is a committee that has been unable to complete its legislative work. Pell not only has had difficulty obtaining a quorum for committee sessions ("Another Day, No Quorum" 1989; Smith and Deering 1990, 103; Dewar 1989) but he also has had trouble getting legislation out of the committee and onto the Senate floor. No foreign aid bill has passed Congress during his tenure. Even more telling, no foreign aid measure was discussed on the floor until the summer of 1991. Total legislative output of the committee has declined as well. As the leadership of the committee has declined, so, too, has its reputation.

Institutional Relationships and the Foreign Policy Committees

While internal dynamics of the foreign policy committees have contributed to their decision-making problems, several incipient institutional changes within the Congress have done so as well. The rise in influence of other committees, the continuing struggle with the Appropriations Committees, and the increased centralization of decision making in the House and the Senate have weakened the foreign policy prerogatives of Foreign Relations and Foreign Affairs.[21]

The Armed Services Committees and Foreign Policy Issues

In the 1980s and early 1990s, the Armed Services Committees in both chambers became important forums for dealing with key issues of foreign policy, and the prestige and influence of the foreign policy committees suffered as a result. One of the reasons was the nature of the issues that dominated the policy agenda. The substantial debate over the defense budget, the Reagan administration's effort to expand conventional and strategic weapons, and that administration's initial aversion to arms control agreements were issues arguably more within the jurisdiction of the Armed Services Committees. Another reason, however, was the ability of the Armed Services Committees to fill the vacuum left by the inaction of the foreign policy committees. Two recent controversies—one arising in 1987 over the attempt to reinterpret a prohibition included in the ABM Treaty, the other involving the congressional role in the Persian Gulf crisis of 1990–91—are perhaps symptomatic of the more expanded role of the Armed Services Committees.

The first controversy dealt with the efforts of the Reagan administration to reinterpret the ABM Treaty in order to proceed with the testing and deployment of the Strategic Defensive Initiative (see Gellner 1989). The issue, however, was more than a technical defense matter; it also involved attempts to limit the treaty powers of the Senate and to redirect national security policy. Yet, the major congressional actions on the matter were centered in the Armed Services Committees, not Foreign Affairs and Foreign Relations. The Armed Services Committees added amendments to the defense authorization bill that, in varying degrees, limited the president to the "traditional" interpretation of the ABM Treaty. The amendments in each chamber differed, and the conference report ended up closer to the less restrictive Senate version. The important point, however, is that the Armed Services Committees played the crucial role in obtaining legislative action on a foreign policy matter.

Foreign Relations and Foreign Affairs were not silent on the reinterpretation of the ABM Treaty yet they failed to take decisive action. A House Foreign Affairs subcommittee held hearings on the matter but went no further. The Senate Foreign Relations and Judiciary Committees held joint hearings, and Senator Joseph Biden (D-Del.), a member of both committees, introduced a resolution challenging the new treaty interpretation. While Foreign Rela-

---

21. On these themes of institutional change, see, for example, Stanfield (1990) and C. Madison (1991b) upon which I draw in this section.

tions reported the resolution, no debate on it was ever held on the Senate floor.[22]

The second recent controversy involved the congressional debate in late 1990 and early 1991 over the initiation of the Gulf war. Once again, the Armed Services Committees took the lead role in the congressional debate. The Senate committee, in particular, was the first congressional panel to hold hearings on the question of whether to continue sanctions against Iraq or authorize the use of force. The committee obtained testimony from two former chairmen of the Joint Chiefs of Staff (General David Jones and Admiral William Crowe), a former secretary of defense (James Schlesinger), and a former national security adviser (Henry Kissinger). The House Armed Services Committee also held hearings in mid-December 1990 with several panels of distinguished political and military witnesses. The chair of House Armed Services, Les Aspin (D-Wis.), also issued three carefully reasoned papers assessing the options facing the administration (Aspin 1991b).

Again the foreign policy committees were far from silent. Both held hearings, though they were initiated after the Senate Armed Services hearings had begun.[23] Foreign Relations, in fact, obtained testimony from such distinguished former policymakers as Robert McNamara and Zbigniew Brzezinski and from several academic experts. Nonetheless, neither set of hearings drew the same kind of attention as those held by the Armed Services Committees. On a crucial foreign policy issue, the foreign policy committees had been displaced.

The Appropriations Committees and Foreign Policy Authorizations

Another set of committees that has weakened the influence of Foreign Affairs and Foreign Relations is the House and Senate Appropriations Committees. The biggest challenge here is the increasing use of the authorization waiver by the Appropriations Committees to fund foreign policy operations, particularly foreign aid. Under congressional rules, all appropriations bills require prior authorizations. As I have argued, Foreign Affairs and Foreign Relations have not always been successful in getting foreign aid authorization bills through the Congress, especially during the 1980s. As a result, the Appropriations

---

22. The issue, however, was not entirely lost. The Senate Foreign Relations Committee did attach a reservation to the Intermediate Nuclear Forces Treaty limiting future reinterpretation of that pact without Senate involvement.

23. It is fair to note that Foreign Affairs' Subcommittee on Europe and the Middle East held periodic hearings on the Persian Gulf crisis from August through December 1990, before those convened by Armed Services. These drew neither the attention nor the prestigious witnesses attracted by the other hearings.

Committees often have sought waivers of the authorization bill in order to appropriate funds. The practical effect has been to reduce the influence of the authorizing committees and to increase the power and influence of the Appropriations Committees. In the context of foreign aid, in particular, the effect has been to increase the power of the Foreign Operations subcommittees of the two Appropriations Committees. Indeed, Congressman David Obey (D-Wis.) recently has been characterized as "the most powerful foreign affairs spokesman in the House" because he chairs the House Appropriations Subcommittee on Foreign Operations (Stanfield 1990, 2916). Obey's Senate counterpart, Patrick Leahy (D-Vt.), cannot be far behind in light of the Senate's failure to pass a foreign aid authorization bill during the past six years.

The controversy over waivers on authorizations, of course, is not a new one. A similar debate occurred in the 1970s (Henderson 1979, 6). But the debate has reached a new intensity since no foreign aid authorization bills have been approved lately. During a recent debate over an authorization waiver for ESF monies to Panama and Nicaragua, Congressman Levine complained that

> the routine and almost unquestioned waiver of basic authorities threatens to destroy the appropriations procedures established by the Congress and to undermine completely the role of the authorizing committees in this process. (*Congressional Record* 1990, H3013)

In this instance, the authorizing legislation for these funds was stalled by a dispute over attaching "extraneous" amendments to it (in particular, one seeking to restrict funds to El Salvador after the killings of six Jesuit priests). After an extended exchange among the authorizers over who was at fault, the effort to stop the waiver was abandoned and the appropriation was approved.[24] This kind of controversy—and this kind of outcome—has become commonplace in matters of foreign aid, further enhancing the role of the Appropriations Committees and eroding and frustrating the role of the foreign policy committees.

Sometimes the debate between appropriators and authorizers occurs the other way around, with appropriators complaining about the restrictions imposed by the authorizers. In particular, appropriators do not like the use of dollar earmarks—specific stipulations on how money may be spent—on foreign aid legislation or the setting of dollar floors for particular activities. Such additions by the authorizers intrude on the responsibilities of the appropriators whose job it is to distribute funds. This controversy was played out dramatically in 1989 over the State Department bill.

---

24. I am indebted to Ellen Collier for bringing this floor debate to my attention.

In this case, Senator Hollings objected to the authorizing bill because it contained a provision requiring that the Board for International Broadcasting must have an authorization bill of its own in the future. As an appropriator, this provision was unacceptable to Hollings, with the result that the authorizing bill was held up until February 1990. Indeed, it was only completed after the Senate Foreign Relations Committee dropped the disputed provision from the bill.

The ongoing dispute between the authorizing and appropriating committees is a greater problem in the Senate than it is in the House, however. Over the last four or five years, the staff of Foreign Affairs has developed an informal arrangement for including members of Obey's subcommittee in their deliberations on the foreign aid authorization bill. As a consequence, the two committees have largely been in sync once the bill reached the House floor, and the Foreign Affairs Committee generally has obtained what it has wanted in the House appropriations legislation. By contrast, Foreign Relations has had more difficulty because it has not been in a position to pass a foreign aid bill on the floor. While its staff also coordinates its activities with the Appropriations Committee staff, it has had little with which to bargain due to its failure to approve authorizing legislation.

Reprogramming and the Foreign Policy Committees

Another problem for the authorizers (and for the appropriators as well) is the reprogramming of foreign aid funds by the executive branch. Under current legislation, the committees dealing with foreign policy and appropriations must be notified fifteen days before the executive branch changes the level of economic or military funding for a particular program, initiates a particular program under a general (or "blanket") appropriation, or increases funding for a given country. The notification requirement does not cover all changes. It is restricted to those exceeding $1 million in a program or $5 million for a particular country. Nonetheless, the executive branch uses the procedure extensively. In the mid-1980s, for example, seven to eight hundred notifications of revised economic assistance were sent to Congress each year. On the military side, the numbers are much smaller—less than ten notifications per year. Those numbers understate the extent of military reprogramming, however, since multiple changes were sometimes incorporated into one notification. In short, reprogramming is used frequently by the executive branch to change the mix and amounts of foreign aid.

In theory, Congress or any of the four committees that receive these notifications could object to the reprogramming and put a "hold" on it. In practice, though, few holds actually have been placed. From the perspective of the authorizing committee, then, this technique of transferring funds from one account to another or from one country to another further erodes its control over the process.

The Centralization of Policy-Making and Foreign Affairs

The third incipient institutional change is the increased centralization of policy-making within the House and the Senate. In the foreign policy area, this change has meant that the leadership increasingly has shaped the congressional response on key issues through direct personal involvement, the appointment of task forces outside the committee structure, or the use of leadership-appointed, select committees. Inevitably, this kind of action has come at the expense of the foreign policy committees. Two of the most contentious and salient issues of the late 1980s and early 1990s were handled in one or more of these ways: the debate over policy toward Nicaragua (including the investigation of the Iran-Contra affair), and the authorizing legislation for the Gulf war in early 1991.

Three episodes from the Nicaraguan debate illustrate this shift in congressional process.[25] First, in its investigation of the Iran-Contra affair, the congressional leadership bypassed the foreign policy committees and turned instead to select committees (C. Madison 1987a, 1271). In fact, the foreign policy committees had few members on the two select panels. Only two (one majority and one minority) members of Foreign Relations sat on the Senate panel and five (two majority and three minority) members of Foreign Affairs were chosen for the House panel. Put differently, only a fifth of the Senate panel and a third of the House panel were drawn from the committees that presumably should be most involved in this key foreign policy issue. In short, one of the most critical foreign policy oversight activities of the Congress in the 1980s was accomplished essentially outside the control of the foreign policy committees.[26]

---

25. Before the Nicaraguan policy episodes discussed here, the intelligence committees—particularly the House Intelligence Committee—had been responsible for shaping congressional policy through the passage of the series of Boland amendments from 1982 to 1986. In this sense, the intelligence committees—once again at the expense of the foreign policy committees—played a key role in the policy process.

26. Interestingly, the recent congressional decision to investigate a possible 1980 deal between Iran and the Reagan campaign over the release of American hostages ("the October surprise") initially was announced as being made by the appropriate subcommittees of Foreign Affairs and Foreign Relations. Apparently the leadership announced this decision to reduce the publicity surrounding this matter and to eliminate any political fight over funding the investigation (Povich 1991). Later, however, the House leadership announced that a task force (chaired by Lee Hamilton of Foreign Affairs and involving other members from that committee) would be established as an alternative investigating device for that chamber. As these actions indicate, the centralized congressional decision making on foreign policy questions would apparently con-

The pattern of centralized decision making over Nicaraguan policy continued in another way in 1987 and 1988. In the spring of 1987, House Speaker Jim Wright (D-Tex.) became directly involved in efforts to encourage peace negotiations between the Nicaraguan government and the Contras. Originally invited by the Reagan administration to aid such efforts, Speaker Wright formulated a peace plan and proceeded to consult with officials from Nicaragua, Costa Rica, and the State Department. While Wright's plan, and his diplomatic activity, met with objections from several quarters (and ultimately was stillborn), his efforts were given credit for stimulating the Central American peace plan that was signed in August. The direct and personal involvement of the Speaker of the House in this foreign policy matter, without much involvement of the foreign policy committees, was indicative of a new kind of centralized policy-making.

A year later, as Congress was again embroiled in a dispute with the White House over providing funds to the Nicaraguan Contras, Speaker Wright appointed a task force headed by the chief deputy majority whip, David Bonior, to shape a Democratic policy response. While Wright did appoint at least one member of the Foreign Affairs Committee (Lee Hamilton) to serve on this task force, the effort really was intended to gain more centralized control over policy.[27] Indeed, about one month after the appointment of the task force, in February 1988, a bill was on the floor for House consideration. In less than another month, a bill was approved by Congress.

The most dramatic recent evidence of centralized decision making—once again reflecting the diminishing policy role of the committees—occurred during the handling of the authorization-of-force resolution for the Gulf war. Not only, as I have noted, did the Armed Services Committees capture much of the limelight in the debate but Foreign Affairs and Foreign Relations essentially were left out of the development of legislation to oppose or support the use of force.

The legislation, instead, largely was handled by the leadership in both chambers or by members particularly active on foreign policy matters (see C. Madison 1991b, 1434). In the House, two key members of the Foreign Affairs Committee sponsored competing resolutions and in both instances they were joined by members of the House leadership. One measure, calling for continued sanctions against Iraq, was cosponsored by Lee Hamilton, the ranking

---

tinue. By the end of the 1991 session, however, these plans were derailed because neither the House nor the Senate approved resolutions authorizing these inquiries (see Doherty 1991b). In early 1992, however, the House finally approved the task force approach with Hamilton as chair and members of the Foreign Affairs Committee participating. In the Senate, the Near Eastern and South Asian Affairs Subcommittee was assigned to carry out this probe (see Doherty 1992a).

27. In the House, too, a leadership task force was established for shaping policy toward El Salvador, headed by Joseph Moakley (D-Mass.).

majority member on Foreign Affairs and chair of the Europe and Middle East Subcommittee, and by Richard Gephardt (D-Mo.), the House majority leader. The other resolution, which called for authorizing force, was cosponsored by Stephen Solarz, chair of the Asia Subcommittee, and by Robert Michel (R-Ill.), the House minority leader. In the Senate, members of the Foreign Relations Committee were not involved directly in sponsoring the resolutions but instead members of the Senate Armed Services Committee were on opposite sides in the debate over two resolutions offered in that chamber. The competing resolutions consisted of one cosponsored by George Mitchell (D-Maine), the majority leader, and Sam Nunn (D-Ga.), chair of the Armed Services Committee; and another cosponsored by Robert Dole (R-Kan.), the minority leader, and John Warner (R-Va.), ranking minority member of the Armed Services Committee.

According to committee sources, the House committee was at least involved in the discussion of the legislation but the Senate committee was left almost entirely in the dark. Indeed, when George Mitchell set up a special committee to deal with the issue, he left out the Foreign Relations Committee. Afterward, Senator Pell expressed mild frustration over this approach but also his acquiescence: "I would have preferred that we have first crack at it, but I didn't make any issue of it" (quoted in Blumenthal 1991, 25).

Conclusion: Improving Committee Operations for the 1990s

Both committees face formidable challenges in maintaining or recapturing their foreign policy roles in the 1990s. Neither the quality of leadership, nor the political gulf among members, nor the pressure for centralization of foreign policy-making can be changed quickly or easily. Yet the new issues facing the United States in the post–cold war era and the changes in the leadership, composition, and operation of the committees ought to afford Foreign Affairs and Foreign Relations an important opportunity to reassert their role.

As the United States begins to reformulate its strategic and structural policies in the aftermath of the cold war, Congress, and particularly the foreign policy committees, are in an advantageous position to play a major role in shaping foreign policy in the decade ahead. In the absence of a communist threat to serve as the overarching justification for action, a clear and consistent rationale must be developed to justify the U.S. military structure at home and abroad, the nature and extent of American commitments overseas, and the composition and targets of foreign aid. In all of these areas, members of Foreign Affairs and Foreign Relations have the expertise to exercise significant influence. As intermestic issues such as global trade and global ecology continue to move to the top of the policy agenda, members of Foreign Affairs and Foreign Relations also are well positioned to participate effectively in the coming congressional debates.[28] Indeed, the foreign policy committees ought to play a central role in their consideration.

Current changes in the composition and operation of the two foreign policy panels further advantage the committees as one looks to the next decade. Foreign Affairs has just appointed a new chair and ranking minority member. These changes alone are likely to energize the committee. In addition, the membership of Foreign Affairs has changed with more than one-quarter joining the committee for the first time at the opening of the 103d Congress in January 1993. This change, too, is likely to encourage a break from the past and allow members to embark upon new policy initiatives. While Foreign Relations continues to suffer from weak central leadership, several senators who were given new responsibilities in the devolution of committee power in 1991 are now in a position to give more vigorous leadership on the new issues facing the United States in the 1990s. By doing so, they also will restore some policy credibility to Foreign Relations.

An implicit assumption throughout this analysis has been that both committees ought to play a larger role in the shaping of U.S. foreign policy. Although the incipient changes—globally and within the committees—seem to facilitate a larger role, four modest structural and procedural changes ought to be considered by both panels as a means of aiding this process in the short term. First, Foreign Relations needs to decentralize committee functions. It ought to consider making permanent the informal subcommittee arrangements that were put into place in 1991. Giving more authority to the subcommittees will assist the committee in dealing with the sharp political divisions within the panel and the lack of strong centralized leadership. With this arrangement, political coalitions within and across party and ideological lines could be forged early in the process and more individuals may have sufficient incentive to provide leadership on these measures as they reach both the full committee and the Senate floor. Further, even if much of the blame for the committee's current difficulties could be placed upon the weak leadership of Claiborne Pell (or alternately on the obstructionist efforts of Jesse Helms), it is unlikely—given the present committee composition and the mixed record of previous chairs in the 1970s and 1980s—that strong leadership will reemerge within the committee in the future. In this setting, shared leadership and shared legislative responsibility through more creative uses of the subcommittees should be the preferred strategy for Foreign Relations.

Second, Foreign Affairs should move toward greater centralization. Al-

---

28. Intermestic issues are those that affect international affairs but also directly affect the domestic well-being of Americans (Manning 1977).

though Fascell reined in the subcommittees in most instances, the length of the decision-making process frustrated some members. Establishing formal deadlines for subcommittee work on foreign aid legislation, for example, and involving the full committee staff and its leadership in subcommittee activities more directly would improve overall committee operation. Without greater efforts to shape subcommittee actions, and if leadership falters in the future, the Foreign Affairs Committee could find itself facing the same stalemate that the Foreign Relations Committee has confronted throughout the late 1980s and early 1990s.

Third, both committees need to reaffirm and strengthen the authorization process. In order to make the authorization process more credible to the Appropriations Committees, however, both Foreign Affairs and Foreign Relations need to be less willing to grant waivers to expedite appropriations measures and more willing to complete the authorizing work in a timely fashion. One way for the committees to do so would be to streamline legislation by reducing the extensive use of earmarks and by focusing instead upon general policy guidelines. The recommendations of the *Report of the Task Force on Foreign Assistance* (U.S. Congress House Committee on Foreign Affairs 1989b), cochaired by Lee Hamilton and Benjamin Gilman, already call for new, foreign, economic and military assistance with this kind of focus but the recommendations have not yet been incorporated into law. Foreign Relations has embarked on an effort to rewrite the foreign aid bill, and the House proposals ought to serve as a guide to that rewrite as well. In light of the emergence of the post–cold war era no better time exists for initiating these changes. Finally, another aid to the committees in completing their legislative agenda would be to develop a closer working relationship with the Appropriations Committees, particularly the subcommittees, as the policy process unfolds within a particular Congress. The House committee has already adopted informal, but regular, consultation procedures with the Foreign Operations Subcommittee, and the Senate ought to do likewise. Indeed, consideration might well be given to formalizing these processes.

Fourth, oversight by both committees might well be redirected. While the House committee does a better oversight job than does the Senate committee at the present time, both panels' activities in this arena could be strengthened. With a newly structured foreign aid authorization bill, for example, both committees would be in a better position to focus upon the substantive goals of that legislation by monitoring the success or failure of implementing new aid strategies within individual countries. The Hamilton-Gilman Report (U.S. Congress House Committee on Foreign Affairs 1989b, 33) actually suggests a new oversight subcommittee to undertake this task but this recommendation has the potential of weakening the role of the regional and functional subcommittees for relatively little gain and perhaps substantial internal conflict. In addition, the whole process of monitoring the reprogramming activities of the executive branch might be improved under this arrangement.

Finally, these committee and legislative changes may have other benefits. If the committees were more successful in fulfilling their legislative agenda, other House and Senate committees with foreign policy and national security interests would be less likely to intrude upon the jurisdiction of Foreign Affairs and Foreign Relations. Similarly, the House or Senate leadership would be more likely to use the committees to address the most crucial foreign policy issues facing the country.

CHAPTER 7

Decision Making in the Armed Services Committees

Christopher J. Deering

On 23 February 1992, the Sunday *New York Times* carried a headline that read "Top Congressman Seeks Deeper Cuts in Military Budget: Counters Bush Proposal" (Tyler 1992). The article went on to detail cuts that Les Aspin, the Democratic chair of the House Armed Services Committee, thought possible to save substantially on defense while still leaving the United States a military superpower. What should one make of such pronouncements? By himself, is Aspin powerful enough to make such changes stick? The *Times* article suggests not. Or is a politician such as Aspin simply blowing smoke? Again the article suggests not.

Tradition and common lore tell us that Congress is ill designed to play a responsible role in national security policy, that it is intent on shoring up local interests and micromanaging Pentagon decisions—bases, contracts, porting arrangements, and the like. If that is true, then how can the chair of the Armed Services Committee suggest deep cuts that will maintain U.S. military superiority? Is Aspin some raving liberal who accidently became chair? Or can the committee, or at least its chair, be a responsible participant in defense policy-making? What, ultimately, is the tension that exists between national security and local security?

One of the most influential treatments of national security policy-making appears in Samuel P. Huntington's *The Common Defense: Strategic Programs in National Politics* (1961). In that work, Huntington argues that "military policy can be roughly divided into strategy and structure" (p. 3). Strategy, he tells us, focuses upon the units and the uses of force. Structure focuses upon the "men, money, and material which go into the strategic units" (p. 4). Most importantly, he argues that structural policy is born out of the domestic policy process while strategic policy is "executive in locale but legislative in character" (p. 126).

Congress's role in national security policy is long standing but—compared with other aspects of congressional scholarship—relatively little storied. Congress's principal agents on such matters, particularly during the post–

World War II period, have been the House and Senate Armed Services Committees. Not surprisingly, these two committees will be the focus of policy-making attention as the United States enters a new strategic era. This chapter focuses upon them.

It is Huntington's characterization of military policy-making that long ago established our vision of Congress's participation generally, and the Armed Services Committees' in particular, as "real-estate" oriented. The committees trade primarily in the distributive politics characterized by subgovernments (see Adams 1977; Ripley and Franklin 1991). As a result, argued Huntington, the committees were *politically* incapable of determining force levels and strategic programs. Whether suited to the job or not, the Armed Services Committees have changed the way they participate in defense policy-making. As Huntington wrote, the committees had not yet embarked on their road to annual authorization. The complexities of nuclear deterrence had yet to emerge fully. And the controversy over our participation in Vietnam was only on the horizon.

This chapter examines the origins and development of the two Armed Services Committees, their constitutional and institutional powers, the behavior of their members, and how their structure has changed. Most importantly, the chapter demonstrates that, even though the two committees have been staunchly supportive of a strong national defense, their role in defense policy-making has changed since World War II. This change is attributable chiefly to a shift away from open-ended authorizations and an insistence on yearly authorization of all defense activities. This approach is not without controversy but it ensures that the Armed Services Committees will be participants in defense policy formulation.

The Origins and Development of Armed Services

In current form the House and Senate Armed Services Committees date from the Legislative Reorganization Act of 1946. By other names, however, their roots can be traced to the American Revolution. Louis Smith, for example, found that at least seventeen special subcommittees were created by the Continental Congress to supervise a wide variety of war-related matters, among them cannon, muskets, hospitals, clothing, beef, and saltpetre, (L. Smith 1951, 173). These special committees were investigative in character and were empowered only to report recommendations back to the assembly. Without identifying precisely when, Smith points out that the Congress found it necessary to consolidate most of the work undertaken by this band of committees (ibid.). Thus, a Board of War and a Marine Committee were formed to oversee land and naval operations. General George Washington frequently had delegations of military affairs committee members encamped with him during the Revolution. Their purpose, of course, was to provide oversight and to ensure that the dictates of the early Congress were being carried out.

Under the new Constitution, the House created Congress's first military affairs committee in 1792 to investigate the defeat of General Arthur St. Clair in a campaign against Northwest Indians. On 10 December 1816, the Senate created a core of standing committees that continues to this day. The committees on Military Affairs, on the Militia, and on Naval Affairs—the forebears of the present committee—were established at that time, as was the Committee on Foreign Relations. In 1858, the committees on Militia and Military Affairs combined to form the Committee on Military Affairs and Militia. *Militia* was dropped from the committee's name in 1872. The House created its committees on Military Affairs and Naval Affairs in 1822. In 1835, the House also created a Committee on the Militia, which was absorbed by the Military Affairs Committee in 1911. In 1947, pursuant to the Reorganization Act, the Military Affairs Committees and the Naval Affairs Committees, in both the Senate and the House, were combined as the Armed Services Committees for their respective chambers. Also in 1947, the National Security Act provided for a roughly parallel, executive branch reorganization by uniting what had been the Department of War and the Department of the Navy in the Department of Defense. The separate establishment of foreign policy committees and military committees marks an institutional distinction between diplomacy and defense. This division of labor has been and continues to be uneasy. Likewise, the principal historical tasks of the State Department, and what is today the Defense Department, demarcate this same division of labor for the executive branch.

For much of its history, the Senate Foreign Relations Committee could make a plausible case for preeminence among the four, dwarfing many times over its cousin in the House. For their part, the naval and military affairs committees provided a modicum of prestige and influence but remained principally "pork barrel" committees throughout their history. The House Foreign Affairs Committee, long discounted, did change dramatically during the post–World War II period—largely because it became responsible for the authorization of tens of billions of dollars in foreign aid. Arguably, however, neither of the foreign policy panels today has the prestige or the influence to compete with the two Armed Services Committees. Perhaps the most obvious indicator of falling prestige is the relative ease with which membership on the foreign policy committees can be gained and the distinctly more difficult time members of both chambers have winning seats on Armed Services.

Constitutional Authority and Jurisdiction

Although, as indicated above, committees were quite common prior to 1789, the Constitution simply empowers the House and Senate to establish their own rules and procedures. Thus, the formal power of congressional committees is granted by the parent bodies and established in the standing rules of the two chambers. Among other things, these rules—typically established by resolutions but occasionally by statute—set the sizes of the committees and formally define their jurisdictions. And, although the rules of the two chambers differ somewhat, they now ensure that committees receive any legislation introduced that falls within their jurisdiction. That jurisdiction is derived from congressional powers enumerated in the Constitution.

Constitutional Authority

Article I, section 8 of the Constitution clearly establishes Congress's responsibilities for national defense.

> to raise and support the army and the navy
> to make rules governing the land and naval forces
> to provide for calling forth, organizing, arming, and disciplining the militia
> to exercise exclusive legislation over all places purchased for forts, magazines, arsenals, dockyards, and other necessary buildings
> to declare war

By tradition and by rule, the last of these responsibilities falls within the jurisdiction of the House and Senate foreign policy committees.

Two additional constitutional provisions are crucial to a basic understanding of the Armed Services Committees' authority. First, the Constitution states that "No money shall be drawn from the Treasury, but in consequence of appropriations made by law. . . . " (It further restricts appropriations for the army—but not the navy—to a period of no more than two years.) Second, the Constitution gives Congress the power "to make all laws which shall be necessary and proper" in executing these activities. In effect, these provisions provide for certain responsibilities and also determine the means for carrying them out. They further ensure that virtually every activity undertaken by the government will take place pursuant to legally established program authority and budget authority. Under current rules, the Armed Services Committees exercise their power only through the creation of program authority. Budget authority—that is, appropriations—is the sole responsibility of the two Appropriations Committees (see chapter 8).

Program authority is the legal basis, provided through acts of Congress, for defense activities performed by various agencies of the government—primarily the Department of Defense and the military services. For example, in 1947, Congress passed the National Security Act, which created the Department of Defense, detached the Air Force from the Army and established it as a separate military service, transformed the Office of Strategic Services (OSS) into the Central Intelligence Agency (CIA), and created the National Security Council. Authorizing bills may have the additional purpose and effect of setting limits on what may later be spent for each of these defense programs. Clearly, program authority, in the form of annual Department of Defense authorization bills, covers a vast array of activities—from buying boots, shoes, and uniforms to the purchase of multi-billion-dollar weapons systems. At least formally, this means that Congress, subject to presidential veto, may create, alter, or abolish any office, program, or activity undertaken by the Pentagon. After authorizing various national security activities, Congress must then provide the necessary funding for those activities. This process of providing budget authority is achieved through appropriations bills.

Armed Services Jurisdiction

The jurisdictions of congressional committees are fixed in the standing rules of the House and Senate. Pursuant to the Legislative Reorganization Act of 1946, the jurisdictions of the House and Senate Armed Services Committees are nearly identical. Indeed, aside from some variation in wording, the only noticeable differences are the inclusion of soldiers' and sailors' homes within the House committee's jurisdiction and the inclusion of maintenance and operation of the Panama Canal zone within the Senate committee's jurisdiction.

Current written jurisdiction makes the two committees responsible for any activity undertaken by the Department of Defense or by the departments of the Army, Navy, and Air Force. The pay, promotion, retirement, and other benefits of members of the armed forces fall within their jurisdiction, as does the Selective Service System. In addition, activities undertaken by other departments and agencies that affect the military uses of space, nuclear energy, research and development in support of the armed services, and strategic and critical materials are within the committees' jurisdiction.

The formal jurisdictions of the two committees have been altered very little since 1946. Each has acquired some authority over the military applications of nuclear energy. These were inherited upon the elimination of the Joint Committee on Atomic Energy in 1977. The committees also lost authority when the House and Senate created the Select Committees on Intelligence, which today have legislative jurisdiction over most intelligence activities.

The Armed Services Issue Environment

National security has been a centerpiece in American national politics since the end of World War II. Containment, the cold war, nuclear deterrence,

Korea, Vietnam, arms control, and post-Soviet security have been controversial, highly salient, and widely discussed. In spite of this centrality, these issues have had a much greater effect on Congress's foreign policy committees than on its military committees. To be sure, episodic disagreements regarding particular weapons systems and occasional debates about U.S. strategic posture have touched the military committees. But for the most part the committees have remained in the background, strongly supportive of national defense and primarily concerned with the domestic side of it. Why is that? And what affect does it have on how these two panels operate?

Issues are important to members of Congress. Even if we accept the notion that members are primarily interested in reelection, issues inevitably play a role. By virtue of varying jurisdictions, committees operate in quite different issue environments. These environments, in turn, determine which private and public sector clients will appear before the committees, whether the interests of those clients will coincide or conflict, and what sort of media attention the committee and its members shall receive. For members these are important matters. Committee agendas determine whether their environments are fragmented or unified, nationally salient or locally defined, and consensual or contentious.

For many members, the best combination of these characteristics would be an agenda with low conflict (low risk), little fragmentation (focused beneficiaries), and high national and local salience (good media). The Armed Services Committees appear almost uniquely suited for such members. The jurisdiction of the committees is nationally salient but also carries intense local interest. By most measures the political environment is neither fragmented nor contentious. The primary claimant is the Pentagon and, service rivalries aside, the military has a fairly unified vision on issues of national security. It is not surprising, therefore, that the committees tend to attract members who are strongly supportive of national defense and that internal committee operations long have been regarded as consensual. Liberal, anti-defense members are not likely to fit into a committee dedicated (for local or patriotic reasons) to increasing the defense budget.

The most important characteristic of the committees' political environment is its limited fragmentation; that is, it is dominated by the Pentagon and the military services. Only seven House committees and four Senate committees have jurisdictions less fragmented than these two panels (Smith and Deering 1990, 80).[1] Committee witnesses provide a good indicator of this monolithic environment. In stark contrast to nearly all other House and Senate

---

1. Fragmentation is measured as a composite of the number of departments and agencies under each committee's jurisdiction and the number of jurisdictional areas listed in the chamber rules.

committees, the vast majority of witnesses appearing before these two committees are from the executive branch—specifically, the Pentagon. Only about 25 percent of the witnesses appearing before the Armed Services Committees represent public interests (Smith and Deering 1984, tables A-4 and A-5).[2] The foreign policy panels and the appropriations panels in each chamber are the only other committees for which a majority of witnesses come from the executive branch. Unlike Armed Services, however, these four committees are among the most fragmented in Congress.

Committee Membership

Identifiable patterns of committee behavior can be traced to the environments within which committees operate and to the motivations members have for joining committees in the first place (Fenno 1973; Smith and Deering 1984). At the very least, relatively high or low demand for committee membership will indicate how popular a committee is within each chamber. This is especially true in the House, where members serve on markedly fewer committees and subcommittees. In this section, the attractiveness, member motivation, and voting behavior of the Armed Services Committees are examined.

Committee Attractiveness

The Armed Services Committees have been and remain among the most attractive committee assignments in the House and Senate. Implicitly, both chambers have recognized this in their rules. Rules established by House Republicans and Democrats call for three levels of committees: exclusive, major, and minor. Each party prohibits members on exclusive committees (Appropriations, Rules, and Ways and Means) from taking any other assignment. Members appointed to major committees may have an additional assignment but only on a nonmajor committee. Both parties have designated Armed Services as a major committee.

The Senate also establishes categories of committees, although its permissive allowance for assignments makes these less meaningful as an indicator of value. Regardless, the Senate Armed Services Committee is a major committee under Senate rules in a system that has no exclusive assignments. A more meaningful indicator is Armed Services' status as one of a handful of committees—Appropriations, Finance, and Foreign Relations are the others—covered by the so-called Johnson Rule. This rule ensures that all

---

2. The pattern is even more dramatic if witnesses before Armed Services are combined with witnesses before the Defense and the Military Construction subcommittees of the Appropriations Committee. The proportion of public witnesses then falls to under 15 percent (Deering 1989, 294).

senators receive an assignment to one of the top four committees in the chamber before any receives a second assignment to one of them.

Committee attractiveness also can be examined more behaviorally. Initial demand for committee positions, requests for transfers to, and the strikingly low level of transfers from, the committee all testify to Armed Services' high level of attractiveness (see Bullock and Sprague 1969; Jewell and Chu 1974; Ray 1982; and Munger 1988). Unfortunately, these behavioral measures have only been used in the House, where limitations on assignments make transfers unlikely once careers are established. Even so, by these various measures, the Armed Services Committee consistently ranks fifth among House committees in terms of attractiveness.

The status of the Committee can be made more concrete by examining actual committee transfers. According to Bullock and Sprague, ten members of the Armed Services Committee transferred to other House committees from the Eightieth to the Ninety-first Congress. Of these, four went to Appropriations, two went to Rules, and one to Ways and Means. The remainder went to Judiciary (one) and to Science (two). The ten transfers represent the fifth lowest number occurring during that period; Appropriations and Foreign Affairs were third and fourth, respectively. Just as important, a clear majority of transfers were to exclusive committees that were arguably more prestigious. From the Ninety-sixth through the 102d Congresses only three members transferred to other House committees. Vic Fazio (D-Calif.) and Ron Coleman (D-Tex.) moved to Appropriations where they now serve on the Military Construction Subcommittee. Republican Lynn Martin (Ill.) joined the Rules Committee.

Systematic data on transfers among Senate committees are not available for earlier Congresses. During the most recent set (the Ninety-sixth through the 102d), however, only three senators transferred from the Armed Services Committee, and the pattern is very similar to that found in the House. In 1989, Idaho Republican Steve Symms transferred to the Senate Finance Committee and Texas Republican Phil Gramm moved to the Appropriations Committee. In each case they retained their other assignments. That same year, New Hampshire Republican Gordon J. Humphrey abandoned Armed Services and Labor and Human Resources for Foreign Relations and Environment and Public Works. It is worth noting that Humphrey retired at the end of the 101st Congress and that his successor, Republican Robert C. Smith now sits on the Armed Services and the Environment and Public Works Committees.

Limited numbers of transfers help to make these committees among the most stable in Congress. Low turnover allows established patterns of behavior to emerge. And those patterns tend to be conservative. But low turnover coupled with high demand also places leaders in a bind. Their response has been to adjust the size of committees in both chambers, largely upward, to reflect current demand. As a result, both committees are roughly 50 percent larger today than they were in the Eightieth Congress, with the House moving from thirty-five to fifty-four members and the Senate from thirteen to twenty members.

Committee Member Preference Motivations

Preference motivations of members long have been shown to affect the way internal decision making takes place on Congress's committees (Fenno 1973; Smith and Deering 1984, 1990). Although members' motivations may evolve during the period in which they serve, virtually all members come to their committees with a set of attitudes and goals. Committees are not ends in themselves, therefore, but a means to an end as far as individual members are concerned.

The available evidence on preference motivations suggests that members' attitudes toward committees have been remarkably stable. The Armed Services Committees have been no exception in this regard.[3] Members of Congress in both the House and the Senate tend to value membership on the Armed Services Committees because it allows them to pursue goals related to their constituents. Time and again, members (or their knowledgeable staff) first mention some district connection as a reason for wanting to join Armed Services.

Over and over, members and staff have mentioned the presence of military bases or other installations in their districts. The economy of the district, they say, is dependent on the defense budget. Or their districts or states contain major defense manufacturing facilities. This is not to say that members never mention the impact of the two committees on policy. But these statements are much less detailed, typically a statement such as "It's an important issue." The tenor of these comments was captured by a Senate aide, who said:

> We're from the South, we have a number of defense facilities and a number of communities are built around those facilities. We're happy to have them there and we want them to grow. We also are interested in a strong national defense.

Recent interviews with knowledgeable committee staff offer no reason to think that this has changed in any way.

The data in table 1 summarize the types of responses offered by new

---

3. The following paragraphs are based on interviews conducted by the author.

legislators regarding Armed Services. Data on the foreign policy and Appropriations Committees are offered for comparison. These data make clear that preference motivations for the House Armed Services Committee have consistently favored constituency, with a strong policy undercurrent. The Senate committee is much more balanced; indeed, Smith and Deering categorize the panel as "mixed," meaning that it appeals to both constituency-oriented and policy-oriented senators.

These conclusions are consistent with an examination of the House committee undertaken by Arnold (1979). Arnold's research indicates that periods of intense base closure are associated with higher demand for committee positions from members elected to military-dependent districts (pp. 125–26). During the most intense period of the Vietnam War, by contrast, the committee was a magnet for more policy-oriented members. Arnold also found that members who left the House committee between 1953 and 1975 generally represented districts subject to little defense influence and that members with installations in their districts were less likely to transfer (pp. 126–27). When they did, however, the shift was typically to Appropriations—a move calculated to enable them to protect those interests. By contrast, members with no installations in their districts were much less likely to transfer to Appropriations.

These preferences create a generally invisible tension within the Armed Services Committees. Strong support for national defense and for local bases or contractors go hand in hand. But what is good for local interests and what is good for the national interest are not inevitably in harmony. During periods of military cutbacks, therefore, tensions arise and members may be inordinately protective and parochial. These same tensions arise for members of the foreign policy committees as periods of international change frequently bring pressures for foreign aid. At present, these tensions are present for both

TABLE 1. Committee Preference Motivations for New Members of the Armed Services, Foreign Affairs, and Appropriations Committees, 92d, 97th, and 101st Congresses

	Constituency			Policy			Prestige		
House Committees	92	97	101	92	97	101	92	97	101
Armed Services	5	11	9	3	7	3	1	0	0
Foreign Affairs	1	2	0	4	8	8	0	0	0
Appropriations	5	5	7	3	6	4	7	11	4
Senate Committees									
Armed Services	4	4	4	4	6	4	—	0	0
Foreign Relations	3	1	0	19	5	2	2	0	0
Appropriations	31	6	3	15	3	3	2	2	3

Source: Smith and Deering (1990, pp. 87, 101).

committees. It is ironic, therefore, that $1 billion in aid for the former Soviet Union was authorized not by the foreign policy committees but by the House Armed Services Committee.

Committee Leadership

Positively or negatively, committees almost always are defined by the person who chairs the panel. Chairs define eras, attitudes, and structures, and they define success or failure. The Armed Services Committees have been chaired by some of the most talented, forceful, and respected members of the House and Senate during the last half century—Representatives Carl Vinson and L. Mendel Rivers and Senators Richard Russell, John Stennis, and Barry Goldwater. For one reason or another, a few have been more notorious—Representatives F. Edward Hebert and Melvin Price, and Senator John Tower. The committees have been led recently by two highly visible and frequently praised legislators—Senator Sam Nunn (D-Ga.) and Congressman Les Aspin (D-Wis.). (Aspin left Congress early in 1993 to become Secretary of Defense; Nunn continues as committee chair.) Regarded by some as competitors over both policy and political turf, the two committees very much reflect their leaders' personalities.

House Armed Services

Congressman Carl Vinson of Georgia was the ranking Democrat on the House Naval Affairs Committee and then on the Armed Services Committee for nearly thirty years—until 1964.[4] Vinson ran the Armed Services Committee in strict accord with the principles of seniority. Backbenchers were discouraged from participating and were required to bide their time. Senior members formed a ruling, generally bipartisan clique. And the committee was staunchly prodefense. Indeed, as noted earlier, the committee (along with its Senate counterpart) carefully reviewed and determined only the military construction aspects of the defense budget.

Vinson was succeeded by the notoriously parochial and autocratic L. Mendel Rivers, a Democrat from South Carolina. By at least one analysis, Rivers's reputation for enriching his state is overrated (Arnold 1979, 122–24) but his reputation as a tightfisted chair seems in little doubt. His death in 1970 may have saved him from the fate of his successor, Louisiana Democrat

---

4. Republicans Walter G. Anderson of New York and Dewey Short of Missouri chaired the House committee in the Eightieth (1947–48) and the Eighty-third (1953–54) Congresses, respectively.

F. Edward Hebert. Hebert, though not as autocratic as Rivers, failed to pass muster with reformers and the unusually large "Watergate Class" of 1974. Thus Hebert, W. R. (Bob) Poage (D-Tex.), and Wright Patman (D-Tex.) were defeated in their bids to return as chairs of the Armed Services, Agriculture, and Banking committees. Although their defeat was regarded as a blow to seniority, each was replaced by the next senior Democrat on their panel. By this route, therefore, Illinois' Melvin Price became chair of the House Armed Services Committee.

The aging Price, who was nearly seventy when he acceded to the chair, served for a decade—from 1975 to 1985. Although loved by his colleagues and regarded as fair and evenhanded, he grew increasingly feeble, first during a period of spending decline and then during a period of rapid acceleration. For several years, grumbling about Price's abilities led to rumors of his possible ouster. Finally, in December 1984, Wisconsin's Les Aspin, with help from Dave McCurdy (D-Okla.), actively moved to win the chair. That effort succeeded in defeating Price on 4 January 1985 by a vote of 121 to 118 after he was renominated by the Democratic Steering and Policy Committee. The Steering Committee met immediately to nominate a new chair and, as had happened in 1974, went to the next senior Democrat, Charles E. Bennett of Florida. Bennett's nomination was countered by Aspin's and in the ensuing vote Aspin won the chair 125 to 103. Aspin's victory was dramatic and unprecedented because he was then only the seventh-ranking Democrat on Armed Services (see Cohodas and Granat 1985, 7–9). Afterward, Bob Edgar (D-Pa.) summed up the feelings of Aspin supporters.

> You need an advocate, you need a spokesman who can go face to face with the administration and the Senate. You need someone who operates with 100 percent efficiency. For several years, Mel hasn't been able to do that. (Cohodas and Granat 1985, 9)

Since then it would appear that Aspin's supporters and opponents have received all of that and more.

First elected in 1970, Aspin was the most visible member of a cohort of policy-oriented "liberal Pentagon critics" to join the committee during the early 1970s; Ronald Dellums (D-Calif.) and Patricia Schroeder (D-Colo.) were added in 1973. This group, episodically bolstered by other liberal members, swam against the tide in Armed Services and they rarely succeeded in attempts to reduce defense authorizations (Glennon 1984, 733–34). Aspin adopted the role of critic, outsider, and media hound (Cook 1989b). In 1983 and 1984, he alienated some liberals when he backed the MX missile. In spite of this, his coalition of supporters in the deposing of Price had a distinctly liberal character.

By early January of 1985, hopes were running high throughout the committee. A restructuring of the subcommittees was anticipated by some, more staff by others, a clear voice in counterpoint to the administration by still others, and even Republicans on the panel were saying nice things (see Towell 1985). But just two months later Aspin engineered a compromise on the MX that was seen as a victory for the administration. His subsequent support for aid to the Nicaraguan Contras and for more defense spending obviously did little to salve this wound. Aspin's liberal supporters were incensed and many felt betrayed. On 7 January 1987, his "pro forma" renomination as chair of the committee was defeated in the Democratic Caucus by a vote of 124 to 130. Remarkably, he was renominated, and then he defeated three other challengers in caucus balloting fifteen days later (Calmes 1987a).

Unspoken in all this was the fact that the committee structure had changed little. Aspin's communications with his colleagues and with leaders were scant. He appeared not to be listening but neither was he talking. And the staff structure apparently did not help. For his part, Aspin claimed to have received the message:

> There are a lot of things I need to do differently in dealing with people. It has to do with the way I deal with my colleagues on a one-to-one basis. A need to be more open, more up front. I need to do more talking, and not just listen and say, 'Uh-huh, uh-huh, uh-huh.' People think the 'uh-huh, uh-huh, uh-huh' means I'm with them. The message is not that you have to toe the party line on issues. . . . What it does say is . . . you can't surprise people. (Calmes 1987a, 139)

Did it help? In 1989, Aspin once again allied himself with the administration, this time becoming the champion of Secretary Richard Cheney's defense request. He lost.

By most accounts, that event really did mark a turnaround. Aspin subsequently made a concerted effort to remold the committee staff. He altered his approach to rank-and-file Democrats and to committee colleagues. He courted party leaders, asked for their help, and mended political fences with key players on the Budget and Appropriations Committees. His new approach ensured that the committee's two most important legislative efforts—the defense authorization and the military-construction authorization—would proceed smoothly. His strategy was to unite the Committee behind a clear Democratic policy position. This was achieved in time-honored fashion: members' needs and positions were solicited, compromises were made when necessary, the leadership was kept informed, and support for the bills was cemented prior to floor consideration. Indeed, according to some observers, floor consideration of the defense authorization bill became pretty boring.

Senate Armed Services

With the exception of the Eighty-third Congress, Democrat Richard Russell of Georgia chaired the Senate Armed Services Committee from 1951 through 1968.[5] (From 1961 to 1968, Russell also chaired the Defense Appropriations Subcommittee.) A staunch supporter of national defense, he served during a time of widespread support for Pentagon programs and the uniformed military services. But it was also Russell who, in 1959, offered the first of a series of amendments that allowed the Armed Services Committees to gain a steady, albeit continuously supportive voice, in defense authorizations.

Russell's health began to fade during the late 1960s, just as Congress's faith began to fade in the capacity of the administration and the Pentagon to provide unvarnished information regarding military policy. Nonetheless, the accession of Mississippi's John Stennis to the chairmanship (Russell stepped down to take over as chair of the full Appropriations Committee) marked little change in style or policy. In 1980, Ronald Reagan swept to victory in the presidential election with the promise of strengthening national defense and brought with him a Republican Senate. The ranking Republican on Armed Services was Strom Thurmond of South Carolina but Thurmond opted to chair the Judiciary Committee. As a result, Texas's John Tower became the first Republican chair of the Armed Services Committee since the Eighty-third Congress.

Like his predecessors, Tower was staunchly conservative. Unlike Stennis, however, he was more partisan in approach. Whereas Stennis would support the president almost without regard for party, Tower was much more supportive of Reagan than of Carter. A former committee counsel characterized Tower as "less committee oriented than Stennis." If the committee's position differed from his own, he simply would not work as hard to defend it. Tower did alter the way the committee looked at issues by changing subcommittee organization. Under Stennis, the committee had a staff organized along mission lines but a set of subcommittees more in line with appropriations accounts. Under Tower, a series of mission-oriented subcommittees was established to encourage the committee to worry more about policy and less about pork barrel.

Tower surprised the political world in 1984 by announcing his retirement, a move that paved the way for the accession of Arizona's Barry Goldwater to the chairmanship. Goldwater was every bit as conservative as Tower, so again the chair would be a staunch supporter of the uniformed military,

---

5. Republican senators Chan Gurney of South Dakota and Leverett Saltonstall of Massachusetts chaired the committee in the Eightieth (1947–48) and the Eighty-third Congresses (1953–56), respectively.

especially the military reserves. But Goldwater differed in his approach to leading the committee. He was more pragmatic and inclined to bargain. Tower relished the links between foreign and defense policy and encouraged the committee to take a broad perspective. Goldwater was more hardware oriented and was at home on the bases, with the troops, and in the cockpit. He was blunt, candid, and known for a colloquial wit. But his tenure as chair was very brief because the Democrats regained control of the Senate in the 1986 elections. By then, Georgia's Sam Nunn had risen to become the second-ranking Democrat on the committee. The senior Democrat, John Stennis, had become the ranking member on the Appropriations Committee (and on the Defense Subcommittee as well) so that, when Democrats reorganized the Senate in 1987, Nunn became chair.

Nunn's rise to the chairmanship was preplanned and perhaps preordained. The grandnephew of House Armed Services chair Carl Vinson, he occupies a Senate seat inherited from Richard Russell. Vinson even helped Nunn lobby other senators for a position on the committee after his election in 1972. Nunn is frequently described as immensely powerful. For some time he has been a Democratic talisman against charges that the party is weak on defense. But he also is regarded as cautious. He weighs the data, sometimes arduously, before reaching conclusions.

Nunn's style as chair is a throwback to an earlier era. The staff is very centralized. Unlike many Senate committees, which routinely feature more centralized staffs than do House committees, Armed Services staff work for Nunn and are not detailed to specific subcommittee chairs. As a result, information is alleged to be at a premium. Subcommittee organization has reverted to a structure similar to that which existed under Stennis. Republicans on the committee fare reasonably well but critics say that the bipartisanship is merely a facade. Others would argue that they fare no better than do all the other Democrats. Indeed, the *National Journal* has dubbed the whole operation "Sam Nunn, Inc." (Morrison 1991b).

Nunn's approach to running his committee, therefore, stands in fairly sharp contrast to Aspin's, and their careers have been quite different. Nunn established his reputation as a Democratic defense guru very early on. Aspin remained a gadfly outsider much longer. Nunn's caution served him well; Aspin's incaution was harmless but earned him fewer devotees and left him without much clout in defense circles. Ironically, their positions may have been reversed in the last two years of the Bush presidency. Aspin's "big think" approach to issues—one characterized as synthetic in comparison to Nunn's deductiveness—paid off during the Gulf war. While Nunn urged caution and supported sanctions, along with most other Democrats, Aspin seemingly went out on a limb and predicted that casualties would be lighter than expected and that victory would be relatively swift. These predictions, the outcome of the war itself (at least in military terms), and Aspin's new-found collegiality all went a long way toward vaulting him at least into parity with Nunn.

Structure and Decision-Making Patterns

Although both the House and the Senate have used committees for more than two hundred years, their structure and operation within each chamber has varied greatly. These differences became even greater during the 1970s when a series of reforms ensured that subcommittees in the House of Representatives would become more heavily and formally involved in the legislative process. No similar movement was experienced in the Senate; indeed, if anything, Senate committees became less inclined to empower their subcommittees (Smith and Deering 1990). In this section, evolution in the structure and operation of the House and Senate Armed Services Committees is examined.

House Armed Services

Prior to the reforms of the early 1970s, the House Armed Services Committee was structured and operated in a very centralized fashion. Chairmen Vinson, Rivers, and Hebert differed somewhat in their style but the committee's method of operation was fairly constant. Very little legislation was referred to subcommittees, the staff structure remained centralized and bipartisan, and the full committee chair ruled with the advice and consent of the committee's most senior members.

From the Eighty-fourth Congress (1955–56) through the Ninety-third Congress (1973–74), Armed Services had a dual structure of subcommittees. One set received numbers rather than formal names and varied from three to five. It is worth noting that, during their time as chair of the full committee, Vinson, Hebert, and Rivers never chaired any of the numbered (i.e., legislative) subcommittees. Parts of legislation or minor bills might be handled in these panels but the most important matters were held for full committee consideration. The numbered subcommittees were chaired by the committee's most senior Democrats. Because of their small number and a high degree of membership stability in the more senior ranks, queues for subcommittee chairmanships became quite long. In fact, on average it has taken longer to become a subcommittee chair on Armed Services than on any other committee in the House—14.2 years. This is slightly longer than the average for Appropriations and substantially longer than that for Foreign Affairs (see table 2).

A second set of special subcommittees that existed throughout this period varied greatly in number and subject matter. In the Eighty-fourth Congress

TABLE 2. Mean Number of Years of Service Prior to Gaining a Subcommittee Chair in the House Armed Services, Appropriations, and Foreign Affairs Committees, 86th–101st Congresses (Ns in parentheses)

Committee	86th–91st (1959–70)	92d–101st (1971–89)	86th–101st (1959–89)
Armed Services	18.00 (4)	13.14 (14)	14.22 (18)
Appropriations	14.11 (9)	11.36 (22)	12.16 (31)
Foreign Affairs	11.00 (6)	07.12 (17)	08.13 (23)

Source: Data collected by the author. Select and special subcommittees and task forces are excluded. Mean years are calculated based upon acquisition of first subcommittee chair; acquisition of subsequent subcommittee chairs is not counted.

there was a single Subcommittee for Special Investigations, chaired by the seventh-ranking Hebert. By the time of the Ninetieth Congress (1967–68) the number of special subcommittees had ballooned to twelve. These considered such diverse topics as military academies, anti-submarine warfare, and military draft-law review.[6] These special subcommittees were similar in one regard: none had legislative jurisdiction.

With Hebert's demise and the culmination of committee reforms, numbered subcommittees and special subcommittees disappeared. Since 1975 the committee has had seven virtually unchanging subcommittees and an occasional special subcommittee. These have fixed jurisdiction, are guaranteed referral of appropriate legislation, and have the authority to mark up and report bills to the full committee.

Today the annual authorization bill is distributed to appropriate subcommittees for their consideration. Aspin, not surprisingly, chaired the Subcommittee on Procurement and Military Nuclear Systems. But he is said to have allowed chairs of the subcommittees (on installations, personnel, research and development, readiness, etc.) ample leeway to construct their parts of the bill. The full committee staff provides oversight and communication, and works intensely to see that the various parts fit when they are reassembled at the committee level.

Aspin used three devices to manage committee business. First, like many other chairs, he held periodic meetings with subcommittee chairs. Second, he employed an informal cabinet of ten to twelve committee members as a sounding board for new ideas and initiatives. And, third, major committee hearings were frequently held by an ad hoc group, the Defense Policy Panel, which has no legislative jurisdiction. These hearings were intended to highlight major strategic issues and to lay a conceptual base for specific decisions.

---

6. Even then, the most senior members continued to control these panels. Hebert, for example, chaired one numbered subcommittee and three special subcommittees.

With these structures and procedures in place, the primary task of this strongly prodefense committee is to fashion legislation that can succeed on the floor. Both party contingents—as will be seen below—are more conservative than their chamber colleagues. Internally, therefore, the committee can operate with substantial consensus. But legislation fashioned in a vacuum might well fail on the floor—as occurred with the defense bill of 1989 mentioned earlier. Recently, the goal has been to avoid floor challenges or embarrassing defeats by cultivating members and enlisting the help of party leaders. That strategy, at least in the last few years, seems to have succeeded.

Senate Armed Services

With the exception of several Congresses of the early 1970s, the Senate Armed Services Committee has consistently employed either five or six subcommittees. Subcommittees on preparedness, the Central Intelligence Agency, and the national stockpile and naval petroleum reserves were consistent features of this system until that time. But Senate reforms in 1976 mandated a decrease in the number of subcommittees and Armed Services responded with panels roughly reflecting appropriations functions: procurement, manpower and personnel, military construction, and research and development. As noted earlier, the subcommittee structure shifted to a more mission-oriented organization under John Tower and Barry Goldwater but has since returned to an organizing scheme reminiscent of the Stennis era. The absence of a military construction subcommittee is a conspicuous exception.

As with Senate subcommittees generally, Armed Services subcommittees have little power. Subcommittees hold most hearings (though broad "force posture" hearings remain in the full committee) but rarely mark up legislation. Staff organization is centralized and loyal to Chairman Nunn while their minority counterparts are similarly tied to Republican John Warner of Virginia. Virtually all committee activities are aimed at passage of the authorization bill. During the 1980s this was frequently a protracted and harrowing task. By the time Stennis and Tower had gone, Nunn's response was to be more prepared than anyone else—an endeavor aided by his small, centralized, and intensely loyal staff.

Committee Members' Behavior

Members of the House and Senate Armed Services Committees long have been noted for their conservatism and hawkish stands on issues of foreign policy and national security. Likewise, their membership has been viewed as dependably supportive of presidents without regard to party. How true are these assumptions?

The first may be examined by comparing scores calculated for each member by the liberal group Americans for Democratic Action (ADA). These scores, published each year and summarized for each Congress, are rough indicators of "liberalism." The data for members of the House and Senate Armed Services Committees are summarized in table 3.

As the data in table 3 demonstrate, the Democratic and Republican contingents on both committees had lower ADA scores for all ten Congresses from the Ninety-first to the One-hundredth. These data must be interpreted with caution since the scores are based upon different sets of votes. For each Congress during this period, Senate Armed Services Democrats have substantially higher ADA scores than do their House Democratic colleagues. A similar but less striking pattern emerged for Armed Services Republicans, as the Senate committee contingent ranked higher on the ADA than did their House counterparts in six of the ten Congresses. As expected, the Republican contingents on both committees received lower ADA scores than did the Democrats in each of the ten Congresses. Finally, Democrats on both committees earned higher ADA scores during the last three Congresses for which data are available.

TABLE 3. Mean Americans for Democratic Action (ADA) Scores for Members of the Armed Services Committees, by Party and Congress, 1969–88

Congress	Democrats				Republicans			
	House	HASC	Senate	SASC	House	HASC	Senate	SASC
Nixon								
91	49.2	35.3	55.2	41.4	20.1	17.1	29.1	27.8
92	51.8	33.2	58.2	42.5	18.2	09.9	24.2	19.6
Nixon/Ford								
93	56.1	40.6	64.6	44.3	21.6	04.2	31.8	05.8
Ford								
94	60.4	41.5	58.6	54.8	19.1	07.8	32.0	07.4
Carter								
95	51.4	34.4	58.1	48.4	19.1	10.2	29.5	06.5
96	59.7	35.8	54.6	46.3	18.6	11.7	28.6	14.4
Reagan								
97	62.9	35.8	69.0	57.3	18.3	11.4	22.5	12.7
98	72.0	49.5	71.7	66.6	15.8	08.9	24.9	15.4
99	70.6	43.1	71.0	61.4	14.9	09.8	19.8	07.9
100	77.7	58.0	75.9	64.7	18.7	14.8	25.8	12.2
Total	60.6	41.1	63.2	52.0	18.8	10.0	26.9	13.0

Source: Raw data for this table were provided by James McCormick and Eugene Wittkopf. The scores are calculated by the Americans for Democratic Action based upon votes selected by that organization. Scores range from 0 to 100 with higher scores indicating more liberal positions.

Comparing these figures to the scores of members of the Foreign Affairs and Foreign Relations Committees confirms an additional popular suspicion, namely, that members of the Armed Services Committees are more conservative than their foreign policy counterparts (see chapter 6 for comparative scores). The difference is much more striking for Democrats than it is for Republicans but it holds for both parties in both chambers throughout the ten-Congress period.

These data continue to support the notion that the House Armed Services Committee is a homogeneous, "preference outlier" (Krehbiel 1990, 155).[7] That is, rather than a liberal and a conservative contingent—each more extreme than fellow partisans within the body—the House Committee's party contingents are each more conservative than their party colleagues in the House. These data suggest that the Senate Committee less dramatically demonstrates this phenomenon largely because the gap between liberals and conservatives *within* the committee is more pronounced. It also means that the "liberal" Aspin had to mold a position from a consensually conservative committee and sell it to a liberal Democratic party in the House. Meanwhile, Nunn must fashion a position within a more ideologically diverse committee and then seek passage within an even more diverse Senate.

Support of the president by committee members on foreign policy issues is far from monolithic. Using data collected by McCormick and Wittkopf, it is possible to examine, by party, support for the president by Armed Services Committee members and by the committees' parent chambers (see table 4). In the House Committee, Democrats were more supportive of the president in seven of the ten Congresses than were their party colleagues. Two of the three Congresses in which they were less supportive occurred during the Carter administration. During those same Congresses, Republican committee members nearly mirrored their party colleagues and, with one exception (the Ninety-first), were substantially more supportive of the Republican presidents than were committee Democrats. They were even less supportive of Carter than were committee Democrats.

In the Senate, the partisan picture is somewhat clearer. Committee Republicans were significantly more supportive of the president during every Congress in which a Republican sat in the White House. They were substantially less supportive of Carter than were committee Democrats, chamber Democrats, and chamber Republicans. Committee Democrats were more supportive of the president than were the rest of their party colleagues in nine of the ten Congresses—the lone exception being the first two years of the Carter administration.

These scores are very similar to those of the foreign policy committees.

---

7. Krehbiel's (1990) data are drawn from a much narrower time period—the Ninety-sixth through the Ninety-eighth Congresses.

TABLE 4.   Mean Presidential Foreign Policy Support Scores for Members of the Armed Services Committees, by Party and Congress, 1969–88

Congress	Democrats				Republicans			
	House	HASC	Senate	SASC	House	HASC	Senate	SASC
Nixon								
91	59.0	57.1	63.6	67.9	59.2	47.1	79.2	75.0
92	47.9	58.7	42.6	62.5	72.3	77.9	72.1	75.4
Nixon/Ford								
93	35.2	37.2	46.3	56.6	51.1	54.8	69.0	69.0
Ford								
94	46.5	49.7	60.9	68.8	66.1	62.9	77.7	85.9
Carter								
95	59.4	45.5	72.0	68.2	36.9	28.7	50.1	21.4
96	67.4	50.4	70.1	71.8	34.0	29.1	54.8	42.2
Reagan								
97	43.2	67.7	43.1	51.1	70.5	78.2	70.1	76.1
98	37.3	59.9	44.3	49.8	77.3	82.9	76.0	80.6
99	22.9	50.3	37.7	44.1	76.0	79.4	79.9	89.4
100	30.8	48.3	49.1	54.6	78.4	82.0	77.1	77.3
Total	44.5	51.2	53.1	59.8	61.6	62.8	70.9	69.9

Source: Raw data for this table were provided by James McCormick and Eugene Wittkopf. Presidential foreign policy support scores are based upon all foreign policy votes on which the president took a position in a particular Congress. Scores range from 0 to 100; the higher the score, the greater the agreement. See McCormick and Wittkopf (1990) for a description of the methodology used to create these scores.

In both chambers, for both committees, partisan differences appear. The gap between the two was apparent but muted during the Nixon and Ford administrations but during the Carter and Reagan years it was much more pronounced. By inclination and performance, members of the Armed Services Committees are supportive of conservative principles and of their president's position. But this trend is more pronounced on national security issues (wherein a strong national defense maintains greater continuity from administration to administration) than it is for foreign policy generally.

Influencing National Security Policy

The capacity of the Armed Services Committees to influence national security policy depends, in great part, on their capacity to draft and pass legislation (see chapter 2). Through legislation, virtually no aspect of national defense lies beyond the committees' reach. Nonetheless, the committees' actual behavior has ranged from being very permissive in its legislative acts to being very precise and prescriptive in its acts. Moreover, once legislation is passed, the two committees must decide whether to monitor executive branch compliance carefully and consistently or only episodically in response to crises, what

McCubbins and Schwartz (1984) have referred to as police-patrol and fire-alarm oversight. Regardless of which tack the committees choose they will be criticized. If they are permissive, critics (mostly liberal) will accuse them of being too deferential to the Pentagon (Adams 1977); if they become more prescriptive, others (mostly conservative) will accuse them of micromanagement (Mellor 1990).

Although this aspect of committee behavior may vary, the evidence presented so far indicates that the committee members' motivations have remained consistent. With few exceptions, members of the Armed Services Committees approach their work with two decision rules in mind: first, to support a strong national defense, and, second, to support military bases and contractors in the home state or district. Throughout the first half of the post–World War II era, implementation of the first decision rule kept the committees at the permissive end of the spectrum in their legislative acts. Hence, as noted in chapter 2, the president and the Pentagon dominated where crisis and strategic policies were concerned. During that same period of time, however, the second decision rule caused them to monitor the structural components of defense policy much more closely.

Our accumulated experience of that period yields a stylized image of the committees as uncritical supporters of the military establishment who receive, in exchange for that support, a continuous flow of defense spending in their districts. The remainder of this chapter examines two innovations by the Armed Services Committees designed to alter this stylized image, recoup influence ceded to the Defense Department and Appropriations Committees, and protect themselves from their urge to preserve the most visible form of defense pork barrel. Each of these innovations—one requiring annual authorization and the other establishing a mechanism for base closings—is procedural in character. But the first is designed to ensure committee involvement while the second is designed to blunt its parochialism.

The Rise of Annual Authorizations

Congress and its military or naval affairs committees long have been in the practice of providing open-ended program authorizations. The reestablishment of a Department of War is numbered among Congress's first acts in August 1789. Its responsibilities were broadly written to include land and naval forces (including ships and supplies) and Indian affairs (White 1948, 125).[8] Subsequent enactments permitted the department to recruit up to cer-

---

8. It should be noted that responsibility for naval affairs was an empty gift since all major U.S. warships had been sold. The only vessels owned by the government were the so-called revenue cutters—precursors of today's Coast Guard—and these belonged to the Treasury.

tain ceilings but these were rarely achieved. This early pattern of open-ended authorizations, accompanied by fire-alarm oversight, became the norm for more than a century. Indeed, by the immediate post–World War II era apparently little had changed. For example, before 1962 the committees authorized for the military services an aggregate ceiling for active duty personnel of 5 million, even though actual levels in peace-time rarely reached half that number (Blechman 1990b, 29–30).

For the most part, the practice of open-ended authorizations has been of little consequence because neither the standing army nor the navy ever amounted to much (see Deering 1988). As a result, any substantial change in the size or character of the military establishment—most importantly mobilization for war—required participation by these committees. By the end of World War II, these circumstances had changed dramatically. From 1947 until the outbreak of the Korean War, the number of peace-time, active-duty, military personnel averaged 1.8 million. From the end of the Korean War until 1965, it averaged 2.8 million. By contrast, active-duty personnel averaged only 285,000 from 1920 to 1940.

The practical impact of open-ended grants of authority and a large standing army was to eliminate the Armed Services Committees from any serious role in national security policy-making. Thus, Huntington's (1961) characterization of defense policy-making gives us a clear sense of the two-track system established by the committees. On strategic and crisis policy, open-ended grants permitted the president and Defense Department a relatively free hand in policy-making attended by fire-alarm oversight. On structural policy, however, close monitoring, accompanied by something very close to police-patrol oversight, became the norm.[9] Indeed, although military construction was a small portion of annual defense spending, Blechman reports that 100 percent of military construction was authorized annually (1990b, 30–31). At bottom, this meant that, except in military construction, the committees made no consistently effective use of their legislative powers and had no procedures in place to ensure Pentagon responsiveness. Moreover, the unity of opinion was such that the committee could only reinforce the Pentagon's views on national security policy. The result, of course, was that opinion elites shaped public opinion in a consistent fashion.

By the early 1960s the committees faced a dual threat to their power. The Pentagon was authorized to operate within very permissive programmatic

---

9. McCubbins and Schwartz argue that fire-alarm oversight is an effective method (1984, 171–73) but their case seems to assume at least some level of conflict between the legislative and executive branch. In this case, the decision rules adopted by committee members, reinforced in the 1950s by anticommunist fervor, limited the willingness of committee members to question the president or the Pentagon on its policy decisions.

authority, a circumstance that reduced the committees to the status of defense cheerleaders. Meanwhile the appropriations subcommittees undermined the authority of Armed Services by going the Constitution one better and establishing a pattern of annual appropriations, a process that frequently also included programmatic guidance. Strategic and political considerations made elimination of the large standing army impossible and only would have returned the committees to the position they held prior to World War II. Thus, the committees seized upon the procedural device of *annual authorization of appropriations* to ensure their capacity to participate effectively in defense policy-making.

The trend toward annual reauthorization began in 1959 with the so-called Russell amendment—named after the venerable chair of the Senate Armed Services Committee, Richard Russell of Georgia. The Russell amendment required the annual authorization of appropriations for the procurement of aircraft, missiles, and naval vessels. From 1962 through 1982, the annual authorization requirement was expanded eleven more times. By one estimate, only 2 percent of defense appropriations required annual authorization in 1961 and virtually all of this accounted for by military construction (Blechman 1990b, 30–31). Today the figure stands at nearly 100 percent. As a result, the Armed Services Committees produce each year what most Hill observers regard as a "must" piece of legislation: the annual defense authorization bill. This bill authorizes the appropriation of roughly one-quarter of the annual federal budget. In fiscal year 1992 that sum amounted to $270 billion, roughly the size of the projected federal deficit for that year. Unlike the foreign aid bill (see chapter 6), this bill has been passed successfully each year for the past three decades or more. Indeed, existing law virtually requires passage.

The move to annual authorization marks an important shift in the potential and actual influence of the Armed Services Committees. It ends open-ended grants, ensures yearly participation, increases the anticipated responsiveness of the Pentagon, shifts the committees to more of a police-patrol style of oversight, while preserving the fire-alarm option, and moves the committees into strategic as well as structural policy-making. Annual authorization is not entirely cost free, however, since it ensures that both committee members and nonmembers may dabble in procurement politics. Sufficient examples exist to make this an area of concern but the most recent evidence suggests that the stylized image of benefits accruing to committee members is overdrawn (see Mayer 1991).

Military Base Closings

For two centuries, military bases (forts, arsenals, reservations, shipyards, and so forth) have been the most visible manifestations of the defense establishment in congressional districts. Not surprisingly, parochialism associated with their construction, location, and relocation has animated legislative decision making for just as long. For example, the establishment of a string of military trading posts along the northwest frontier was among Congress's first acts. In addition to serving military and foreign policy interests, the posts had important economic impacts—albeit in areas not yet admitted as states. Bases, in a variety of shapes and sizes, have been important community assets for a long time.

During the early 1970s nearly 500 military bases were closed in the United States.[10] This reduction was caused by the U.S. withdrawal from the war in Vietnam and made possible by open-ended authority provided to the Pentagon by the Armed Services Committees. Distressed at the perceived economic impacts and convinced that base closings were being used as punishment by the administration, a large number of members rallied to the support of a floor amendment offered by Democratic majority leader Thomas P. O'Neill of Massachusetts. The immediate inducement for the amendment had been a Ford Administration announcement that 160 more bases would be closed. O'Neill's first attempt to counteract this, an amendment to the defense procurement authorization, failed on a floor vote. While his second, slightly revised attempt, an amendment to the FY77 military construction authorization, succeeded, the bill was vetoed by President Ford. Ford's veto message challenged the amendment as a violation of the separation of powers.[11] Revised once again, the amendment finally passed as a requirement for the filing of environmental-impact studies (EIS). These time-consuming studies had the intended effect: from 1977 to 1988 not a single major military base was closed.

In order to overcome congressional protectionism, some new procedure was needed, one that would deny members access to bureaucratic or parliamentary dilatory tactics. That procedure, originally proposed as an amendment to the defense authorization bill in 1987, came in the form of a base-closing commission. The job of the "nonpartisan" commission would be to select which bases to close, combine them in a single legislative package, and permit only an up or down vote on its acceptance. Although the amendment failed, Sam Nunn, Les Aspin, and William Dickinson (the latter the ranking House Armed Services Republican from Alabama) successfully joined forces to create base-closing legislation the following year. In its final form, this legislation:

---

10. This account of base closure legislation is drawn from several editions of the *Congressional Quarterly Almanac.*

11. It is worth noting that a similar amendment had been added to the FY67 military construction bill but it, too, was vetoed—by President Lyndon Johnson.

created a twelve-member base-closing commission

provided for its appointment by the secretary of defense

required the commission to report recommendations by 31 December 1988

required the secretary to approve (or reject) the list in total

permitted Congress forty-five days in which to reject the entire package

severely limited the use of an EIS as a dilatory tactic

On 29 December 1988, the commission recommended the closure of eighty-six bases and the partial closure of five others. The recommendation was endorsed by the defense secretary on 5 January 1989 and by all but four members of the House committee. A resolution to reject the package, that is, to keep the bases open, was then defeated on the House floor, on 18 April, by a vote of 43 to 381. Opposition votes, as expected, came from members slated to lose bases located in or near their districts.

While the 1988 law provided for only a single round of base closings, the 1991 defense authorization bill provided for a slightly revised commission process and three more rounds of cuts—in 1991, 1993, and 1995. The first set of cuts—proposed by the secretary, reviewed by the commission, and approved by the president—was sustained by the House on 30 July 1991 when a resolution to defeat the package was defeated by a vote of 60 to 364. That package included twenty-five major military installations.

The base-closing procedure is essentially a means for the committees and for Congress to make a decision in the public's interest that would not otherwise be forthcoming. Members affected by the cuts are able to engage in the necessary symbolic opposition but the packages are of sufficient size to sustain protest votes against them. Although the initiative has returned to the Pentagon, since the defense secretary promulgates the initial list, the commission shields members by its endorsement, allows for member input, and the all-or-nothing procedure prevents serial consideration of each of the proposed closings.

Conclusion

The move to annual authorization is the most important change for the Armed Services Committees since World War II. Annual authorizations—like appropriations—ensure at least informal oversight of military activities and, more than any other committees except appropriations, establish something approaching police-patrol oversight. Because the committees have fashioned this approach, anticipated reactions necessarily play an important role in defense policy-making. Without annual authorizations, the president and the Pentagon might well be more adventuresome in their approach to national-security policy. This is not to say that Congress routinely gets its way or that the Pentagon is powerless. Far from it. But, whenever new programs or new departures in national security policy are contemplated, they first must pass congressional muster.

President Ronald Reagan's proposal for the Strategic Defense Initiative (SDI) provides a good example of this. Prior to Reagan's 23 March 1983 speech, SDI existed as a congeries of discrete research-and-development programs. As such, they attracted little public attention. Reagan's speech changed all that by calling for amalgamation of the various efforts into a single organization, asking for a fundamental change in our strategy for national security, and requesting a substantial increase in spending on these heretofore unrelated programs. In spite of its highly classified nature, SDI— or Star Wars, as it became known—generated a heated policy debate. And, while the most intense opposition came from outside the Armed Services Committees, close scrutiny by them resulted in consistently lower levels of support than the administration desired. Moreover, the requirement for annual authorization forced the administration to face its critics each year.

In spite of their strongly prodefense memberships, the two panels frequently challenge the administration on particular weapons systems, security strategies, and administrative procedures. While the debates have never been completely free of parochialism, ballistic missile defense, offensive nuclear weapons systems, the strategy of conventional warfare, and the missions and strategy of naval warfare have all been discussed regularly by the committees. During the 1980s, a fundamental reorganization of the military hierarchy was mandated by the committees. And Chairmen Aspin and Nunn heavily influenced the shape and size of the U.S. defense establishment in the first steps of its transition to a post–cold war world.

While there is little likelihood that we shall see a return to the pre–World War II style of defense policy-making, the reduction of international tension following the end of the cold war makes it more likely that the Armed Services Committees will become true partners in the process. Annual authorization will remain in place. Budget pressures will ensure substantial reductions in defense spending during the next five years. And the committees will demand a role. This is not to say that local concerns will go away, for substantial reductions in defense spending will push in the opposite direction. It was no surprise, therefore, that when Senator Strom Thurmond announced that he would assert his right to become the ranking Republican on the Armed Services Committee during the 103d Congress (1993–94) he invoked the interests of his home state in doing so: "I feel it is in the best interest of South Carolina for me to assume this position" (Jenkins 1992).

It is a positive sign of change for the committees that a tension exists between national and local concerns. For years, members of the committee simply ensured that bases in their states remained open or that construction projects were funneled their way. Real estate has not ceased to be important. But members of both panels now also seek a voice on major defense issues. That voice will be of consequence during the next decade and it will be a voice that neither presidents nor defense secretaries can ignore.

CHAPTER 8

Decision Making in the Appropriations Subcommittees on Defense and Foreign Operations

Joseph White

In chapter 2 of this volume, Lindsay and Ripley distinguished among crisis, strategic, and structural policies. They argued that the president dominates responses to immediate threats, or crisis; that Congress has somewhat more effect on the goals and tactics, or strategy, of defense and foreign policy; and that Congress has greatest influence on decisions to procure, deploy, and organize the resources, or structure, of the government's defense and foreign policy establishments.

Foreign policy is hardly the only area in which Congress's greatest power is control of resources. Allocation of resources is better known as the power of the purse, what James Madison (1961b, 359) called "the most complete and effectual weapon with which any constitution can arm the representatives of the people."

If the power is so complete and effectual, however, one might wonder at Congress's differing ability to control different types of policy. The simple answer is that Madison probably thought there were inherent limits on representative bodies, and that this was the best they could do. Yet he and all his colleagues surely believed that control of resources could become control of behavior, that control of structure and strategy, in the editors' terms, were not separated easily.

This chapter focuses on the parts of Congress that most directly and authoritatively allocate resources. The Appropriations Committees in the House and Senate most directly exercise Congress's constitutional power of the purse, in line with the Article I, section 9, provision that "No Money shall be drawn from the Treasury, but in Consequence of Appropriations made by Law."

This chapter's first purpose is to describe how Congress, through these committees, exercises its power over structure. For a series of reasons, ranging from the technicality of many budget issues to the process of brokering "pork barrel" projects, the process concentrates power in appropriations sub-committees, and especially in their chairs and senior staff. The subcommittees tend to focus, however, on management and distributive issues rather than large policy concerns. To the extent that the process addresses controversial policy matters, nonappropriators feel more free to challenge the committees.

The problematic relationship between structure and strategy poses two more concerns. Within Congress, the tension is defined, institutionally, as a competition for influence between the appropriators and the authorizing committees. How Congress shapes foreign policy cannot be understood without considering the endless struggle between the Appropriations Committees, on the one side, and the two Armed Services Committees, the House Foreign Affairs Committee, and the Senate Foreign Relations Committee on the other. These various committees can unite due to shared beliefs, constraints, or enemies. Yet competition always lurks beneath the surface.

Ideally, the authorizers and appropriators could cooperate through a division of labor. The standard sense of that division is similar to the idea of strategy versus structure. "Appropriations says the most efficient way to spend the money," one Appropriations subcommittee chair explained, while authorizers "say what the need is." Another declared that appropriators "have to rely on authorizers for innovation" because "we don't have time to reshape the programs."[1] Yet in practice it is very hard to tell what is a decision about efficiency and what is a choice of goals; after all, the cost/benefit ratio of any activity depends on how we value the benefits. Further, as appropriators explain when asked why they joined their committee, "nothing happens without the money." The relative spheres, and therefore the influence, of appropriators and authorizers are always controversial.

This chapter's third concern is the extent to which Congress, or factions within it, can use appropriations, the direct allocation of resources, to control the behavior of the executive. The power of the purse is better suited to preventing activities that can be identified in advance than to forcing the

1. The interviews consulted for this article were conducted as part of a Brookings Institution project on the appropriations process and American government. All interviews were conducted on the condition of no quotation or attribution without direct written permission. When I identify positions, there are multiple recent holders and, as in this case, I may not identify whether they are in the Senate or the House committee. The interviews were open ended, averaged more than an hour in length, and their subjects included senators, representatives, staff of the relevant subcommittees, and observers in positions such as other committee members, agency staff, and lobbyists. Over forty interviews were specifically relevant to this paper. I would like to thank the Lynde and Harry Bradley Foundation and the Smith Richard Foundation for their support of this project. John Righter provided research assistance; the editors of this volume, Deborah Cichon, Lawrence J. Korb, Thomas Mann, and Patrick Windham critiqued earlier drafts. I am grateful for all help and assume that only I will be held responsible for both the arguments and any infelicities herein.

executive branch to do something in particular. For example, it can prevent tests of an antisatellite weapon (ASAT) but it cannot force agreement on an arms limitation treaty. But, just as this volume's editors have argued that legislation is only part of Congress's influence, appropriators' influence on the executive exceeds the visible resource-allocation decisions.

Appropriations politics is a complex game of trades and side payments often invisible to outsiders. Legislators may threaten sanctions or offer rewards in one area (the secretary's administrative budget, for example) in order to get their way in another. In other cases the administration will anticipate the appropriators' reactions, so that Congress seems to be approving an administration request.

In many cases, however, appropriations battles reveal that nobody controls foreign or defense policy. Neither the president nor Congress can force a bureaucracy to be efficient and effective; even the bureaucracy may not know how to do so. Both sides are highly constrained by public and elite moods, interest groups, and the seeming knowledge of technical elites.

This chapter's analytic concerns must build upon description. The appropriations process is poorly understood even within Congress. While some of the trends and tendencies described here are products of the time during which this study was undertaken, roughly 1985–91, the basic task of appropriating has been unchanged for generations. Its peculiarities create obstacles and opportunities that shape the influence of the committees in their conflicts with both authorizers and the executive.

The Work

Appropriators have a task: passing the bills that finance the activities of the government. If any of the thirteen bills fails, some important government functions will cease. Each bill involves immense detail (mostly specified in the accompanying report) as Congress specifies what each agency can do. Each chamber has the same thirteen subcommittees, one for each bill. The bill is each subcommittee's major product for the year, although there are occasional, emergency, "supplemental" acts. The same people work on the same issues, developing unusual expertise, each year. They describe the process as virtually a production line, moving from the raw materials of the president's budget to the finished product, a conference report and public law.

Five subcommittees have significant roles in defense and foreign policy. Nuclear weapons activities are funded in the energy and water appropriation, the Department of State and United Nations peace-keeping activities in the commerce/justice/state/judiciary bill, and military bases in the military construction bill. This chapter considers the two subcommittees that involve the most money and controversy. The Foreign Operations Subcommittees (Foreign Ops) author an appropriations bill that in fiscal year 1991 (FY91) provided $15.4 billion for both direct (Agency for International Development [AID], foreign military sales credits) and indirect (multilateral banks) foreign aid. The Appropriations Subcommittee for the Department of Defense (DOD) oversees the defense bill, which in FY91 provided $269 billion to fund the vast majority of defense activities.

Gathering Information

Congress can only be influential, at least intentionally so, to the extent that it is informed. The nature of its influence depends upon the information it collects. Each year's budget cycle begins with the presentation of the president's budget and voluminous agency "justifications" of their requests. Each subcommittee member, aided by personal staff, may have areas of expertise. But by far the bulk of the review of the requests is provided by subcommittee staff.

The Senate "professional" staff is composed of aides designated as either majority or minority, appointed after consultation between the full committee leadership and the chair or ranking member for whom the staffperson will work directly. In the House the core is the majority staff, appointed by the full committee chair, supplemented for ranking members by their personal "associate" aides. The House staff is deeper and more experienced but in every Senate subcommittee there is at least one veteran assistant.

Staffs are small. House Foreign Ops has three professional staff; Senate Foreign Ops has two majority and one minority. House DOD has thirteen professionals and Senate DOD a few less (U.S. Congress Joint Committee on Printing 1991).[2] The subcommittees can live with these numbers because their job is basically reactive and critical. The staff and members focus on year-to-year changes in the requests, whether increments or decrements. They gather and sift information from other people. Appropriators are deluged with data from outsiders who want to influence their decisions. If they want more information, the House can turn to a special surveys and investigations operation, both chambers use the General Accounting Office (GAO), and every appropriator has a wide network of contacts within the agencies, particularly in budget offices.

Staff persons claim that grand policy issues are "beyond my pay grade." That's not quite right but they do concentrate on practical, financial questions. Staff ask: can the money really be used, are personnel needs calculated correctly, would another site (even one originally suggested for pork-barrel reasons) cost less? Members appreciate any cuts that can be justified, technically,

---

2. This count is imprecise due to difficulties of classification.

as not distracting from a mission. Such savings can be used either to reduce the total or, more commonly in the past decade, to fund something else.

"Whenever we get a new guy here," a committee investigator remarked, "most want to do policy, to generate a think piece. . . . I say, 'No, No, we're a creature of the Appropriations Committee, it's about money! How'd you use it last year, why do you need $150 million this year?'"

Staff and subcommittee leaders also collect requests from legislators and advocacy groups. Whether the request is a policy or management matter, or of local interest, there is a clear hierarchy of whom to satisfy: the subcommittee chair, then the ranking member; full committee leaders and other subcommittee members; other members of the committee or outsiders whose cooperation is especially important (such as party or authorizing committee leaders); and then everybody else. This ranking reflects who is needed most at different stages in producing the bill: the chairman's mark (draft), subcommittee report, committee report, the floor, and, most important, conference.

Neither looking for the least harmful cuts nor brokering requests for political pork has much to do with grand policy. Yet it still is important for many people whose programs will or will not be funded, and getting good information is not always easy.

Information gathering and sorting is especially difficult for the DOD subcommittees. The gravest problem is the department's size. "It's absolutely brutal," a veteran recalled.

> That first enlightenment is the incredible shock of what you don't know . . . [compared to other subcommittees] Defense is infinitely larger, and there are infinitely more people.

A new member commented:

> It's overwhelming, a whole new language. I know things I didn't *recognize* a year ago. Scores of things that I had never heard of, I didn't know if they were a plane or a boat.

Size also makes DOD unpredictable, both because its parts differ and because it has a hard time coordinating itself. In a House staffer's words:

> the Department is such a slow-moving behemoth—sometimes it takes them a month to respond; you thought an issue was settled and the letters start flying . . . it's just bizarre. . . .

Staff emphasize the different service cultures as well. "It's not just a bureaucracy," one exclaimed. "The Air Force is America—in 1955!"

The other problem is secrecy. Of course, there are attempts to keep secrets *from* Congress, and I was treated to some disquisitions, best not repeated here, on the variety of ways in which the services lie. More distinctive is the part of the budget that Congress itself must keep secret, which inhibits discussion and debate. The "black" budget involves such major procurements as the B-2 and the F-117A, tens of thousands of personnel, and a raft of smaller items.

There always has been an inner core of members and staff who oversee the black budget. "I was on the Intelligence Committee," an elder member recalled, "before the Speaker knew we had one!" The chair, ranking member, and a very few aides still have most of the responsibility but formally all subcommittee members now have access to the classified justifications and the classified annex to the committee reports. In practice few have the time or interest to review them; the visible budget is hard enough to understand.

DOD staff and subcommittee members do not feel disabled by these obstacles because they compare their information not to an ideal but to other parts of the system. Appropriations is the last and, in a formal sense, the most powerful in a long line of overseers. If the services lie to the subcommittee, they probably have misled everybody else, too, including the president.

If subcommittees know they disagree with an agency on policy direction, they look to outside sources of information to counter the agency's arguments. If the Office of Management and Budget (OMB) or political executives have imposed priorities of which neither Congress nor the agency staff approve, there is a set of norms as to how the appropriators get the agency to tell them so.

The most common information problem, however, is less conflictual. The agency has asked for more than the committees can provide, and the committees want to know where cuts would do the least harm. In the absence of other information, they are glad to let the agency choose. In a House member's words, "we urge the services to give us some priorities, what we refer to as 'what is your real heartburn?'"

Sometimes an agency refuses to rank its needs. Then, "the best way to get information is to cut a project." A Senate aide explained that the House "will make big cuts to throw a rock at the Pentagon, saying they want it fixed before we get to conference. And whatever it is gets fixed. . . ." Priorities, a House source claimed, "always comes out by conference."

The process of gathering information concentrates power in the subcommittees. Other members of the committees have little standing to challenge a subcommittee's knowledge (they are busy enough on their own subcommittees). Relative to either the president or the authorizing committees, the appropriations subcommittees, if anything, have an information advantage. If they do, they may be able to make better decisions. Yet most of the information they are gathering involves only the performance and costs, not the purposes, of programs.

Targets

Perhaps the most important and politically controversial decision about defense and foreign policy is how much we will spend on them. This decision has two components: how big our government will be, and, within that parameter, the priorities of foreign aid and military programs.

The aggregate total always has been determined outside the appropriations process because it has little to do with the subcommittees' special expertise. Until the mid-seventies, the upper limit was set by the president's budget.

The passage of the Budget and Impoundment Control Act of 1974, which was followed by a series of interpretations and codifications in the various versions of the Gramm-Rudman-Hollings law, created a new, and much more formal and precise, procedure for setting the totals. Annual budget resolutions provide the appropriators with totals for both budget authority and outlays. If they exceed these totals, known as the 302(a) allocations, their bills are subject to points of order and accusations of budgetary irresponsibility.

Appropriators' control of broad priorities within that total has varied from year to year. Formally, the appropriators set a total for each subcommittee in the 302(b) process, issue a report of those totals, *and those totals are then binding on the House or Senate floor* (U.S. Congress 1991, 262–64).[3] Since it was made binding in 1985, the 302(b) process has made committee decisions decisive with regard to priorities among, say, education, agriculture, and transportation. In some years the 302(b) process has set totals for defense and foreign operations.

For FY89 and FY91–93, however, the shares for defense and foreign aid were settled in the entirely informal process of "budget summits" as grand bargains between the parties and branches of government. Whether appropriators' influence is overridden by summits depends on a macropolitics of partisan competition and institutional aggrandizement that is beyond the committees' control.

On a spectrum of controversy, broad priorities are at the opposite end from the workaday expertise of the appropriators. The rest of Congress is far more likely to have opinions and far less likely to defer to any committee.

---

3. The 1990 budget process reforms created (hopefully) temporary procedures, and thus temporary numbering, that changed 302(b) to 602(b) just as participants were finally coming to understand what 302(b) meant. I have retained the old term because current law supports either usage.

Therefore, even when there is no summit agreement, the appropriators' flexibility is limited.

Such choice as they have will be exercised mainly by the chairman and the front-office staffs. Congressman Jamie Whitten (D-Miss.) maintained control throughout the decade, and Senator Robert Byrd (D-W.V.) gained it when he became chair in 1989. On both sides, subcommittee heads see little to gain from trying to alter the chair's allocation by taking funds from some other subcommittee as long as the full committee chair is "fair."

In meeting these targets, which, from any subcommittee's perspective, are set by outsiders, the panel's task is complicated by the difference between budget authority (BA) and outlays. BA is the amount actually appropriated, say, to allow the navy to buy an aircraft carrier. Money is spent, however, over a period of years as the carrier is designed and built. Therefore, much of the outlay each year stems from BA appropriated earlier, and much of the BA provided each year will not be spent that year.

Since outlays create the deficit, the 302(a) allocation limits them as well. This dual score keeping gives budget analysts in the Budget Committees, the Congressional Budget Office (CBO), and the OMB a part in devising formulas for estimating outlay rates for each budget account, and then in reviewing the bills for compliance with the targets. Most matters are agreed upon among the technicians but the appropriators resent the interference.

Worse, since BA is the promise to constituencies, and outlays are what concerns deficit reducers, the 302(a) allocation on outlays is always less than realistic given the BA figure. Next the imbalance is ratcheted through the 302(b) process, for as the committee allocates BA and outlays to each subcommittee the imbalance has to show up somewhere. Usually it is spread among most subcommittees. They then face claimants demanding all the BA "allowed" by the allocation. They have no way to provide that BA, however, without either exceeding the outlay limit or intentionally funding "slow-spending" accounts.

Unfortunately, slow-spending accounts may not be those it makes the most sense to fund. The result infuriates appropriators. "There is this big mismatch," a Foreign Ops aide explained. "The BA is about enough but the outlays are way out of whack." As a result, they are "driven to adjust the funding levels, to far too great a degree, purely on the basis of mechanical numbers, making the numbers add up." DOD appropriators cite the two aircraft carriers they funded for FY88 as classic examples of funding a slow-spending item to raise BA and lower outlays.

Targets and score keeping, ironically, show both the limits and the extent of structural concerns. What might seem to be the most important information about structure—which weapons work best—has little role in setting spending totals. Totals are influenced far more strongly by broad perceptions of threat, a more strategic (if often irrational) consideration. Yet, because of the need to meet targets, the force structure is shaped by an entirely unstrategic consideration, how long it takes to spend money for different purposes.

The Markup

Both the need for and the technicality of "making it fit" centralize power in the chair and staff. Subcommittee members do not know all the spend-out algorithms. Nor does anyone other than the chair see all the demands for spending. Only the chair can use the staff to develop arguments against a member's proposal.

The chair has an especially great advantage on member-interest matters. Two people care: the chair and the requester. If the requester challenges the chair in markup, the other members have to decide whom to support. Since the chair can do them more good or harm later, members will support him unless he violates a norm of fairness or the challenger has a strong case on the merits. Challenges do occur. In defense, where nobody believes that even the chair can understand the whole bill, a House member reported, "if you've got a direct interest you fight for it. No hesitation." Yet, "you only get so many times at bat," so the chair decides most items. And the chair's power over district interests gives him inducements and sanctions with which to gain votes on more controversial matters.

While the chair is preeminent in all appropriations subcommittees, member input varies. House members, for whom Appropriations is their only committee and who have fewer subcommittee assignments, are far better informed, and therefore more active, than senators. The DOD bill is so complex that nobody believes even the chair can master it. Therefore member participation is greatest on House DOD.

One member noted that the staff:

> do the green eyeshade stuff . . . and say "we think this program's in trouble, it should be cut," and we'll go along. . . . We adjust up or down, but they have a lot of sway. We might object to twenty percent of what they do, a lot of those being big policy issues. . . .

Within this process Republicans are at some disadvantage if they feel compelled to support the president's budget but they rarely do. Appropriations subcommittees operate in an unusually nonpartisan manner; Republican members, for example, broadly praise the majority staff.

Senate chairs are far more vulnerable than are those of the House. They are more likely to have agendas beyond the bill and the Senate provides far more opportunities for obstruction. "There are lots of ways one senator can embarrass another, frustrate him from getting something done," a Senate DOD member commented. Senators are also much busier than House members, so members influence the Senate mark more by the chair's efforts to accommodate them than through activity in the markup meeting. The Senate DOD meeting is much shorter than that of the House; in 1989 it lasted an hour and twenty minutes (for nearly $300 billion!). There was little controversy, as other senators accepted Chairman Daniel Inouye's (D-Hawaii) assurance that he had personally reviewed everything in extensive meetings with the "very talented staff of very dedicated professionals."

Senate, like House, DOD staff see members largely as pushing particular projects; in the Senate "we try to accommodate the members without overriding professional considerations." This is how bills are passed, a senator explained:

> In some cases you need glue, so people stick with us. It may mean a little for this campus. Or you carry a production line one more fiscal year. Though never so that you're making havoc with the bill.

Staff disagree with that opinion less than outsiders might expect, in part because the distributional stakes can be large. Sometimes, one aide remarked, a cut may mean that "a *town* can go away . . . compounded with other decisions, it can destroy that manufacturer, those workers, that industrial base. . . ." The administration will attend to such side effects of policymaking to maintain a lever on Congress but Congress is more sincerely interested than is the Pentagon.

Foreign Ops members participate less than those on DOD, both because their bill is smaller and because they have less glue to spread around. The lack of political advantage in serving is commonplace. "People were sort of avoiding Foreign Ops," one member replied when I asked how he got on the subcommittee. Foreign Ops members are interested in policy and figure they can influence it as much there as on Foreign Affairs. Reflecting those interests, certain members are considered influential on specific issues. Senators are less likely to see Foreign Ops as a substitute for a seat on Foreign Relations, which presides over treaties and appointments. Yet senators' desire to have a finger in everything means they still will have some interest.

It is hard to buy votes when there is little district interest. Gathering information on operations so as to make decisions on efficiency grounds also helps little. Other nations are sovereign, so the committee "can't go in and cut projects," even if they are turkeys. In other cases, like that of Israel, aid is not project based and "could be used for *anything*." Staff are not sure they want to know what it is used for. Therefore, Foreign Ops decisions become more symbolic, involving decisions about which countries we like, and how much, or "level of effort—effort on nutrition assistance, health assistance, etc." Since decisions are more symbolic than they are based on logrolling or efficiency, they may become partisan. In the mid-1980s, House Foreign Ops chair David Obey (D-Wis.), although personally a believer in foreign economic aid, pushed for cuts so that the administration would suffer for its refusal to raise taxes. In spite of substantive doubts, the very liberal Democratic contingent on the subcommittee supported Obey out of personal respect and shared frustration. Partisanship was exacerbated by personal and political clashes between Obey and the ranking member, Jack Kemp (R-N.Y.).

Yet appropriators normally seek compromise because they have to pass their bills. After 1987, budget summits settled the foreign aid total for Obey. Perhaps equally important, he maintained good relations with the new ranking member as of 1987, Mickey Edwards (R-Okla.). Although Edwards is a former president of the American Conservative Union, he shares with Obey an institutional loyalty to Congress over the president.[4] And, while highly partisan issues such as El Salvador remained, shared irritation with the agencies, inherent in the oversight relationship, drove Edwards and Obey closer. "I don't know what I'm going to do," Edwards was described as saying, "every year I find myself more in agreement with David Obey than with the State Department."

Obey still has the votes in subcommittee, and everyone knows it, but, given congressional distaste for his bill, he wants all the allies he can get. This desire is even stronger on Senate Foreign Ops, which also has had a much closer partisan balance, and smaller ideological cleavage, during the past decade. Bob Kasten (R-Wis.) and Daniel Inouye and then Patrick Leahy (D-Vt.), and their staffs have worked together to write the bill. An aide commented that Chairman Leahy "knows this bill is tough to vote for . . . we want Senator Kasten's support for this unpopular bill. And all the other senators."

Summary

Appropriators search for economies and pursue their personal preferences but above all else they aim to satisfy whomever they must in order to pass their bills. They need majorities on the floor and a signature from the president. At the same time, the floor and the president need them, for bills cannot be written on the floor and the president cannot legislate. Therefore, the subcommittees expect to exercise some authority over policy and pork as a fee for brokering an agreement. Where that influence is exercised depends, above all,

---

4. "Imagine," Obey quoted Edwards at one talk I heard, "Lyndon Johnson with an item veto. . . ."

on the extent and intensity of preferences outside the Appropriations Committees.

Most legislators care or know little about the details of each appropriations bill. If a small group of members cares intensely about a weapon or a country, and the appropriators have no preference, the latter may go along. But, if the appropriators do care, only issues that excite large interest groups or involve clear and widely publicized policy stakes, such as aid to Israel or the MX missile, will interest members enough to produce a challenge to Congress's specialists. Normally, as a Senate appropriator remarked,

> there aren't that many weapons systems that members of the Congress have concerned themselves with. There are over a thousand procurement items in the bill. . . . And of the thousand, the Congress would without question or debate pass favorably on, ummm—980 of them? The remaining twenty would be difficult in degrees, from the B-2 to whether the Seawolf will be built by Electric Boat or Newport News.

There are, however, two sets of specialists. We turn, therefore, to the relationship between appropriators and the authorizing committees.

Authority within Congress

Members of the Armed Services, Foreign Relations, and Foreign Affairs Committees, like the appropriators, can claim special expertise in, and will be interested about, many of the less-publicized aspects of defense and foreign policy. Further, in these areas there is unusual difficulty in distinguishing between strategy and structure. The military has no output during times of peace, so the only observable object of control is the structure of forces with which, someday, they might achieve some output. Therefore, the Armed Services Committees try to specify inputs, which the appropriators think is their job. Foreign Ops poses the reverse problem: since the appropriators cannot make decisions on the basis of performance and efficiency, they end up poaching on the authorizers. How the inevitable conflicts are resolved depends on factors ranging from the prestige and skills of the competing leaders to the nature of the particular disputes.

Authorizers vs. Appropriators: DOD

In recent years, the Armed Services Committees have asserted power more successfully than have House Foreign Affairs and Senate Foreign Relations. One House DOD aide called "the interaction with the authorizing committee" the thing that made his job most difficult: "We always get crossways with them." The Armed Services Committees claim that the appropriators are funding programs or projects that are unauthorized, or in larger amounts than are authorized. The conflict matters not just because the authorizing chair may challenge the bill on the floor but because so much of the appropriations process works not through law but through less formal agreement.

Conditions change, or are not quite understood, and both the executive and legislative branches may want flexibility that the law does not provide. Congress, therefore, appropriates in large chunks (such as $5,825,171,000 for "Other Procurement, Navy") on the understanding that the money will be spent either as planned in the justifications or as specified in the legally nonbinding report that accompanies the bill. Using the report allows the executive and the committees to change their minds, if conditions require, without the difficulties of passing new legislation. Agencies conform because the report is the only statement of congressional intent and because Congress can punish the agency next year if it disobeys.

If the authorization and the appropriation disagree within the language of the laws, two simple decision rules are invoked: the appropriations bill controls the numbers, and the later bill (which means the appropriation) wins on other matters if it explicitly contradicts the earlier bill. Because Congress cannot bind itself, its latest statement wins. But, since report language is not formally binding, when the authorization and appropriation have contrary language there is no obvious winner. The Armed Services Committees argue that if they set a limit in their report the services cannot spend more even if the appropriations report says they can.

The appropriators have large advantages in any conflict. If the issue is the normal one of a maximum amount, the authorizers have no argument when the appropriation is lower. If the appropriation is higher, it is not in the interest of the military to accept the Armed Services Committees' insistence that they ask the authorizers' permission to exceed the authorization report. Perhaps because its leaders thought the authorizers were their advocates and the appropriators their enemies, the Pentagon complied with the authorizers' demands for a time in the 1980s, but that has stopped.

By filling each bill to its 302(b) limit, the appropriators ensure that anyone who offers an amendment to increase spending on some item must offset it with a cut. Offsets are hard to find, and they buy enemies who side with the appropriators against the change, so those who want some district item that is not in the committee bill have little prospect of winning. Appropriators then can glue people to their bill, especially since members with nothing at stake in the military jurisdiction may want something somewhere else—agricultural research, national park facilities, a new wing for a veterans hospital—with which Appropriations can help them while Armed Services cannot.

For a while the Armed Services Committees worsened their position further by authorizing far more than the total appropriation, which meant that their reports could not claim to provide a sensible guide to dividing the money. With the advent of budget summit agreements, however, beginning with the FY89 round, the authorizers began marking to the same total as the appropriators, restoring much of the formers' credibility. The Armed Services Committees also have threatened to put their own numbers in the law and challenge the appropriators if they do the same. And they have threatened to legislate floors as well as ceilings for accounts.

In the absence of a big, visible, policy issue, authorizers can employ the procedural argument that the appropriators are poaching and, if not stopped, will intrude upon other members next. Appropriators acknowledge the power of this argument, emphasizing that there are many more authorizers than appropriators. The argument is not relevant if, as was the case in Foreign Relations for most of the 1980s, the authorizers have not passed their own bills. Armed Services bills do pass, and since 1987 have benefited further from the personal standing of Senate Armed Services chair Sam Nunn (D-Ga.). As neutral senators tend to side with Nunn, out of trust in his moderation and expertise, the appropriators do not want to fight him on the floor on *his* bill.

Therefore, ever since the Armed Services Committees accepted budget constraints, the balance and battles have been extremely complex. The appropriators and authorizers have signed, and then disputed the meaning of, formal agreements. It remains the case that, formally, the appropriators have the advantage on the issue of numbers. If the disagreement is not a matter of money, however, the real winner is the military. When I asked one official if, in such cases, they chose the side they preferred, he replied, "You bet." That may explain why, by 1991, bargaining on conference reports for the authorization and appropriation was simultaneous, as House and Senate authorizers and appropriators tried to strike deals across bills.

Authorizers vs. Appropriators: Foreign Operations

During the 1980s, the House Foreign Affairs and Senate Foreign Relations Committees became supplicants to the Foreign Ops subcommittees. Between 1982 and 1990, foreign aid authorizers passed only a 1985–86 measure. The appropriation for FY79 comprised 11 pages in the statutes at large, with 27 headings and 26 general provisions. As the authorization disappeared, the Foreign Ops bill grew to take its place: by FY90 it was 71 pages long, with 61 headings and 110 general provisions. It included provisions about the conflicts in Afghanistan and El Salvador, and military assistance to Mozambique;

declarations concerning Haiti, global warming, AIDS initiatives, and drug production in foreign nations; and a raft of other restrictions and urgings.

Virtually all players (everyone I interviewed) would agree that power in the 1980s moved from the authorizers to Foreign Ops, and that the shift was due to the collapse of the authorizers. A Republican aide on House Foreign Affairs spoke of their "frustrations at our own inability to pass an authorizing bill, and having to yield to the appropriators." One senator remarked:

> After a while it became routine, it was expected that we legislate all over the place . . . it's the little old Foreign Ops [sub]committee, which is never on TV, that sets the foreign policy of the United States.

The shift was caused by a crowded legislative calendar resulting from the budget mess, extreme policy differences between the Reagan administration and Congress, and the collapse of the Foreign Relations Committee under the leadership of Claiborne Pell and Jesse Helms. Foreign Relations' collapse disabled Foreign Affairs because, given no prospect of Senate passage, House leaders hesitated to make their members vote on Foreign Affairs' version of the unpopular foreign aid authorization.

Legislators did not want to vote for a Foreign Ops bill, either, but the appropriators could insert their bill into a continuing resolution (CR) that had to be passed and signed. Under House rules, a CR is not subject to the restrictions against authorizing on appropriations, so inhibitions against using appropriations to make policy weakened further.

In many cases, especially in the House, Foreign Ops did what the authorizers would have done if given the chance. Chairman Obey, in particular, is widely believed to have consulted closely with Foreign Affairs chair Dante Fascell (D-Fla.) so as to limit conflict. Appropriators, oriented as they are toward passing their bills, rarely welcome extra controversy. Observers ranging from lobbyists, to budget officers, to House leaders report that, while as politicians the appropriators naturally seek influence, on balance they are skeptical of requests to do things that might excite opposition because they are unauthorized. This attitude was epitomized (on a matter he did not care intensely about) by House Appropriations Committee chair Jamie Whitten who, when asked how he voted on Contra Aid, replied "every which way"— whatever would pass the bill.

Yet, even if appropriators are asked by authorizers to do something, and try to do so in conference, the latter resent the relationship. As authorizers cannot know from experience that compromise is necessary, they will suspect that they were sold out. The appropriators favor themselves over the authorizers on member-interest matters. And, as one observer put it,

Obey listens to Fascell, and can say he's accommodated him. But Fascell only wants four things. And if Obey disagrees with one real bad, Fascell gets three out of four.

The Variability of Influence

The different conflicts in the DOD and Foreign Ops jurisdictions should not be overexplained. Many of them had to do with the random factor of the authorizing chairs' skills and interests.

The 1980s were also a time of severe budgetary conflict, which strengthened the appropriators within Congress. In practice, appropriations rarely suffer important amendments. The Senate allows a lot of little changes— opportunities, one senator said, to let colleagues "publicly display their influence" by sponsoring something that passes by "those ridiculous votes of 97 to 0." In 1988 and 1989, the Senate handled more than thirty amendments to the DOD bill, while the House had three. But few are major in either chamber, and the prospect that they would be overturned on the floor was further reduced in years when the Foreign Ops and DOD bills never hit the House floor at all, being packaged in a CR so that the president could not get the defense and foreign policy spending he wanted without accepting domestic spending he did not want. CRs in the House normally have restrictive rules on amendments, limited time for debate, and even more urgency than general appropriations.

Procedural matters like the CR, tactical matters like Armed Services deciding to allocate the right total, and random factors like leadership all affect the distribution of authority. The process is too complicated for simple rules. "Everybody gets in the act to the best of their ability," a senior authorizer explained. "It's a broad consultative process, wheels within wheels. . . . The administration, the Republicans, everyone is in the act."

Yet within that variability it is possible to identify patterns. And those patterns fit the distinctions in terms of items of greater and lesser interest, the broad notions of strategy versus the gritty detail of structure, made before.

As an example, we can compare the 1989 (FY90) DOD bill with the authorization. The bills provided identical amounts for the highly controversial Strategic Defense Initiative (SDI) and nearly identical provisions on mobile ballistic missiles. They contained very similar provisions on two major disputes between Congress and the administration that outsiders tended to dismiss as pork-barrel issues, the V-22 Osprey and the F-14D. On funding for the stealth bomber, the appropriators varied only on the technical level, reducing the allowance for spare parts by $82 million.

In all of these cases, controversy was so extensive that the issue was settled, in essence, by mobilization outside the committees. Results might be closer to one or the other's initial preference but the winning side made sure it won in both arenas.

The bills differed on a number of technical matters. Appropriators provided $70 million less new BA for the same number of M-1 tanks but allowed spending of $109 million in unobligated balances. They provided $3 million less for 420 Phoenix missiles and appropriated $796 million to buy 900 AMRAAM missiles, not 965. They delayed buying $202 million worth of components for the Seawolf-class submarine. In a number of other, less controversial cases, like the ATACMS long-range missile, there was no technical disagreement and the appropriations report matched the authorization. In neither case was structure changed in a dispute over strategy.

Yet substantive differences were large enough to affect strategy on some items that generated little interest outside the committees. Appropriators gave $1.49 billion for Apache helicopters instead of the $701 million the authorization provided for, two coastal mine sweepers instead of the three, authorized $600 million to build four cargo ships and two tankers instead of $35 million to begin designing them, and funded many items for the national guard and reserves. These are clearly different matters from SDI, a broad partisan issue, or the F-14D, a distributional issue of such size that the entire New York delegation was striving to influence both committees.

We can generalize that, on the really big issues, the result depends not on either committee but on compromise between Congress and the administration. Sometimes these will be settled in the authorization bill and the appropriators follow that agreement. Sometimes, as on arms control in 1986, the administration will not settle with the authorizers and Congress turns to the appropriators to carry on the fight. In the latter case the key subunit of the House was neither the Armed Services Committee nor the DOD subcommittee; it was the Democratic caucus.

The appropriators gain more influence, then, as the issue becomes more concrete (what is bought where) and less "strategic," easily related to policy goals. Their special expertise, program performance and management, is more directly relevant to structure than to strategy. Their power, based on the indifference of other congressmen, is greatest on matters of low controversy, particularly those that affect only one or a few districts.

Powers of the Purse

To what extent, then, can the Appropriations Committees, or Congress working through them, determine the policies to be pursued by the executive branch? The answer depends on some of the same factors that allow the appropriators to prevail in conflicts with the authorizers, particularly, whether the issue can be reduced to a concrete funding decision. There is even an executive branch analogy to the question of whether the authorizers or appropriators can win support on the floor. Conflicts rarely reach the level at which the president, with a strong personal preference, will battle Congress. Usually some aspect of the executive and some part of Congress conflict, and then support from the rest of their establishments is important. Appropriators often expect to find executive allies. Asked whether instructions are normally followed, a subcommittee clerk replied, "Sure they'll do it. *Someone* there wants to!"

Issues of executive-legislative conflict encompass some dimensions of the legislature's influence. Congress must be concerned with whether the executive follows instructions or if it can prevent implementation of instructions through use of the veto. This section argues that, to the extent that an instruction can be made to depend on resource allocation, Congress has the upper hand.

But a focus on executive-legislative conflict distorts the question of policy influence. First, it ignores the multidimensional aspects of policy. Often Congress or the appropriators balance concerns, accepting limits on some and having their own way on others. Second, to emphasize legislative-executive conflict is to underestimate the extent to which each branch is constrained by larger societal forces.

Multidimensional Choices

Appropriators see most decisions as a combination of decisions. One aide illustrated how they favor some decision premises over others when I asked what kind of decisions are hard:

> All right. The B-2. Do you accept the notion of the triad? All of the senior military leadership does. All the people in the think tanks do and have. I don't. But the amount of time and information I would have to amass to fight that, the credibility I would have to achieve, is beyond my capability. So I have to accept the notion of the triad. Having done that frames my questions, and, from that, it's clear we do need the B-2. How many, I don't know.

He has opinions but on such a controversial matter he cannot enforce them. He thought they should build five B-2 bombers: "From the staff's perspective, if you're going to build them, build them fast." But, "once the decision for two was made in the Pentagon, there wasn't a prayer." If a program is controversial and budgets are tight, the Senate surely will not vote for *more* than the number the Pentagon requests.

The B-2 is an extreme case. On other matters, in which the subcommittees have far more flexibility, they balance policy, politics, and personalities. Do we want more main battle tanks?

No, that's for war in central Europe . . . someone wants you to fund ammunition for a tank that will be built in Lima, Ohio. You know they can't produce the ammo or the guns as fast as they want. You write back and say you will do what you can, but you do less cannons and ammo, and put some of them on M-181s. He has done his part. You've done yours because you use analysis to justify the level and can say why it's inadvisable to do more. . . .

Now what if you only have enough money to buy a hundred lots of ammunition, and there are two plants, and it only makes sense to buy that amount at one, and both plants have members on the subcommittee? You try to find something else they can make in the less efficient plant, so you can save money for the taxpayers by putting the ammunition in the more efficient plant.

Appropriators make decisions in many dimensions, some more and some less under their control.

It is impossible, therefore, to speak of the absolute power of appropriators, or of Congress, in an appropriations decision. Every choice is actually part of a long chain of choices, some made in the appropriations process, some outside it.

Yet we also should be aware of the difference between an absolute and relative assessment of power. On an absolute scale, the subcommittees' power is quite constrained. On a relative scale, as the persons who broker competing claims, they may have more influence than anyone else.

An observer made the point nicely in discussing David Obey's cooperation with Dante Fascell. Obey, he said,

wants a policy from the authorizing committee. . . . Appropriators make their living not making policy, but picking at it, and doing oversight. And there's a reason: that's the best of both worlds. They can never lose the power because they've got the money; but they don't get the responsibility. . . . The business of Appropriations is to look at the authorization, and look at the administration's budget, and say, "No, that one is a dog. Our investigators say. . . ."

The committees inherently are "second-guessers, and that is the nature of the business. They want to be."

The appropriations process gives the committees second, or rather last, guesses. After agencies propose and OMB adjusts, authorizers authorize (or fail to) and the president responds. After the appropriators themselves grill the agencies and outsiders, and propose cuts to force the executive to prioritize, appropriations conferees present a bill to the president and Congress.

The Last Move

Using their last move, the appropriators and their process of allocating resources can shape strategy in two ways. The first is direct. To the extent a strategy requires resources, it can be prevented by denial. Thus the Reagan administration was not allowed to make arms control more difficult by building antisatellite weapons. The second lever is indirect. The administration may have the means to pursue some strategy that Congress disapproves but it may refrain because it can be punished on some structural matter that it also values.

In Congress's attempts to control the administration, in spite of many difficulties, it seems fair to conclude that, to the extent that policy depends directly on provision of resources, Congress has at least a veto. Elaborate understandings for "reprogramming" military funds reflect this premise of congressional dominance: if the Pentagon did not believe it was supposed to obey the reports, it would not ask for variances. It would just make the changes, and that would be the last move.

The Veto

In principle the president may seem to have the last move, his veto. Yet the veto depends on the president being more willing than Congress to live with the consequences, and in defense and foreign policy that is rarely true. "We're in a different situation from other subcommittees," one staffer commented,

> in that the foreign aid bill and the defense bill, those are the two jewels in the president's crown. . . . So by and large they don't have the leverage, it's the other way around.

If anything, the president's desire to see those bills passed increases Congress's ability to exert the second kind of influence on strategy. It is hard to imagine Ronald Reagan having agreed to the Boland amendments were that not necessary in order to get other things he wanted.

The veto also can be used for only a limited number of issues at one time. Participants at all levels of the process, including OMB, agree that an administration can threaten a veto credibly over perhaps five issues on a normal bill. On DOD it may get ten or fifteen, and of course it can rally other forces, such as contractors, to pressure Congress. But participants assume that, if the president threatens a veto over too many issues, Congress, on a bipartisan basis, will get fed up. There are very few issues on any bill on which the president can threaten credibly to rally public support.[5]

Implementation

Rather than veto, the administration may stretch interpretations and present Congress with a fait accompli. Asked about bases in Honduras, a representative replied that "We supposedly have not funded permanent facilities in that part of the world." When I noted that he sounded skeptical, he responded that it was a gray area but "the services will shoot square with you . . . usually."

Yet, even in the black budget, Congress has leverage. Appropriators not only have the House Surveys and Investigations staff, which is laden with FBI types, to check up on the national-security community but they also have sanctions. As a Pentagon source elaborated, "If you disagree with the members who really care, you risk they will go public." That will happen if "there hasn't been a satisfactory conclusion" to a dispute, or if the executive simply defies what "the people responsible for it [in Congress] decided." So direct denial of funds is possible, and this power is enhanced by the ability to take revenge in the public accounts. Budgeteers agree that there is always something, in the office of the secretary or elsewhere, that a department or agency wants but cannot publicly demand.

Appropriations' control declines as structure becomes less important. Intelligence operations is a case in point. Here, the short-term deployment of resources is analogous to Lindsay and Ripley's notion of crisis policy, and Congress is at a huge disadvantage. One House leader was appalled when he was briefed about CIA activities: "After six months I said 'this is crazy, I can't do anything about these.'" Appropriators shunt the responsibility for operational oversight onto others in Congress. As one aide said, "We have no need to know the operational and don't want to. That is properly the venue of the authorizers." To staff members, at least, their jurisdiction is entered when someone asks for money—or when someone is shown to have deceived them on a previous request.

There is a muddy middle ground in which Congress can restrict funds in

---

5. Since neither side can live with the failure to accomplish anything, the actual power of the veto depends on the participants' perception of the likely reversion point if the appropriation does not pass. The normal, though hardly inevitable, reversion point is a continuing resolution at the current year's level. Given inflation, that really is a small cut. During the Reagan years, when the president asked for big increases, the current level would have been far worse for him than any likely compromise. As defense heads into an era of large reductions, however, a mere 3 or 4 percent real cut may look good. Under the rare circumstances of the 1990s, therefore, the veto may become more useful.

advance to prevent operations. But denial must be clear and violation visible. The Boland amendments, denying funds for the Contra war on Nicaragua, may seem to have been an example of Congress's weakness. Yet the need for secrecy kept administration efforts small (and perhaps incompetent), and the administration got into a great deal of trouble over very little money. The administration clearly did not feel it could defy the ban directly, and the Contras were maintained more by means of Congress fudging notions of "humanitarian" aid than by executive evasion of instructions.

The Difficulty of Forcing Action

While Congress has ways in which it can prevent, or at least punish, the administration for implementing a policy in violation of its instructions, it is much less capable of forcing the executive to implement a policy that requires administrative discretion. For example, it cannot force agreements with parties over whom Congress has little leverage or oversight control. That is true of most matters involving foreign countries. In such cases the administration may choose to fail and Congress cannot decisively assign blame.

Thus, Congress was able to use appropriations to limit the war in Nicaragua but not to create peace. Majorities could prevent ASAT deployment but they could not force President Reagan to conclude arms control treaties. The Military Construction subcommittees have long insisted that allies should pay more of the cost of basing U.S. forces in Europe but administrations more interested in limiting conflict within NATO have accomplished little.

In some cases the inability to conclude such agreements may be legitimate: the other nation simply may not go along. That brings us to the consideration of limits on the ability of anyone, Congress or the president, authorizers or appropriators, to implement policy effectively.

Joint Difficulties

All participants in appropriations politics face changing budget constraints and shifting public attitudes toward their jurisdictions. "Some years you can sell cuts in defense," a veteran aide shrugged, "and some years you can't." The assessment of relative threats, and thus the need for different types of weapons, are shaped greatly by the Pentagon and the intelligence community. Willingness to fund Israel is affected both by that nation's behavior and by skillful lobbying by its advocates.

Another limit is incompetence. Even on a purely structural, entirely visible item such as the army's Division Air Defense (DIVAD) system, Congress may be thwarted because there is no way to force the army to get something right. Nor would punishing the State Department for allowing the

Soviets to build eavesdropping equipment into its walls in Moscow produce a functioning embassy. Defunding a program does not help if the program's mission is essential. The problem of incompetence in the Philippine government and its misuse of U.S. aid would not be solved by cutting off funds but it would damage the U.S. mission of support for that government.

In some cases incompetence may seem to thwart Congress alone but it is a problem for the president as well. Even the most dedicated Reagan-hater could hardly assume that the president wanted DIVAD to fail.

All arms of the U.S. government are limited by public opinion. It is doubtful that the president, authorizing committees, and appropriators combined could convince the rest of Congress to fund big increases in unpopular foreign aid. Defense spending fluctuates much more than does domestic spending because the public's desire for and trust in the military have varied in response to events such as Sputnik, the Vietnam War, détente, Afghanistan, Iran, the procurement scandals of the 1980s, and now the collapse of the Soviet Union. The president and members of Congress try to shape these moods, as with Ronald Reagan's speeches and congressional publicity for spare-parts scandals, but they are only partially manipulable.

It is natural for legislators to assume that executive branch blunders, or contrary public moods, favor the president. Yet often both sets of political executives are in the same boat: neither's powers of the purse are sufficient to attain joint objectives.

Conclusion

The policy-making process is, indeed, one of "wheels within wheels." Neither the "little old Foreign Ops subcommittee" nor anybody else "set[s] the foreign policy of the United States." Yet the appropriators can delay presidential initiatives, kill (or at least starve) the occasional "turkey," shape the managerial or distributive aspects of structural policy, and significantly influence a vast array of middle-range decisions (such as the size of the national guard and reserves) that are not subject to broad partisan dispute.

There is little doubt that the Appropriations subcommittees on Defense and Foreign Operations significantly affect structural matters in foreign aid and defense policy. And, on occasion, as with the MX and El Salvador, Congress uses the appropriations process to assert its power over strategy.

The future of the appropriations process is likely to vary in accordance with the three main concerns of this chapter. Unless legislators suddenly develop immense cognitive capacity, or lose the interest in distribution that enables appropriators to win battles through sidepayments, the internal workings and authority of the committees is unlikely to change in any significant manner.

The balance between authorizers and appropriators, however, will continue to swing with the relative prestige and skill of committee leaders. Foreign Affairs and Foreign Relations have nowhere to go but up, and so they probably will.

As for conflict with the executive, the "new world order" seems likely to make both defense and foreign policy seem more and more like domestic issues. For instance, structure, in the form of what gets built where, will become a more legitimate (and pressing) concern as defense cuts shock local economies and the security rationale for spending becomes less convincing. As the nation turns even more sour on foreign aid, the president may have to defer more to Congress to get what he wants. On balance, the influence of both Congress and the appropriations process is likely to increase.

Yet increased influence relative to the president is not the same as making policy. It is hard to make recognizable policy without any guiding theory, and the collapse of the Soviet Union, combined with American economic insecurities, leaves politicians with few guidelines. The immense information-gathering effort of the appropriations committees has never been oriented toward providing understanding. The process will allocate resources but the effects may become less and less predictable.

CHAPTER 9

Congressional Party Leaders in the Foreign and Defense Policy Arena

Barbara Sinclair

The contemporary Congress, scholars agree, plays a more active and independent role in foreign and defense policy-making than did the Congress of the 1950s and 1960s. Though systematic substantiating studies are lacking, most observers would agree further that the role of congressional party leaders has grown as well. Certainly their visibility as critics and supporters of the president's foreign and defense policies has increased enormously. I will argue here that Democratic party leaders in Congress are more actively involved in such issues than were their predecessors of the pre–Vietnam War period, that they are more likely to oppose the president on such issues than their predecessors were, and that this new role reflects the expectations of their members.

Elected by the members of their party in the chamber, congressional party leaders are best understood as agents of those members. Their role is dependent upon their members' desires and expectations and these can vary over time. To be sure, aspects of the role of the majority party leadership are institutionalized; party leaders are expected to carry out certain coordination functions, particularly floor scheduling; and they are expected to play a role in vote mobilization. In general, members expect their leaders to assist them in passing legislation that furthers members' reelection and policy goals but to do so in a way that does not unduly constrain members in pursuing their goals through their own activities. That is, members expect both help in passing legislation and considerable autonomy of action and freedom from coercion.

This essay is based in part on participant observation (as a congressional fellow in the office of the House majority leader in 1978–79 and in the Speaker's office in 1987–88) and on interviews conducted with members, staff, and informed observers between 1978 and 1991. I thank all those kind enough to give me some of their precious time. I also would like to thank the Research Committee of the Academic Senate of the University of California, Riverside, and the Dirksen Center, both of which provided financial support for some of my many research trips.

Thus, party leadership always involves a balancing act. However, members' views of the optimal balance can vary over time, and as members' wishes and expectations change so does leadership behavior.

When Congress, in the 1970s, set about reclaiming some of its constitutional powers over foreign policy and national security, it explicitly vested new responsibilities in its leaders. The majority party leadership's changed role is, however, the result not primarily of its new legal responsibilities but rather of a complex of internal institutional changes interacting with changes in the political environment that altered what members expect of their leaders. Briefly stated, the House reforms of the 1970s combined with the adverse political climate of the 1980s—divided control and a conservative, confrontational president—made passing legislation satisfactory to House Democrats increasingly difficult. In response to their members' need for assistance, the majority leadership became more active and more central in the legislative process (see Sinclair 1991). Some of the most contentious issues of the 1980s were foreign and defense policy matters on which a substantial majority of House Democrats strongly disagreed with the Republican president. On such matters, those members expected and received help from their leadership—in passing legislation and in explaining their position to the media and thus to the public. Because Republicans controlled the Senate during much of the 1980s, House Democrats and their leaders took the lead in challenging the president on issues such as aid to the Nicaraguan Contras and arms control. With the regaining of Democratic control of the Senate, and especially with the election of George Mitchell (D-Maine) as majority leader, the House's dominance lessened. Senate Democrats also expect their leader to act as their spokesman, attempting to frame the debate to their advantage, and Mitchell has done so on a number of controversial foreign policy issues.

Because foreign and defense policy make up a larger share of the contested congressional agenda, Republican leaders also have become more active on such issues. Their role has not, however, changed in a major way; they usually act as lieutenants of the Republican president. Republican congressional leaders are, of course, also agents of their members. Since the president is the leader of their party, the congressional party leaders, in carrying out their responsibilities to their members, usually actively support the president. When their members disagree with the president on foreign or defense policy, the congressional leaders may well attempt to change his mind, and occasionally they will have no choice but to oppose him. But publicly embarrassing the president or reducing his clout by defeating him legislatively is seldom in the leaders' or their members' interest. Increased partisanship on foreign and defense policy issues, in fact, augments existing incentives for the Republican leadership to work closely with the White House.

When Partisanship Stopped at the Water's Edge

Franklin Roosevelt's long, activist presidency established the expectation that the congressional leaders of the president's party will act as his lieutenants in the legislative process. To be sure, as congressional party leaders are elected by their fellow partisans in their own chamber, they owe their first loyalty to them. However, during World War II and its immediate aftermath, rank-and-file Democrats generally took their cues on foreign and defense policy from their presidents, and their leaders were not confronted with a conflict. From the mid-1940s through the mid-1960s, when one party controlled both Congress and the presidency, majority leaders acted as loyal and largely uncritical lieutenants of the president on foreign and defense policy (see Albert 1990, 208–13, 263–64; Sundquist 1981, 103–26).

In the early post–World War II period, leaders of the majority party who served with a president of the other party lacked a recent model and had to invent their own roles. To a very large extent they, too, acted as loyal supporters—if not quite lieutenants—of the president on issues of foreign and defense policy. The widely accepted perception that in a dangerous world the president must and does play the dominant role (a view that came out of World War II and was increasingly accepted during the cold war) and a bipartisan consensus on the broad outlines of policy shaped the party leaders' definition of their role (Franck and Weisband 1979; Sundquist 1981, 120–23).

In return for support, most presidents of the 1950s and 1960s apparently did keep party and committee leaders informed but engaged in little true consultation. Even the oft-cited instance of Eisenhower consulting with the congressional leadership about involvement in Vietnam in 1954 may have involved less real consultation than is often portrayed (Sundquist 1981, 113–14). Nor did the leaders expect true consultation if that implied a voice in decisions. In 1962, in response to President Kennedy's sending fifteen thousand troops to train the Vietnamese army, Senate Majority Leader Mike Mansfield (D-Mont.) praised Kennedy—and Eisenhower also—for keeping Congress informed. But, he added, "it is the President's responsibility to decide and to act. It is ours to advise . . . and, to the extent it is constitutionally required, to consent." Congress should not

> look over the President's shoulder 24 hours of a day and . . . tell him how to conduct the foreign policy of the United States. That is the President's responsibility. . . . It is in the Nation's interest that he be supported in exercising it. It will be a disservice to the Nation . . . to impede him, for whatever reason, in exercising it. (quoted in Sundquist 1981, 121)

The Breakdown of Consensus

The Vietnam War destroyed the foreign policy consensus. Seemingly interminable, unwinnable, and in the eyes of some immoral, the war eroded the confidence most elites had in the presidency as the font of foreign policy wisdom. Consequently, the basis for the extreme congressional deference to the presidency in foreign and defense policy was undermined. Over time, opposition to the Vietnam War led many to reassess the direction of U.S. foreign and defense policy more generally. Assumptions that had been widely accepted came to be questioned and previously noncontroversial decisions provoked heated conflict. The size of the military budget, the need for a wide variety of expensive and deadly weapons systems, and U.S. aid to repressive regimes were brought into question (see Sinclair 1982).

The Senate was the locus of early congressional opposition to the Vietnam War. As early as March 1964, two Democratic senators demanded total U.S. withdrawal from Indochina and, in early 1966, Senate Foreign Relations Committee chairman J. William Fulbright (D-Ark.), who had managed the Gulf of Tonkin Resolution on the Senate floor, became an outspoken critic and held televised hearings on the war.

By 1966, Senate Majority Leader Mike Mansfield also had become a public opponent of the war. Public opposition by a top party leader to a central foreign policy of a president of his party was, certainly, a break with the prevalent pattern. And President Lyndon Johnson was not at all pleased. Yet Mansfield expressed his opposition to the war in his role as an individual senator and not as a party leader. Precedents for such a distinction and such behavior did exist. In the 1950s, William Knowland (R-Calif.) moved from the front-and-center desk he occupied as Republican leader to another position in the chamber in order to criticize Eisenhower's foreign policy. During Johnson's presidency, Mansfield left the lead opposition role to others, to Fulbright particularly. In his capacity as majority leader, he sometimes aided the administration on the Senate floor, offering a compromise amendment to head off a stronger antiwar amendment, for example (*Congressional Quarterly Almanac 1967,* 207).

The House Democratic leadership, in contrast, steadfastly supported the Johnson administration's Vietnam policy. It largely prevented floor votes on Vietnam policy—an easy matter in the days before recorded teller votes on amendments. But increasing numbers of House Democrats were beginning to have doubts about administration policy. As early as 1966, seventy-eight of them expressed their uneasiness in a letter to the president (*Congressional Quarterly Almanac 1966,* 392). The growing split among Democratic members seems to have had no impact upon the leadership's stance; certainly it did not weaken the leaders' support for the president. Making a relatively rare floor speech in support of a bill authorizing funding for the war, Speaker John McCormack (D-Mass.) said that the vote would "convey to the . . . enemy and also the rest of the world that America is united" (*Congressional Quarterly Almanac 1966*, 392).

The election of Richard Nixon as president brought with it divided control and increased conflict on domestic issues. Conflict over the Vietnam War continued and, in the wake of the bombing of Cambodia, intensified. More and more, debate revolved not just around Vietnam policy per se but around questions of presidential and congressional powers and prerogatives in foreign and national security policy. Nixon's attempt to impose his domestic policy priorities by administrative fiat, especially impoundment, when he could not prevail in the Democratic-controlled Congress, generated among members an intensified concern about the loss of congressional prerogatives to the executive.

This concern about the shifting balance of power between the president and Congress contributed to the transformation Congress underwent in the 1970s (see Sinclair 1991). Personal and committee staffs were enormously expanded, making members of Congress much less dependent upon the executive branch for information and greatly enhancing members' and committees' independent legislative capabilities. Support services were expanded and strengthened. The Congressional Research Service (CRS) and the General Accounting Office (GAO) were upgraded and the Congressional Budget Office (CBO) and the Office of Technology Assessment (OTA) were created. As a result, Congress gained access to expertise that was independent of the executive in a range of key areas. The Budget and Impoundment Control Act of 1974, which created the CBO, limited the power of presidents to impound—or refuse to spend—funds appropriated by Congress, a power that Nixon had attempted to expand. More importantly, the act set up a mechanism by which Congress can make decisions about the overall level of spending, taxes, and the deficit as well as about spending priorities. This made it possible for Congress to challenge the president's recommendations in a comprehensive rather than a piecemeal manner.

The appearance on the Washington scene of increasing numbers of interest groups—and of some new think tanks as well—with a central interest in issues of foreign and defense policy also increased Congress's capacity for independent decision making in these areas by providing another source of information. Of course, the existence of these groups also provided an incentive for members of Congress to involve themselves in such issues.

As Congress reasserted itself in foreign and defense policy-making, it created a variety of new processes and structures (Blechman 1990b, 9–20). The War Powers Resolution of 1973 required the president to consult with and report to Congress concerning the introduction of U.S. armed forces into hostilities and stipulated that unless Congress approves the use of force within a specified time the president must terminate it. Via the 1974 Nelson amendment and the 1976 Arms Export Control Act, Congress gave itself the power to veto arms sales proposed by the president (Blechman 1990b, 113). The Senate in 1976 and the House in 1977 established Intelligence Committees to oversee the activities, including covert operations, of the intelligence agencies; the CIA was required to notify Congress of covert operations (Blechman 1990b, 13).

The War Powers Resolution requires the president to report to the Speaker of the House and the president pro tempore of the Senate. The legislation setting up the Senate Intelligence Committee made the Senate majority and minority leaders members ex officio and gave them the power to appoint seven of the committee's fifteen members. The Speaker appoints the chair and the majority party members of the House Intelligence Committee; the majority leader and the minority leader serve as nonvoting members ex officio.

In Congress's reassertion of its authority over foreign and defense policy, the House Democratic leadership did not play a lead role. When control of the presidency passed to the Republican party, the top Democratic leaders continued to support the president's Vietnam policy and employed their procedural powers and their prestige on its behalf. In 1970, for example, any real debate and a vote on the Cooper-Church amendment was blocked through the use of a procedural ploy (*Congressional Quarterly Almanac 1970*, 947–48). Presumably the leaders believed Nixon's policy was correct; however, their support was clearly, and perhaps predominately, predicated upon the assumed necessity of presidential supremacy in foreign and defense policy. Opposing an antiwar amendment on the House floor in 1971, Speaker Carl Albert (D-Okla.) argued against tying the president's hands in any way (*Congressional Quarterly Almanac 1971*, 310–11).

In 1971 and 1972, a majority of Democrats repeatedly opposed their party leadership on Vietnam-related votes. When, in 1971, the party leaders blocked a direct vote on the Mansfield amendment via the use of parliamentary rules, Democrats voted 160 to 76 against them (*Congressional Quarterly Almanac 1971*, 324). In 1972, the Democratic Caucus, by vote, requested the Foreign Affairs Committee to report an end-the-war bill. When the committee did so as part of a foreign aid bill, both Speaker Albert and Majority Leader Hale Boggs (D-La.) voted to drop that provision despite pressure from their membership (*Congressional Quarterly Almanac 1972*, 470). In 1973, Speaker Albert switched his position. The new Democratic Steering and Policy Committee, on an 18 to 3 vote, supported an amendment cutting off funds for the war. The Democratic Caucus voted its support by a vote of 144 to 22. The House passed the amendment (*Congressional Quarterly Almanac 1973*, 95–99).

Speaker Albert simply may have changed his mind. However, opposition to his position by a clear majority of his members, and the new availability of arenas—the Steering and Policy Committee, the reactivated caucus—in which rank-and-file members could make their views clear and potentially hold their leaders accountable, seem likely to have influenced Albert's switch.

Institutional Reform, Political Adversity, and the Changing Role of the Party Leadership

Concern about presidential encroachments upon congressional powers in foreign and defense policy was only one of a complex of motives that sparked the congressional reforms, and new processes and structures in the foreign and defense policy areas were only a small part of the institutional alterations that resulted.

Policy-related dissatisfactions were the initial motivating force behind the reform movement in the House. Liberals complained that the seniority system and the committee assignment process resulted in committee chairmen and the membership of the most important committees being unrepresentatively conservative. And no procedure or forum for holding chairmen or committee majorities responsible to the party majority existed. Between the late 1960s and the mid-1970s, reformers, most of whom were northern liberals, made a series of changes intended to enhance the responsiveness of the House legislative process to the policy preferences of party majorities. The chairmen of committees and the appropriations subcommittees were required to win majority approval in the Democratic Caucus in order to hold their positions. A provision for regular meetings of the caucus provided a forum in which rank-and-file members could express their views to Democratic committee contingents and the leadership. The committee assignment function was shifted from Ways and Means to the new Steering and Policy Committee, which the Speaker chairs and a number of whose members he appoints. The Speaker was granted the right to nominate all Democratic members and the chairman of the Rules Committee subject only to ratification by the caucus, thus giving the leadership true control over the scheduling of legislation for the floor.

In addition to policy dissatisfactions, desires to increase rank-and-file members' opportunities for meaningful participation in the legislative process motivated the reform movement. In an effort to spread positions of influence, members were limited to chairing no more than one subcommittee each. The subcommittee bill of rights removed from committee chairmen the power to appoint subcommittee chairmen and gave it to the Democratic Caucus of the committee; it guaranteed subcommittees automatic referral of legislation and adequate budget and staff. The supply of resources available to Congress and its members, most importantly staff, was expanded and distributed much more broadly among members. The institution of the recorded teller vote in the Committee of the Whole changed the dynamics of the floor stage, increasing the incentives for offering amendments and often for opposing the committee's position. Sunshine reforms opened up most committee markups and conference committee meetings to the media and the public, encouraging members to use those forums for grandstanding as well as for policy entrepreneurship.

By the mid-1970s, the reforms had transformed the legislative process in the House. Increased participation by rank-and-file members at both the committee and the floor stage, the growing attractiveness of the free-lance entrepreneurial style, and large numbers of inexperienced subcommittee chairmen multiplied the number of significant actors and radically increased uncertainty. The large number of amendments offered on the floor and pushed to a roll call vote was a particular problem, threatening to fundamentally change or altogether unravel legislation (see S. Smith 1989a, 15–48). Although the reforms had granted the party leadership new powers, policy splits among Democrats and members' desires to participate extensively in the legislative process constrained their use. Initially leery of exploiting their new leverage, the majority leaders over time began to develop coalition-building strategies appropriate to the changed circumstances. By including large numbers of rank-and-file members in the coalition-building process, leaders got the help they so badly needed and gave those members the opportunity for participation that they sought (see Sinclair 1983, 1991).

If the reforms complicated coalition building for the majority party in the 1970s, the combination of the reforms and the adverse political climate of the 1980s made passing legislation favored by majority Democrats exceedingly difficult. With a conservative, confrontational, opposition party president in the White House, a Senate also controlled by the other party, and, as the decade wore on, huge and recalcitrant budget deficits, Democratic committee contingents, committee leaders, and the membership badly needed help in passing satisfactory legislation. The new powers given to the leadership during the reform period made them capable of providing significant assistance. The leadership's control of the Rules Committee allows it, if supported by a majority, to determine the ground rules under which legislation is considered on the floor. It thereby can shape floor choices (by specifying that certain amendments will and others will not be allowed, for example). Increasingly, Democrats were not only willing to allow their leaders to make aggressive use of their powers but expected them to do so.

The caucus and the expanded whip system provide forums in which rank-and-file members can convey their views to, and exert pressure on, committee and party leaders. The caucus meets monthly, it can be convened for a special meeting upon petition by fifty members, and it can, though it seldom does, instruct committees or party leaders. The whip system, which now includes approximately 40 percent of the Democratic membership, meets weekly. Intense member sentiment, as expressed in one or both of these forums, can serve as a spur to leadership involvement in a specific legislative battle and can also provide the leadership with considerable leverage should the relevant committee be inclined to be less than cooperative.

The pressure for greater leadership involvement and legislative aid did not come only from the rank and file, however. To be considered influential, committee and subcommittee chairmen need to pass their legislation; in the adverse climate of the 1980s and continuing into the 1990s, they often need the leadership's help to do so. When, as is now frequently the case, legislation is referred to more than one committee, leadership coordination, and often the brokering of compromises, may be needed to get legislation to the floor. To increase the chances of floor success, party leaders can help committee leaders by getting them a favorable rule, by providing information through a whip count, and, when necessary, by orchestrating an elaborate vote-mobilization effort through the whip system.

The party's increased ideological homogeneity—a result of a change in southern Democrats' electoral constituencies and a shrinking of the feasible issue space in a conservative era—was very likely a prerequisite to the emergence of a highly active leadership centrally involved in the policy process (on the trend in party cohesion, see Rohde 1988).

After 1982, the voting cohesion of House Democrats began to increase. By the late 1980s, it reached levels unprecedented in the post–World War II era. For the period 1951 through 1970, House Democrats' average party unity score was 78 percent; this fell to 74 percent for the period 1971–82. After the 1982 election, the scores began rising and averaged 86 percent for the period 1983–91. During this same period, the proportion of roll calls on which a majority of Democrats voted against a majority of Republicans also increased, averaging 55 percent compared with 37 percent during the 1971–82 period. As policy differences among Democrats declined, so did fears that the exercise of strong leadership would pose a threat to individual members' policy or reelection goals.

As Democrats became more cohesive and their leadership became stronger, the role of House Republicans shrank. Because the House is a majority-rule chamber, as long as the majority party commands a floor majority, the minority can exert little influence. When Republican House members opposed their president, they could embarrass him; when they supported him, they still needed Democratic help to pass his requests. The job of the minority leader, as Congressman Bob Michel (R-Ill.) interpreted it, was to try whenever possible to hold his troops together in support of the president and hope for enough Democratic defections to make the difference. The Democratic party's increased ideological homogeneity made that a considerably less frequent occurrence after 1982 than it had been in the 1970s. And the minority leadership lacked any significant tools for engineering the needed defections. After the Democrats regained Senate control, their voting cohesion also increased. Senate Democrats' party unity, which had averaged 75 percent over the period 1971–86, averaged 83 percent in the succeeding two Congresses. However, the institutional changes that the Senate had undergone in the 1970s did not include a substantial augmentation of the majority leadership's power. Senate rules that give great blocking power to individual senators force the majority leader to work with the minority leader to an extent unimaginable in the House. In the realm of foreign and defense policy, as in domestic policy, the Senate minority leader has more influence within his chamber than his House counterpart has, influence he usually employs to help further the common legislative goals of his members and the president.

To pass the legislation his members want, the Senate majority leader is heavily dependent upon his members' natural cohesion. He lacks the institutional powers the House leadership commands to structure choices so as to increase the probability of success. On the other hand, he does have some advantages in fulfilling the spokesman role.

Majority Party Leadership and Foreign and Defense Policy in the 1980s and 1990s

The current, more activist role of the majority leadership on issues of foreign and defense policy stems, I have argued, from members' increased expectations for legislative assistance in an era in which Congress is more active on such issues and at a time when such issues more frequently split congressional Democrats and the president. Table 1 presents data that tend to substantiate these points. Over the course of the last two decades, foreign and defense policy issues have become a larger part of the congressional agenda of major

TABLE 1. Foreign and Defense Policy Issues in the House[a]

Years	Congress	% of Agenda Items	% Pitting 2/3+ Democrats vs. President	% with Major Leadership Involvement
1969–70	91	16	0	12
1975–76	94	19	22	0
1981–82	97	18	38	12
1987–88	100	23	67	78
1989–90	101	22	45	73

[a]See note 1 for definitions and coding.

legislation.[1] Were the period analyzed to begin before the Vietnam War, the trend presumably would be even stronger. The frequency with which these issues pit two-thirds or more of House Democrats against the president has increased enormously. During the first Nixon Congress, no foreign policy or defense issue produced such a partisan division; between 1987 and 1990, on average more than half did. And, as such issues became more partisan, the frequency of major leadership involvement also increased greatly.

The current role of the majority leadership on questions of foreign and defense policy primarily derives from, and is best understood as, simply one manifestation of the current activist leadership role, which, in turn, is largely a product of contemporary member expectations. Members expect their leadership to help them pass legislation that furthers their legislative goals. Increasingly they also expect their leaders to act as spokesmen, explaining party positions to the media, and thus to the public, thereby advancing their policy goals and often providing political protection. In addition, members expect their leaders to protect the institution and its prerogatives, and to do so without exposing them to electorally risky circumstances.

The forces that push party leaders toward involvement in issues of foreign and defense policy are not fundamentally different from those that encourage leadership involvement in domestic issues. How the leaders act and the way they explain their activities, however, are frequently constrained by the president's special standing in these policy domains. Congress collectively, members individually, and the opposition party leadership are much less reticent about challenging the president on foreign and defense policy issues than they used to be. Nevertheless, the president, in addition to his

---

1. *Congressional Quarterly*'s list of major legislation, augmented by those measures on which key votes occurred (again according to *Congressional Quarterly*) is used to define the agenda. This produces a list of legislation considered major by close contemporary observers. Some leadership involvement is distinguished from no involvement based upon answers to the following questions: (1) Was the bill a part of the leadership's agenda? (2) Did the Speaker or the Majority Leader advocate passage during floor debate? (3) Did *Congressional Quarterly*'s account report the leadership as being involved? If any one of the answers to these questions was yes, the leadership is considered to have been involved. Major involvement is distinguished from minor involvement on the basis of the mode or modes of involvement reported by *Congressional Quarterly*. Four modes are distinguished: (a) the leadership uses its control over scheduling, the Rules Committee, or some other procedure to advantage the legislation; (b) the leadership is involved in a floor vote mobilization effort; (c) the leadership is centrally involved in some other aspect of legislative strategy; or (d) the leadership participates in shaping the content of the legislation by talking or negotiating with or among the committee(s), or with the Senate, or with the president. Major leadership involvement is defined as engaging in shaping legislation (e.g., mode *d*) or any two of the other activities (e.g., questions 1 or 2, and modes *a*, *b*, or *c*). For details of the study, see Sinclair (1991).

other advantages, has special standing with the American public in these issue domains and the opposition party leadership, as guardian of the party's image, must take this into account in its decisions.

Furthering Members' Legislative Goals

When, on a contentious issue, a substantial Democratic consensus exists or the issue is of great importance to a significant segment of Democrats, members expect leadership help. Whether the issue is foreign or domestic does not affect the expectation that the party leadership will employ its resources to further their members' legislative goals.

Some issues that fall into the domain of foreign and defense policy have major domestic ramifications. Members of Congress are deeply concerned about such issues because of their constituency impact, their importance to key interest groups, and, consequently, their possible effect upon chances for reelection. Foreign trade policy has always had domestic ramifications but in recent years, as U.S. competitiveness declined and jobs in manufacturing were lost, constituency, interest group, and member concerns increased enormously. When Speaker Jim Wright (D-Tex.) made an omnibus trade bill the centerpiece of the Democratic agenda in the One-hundredth Congress (1987–88), he clearly was responding to his members' strong desire for action on the issue. The large number of committees that would be involved in drafting such legislation, the Reagan administration's opposition, and Democrats' desire not just to pass the legislation but to get credit for it as well all dictated early, continuous, and central leadership involvement. Wright met with the relevant committee chairmen at the beginning of the Congress to lay out a timetable and to plan strategy. Staff monitored committee proceedings and helped to work out conflicts as they occurred. Wright himself stepped in when that seemed necessary, periodically meeting with committee leaders individually and in groups, and keeping the spotlight on the issue in his many contacts with the media. The leadership orchestrated the elaborate floor effort and made the key decisions about conference strategy. Most Democratic members and affected committee leaders applauded rather than resented such intensive leadership involvement because they perceived it as necessary to the enactment of legislation they badly wanted.

Post–Vietnam era congressional activism extends will beyond issues with such direct domestic economic implications. Strategic policy, according to Lindsay and Ripley (chapter 2), "specifies the goals and tactics of defense and foreign policy." A major legacy of the Vietnam era was less consensus and more conflict among foreign policy elites, elected decision makers, and the attentive public about the goals and tactics of defense and foreign policy. With increasing frequency, conflict cuts along predominantly partisan lines.

On many of the highly contentious noneconomic strategic issues, interest groups are active, though these are primarily ideological groups. On such issues, as on those with direct economic implications for their districts, Democratic members expect their leadership to help them advance their legislative goals.

Arms control policy during the 1980s provides a good example. The early Reagan administration's rhetoric about the evil empire and the survivability of nuclear war raised concerns among many congressional Democrats and among segments of the public as well. The latter coalesced into a strong grass roots movement that advocated a nuclear freeze and pressured Congress to pass a profreeze resolution (Blechman 1990b, 84–87). For a substantial majority of Democrats, passage of the nuclear freeze resolution would have significantly furthered both their policy and their electoral goals. It would have put pressure on the administration to pursue a less belligerent path and it would have pleased an active and passionate constituency. The freeze resolution was brought to the House floor in August 1982, where it lost narrowly on a 202 to 204 vote, with Democrats supporting the freeze by more than a 3 to 1 margin.

After the election of 1982, in which Democrats picked up twenty-six House seats, the leadership and the chairman of the Foreign Affairs Committee put the freeze resolution on a fast track, bringing it to the floor in March 1983. Aware that they could not defeat the resolution outright, the administration and House Republicans pursued a strategy of amending it into meaninglessness. The Democratic leadership was active in vote mobilization but, because the initial rule for floor consideration of the resolution was an open rule allowing all germane amendments, defeating the Republicans' strategy required building coalitions to defeat what often were reasonable-sounding amendments over and over again, an impossible task. Floor consideration extended from 16 March to 4 May 1983. The leadership eventually went back to the Rules Committee for a second rule to restrict amendments. The freeze resolution did pass on 4 May with Speaker Thomas P. O'Neill (D-Mass.) making the final argument for the freeze proponents. It had, however, been heavily amended and it died in the Republican-controlled Senate.

Arms control advocates then shifted their attention away from the freeze toward attempts to require the administration to abide by various treaties, signed and unsigned (ABM and SALT II), in order to restrict the development and deployment of the Strategic Defense Initiative (SDI) and to place a moratorium on tests of antisatellite weapons. Instead of a free-standing bill or resolution, they used as their legislative vehicles the Department of Defense (DOD) authorization and appropriations bills. For their strategy to work they were heavily dependent upon leadership aid. The conservative Armed Services Committee would not include arms control provisions in its bill. Consequently, these would have to be added as amendments on the floor and, to do so, the leadership's vote mobilization operation and its control over the Rules Committee were crucial. Because presidents can easily veto the DOD authorization bill, for the arms control provisions to have a reasonable chance to become law they also needed to be included in the DOD appropriations bill. The party leadership could persuade or pressure the Appropriations subcommittee chair to include those provisions in his bill, and persuade the House conferees to insist upon retaining the provisions, with a much greater chance of success than could rank-and-file advocates.

In response first to the uncertainty wrought by the 1970s reforms and then to the adverse political climate of the 1980s, the Democratic leadership developed a sophisticated vote mobilization operation. The regionally elected zone whips continued to conduct the initial count of Democrats' voting intentions and an issue-specific task force drawn from the much expanded whip system and from other especially interested Democrats was primarily responsible for vote mobilization. Task force members refined the count and, when necessary, worked to persuade enough of their colleagues to attain a majority. In this effort they worked closely with outside groups and were supported by a small but highly sophisticated group of leadership staffers.

From the mid-1980s on, such leadership task forces worked on selected arms control amendments with an impressive record of success (see Blechman 1990b, 89–107). The decision concerning the amendments on which to work was made through consultation among the party leadership, House activists on this issue, and the groups that made up the arms control community. To a large extent the leadership allowed the latter two groups to set priorities among the large number of possible and desirable amendments, insisting only that the number be kept reasonable and that they all be measures that could command widespread support among Democrats. In 1988, task forces advocated seven amendments during the approximately two-week period that the DOD authorization bill was on the floor and won on six of them.

The leadership's control over the Rules Committee, and consequently over the character of the rule governing floor debate, also can be employed to advantage legislation it favors. In recent years, the DOD authorization bill has been considered under extremely complex rules that give many members an opportunity to offer amendments but also confer a strategic advantage on a politically adept floor manager, an advantage that committee chair Les Aspin (D-Wis.) has employed to promote arms control amendments advocated by leadership task forces.

The rule for consideration of the defense authorization bill in the spring of 1987 is a case in point. After the Armed Services Committee reported the bill, about four hundred floor amendments were proposed. If the Rules Committee had granted a simple open rule allowing all germane amendments, floor consideration would have gone on for weeks, with totally unpredictable legislative results. The rule allowed about two hundred amendments, set time limits for various of them, and specified, or gave the committee chairman the discretion to specify, the order in which they were to be considered. The decisions on order provided important strategic opportunities to structure choices. "The House doesn't want to go on one tack for too long," bill manager Aspin explained.

> If it hits a couple of votes going left, the boys are then looking to tack back and go to the right. The rhythm of the place is important. You will want to structure a debate so you catch the wave. It's like surfing. (Greenhouse 1987)

The rule contained several "king-of-the-hill" provisions, which specify that a number of alternatives would be voted on ad seriatim, with the last alternative receiving a majority declared the winner. Clearly the order in which alternatives come to a vote was critical.

Debate on the defense bill lasted for two weeks, a long period for the House but almost certainly shorter than the debate would have been under an open, unstructured rule. Although 124 amendments were offered, the process was orderly and controlled, and the arms control amendments favored by the leadership were adopted.

The requirement that committee chairmen and Appropriations subcommittee chairmen be approved by majority vote in the Democratic Caucus gives the leadership leverage in persuading members to be responsive to party sentiment. Thus, conservative Bill Chappell (D-Fla.), who became chair of the Defense Appropriations subcommittee in 1986, was consistently, if not always happily, responsive to leadership requests in the arms control area, including such provisions in his bills and following leadership guidance in conference. After the House Armed Services Committee allowed all of the arms control amendments approved by the House to be removed in conference in 1985 (an action that contributed to the caucus challenge and near deposal of the committee's new chairman, Les Aspin), Speakers regularly made use of their power to appoint special conferees so as to protect House decisions (Blechman 1990b, 38–39; also see Lindsay 1991, 58–59).

During much of the 1980s, arms control policy divided the parties, and particularly House Democrats, from the Republican administration. It was an issue about which many Democrats felt strongly and one from which many also perceived a political payoff. It is under such circumstances that House Democrats expect their leaders to actively help them advance their legislative goals. In fact, the leaders responded, employing their resources on behalf of their members' policy aims. Legislation imposing sanctions on South Africa and the effort to cut off aid to the Nicaraguan Contras are other examples of the party leadership becoming deeply involved in nondomestic issues in response to member expectations that leaders will act as agents of the membership to further their legislative goals.

The dynamics that deeply immersed the leadership in the controversy over defense spending, while also fundamentally based on member expectations, were more complex. From its inception, the budget process in the House has been highly partisan and the party leadership has been deeply involved. In the 1980s, Reagan made use of the process to attempt to impose his priorities upon Democrats, most of whom bitterly disagreed with him. Reagan's early successes put defense spending on a sharply increasing trajectory and led to huge deficits that insured a continuing battle over priorities. In a context of scarcity, budget resolutions and the legislation required to implement them (reconciliation and appropriations bills) became more contentious and even more partisan. After the 1982 elections, when Reagan could no longer command a majority in the House, stalemate resulted. To pass the necessary money bills, the leadership resorted to continuing resolutions that incorporated all the appropriations bills into one huge package.

In the 1980s, then, a large proportion of significant legislative decisions were made in a small number of omnibus bills. Because of the large number of issues involved, and (in a context of scarcity) their consequentiality, committee leaders were not always capable of crafting such legislation and they were highly dependent upon the party leadership for floor passage. The necessary tasks of crafting compromises on the most difficult issues often fell to the party leaders, as they possess a coordination capacity beyond that of committee leaders. Even more important, when painful and highly consequential decisions about priorities had to be made by a small group of members, Democrats were more willing to delegate those decisions to their elected party leaders than to committee leaders. Thus, when budget summits became routine in the late 1980s, the key negotiators for the House Democrats were the party leaders (Sinclair 1989a, 1991; Palazzolo 1989).

Throughout the decade, a key recurring conflict in decision making on the budget concerned the level of defense spending and the trade-off between domestic and defense spending. By virtue of its central role in budget decisions, the House majority leadership was deeply involved in that conflict and influential in its outcome. In this area, the leaders clearly acted as agents of their membership, attempting to achieve results that a large majority of Democrats could support and that were defensible as party policy.

Framing Debate and Opinion

The long period of Republican control of the presidency led to another change in the role of Democratic congressional leaders. Members expect their leaders to act as spokesmen, enunciating and explaining party positions to the media, and thus to the public, and framing debate so that it benefits Democrats and their preferred policies. Reagan skillfully used the enormous media access a president commands to denigrate Democrats and their policy positions. Aware that their leaders' access to the media far surpassed their own, rank-and-file members demanded that they act to counter Reagan (Sinclair 1992).

When the parties differ on salient issues of foreign or defense policy, the spokesman role is problematic for congressional leaders. The special legit-imacy the president commands in nondomestic policy, the common belief that domestic criticism may weaken the U.S. position abroad, and the president's much greater media access (and consequently his much greater ability to explain his position and frame opinion) all make opposing the president on major foreign and security issues politically perilous. The party opposing the president can easily appear to be carping at best and unpatriotic at worst.

In order to protect the party's image, though not only for that reason, all recent opposition party congressional leaders, even while opposing the presi-dent's stance, have emphasized their desire for bipartisanship and the rarity of partisan splits on such issues. As Speaker Thomas Foley (D-Wash.) recently expressed it:

> But perhaps I could make one statement that I've made before and that I strongly believe, and that is that for much of the debates in recent foreign policy terms we overlook the fact that, in my view at least, there is a great and enduring consensus in principal foreign policy objectives in the United States and has been since the end of World War II. The Demo-cratic and Republican parties have had their disputes over foreign policy to be sure, some of them very heated. The example of our disputes over the Contra issue and the policy toward Nicaragua and Central America is an example, or our differences over South Africa and the sanctions policy could be mentioned. But they are exceptions to a general rule that Demo-crats and Republicans, Democratic administrations and Republican ad-ministrations, Democratic Congresses and Republican Congresses—the few there have been—have supported the notions that policy toward Europe, toward Japan, toward the great issues of the post–World War II period have been policies of large consensus. (Foley 1991,1–2)

Foley's oft-repeated contention that, in foreign and security policy, bipar-tisan agreement is more frequent than conflict is clearly correct. The bulk of such policy never becomes controversial at all. Congressional leaders of both chambers and parties provided immediate, strong, and vocal support for Presi-dent Bush's response to the Iraqi invasion of Kuwait. Support for the invasion of Panama and the overthrow of Noriega was similarly bipartisan.

With a few such exceptions, however, partisan conflict receives a great deal more media coverage than does cooperation. And it is in instances of conflict that the spokesman role assumes its greatest potential importance. In many such controversies public opinion becomes a critical battleground. Whichever side is most successful in shaping perceptions, and thus setting the terms of the debate, is the likely legislative winner. In the battles over Contra aid and South African sanctions that was clearly the case.

During the 1980s and continuing into the 1990s, the House Democratic leadership has worked to increase its capacity to play the spokesman role effectively. To the Speaker's daily press conference have been added special lunches with selected reporters and frequent appearances by the top leaders on weekend interview shows. A group of activist, media-savvy Democrats meets with the majority leader daily when the House is in session to agree upon a message for the day and to plan press-related efforts. Although members want their leaders to act as spokesmen, however, they do not thereby take a vow of silence. The problem of getting everyone "to sing from the same hymn book" is a perpetual one. Coordination cannot solve the problem when the party is split but when there is considerable agreement it can help. While the congressional leadership still cannot compete with the president on an equal footing, these efforts have modestly narrowed the gap. When external developments work in favor of the Democratic position, as they did on Contra aid and South African sanctions, the leadership is now more capable of amplifying the effect of positive developments via their media efforts.

During most of the 1980s, the House Democratic leadership was far more prominent than that of the Senate both as spokesmen and as direct legislative leaders. Republicans controlled the Senate from 1981 through 1986. Like the House, but even more so, the Senate underwent an institutional transformation in the 1960s and 1970s that greatly enhanced rank-and-file senators' opportunities to participate in all stages of the legislative process (see Sinclair 1989b). Unlike their colleagues in the House, however, senators did not enhance the powers of their majority leaders, and thus did not make them more capable of assisting their members in reaching their legislative goals.

Republican control of the White House nevertheless led Democratic senators, as it had their House colleagues, to perceive a need for their leaders to act as spokesmen. The Foreign Relations Committee chairman's lack of forcefulness as a counter to the administration may well have contributed to that perception. Certainly George Mitchell's election as majority leader in 1989 owed something to his colleagues' belief that he would be the most effective media spokesman among the candidates under consideration.

Although criticized by many of his colleagues for being overly cautious initially, Mitchell became the Democrats' most prominent spokesman on a number of foreign policy issues. In 1989, he took the lead in criticizing

President Bush's meager aid request for Poland and Hungary as well as his cautious, wait-and-see attitude toward changes in the Soviet Union and Eastern Europe (*Congressional Quarterly Almanac 1989,* 509). In this he enunciated the sentiments not only of his own party but of many Republicans as well. Broadly based criticism forced Bush to increase his aid request several times. Even so, Congress approved considerably more than he wanted. Mitchell also took the lead in criticizing Bush's policy toward China—the president's initial unwillingness to take a strong stand in response to the brutal crackdown on dissenters, his reluctance to guarantee asylum to Chinese students in the United States, and his desire to extend unconditionally most-favored-nation trade status (*Congressional Quarterly Almanac 1989,* 520; Mitchell 1991).

The Senate's special powers in the domain of foreign and defense policy, combined with the media's preference for senators over House members, gives the Senate majority leader an advantage over the House majority leadership in playing the spokesman role. Given that the Senate majority leader's institutional powers and resources are meager compared to those of the Speaker of the House, he must rely more heavily on that role to influence policy outcomes. To the extent that he can frame issues in public debate so as to advantage the position favored by his members, the meagerness of his institutional powers becomes less important. Doing so successfully in opposition to the president is, however, very dependent upon special and relatively rare circumstances. Thus, most of the time he is more limited than his House counterparts in his ability to assist his members in attaining their legislative goals.

Protecting Congressional Prerogatives

In foreign as in domestic policy, guarding congressional prerogatives from presidential encroachment is a duty that falls upon the leadership of the majority party. Members want their leadership to do so, though sometimes more in the abstract than in a specific instance. The leaders are aware that history's judgment upon them will be strongly affected by how successful they are in protecting the institution's power. Yet vigorous action to guard congressional prerogatives in foreign and security policy can be fraught with politically dangerous consequences.

Congress's attempt to reassert its war powers has presented the institution and its leadership with its greatest difficulties. Although it was capable of passing the War Powers Resolution, Congress has never been able to enforce its provisions (Blechman 1990b, 307, 167–201; Katzmann 1990). No president has conceded the act's constitutionality. When faced with situations covered by the resolution, but without the president acknowledging it, Congress has, for understandable political reasons, refused to force a constitutional showdown. In the 1987 case of U.S. military involvement in protecting shipping in the Persian Gulf from Iranian and Iraqi attack, for example, Congress, with the help of its leaders, strenuously avoided invoking the act (Blechman 1990b, 3–7, 184–87). By setting into motion the sixty-day clock, Congress would be required to vote on the continued U.S. presence, and, assuming that the president complied with the decision, it would have to share responsibility for whatever ensued. Given the Congress's inability to influence on a day-to-day basis the consequences of a big decision such as committing troops or forcing their withdrawal, the tendency to avoid such responsibility is understandable.

Iraq's invasion of Kuwait, and its aftermath, presented the majority party leadership with a complex strategic situation requiring a delicate balancing of its partisan and institutional roles. The leaders of both chambers and most of their members fully supported President Bush's initial response to the invasion. However, when Bush doubled the number of troops in the Persian Gulf after the 1990 elections, without consulting Congress, the criticism began.

Administration spokesmen argued that the president needed no additional authorization from Congress to commit troops to battle. Majority Leader Mitchell repeatedly warned that "Under the American Constitution, the president has no legal authority—none whatsoever—to commit the United States to war. Only Congress can make that grave decision" (*Congressional Quarterly Weekly Report,* 29 September 1990, 3140; 6 October 1990, 3240; 27 October 1990, 3630; 3 November 1990, 3709).

That Bush intended to go to war against Iraq became increasingly clear. Congress as an institution, and specifically its leaders, were thus confronted with an increasingly pressing but unpalatable choice. If Congress did nothing in this situation, it was clearly, if tacitly, conceding that the power to wage war had shifted to the president. A vote on whether to authorize the president to use troops, however, also entailed potentially serious consequences. A negative vote would likely precipitate a constitutional crisis, and it certainly would place responsibility for the consequences upon the presumably Democratic majority that carried the vote. Whatever the outcome, a vote would put members on the spot, and, unless it were handled carefully, it might severely damage the party's image.

The decision on a vote fell to Majority Leader Mitchell and Speaker Tom Foley. Their partisan and institutional positions generally, and their central role in the floor scheduling of legislation specifically, made them the ultimate decision makers, though, of course, they consulted broadly. "There was never a question of whether to have a vote, only of when," claimed an aide to the Speaker. Both leaders felt strongly that Congress had to vote in order to protect its constitutional role. On the other hand, Foley especially opposed an early vote; he wanted, he said, a vote members would interpret as a decision on whether or not to go to war and not in some other fashion. According to some observers, the leaders delayed the vote until the outcome was a foregone conclusion, thus avoiding a possible constitutional crisis.

By January, most members supported taking a floor vote. Democrats were, in fact, much more united upon the constitutional necessity for congressional approval than upon the substantive question of war with Iraq. Mitchell and Foley worked to ensure that both sides would get a full and fair opportunity to present their cases on the floor. Foley, for example, persuaded the leaders of the House Foreign Affairs Committee to report two resolutions rather than a single resolution supporting the president's position. Although the majority leaders in both chambers were unanimously in favor of continued sanctions and against granting Bush immediate authorization to use force, they repeatedly and publicly emphasized that this vote was a matter of conscience and that no party position existed. This strategy was aimed at reducing to a minimum any bitter residue from the inevitable intraparty split and at protecting to the greatest extent possible the party's image.

By means of their adroit balancing act, Foley and Mitchell at least contained the damage the Gulf situation could have done to the Congress, the Democratic party, and its individual members. Given all the forces that work against congressional influence on crisis policy, such a result probably represents a significant accomplishment. Certainly most of the Democratic membership was satisfied with how their leadership had handled the matter.

Policy Leadership and Its Limits

Members expect their leaders to employ the resources they have been granted to further their legislative goals. On foreign and defense, as on domestic, issues, leaders are expected to provide coordination and coalition-building services on behalf of members' policy aims. Leaders also are expected to act as spokesmen, explaining their membership's position to the media and the public. Members' and leaders' own expectations that the leadership role entails protecting the institutions' prerogatives sometimes dictates leadership action at least somewhat independent of contemporaneous member preferences. But do party leaders ever exert true policy leadership? Can they?

Speaker Jim Wright's involvement in U.S. policy toward Nicaragua in 1987–88 is an example of policy leadership that went far beyond the facilitator role; he seemed at times to be acting in opposition to the wishes of his membership. He was roundly criticized by the administration and its supporters for overstepping the legitimate bounds of his role. Thus, an examination of this instance should reveal the possibilities and limits of aggressive foreign policy leadership by congressional party leaders.

Over the course of the Reagan administration, the House Democratic leadership became increasingly involved in the controversy over aid to the Nicaraguan Contras as the issue became more and more important to a sizeable segment of its membership. For these Democrats, both policy and electoral goals were at issue. While they cared deeply about the issue themselves, a highly active constituency of peace and church groups developed around it as well. An informal working group evolved into the leadership-designated Nicaragua Task Force. Chaired by David Bonior (D-Mich.), whom Wright appointed chief deputy whip in 1987, this was a permanent task force with about seventy-five active members. It monitored events in Central America, it attempted to influence media coverage of Contra aid by disseminating the opponents' side of the story, and, of course, it carried out the mobilization effort on the frequent Contra aid votes.

By the summer of 1987, administration prospects of getting House approval for more military aid to the Contras looked relatively poor (see Brenner and LeoGrande 1990, 231). At that point an emissary from the Reagan administration came to see Speaker Wright and suggested that Wright join Reagan in developing and sponsoring a joint peace plan for Central America. The rest of the Democratic leadership and the great majority of other Democrats with whom Wright conferred feared that the White House was attempting to entrap the Speaker—that the administration would one way or another ensure Sandinista rejection of the peace plan and then use the rejection as an argument for more Contra aid. Wright believed that there existed a real chance that the Central American countries would agree to some peace plan. He consented to the joint endeavor with the administration.

After intensive negotiations between the Speaker and the administration, President Reagan on 5 August announced the plan. On 7 August the Central American leaders signed a peace accord based upon a plan proposed by Costa Rican president Oscar Arias. Wright immediately, repeatedly, and very publicly embraced the accord, making it impossible for the administration, which was clearly unenthusiastic, to reject it outright. The Esquipulas Accord specified a number of conditions that had to be met and set an early January deadline for compliance. During the fall, as various problems inevitably cropped up, the Reagan administration sniped publicly. Some believe that it attempted to undermine the accord behind the scenes. Wright did what he could to support the peace process. When, in mid-November, he met with Nicaraguan President Daniel Ortega, Contra leaders, and Cardinal Miguel Obando y Bravo, the mediator, Wright was subjected to a barrage of often vicious criticism from the administration and its supporters. Accused of infringing upon the president's prerogatives, of "taking on the role of mediator for the Sandinista government," Wright replied that he was simply attempting to act as a facilitator and not as a negotiator (Felton 1987, 2790).

In early 1988, President Reagan asked for renewed military aid for the

Contras, claiming that it was necessary to strengthen their bargaining position. Democrats opposed this because it appeared to violate the terms of the Central American peace agreement, which called for a halt to all outside aid for insurgent groups in the region. Fearing that approval would torpedo the peace talks, the leaders mounted an all-out mobilization effort and, on 3 February, defeated Reagan's proposal on a 211 to 219 vote.

To amass a majority, Wright had promised a group of moderate Democrats a quick vote on a package of humanitarian aid to the Contras. David Bonior headed a broadly based task force that put together such a legislative proposal. Although Wright and Bonior invited Republican and administration participation, few Republicans were willing to do so. Brought to the floor on 3 March, the package was narrowly voted down, 208 to 216, by an overwhelming majority of Republicans, who claimed it was inadequate, and by a minority of Democrats unwilling to vote for any Contra aid.

The "victory" scored by the administration and the Republicans was a pyrrhic one since it left the Contras with no aid whatsoever. When on 23 March the Sandinista government and Contra leaders signed a cease-fire agreement aimed at concluding their war, the issue of military aid was removed from contention and the administration and House Republicans in talks with the House Democratic leadership agreed to a humanitarian aid package that was essentially identical to the Bonior plan rejected in early March.

The final act in this drama occurred on 24 March 1989 when, after four weeks of intensive negotiations, President Bush and congressional leaders agreed on another Contra package, one that provided continued nonmilitary aid. Bush, in essence, finally and irrevocably abandoned the Reagan policy of attempting to oust the Nicaraguan Sandinistas by military force. In return, Democrats gave Bush sufficient nonmilitary aid to protect him—and their own vulnerable members—against right wing allegations that the "brave, freedom-fighting" Contras had been abandoned.

Clearly Wright's leadership went beyond what his members' expectations dictated. A speaker less interested in, and knowledgeable about, Central America, or one more wary of risk, would have turned down the administration's offer to collaborate on a peace plan. That was the advice Wright received from most of his Democratic colleagues. Yet Wright's actions throughout his involvement were aimed at solving a problem the Democratic party and many of its members faced, a problem acknowledged by the other leaders and many members. The great majority of Democrats opposed Contra aid but legislative success on the issue was fraught with the potential for serious political damage. If Democrats simply had cut off aid, they would have been held responsible for whatever ensued. Wright took a gamble that many of his members thought too risky but he did so to solve a problem they acknowledged and to attain for them a policy goal they highly valued. Had those two conditions not held, Wright could not have taken the activist role he did. Even so, the extreme hostility that his involvement provoked among Contra aid supporters, and the role this played in his downfall, may deter future congressional leaders from emulating him (see Berry 1989).

Conclusion

Congressional party leaders are now more active, more involved, and more visible on issues of foreign and defense policy than they were in the era before reform. But they are functioning as agents of an active and involved membership not as independent policy entrepreneurs. To be sure, unless a strong intraparty consensus exists, discerning their membership's position is not a purely mechanical exercise but involves interpretation and, consequently, some leeway. Sometimes the dictates of helping significant groups of members attain their legislative goals and the dictates of guarding the party image can conflict; in recent years, for example, trade issues sometimes have presented Democrats with such a conflict. In national politics, the protectionist label is clearly detrimental, and thus to be avoided. Many Democrats, however, take what economists label a protectionist position on specific legislation for compelling constituency reasons. Such conflict situations require leaders who can choose and offer them the opportunity to exercise creativity. When President Bush asked for fast-track authority to negotiate a free trade agreement with Mexico, Majority Leader Gephardt (D-Mo.) attempted to balance the dictates of protecting the image of his party and of furthering his membership's policy goals by supporting the administration request but only after Bush had signed a letter agreeing to safeguard the economic and environmental concerns of members during the negotiations. The dictates of protecting the prerogatives of the institution also can conflict with the dictates of furthering members' immediate policy and election goals and so may also offer leaders an opportunity to choose and to exercise creativity. Yet, even in such instances, leaders are acting as their members' agents, attempting to help them achieve their own aims not those of the leadership.

The issues of foreign and defense policy taking center stage in the post–cold war era are, by and large, ones on which members of Congress will want to be centrally involved. Some—trade, immigration and the defense build-down—directly affect their constituents. Others—global environmental issues, for example—have great appeal to policy-oriented members. The lack of a superpower enemy armed with nuclear weapons further reduces the credibility of presidents' favorite argument for congressional deference to executive leadership—that a united front is essential in a dangerous world. When they see a policy or an electoral benefit to be gained, members of Congress will not hesitate to involve themselves in the new set of foreign and defense policy issues. Consequently, party leaders acting as agents for their members also are likely to become involved.

What does the more assertive party leadership role mean for presidential-congressional relations on matters of foreign and defense policy? When the majority leadership speaks for and acts on behalf of a united majority, it will continue to be a potentially formidable competitor to the president. The leaders' strength derives directly from their role as agents of a majority. Consequently, if the leadership is backed by a determined majority, the president will be well advised to listen, to consult, and even to deal with the congressional leadership. The leaders themselves prefer, whenever possible, to work with the president. Opposition on foreign and defense policy issues always carries some risk of damage to the party's image, and individual members, who are often less sensitive to that risk, may be less inclined to compromise and cooperation.

Part 4.
Issue Areas

CHAPTER 10

Congress and Defense Policy-Making for the Post–Cold War Era

Paul N. Stockton

With the collapse of the Soviet military threat, dramatic changes in American forces and defense policies are inevitable. Congress is already contributing to that change on a piecemeal basis by altering the funding of specific weapons programs. But what of overall defense policy? How might legislators work with—or against—the president to set basic guidelines for restructuring U.S. forces? And how will Congress carry out those changes given the incentives that members have to protect defense-related jobs for their constituents? This paper examines the post–cold war struggle between the legislative and executive branches to formulate and implement overall defense policy (which entail assessing future threats to national security, deciding how much to spend in response, and identifying the basic characteristics that U.S. forces should acquire).

Lindsay and Ripley argue in the second chapter of this volume that on strategic policy issues, which involve the goals and tactics of policy, the president holds the upper hand because he benefits from a natural tendency toward inaction on Capitol Hill. This would seem to be especially true in matters of defense policy. Before the breakup of the Soviet Union, many analysts argued that legislators tend to ignore broad policy issues (e.g., Art 1985a, 1985b; Blechman 1990b; and Friedberg 1991). Moreover, even if the collapse of the Soviet threat has made legislators more interested in overall defense policy, the president has enormous advantages in formulating and promoting such broad initiatives. Indeed, Lindsay and Ripley argue that the president's greatest single strength on strategic policy is that he initiates it. Given these constraints on the role of Congress, why and how might legislators battle against the president to formulate overall defense policy?

I argue that, far from ignoring broad policy issues, legislators such as Congressman Les Aspin (D-Wis.) and Senator Sam Nunn (D-Ga.) took the lead in responding to the end of the cold war and formulating a new approach to defense in early 1990. However, President Bush created the opportunity for that congressional activism by failing to offer a sufficiently far-reaching response of his own. By examining how such "policy vacuums" influence congressional behavior, how Bush struggled to recapture the lead in defense policy-making, and how members of Congress generate anticipated reactions by the president, this chapter offers some broader conclusions about the interplay between the legislative and executive branches in matters of policy formulation.

Crafting post–cold war defense policies, however, will not automatically lead to their implementation. Many of the same analysts who criticize Congress for ignoring broad defense issues argue that legislators are all too interested in "pork," that is, in defense programs that provide jobs for their constituents and thereby help those legislators get reelected. Such parochial behavior could torpedo efforts to implement broad policy initiatives. This chapter argues that, while individual legislators have pork incentives for some programs, especially those crucial to the economic health of their own districts, those incentives are often inadequate to explain the behavior of Congress as an institution. Policy concerns can have a decisive impact on congressional funding decisions. Yet, so much room for policy disagreement surrounds the implementation of a post–cold war military strategy that continued conflict between the president and Congress is inevitable.

The first section of the chapter examines why legislators are usually expected to have little interest in formulating policy and far more interest in warping the policy implementation process in order to satisfy narrow, constituent-oriented concerns. The second section contrasts these expectations with the way Congress and the president have struggled to reshape overall defense policy since the collapse of the Berlin Wall. The third section analyzes how Congress is implementing such changes in specific programs vital for defense restructuring.

Defense Policy on the Hill

Writing before the demise of the Soviet Union, Robert Art, Barry Blechman, and other analysts argued that Congress rarely focuses on broad, defense-policy issues. As Art puts it, Congress looks "mostly at the details of defense spending but rarely at the big picture" (Art 1985a, 227; Art 1985b, 139–46). That assessment may appear surprising given the general growth of congressional activism and independence in defense issues over the past twenty years. Art claims, however, that precisely because Congress has devoted more time and resources to overseeing the defense budget, and has focused to a growing extent on controlling the details of that legislation, members have had less opportunity to address broader policy issues.

This skewing of priorities reflects the underlying incentives for congressional action. Art contends that few members of Congress address policy issues because it so rarely helps them to get reelected; their constituents pay little attention to defense strategy. In contrast, constituents care a great deal about getting and keeping defense-related jobs. Moreover, by catering to such "parochial" constituent interests instead of worrying about broader policy issues, members of Congress can improve their prospects for reelection. Blechman summarizes the result: "Congress continues to get lost in the 'trees' of detailed defense programs, losing sight of the 'forest' of broader issues in defense planning and military strategy" (Blechman 1990b, 27–28).

James Lindsay offers a compelling critique of this assessment. Lindsay identifies a number of incentives that exist for members to tackle policy issues. One is parochialism: to defend a favored program and attack rival initiatives, members often turn to policy arguments to help win broader support. A second incentive is ambition: policy issues can, in fact, help members get reelected and gain power within Congress. The third is duty: members consider dealing with policy issues a part of their job (Lindsay 1990a, 19–27).

However, these incentives may be strongest for congressional action on specific programs and relatively narrow issues (such as cost overruns) rather than for challenging something as broad and abstract as overall defense policy. Members might conclude that such big-picture policy issues have only a remote connection to the programs they (and their constituents) care about, which are more directly affected by funding actions on specific line items. Art contends that the Armed Services Committees began to adopt annual line item authorizations

> precisely because their members felt that general policy reviews were ineffective and put them at a competitive disadvantage with the Appropriations Defense Subcommittees, which actually controlled policy because they had the say over the details of spending. In short, annual authorizations were begun because policy oversight had failed. (Art 1985a, 241)

Arguing that this move away from policy oversight had led Congress too far from its responsibilities for the big picture, Sam Nunn, chair of the Senate Armed Services Committee, began attempting to focus greater congressional attention on overall defense policy in the mid-1980s. But the perceived irrelevance of such oversight efforts persisted. A former staff member recalls that, although the committee hearings on strategy were "cogent, they have not had any impact on the system" (Mellor 1990, 127).

Even if members have an incentive to focus on big-picture policy issues, the problem remains of how to address them. Analysts generally tend to discount the ability of Congress to create an overarching defense policy of its own. Lindsay argues that members lack the time and resources to "delve into defense policies and programs to anywhere near the extent" that the Department of Defense can. He also argues that Congress lacks the hierarchical characteristics that allow bureaucracies to formulate such policies (Lindsay 1990a, 10–13; see also Heginbotham 1984, 251–61). That nonhierarchical organization makes it "virtually impossible" for Congress "to establish an overall military strategy and broad set of policies, and then derive a coherent set of programs to implement them" (Blechman 1990b, 55).

More important, Congress does not have sole authority over such matters. The president, as commander in chief, is in a unique position to propose defense policy changes and garner support for them. The president also is less encumbered by the sort of institutional constraints that plague Congress. With the more hierarchical structure of the executive branch, the availability of vast information and expertise in the Department of Defense (DOD) and the opportunity to use the yearly budget request as a framework for recasting defense policy, the president appears better positioned to formulate such initiatives.

A further advantage is that Congress (recognizing its own limitations) often defers to the president in setting overall policy. Senator Richard Russell (D-Ga.) offered the classic rationale for congressional self-abnegation in the defense realm: "God help the American people if Congress starts legislating military strategy." And, while legislators have displayed greater activism and independence on defense issues since Russell's retirement, Congress continues to expect the president to formulate overall policy. That expectation was enacted into law in the Goldwater-Nichols Act of 1985, which requires the president to issue a comprehensive, national security strategy report with each year's budget request, relating the threat and U.S. national objectives to defense spending, arms control, and other security initiatives (General Accounting Office 1991, 2).

However, formulating an overall defense policy does not necessarily lead to its implementation. Such policies can only affect the U.S. force structure if they are transformed into budgetary reality through changes in funding levels for individual programs. Thus, although the president is responsible for executing policy, Congress also plays a de facto role in implementing broad policy shifts by altering defense budget line items and making other detailed, legislative changes. But legislators have their own reasons for focusing on the details of program spending. Critics of Congress argue that, because legislators have strong electoral incentives to seek benefits for their constituents, they often attempt to increase spending on weapons produced in their districts or otherwise manipulate the defense budget to serve narrow, parochial concerns. This fixation with budgetary details creates a further impediment to defense policy-making. Congress is "sacrificing overall consistency and coherence of national policy for narrow interests and short-term objectives. This is a natural consequence of the political calculus that inevitably dominates congressional decisionmaking," that is, the need to "protect the interests of constituents" (Blechman 1990b, 21, 45).

Recent research suggests that parochial concerns are less decisive in driving congressional behavior than has been previously assumed (Lindsay 1990a, 1990b, 1991; Mayer 1991). Although members of Congress may have electoral incentives to win funds for defense contractors in their districts, the way defense contractors actually are selected limits their ability to intervene in that process (Mayer 1991). Moreover, once the contracts have been awarded for a particular weapons program, the spending for that program usually is concentrated in a small number of districts. Thus, while a few members of Congress will have strong incentives to protect the program, the vast majority of members will have no constituent interests at stake. And, even when members do have pork interests, they often vote against them (Lindsay 1991, 96, 111, 141).

However, legislators may find it increasingly difficult to ignore constituent interests in the future. As the defense budget shrinks in the post–cold war era, battles over which programs will survive are likely to become sharper than ever, exacerbated by constituent pressures to preserve defense-related jobs. President Bush attacked Congress for caving in to such pressures. In July 1991, after Bush proposed funding cutbacks for weapons he deemed unnecessary, he denounced the House of Representatives for parochialism in rejecting those cuts and called for a budget that "defends people, not pork" (*Defense Daily* 1991b). Congressional parochialism may become still more pronounced as presidents attempt to portion out further spending reductions. For example, when President Bush attempted in 1992 to rescind funding for Seawolf submarine construction in Connecticut, Senator Christopher Dodd (D-Conn.) and other members of his state's delegation fought tooth and nail against the cuts (McGrory 1992).

These critiques of Congress suggest two related hypotheses about the making of overall defense policy in the 1990s. First, because of the electoral incentives to focus on narrow, constituent interests, the organizational constraints on congressional policy-making, and the advantages held by the president in policy formulation, Congress will play no more than a minor role in crafting such overall policy. But those same electoral incentives will drive Congress to manipulate (and distort) the program funding changes essential for carrying out a new defense strategy. While Congress will ignore policy formulation, it will pay all too much attention to policy implementation.

Formulating a New Approach to Defense

The process by which Congress and President Bush hammered out the defense budget for fiscal year 1991—the first budget following the collapse of the Berlin Wall—offers a preliminary basis for testing these hypotheses. When

President Bush submitted his budget request for FY91 in January 1990, he said that the request was intended to be "a defense budget that begins the transition to a restructured military. . . ." (Nunn 1990b, S 2967). However, when Secretary of Defense Dick Cheney testified in support of that request on Capitol Hill, he noted that the budget largely continued past policies. Cheney stated that, despite the changes in Eastern Europe and the Soviet Union, Soviet military power remained formidable (Cheney 1990b, i–ii). Furthermore, in the face of uncertainty surrounding the decline of the cold war, Cheney testified that this was "the worst possible time to contemplate changes in defense strategy" (Nunn 1990b, S 2967).

Cheney's stance provoked sharp criticism on Capitol Hill. Almost immediately, members began calling for a thorough revision of defense policy—and specifying what they thought the new U.S. military strategy ought to be. Prominent among these members was Senator Nunn who gave a series of speeches on the Senate floor in early 1990 in which he assessed future U.S. security requirements and proposed "major changes in our military strategy" (Nunn 1990a, 1990c). Other Armed Services Committee members soon began offering their own visions of what U.S. strategy ought to be. Even Republican members such as John McCain (R-Ariz.) and William Cohen (R-Maine) called for drastic revisions of administration policy and issued defense budget proposals to carry out their reassessment of U.S. strategy (Dewar 1990).

This congressional drive for a new approach to defense quickly moved beyond rhetoric. After attacking the testimony of Cheney and other defense officials in a series of defense policy hearings, the House and Senate Armed Services Committees began in the spring of 1990 to draft their own versions of the defense budget. Differences soon emerged between the two committee "marks," with Nunn pushing for smaller cuts than did Congressman Les Aspin, chair of the House Armed Services Committee. Nevertheless, the defense authorization bills that emerged from the two committees reflected a different sense of program spending priorities (and lower overall spending levels) than those proposed by the president.

Members of Congress were not alone in pressing for change. Despite Cheney's public dismissal of the need to rethink U.S. defense strategy, a number of officials in the Bush administration and DOD already were carrying out such a reappraisal in early 1990. The internal administration disagreement over the need for policy change became public in March 1990 when William Webster, director of the Central Intelligence Agency (CIA), declared that the decline of the Soviet threat was irreversible (Tyler 1990). The appearance of dissension in the executive branch, however, only encouraged members of Congress to press for change, particularly as Cheney persisted in defending the FY91 budget request.

One impetus for this congressional activism was the belief that, despite Webster's assessment, the administration was continuing to underestimate the decline of the Soviet threat. Nunn told his colleagues on 22 March 1990 that the administration's assessment of the Soviet threat was "rooted in the past," and that "the development of a new military strategy that responds to the changes in the threat has not yet occurred" (Nunn 1990b, S 2966). Aspin considered the administration's threat assessment so unrealistic that he commissioned one of his own, conducted by a special panel of the House Armed Services Committee. This report (from which Republican members dissented) found the threat in rapid decline and concluded that the "Bush Administration has been overly cautious, even grudging, in its appreciation of how the Soviet threat is changing" (Defense Policy Panel 1990, 12).

Congressional interest in the declining threat was closely tied to another Hill concern: reducing defense expenditures. The president's FY91 budget request, submitted in January 1990, called for $296.4 billion in budget authority for DOD spending. (This is formally known as function 051 of the budget; the administration requested $306.9 billion in budget authority for function 050, which includes not only DOD but also nuclear weapons spending by the Department of Energy and other defense-related activities.) Although that figure represented a 2 percent real decrease from the FY90 DOD budget, Cheney emphasized that no further cuts could be made without endangering U.S. security (Cheney 1990b, i–ii). That stand was immediately attacked by Nunn, Aspin, and Jim Sasser (D-Tenn.), chair of the Senate Budget Committee. Sasser argued that the decline of the Soviet threat should permit an additional $12 billion defense cut for FY91, with House Democrats proposing still deeper cuts for subsequent years (Rasky 1990a, 1990b).

Given this desire to reduce defense spending and reassess U.S. military requirements, Aspin and Nunn were rankled by Cheney's testimony that it was the "worst possible time" to consider fundamental policy changes. Nunn attacked that position as incomprehensible, and argued that the administration's defense policy was riddled with "big blanks." Aspin reached a similar conclusion, arguing that "there are new realities in the world, but no new thinking at home to match them" (Moore 1990). From this perspective, the Bush administration had created a policy vacuum by failing to respond to the end of the cold war.

That failure created both the opportunity and the impetus for Congress to step into the breach. According to Congressman Norman Dicks (D-Wash.), "Congress abhors a vacuum"; when the executive branch fails to offer a policy initiative that Congress deems necessary, legislators will do so on their own (*Defense Daily* 1991a). But why is this the case? After all, according to analysts who argue that Congress is uninterested in policy, legislators lack the incentive to address such issues because doing so usually is irrelevant to the process of getting reelected. The need for reelection cannot account for the push by Nunn and Aspin in 1990 to revolutionize U.S. defense policy. Both have safe seats. Regardless of whether their constituents care about defense policy, neither was at sufficient risk of defeat to be motivated by electoral concerns alone.

However, as noted in the previous section, Lindsay argues that parochialism, ambition, and duty also can encourage members to address policy issues. Incentives to pursue policy issues on behalf of parochial goals would appear strongest for particular spending programs rather than for overall defense strategy. Nevertheless, other incentives can exist for action at that broader policy level. One possibility is that members of Congress address policy issues because they believe doing so is part of their job. A number of members cited that motivation in justifying their policy initiatives in early 1990. Republicans and Democrats alike argued that, because of the absence of long-range policy guidance from the president, it was becoming difficult for them to fulfill their legislative responsibility to draft the defense budget (Pasztor 1990). Someone had to step into the policy breach and provide the necessary guidance. As Senator Nunn told his colleagues,

> The Armed Services Committee will meet our responsibilities to the Senate in the authorization process for national defense programs. In the absence of administration decisions on major program and force structure issues, the committee will have to rely on our own best judgments about changes in the threat and our military strategy, and the implications of these changes for the future structure of our military forces. (Nunn 1990b, S 2970)

Political incentives can also encourage attention to policy matters. Although the need to get reelected may not drive much congressional interest in policy, members have other political goals. Legislators may believe that addressing policy issues can make them appear more statesmanlike, thereby improving their chances for winning higher office, or gaining (or preserving) their power within Congress (Lindsay 1990a, 22–23). The latter incentive may have contributed to congressional activism in early 1990. During that time speculation arose that Senator Nunn was seeking an especially visible role on defense policy in order to consolidate his influence over his colleagues, and to position himself as a "super-Senator" akin to the status of his predecessor, Senator Russell (Rasky 1990c). Aspin faced a more urgent need to maintain his power within Congress. During the 1980s, House liberals twice attempted to oust him from the Armed Services Committee chairmanship (Towell 1990). With the end of the cold war, and the clamoring of House

Democrats for a peace dividend, Aspin's push for a defense policy revolution helped cement his leadership position (Morrison 1992).

That desire for a peace dividend highlights another key motivation for Congress. Despite the assumption that defense policy issues are usually irrelevant to getting reelected, such issues sometimes can attract enough public support to encourage congressional action, as occurred in the case of the nuclear freeze movement (Waller 1987). Public support for major shifts in the defense budget can gain special attention on Capitol Hill. In the early 1980s, when public support for increased defense spending was strong, members of Congress were quick to follow President Reagan's lead in boosting such spending. However, after the fall of the Berlin Wall, opinion polls showed unprecedented support for slashing the defense budget (Graham 1990). President Bush's FY91 request ran counter to this opinion surge and created a juicy political opportunity for congressional Republicans and Democrats to propose much deeper military cuts.

The President Strikes Back

Of course, members of Congress were not alone in recognizing the need to revise overall defense policy. Even as Secretary Cheney was defending the FY91 request and resisting congressional demands for change, a handful of civilian defense officials and military officers (led by Gen. Colin L. Powell, chairman of the Joint Chiefs of Staff) were secretly drafting a new military strategy for President Bush. Bush unveiled the results of that effort in a speech in Aspen, Colorado, on 2 August 1990, the same day that Iraq invaded Kuwait.

Bush called for changes in three key elements of overall defense policy: spending levels, the assessment of the threat, and the basic characteristics of U.S. forces (Bush 1990). The new strategy proposed cutting back the U.S. force structure by 25 percent by FY95, and reducing the percentage of Gross National Product (GNP) devoted to defense to its lowest level "since before the attack on Pearl Harbor" (Cheney 1991, ix). This spending cut was made possible by a drastic reassessment of the Soviet threat. General Powell argued that the "absolute, total demise of the Cold War" meant that U.S. forces no longer needed to be capable of fighting a global-scale, short-warning conflict (Powell 1990, 13). Accordingly, Bush proposed a major restructuring of U.S. forces. Those forces not only would be much smaller by 1995 but they also would be of a different character. Sharply downsized, regional forces would be maintained in the Atlantic and Pacific areas with a highly mobile contingency force created to fight what Bush called "come as you are conflicts" in the Third World (Bush 1990, 132).

Both the timing and the substance of this proposal offer some broad insights into the constraints on the president and Congress in formulating policy. Why was Bush so much slower than legislators such as Nunn to propose a response to the end of the cold war? After all, the president usually is thought to be better positioned to offer defense policy initiatives. He can take advantage of the more hierarchical structure and special expertise of the Defense Department to formulate his initiatives and he can use the annual budget request to launch them.

However, the budget request is difficult to recast in quick response to events such as the collapse of the Berlin Wall. The planning, programming, and budgeting process that helps shape that request is a complex procedure that takes eighteen months to complete (Art 1990, 29). Even if administration officials had wanted to rewrite the FY91 request in response to the Eastern European upheavals of late 1989, they would have encountered serious procedural impediments to doing so (General Accounting Office 1991, 1–10). Moreover, no consensus existed on the need for such a quick and dramatic revision. Although CIA director Webster declared in early 1990 that the Soviet threat was collapsing, Cheney and the joint chiefs disagreed with his assessment. And, while the services possess special expertise on military issues, they also hold strong positions on them, particularly in matters involving force reductions. Consequently, the president may find it necessary to bypass such organizations in formulating new policies. Bush's August initiative was drafted in the spring and summer of 1990 by a handful of civilian officials and officers from the Joint Chiefs of Staff; the army, navy and air force leadership was excluded from the process (Pocalyko 1992; Tritten 1992).

The disadvantages of Congress in policy formulation seem less onerous from this perspective. Although the president's budget request offers a once-a-year vehicle for proposing broad policy changes, the lengthy process by which Congress critiques that request (and drafts its own version of the budget) provides an almost continuous opportunity for new initiatives. The less bureaucratized structure of Congress also helps individual members take advantage of this opportunity. Legislators have greater freedom to propose sudden policy shifts without first having to go through a formal decision-clearing process that can give suborganizations the opportunity to impede or reshape such initiatives. Nunn and Aspin were less constrained by bureaucratic impediments than was Secretary Cheney. On the other hand, Nunn and Aspin lacked the in-house expertise available to the secretary of defense. The ability to formulate policy initiatives more rapidly does not mean that those initiatives will be better crafted. Yet, when President Bush decided that a new defense strategy was needed, he also found it necessary to bypass much of the expertise available in the armed services. The advantages of the president in formulating policy are less decisive than is commonly supposed.

While these factors help to explain why Bush was comparatively slow to offer a new strategy, the question remains as to why he pushed his initiative as *soon* as he did. Why did he not launch his proposal six months later, with the FY92 budget request, rather than jumping into the middle of the congressional budget process for FY91? Concerns about the difficulty of incorporating such large policy changes into the FY92 request might have encouraged Bush to make an early, and highly visible, announcement of his new overall strategy that would undergird that request.

However, other factors played a role—suggesting some broad implications about the power of Congress in policy formulation. Although legislators such as Aspin and Nunn attempted to reshape U.S. defense policy in early 1990 through direct action, by offering their own proposals and attempting to recast the defense budget accordingly, legislators also can affect policy indirectly by influencing the proposals made by the president. As Lindsay and Ripley argue in chapter 2, one potentially important source of indirect influence is framing, that is, raising the visibility of an issue with the intention of forcing it onto the presidential agenda or changing the administration policies associated with it. Congressional Democrats and Republicans alike raised the issue of overall defense policy to new heights in early 1990. Through repeated speeches, press releases, and committee hearings on the defense budget, those legislators excoriated Bush's "business as usual" FY91 request, and they highlighted the need for a quick and dramatic revision of U.S. military strategy.

Congress also can affect presidential initiatives indirectly by generating anticipated reactions in the executive branch. As chapter 2 argues, the mood on Capitol Hill determines which policy options are feasible for the executive branch; when Congress is strongly opposed to an initiative, presidents may trim their sails and revise (or drop) a proposal accordingly. Members of Congress went out of their way to attack the FY91 request as politically unrealistic and insupportable.

However, legislators often criticize presidential initiatives without any apparent effect. The key to congressional leverage in early 1990 was the ability, and evident willingness, of Congress to dump Bush's FY91 request and enact their own version of what a post–cold war budget ought to be. The policy-making train was leaving the station—with or without guidance from the administration. And, while Bush could have vetoed the resulting budget, any such veto would have done little to put his positive stamp on U.S. policy. Months before the president unveiled his August initiative, Congress made it clear that there would be a new approach to defense. The only question was whether the president would be a player and abandon his previous stand in favor of a more politically sustainable vision of U.S. strategy.

When Bush did just that, by offering the August proposal, his action highlighted some important powers the president retains over policy formulation. The congressional activism over defense policy in 1991 was spurred by the failure of the administration to offer a proposal of its own. But, if the president can create a policy vacuum, he also can fill it, and thereby shrink the opportunity and impetus for Congress to step into the breach. Bush's August initiative reduced the impetus for congressional activism on each of the issues central to overall defense policy: the threat, spending levels, and force characteristics.

The Bush proposal recognized the decline in the Soviet threat in a way that the FY91 request had not. Administration officials and the officers of the Joint Chiefs of Staff adopted a sharply reduced assessment of the Soviet threat, and in the months after the August initiative they defended it by citing the complete collapse of the cold war threat (Powell 1990). They also highlighted the claim that Bush's proposal responded to this demise with a "total rethinking" of U.S. defense policy. No longer could congressional leaders accuse the administration of ignoring the changes in the Soviet Union.

The August proposal also endorsed a sharp reduction in defense spending. In early 1990, Bush helped make it politically attractive for Congress to focus on defense policy because his FY91 request was so contrary to public-opinion trends favoring greater spending cuts. Bush shrank that congressional opportunity with his August initiative. By calling for a 25 percent reduction in forces, that proposal set the stage for the administration's subsequent "budget summit" agreement with Congress, which envisioned a cut in defense spending of over 20 percent in real terms between FY91 and FY95 (*Inside the Pentagon* 1991, 13).

Furthermore, the August proposal called for changes in the basic character of U.S. forces, with some of those changes addressing the same issues raised by legislators earlier in 1990. In particular, by emphasizing the need for highly mobile forces capable of quick response actions in the Third World, Bush's initiative was consistent with the demands for restructuring made by Nunn, Aspin, and many of their colleagues. This is not to suggest that General Powell and the others who drafted the August proposal did so by parroting speeches from the *Congressional Record*. They performed their own lengthy analysis of the problems confronting U.S. strategy, and they devised a number of proposals distinct from those of Congress (such as the requirement to be able to "reconstitute" forces for large-scale conflicts). Nevertheless, the August proposal was sufficiently consistent with the congressional demands for change that Bush further narrowed, and co-opted, the impetus for congressional policy-making. That co-optation was evident when Senator Nunn told his colleagues in September 1990 that Bush's new strategy "was very similar to some of the things I was talking about earlier this spring" (Corddry 1991, 6).

Yet, as Nunn's statement suggests, the powers of Congress and the president over policy formulation are bound together in an important respect. The president can fill the policy vacuum that otherwise would create the opportunity and impetus for congressional activism, and he can frame his proposals so as to co-opt that activism. But he does so at the price of giving his critics in Congress indirect influence over his proposals. When the president abandons his previous stance and offers a proposal that coincides with key congressional preferences, he can narrow the impetus for further congressional action but in so doing he gives his critics at least some of what they wanted. Co-optation and anticipatory response are two sides of the same policy-making coin.

Implications for Future Defense Policy Formulation

Two factors might alter this pattern of executive-legislative policy-making in the years to come. First, with the election of Bill Clinton the problems of "divided government" might be headed into at least temporary remission. In the battle over defense policy in 1990, a Republican president confronted Democratic majorities in the House and Senate. The partisan element in such battles might decline now that the Democrats control both the executive and legislative branches. However, the 1990 dispute was not motivated solely by partisanship. A number of Senate Republicans joined Democrats in attacking President Bush for not reformulating defense policy, and they offered their own proposals for change. Disputes over policy formulation emerge along institutional as well as party lines. Thus, the end of divided government will not necessarily prevent future legislative-executive conflicts nor will it eliminate the patterns of co-optation and anticipatory response that help resolve them.

More critical to the interaction between Congress and the president is the question of whether dramatic policy vacuums are likely to reemerge. Although Congress took the lead in reformulating defense policy in 1990, that activism responded to a rapidly unfolding revolution in world affairs. Such events do not occur every day. It may be that congressional behavior in 1990 stemmed from a unique set of circumstances, and that this uniqueness explains why legislators acted differently from what previous studies of Congress would suggest. How likely is it that an equally powerful spur to congressional activism will reemerge?

The policy vacuum in 1990 had three characteristics of particular relevance to this question. First, it emerged suddenly. The collapse of the Berlin Wall and death of the cold war were so rapid, and unexpected, that Congress could exploit its less bureaucratic structure to offer a quicker policy response than could the administration. Second, these events raised policy issues that were highly salient in terms of incentives for congressional action. Members such as Aspin and Nunn argued that they simply could not do their jobs without rethinking overall defense policy. And, with the possibility of carving out a reduction in defense spending, legislators had particularly strong incentives to address such matters. Third, legislators not only considered these issues important but they recognized a huge (and politically attractive) opportunity for substantive disagreement with the administration. Secretary Cheney's call for business as usual in the FY91 budget was a move profoundly out of step with many legislators' perspectives on the threat, defense spending levels, and the need for fundamental changes in the U.S. force structure.

The president could again fall into sharp disagreement with Congress in assessing the threat, thereby giving Congress fresh opportunities to formulate a policy response of its own. That possibility was highlighted by the failed August 1991 coup in the Soviet Union. While Aspin, Sasser, and other legislators argued that the Soviet threat had declined so much further that additional defense cuts were warranted, Secretary Cheney argued that it was far too soon to make such a judgment and that the president's FY92 budget request ought to be upheld (Gelman and Smith 1991). But, by the end of 1991, administration officials sharply downgraded their estimate of the former Soviet threat and minimized this impetus for congressional activism. And, while members of Congress may eventually attack the president for overestimating non-Soviet, third world threats, the persistence of regional instabilities and continued proliferation of advanced weapons (including weapons of mass destruction) could dampen such criticism. Indeed, if a dramatic shift in the threat again attracts congressional interest, that shift might come from an unexpected *rise* in the threat that will generate renewed support for defense spending.

Defense budget-cutting also will offer an uncertain impetus for congressional action. Despite the continued decline of the Soviet threat, Congress voted down every effort in 1991 to divert funds from defense into domestic programs by amending the Budget Enforcement Act of 1990 (which resulted from the budget summit). Such efforts were rejected again in 1992 (Hager 1992b). Even liberals such as Congressman Leon Panetta (D-Calif.) opposed additional cutbacks because of their reluctance to unravel the hard-won, multiyear agreement. However, other factors contributed to the reluctance of Congress to enact sharper defense cuts—factors that could endure for years to come. One is the effect of defense cutbacks on jobs. According to Senator James Exon (D-Neb.), who offered a key amendment to cut FY93 defense spending below the administration's request, senators rejected his initiative because they feared too many of their constituents would lose defense-related jobs, a fear that the administration encouraged by offering "an artful, emotionally charged, yet inherently dishonest snow job" exaggerating such effects (Pianin 1992). When President Bush attempted in early 1992 to rescind spending for weapons he deemed unnecessary for the post–cold war era, even liberals such as Senator Dodd fought to preserve the Seawolf submarine and other employment-producing programs (McGrory 1992).

If the U.S. economy expands sufficiently to create civilian-sector jobs for defense workers, this pressure on Congress to sustain military spending will decline. However, another potential constraint will remain on congressional budget-cutting initiatives: presidential co-optation. As Sasser, Aspin, and other legislators clamored for deeper defense cuts in late 1991, President Bush took the wind out of their sails by offering a surprise, six-year, $50 billion defense reduction beyond the cuts he had endorsed already (Schmitt 1991c, 1992b). Senator Nunn then decided to support the administration's request for FY93. And, while the House Armed Services Committee voted to cut more than $7 billion from that total, DOD officials declared that they were "pleased that the committee approved so much of the President's package" (*Defense Daily* 1992). As in 1991, presidential co-optation limited the incentives for congressional activism. Yet this co-optation also represents an indirect victory for those legislators who wanted deeper defense cuts. Regardless of the ebb and flow of congressional pressures to cut defense spending, the patterns of co-optation and anticipatory response between the president and Congress will persist, offering both sides powerful (if indirect) sources of influence over policy formulation.

Policy disagreements are most likely to emerge over the characteristics of U.S. armed forces. Although Nunn and other congressional leaders stated that some elements of Bush's August 1990 proposal responded to their policy concerns (such as the need for greater force mobility), other administration initiatives lie beyond this "protected" realm of congressional co-optation. Moreover, even if Congress were to accept the general precepts of Bush's strategy, gaps and controversies in specific defense policy issues are likely to persist. The future of naval aviation is a prime example. Under the administration proposal, carrier-borne aircraft will play a key role in providing the United States with mobile, flexible, striking power. However, because of cost overruns, mismanagement, and other problems, the service's top four aircraft programs were axed in 1990 and 1991. Senate Armed Services Committee member John Glenn (D-Ohio) and others have castigated the navy for its "atrocious" record in providing such aircraft for the future (Pasztor 1991a).

While Congress and the president will have plenty of room for disagreement over U.S. force characteristics, it is less clear that legislators will have strong incentives to address such issues. The future of naval aviation is an important issue but it offers far less dramatic appeal than the disintegration of the Warsaw Pact. And, while members of Congress still may hope to pursue higher office or other political goals by addressing big-picture issues concerning U.S. force characteristics, their opportunities to do so rarely will be as inviting as they were when President Bush appeared to ignore the end of the cold war.

Nevertheless, other incentives for congressional activism will keep force structure issues salient on Capitol Hill. To the degree that members continue viewing policy oversight as an essential part of their job, and as a prerequisite for fulfilling their responsibilities in defense budgeting, Congress will scrutinize even relatively narrow force modernization problems. It was in the context of naval aviation that Congressman Dicks warned that Congress abhors a vacuum and that the failure of the executive branch to exercise better leadership would spur Congress to dictate policy on its own (*Defense Daily* 1991b). Moreover, broader issues of defense continue to attract congressional attention. In 1992, Aspin issued a series of proposals to restructure U.S. strategic and conventional forces based on a "ground-up" rethinking of defense requirements (Aspin 1992a, 1992b).

Another possible incentive for congressional activism is more troublesome. Changing the force structure will require changing the sorts of weapons that the United States pays to develop and produce. The prospect of manipulating these funding shifts will attract strong congressional interest, as it did in the case of the Seawolf submarine. Critics of Congress argue that, because legislators have strong electoral incentives to seek benefits for their constituents, they often attempt to increase spending on weapons produced in their districts or otherwise recast the defense budget to serve narrow, parochial concerns. How valid will this assessment be in the post–cold war era? As the United States begins to carry out changes in overall security policy, how will congressional parochialism affect the implementation process?

Implementing New Defense Policies

The shifts in overall defense policy proposed by legislators and President Bush in 1990 involved big picture issues: slashing the resources devoted to military spending, reordering the perceived threats to U.S. security, and changing the structure and composition of the armed forces. But implementing these shifts in overall policy (those affecting particularly force structure) will require changes at the more mundane level of budget line items. Indeed, unless spending on individual programs is altered in accordance with overall policy recommendations, such policy initiatives will remain little more than rhetoric.

The need to shift spending on individual programs will create opportunities for parochial behavior on Capitol Hill. However, Lindsay and Mayer have challenged the assumption that pork barreling drives congressional behavior on defense issues. Although members of Congress may have electoral incentives to win funds for defense contractors in their districts, the methods by which defense contractors are selected limits congressional influence over that process (Mayer 1991). Nor do members always vote according to pork incentives. Particularly in the case of nuclear weapons programs, statistical analyses find that constituency benefits do a poor job of predicting how members vote, with legislators' general views on defense policy offering a much better predictor (Lindsay 1991, 110–11, 127–32).

Members are most likely to follow pork incentives when the electoral costs of opposing constituency interests are greatest, for example, when a particularly large number of constituent jobs are at stake, as in the closing of a large military base. However, most constituencies do not depend on contracts for a particular weapons program to the extent that many constituencies depend on military bases. Where a weapons program does sustain numerous jobs in a district, legislators who represent those constituents can have powerful electoral incentives to protect the program. However, the jobs for most weapons programs are concentrated in a very limited number of congressional districts. Thus, while a few members of Congress will have strong incentives to protect the program, the vast majority will have no constituent interests at stake. Members with constituent interests in different programs might attempt to "logroll," trading support for each other's weapons programs. However, Lindsay argues that "since the cancellation of one weapon does not herald the cancellation of others, legislators have less reason to logroll. They know that they can vote against, say, the MX, without jeopardizing, say, the F-16" (Lindsay 1991, 140–41). Individual members sometimes vote parochially; Congress as an institution is much less likely to do so.

While Lindsay predicates this analysis by stating that "DOD rarely lobbies Congress to discontinue a weapons system" (Lindsay 1991, 140), that reticence is disappearing. Under President Bush's FY92 budget request, DOD pressed Congress to eliminate thirteen major weapons programs and make sharp spending reductions in the national guard and other force elements (Finnegan 1991). Those cuts reflected Bush's initial effort to begin restructuring U.S. forces for the post–cold war era, which he continued in his 1992 spending recision-request and his FY93 budget proposal. Many more such cuts are in the offing. With the disappearance of the Soviet threat and the rise of new security concerns, the need to reallocate funding among various weapons programs (not all of which remain necessary) will intensify. The competition for money among these programs will be all the stronger because overall defense spending levels are declining. Some weapons in this battle for money will be winners; others, tied too closely to the disappearing Soviet threat, will be losers. And losing programs will represent lost jobs in congressional districts. As the defense pie shrinks and the competition for weapons funding intensifies, how will Congress divide the slices? Will individual, and institutional, pork-driven behavior become more common?

The FY92 defense budget provides some preliminary case studies for addressing such issues and examining the broader congressional role in post–cold war defense policy implementation. The following section examines the ways in which Congress has dealt with some high-profile, budget-cutting proposals in two areas vital for defense restructuring: personnel and weapons programs.

Personnel: Cutting Reserves

In the FY92 budget request, the Bush administration proposed cutting the reserves by 107,000 persons in FY92. According to Secretary of Defense Cheney, those cuts were needed not only to reduce overall spending but because reserve forces will not play as prominent a role under the new national security strategy. That strategy emphasized the need for U.S. forces to respond quickly to regional conflicts. Cheney argued that reserves and national guard units are unsuitable for such operations, and that the Gulf war underscored the need to diminish the combat roles assigned to reserves in the future (Healy 1991; Schmitt 1991a).

Congress rejected this proposal. In the FY92 defense authorization bill, approved by the House on 22 May, members agreed to restore two-thirds of the reserve and national guard troops Cheney had sought to cut (Schmitt 1991b). The defense appropriations bill passed by the House on 7 June went a step further, entirely eliminating the administration's proposed cutbacks and adding $645 million for 1,065 new members of the reserves and the national guard (Towell 1991a). Cheney struggled to persuade legislators to restore the cuts in the final FY92 defense appropriations bill. Nevertheless, that bill limited Cheney to a reduction of no more than sixty thousand, only 60 percent of the cut originally requested. The final bill also gave reserve and guard forces more than $700 million more than the amount requested for personnel and operating costs, and $1.9 billion more than the request for weapons for those forces (Towell 1991b, 3646).

Congressman G. V. (Sonny) Montgomery (D-Miss.) took the lead in protecting the reserves and the guard in the House. Montgomery argued that

> the best way to spread around defense spending is to have National Guard and reserve units in our different communities, where those reservists can receive additional income, educational benefits and serve his or her country. (Sia 1991)

Advocates of reserve cuts (and base closings) also recognized the power of those political considerations. According to Senator Daniel Inouye (D-Hawaii),

> cutbacks translate into loss of jobs and loss of economic base, and politically, that is of considerable concern to most, if not all, members because it affects constituents. And the people screaming the loudest are the ones who are quick to cut the defense budget, but not in my back yard. (Sia 1991)

Nevertheless, opponents of reserve and national guard reductions cited more than pork considerations in their defense. They also argued that it was good defense policy to maintain existing reserve levels. Montgomery and his supporters disagreed with Cheney's claim that the reserves had performed poorly in the Gulf war and cited earlier statements issued by Cheney hailing their contribution. Congressional opponents also argued that, with cuts in the defense budget under the new defense strategy already in place, it was more important than ever to maintain reserve and national guard forces because they offer a relatively cheap way for the United States to maintain a pool of trained military personnel (Sia 1991; Towell 1991a).

Programs: The V-22, Sealift, and Beyond

The overlap between pork and policy considerations was particularly strong in the case of the V-22 Osprey, tilt-rotor, transport aircraft. Every year he was in office, Secretary Cheney attempted to eliminate the V-22's funding, arguing that the United States simply could not afford the $33 billion program. Congress consistently rejected that recommendation and voted to continue funding the V-22. The FY92 defense appropriations bill passed by Congress provided $625 million for the aircraft (Towell 1991b, 3649).

What accounted for this support? For the leaders of the V-22 fight, the most immediate answer was jobs. Congressman Curt Weldon (R-Pa.), a key supporter of the program, represented a district that was home to Boeing Helicopter, a V-22 prime contractor (Scarborough 1991). Another leader was Congressman Peter Green, (D-Tex.) whose Fort Worth district benefited from five hundred V-22 jobs at Bell Helicopter Textron (another prime contractor) and would gain up to five thousand jobs if the aircraft went into full production (Towle 1991).

However, while these two members had strong parochial incentives to support the program, such incentives were far weaker for Congress as a whole. Spending on the V-22 was heavily concentrated in Texas and Pennsylvania and the program offered few jobs or related benefits for congressional districts in other states (Scarborough 1991). Some members of Congress, including Ted Stevens (R-Alaska), ranking member of the Senate Defense Appropriations subcommittee, backed the program because they believed it would lead to civil aviation spinoffs important to their states. Nevertheless, far more members of Congress supported the V-22 than had explicit, pork-related incentives to do so. If members voted only for those weapons that provided them with immediate constituent benefits. the V-22 would have been canceled.

One possible explanation for the V-22's survival is that its core backers were able to logroll with other members, building a winning coalition by trading support for similarly endangered programs. However, neither Weldon nor Green were in a particularly strong position to create such a coalition or reward their colleagues' support. Weldon was a Republican in a Democrat-dominated institution. Green was a very junior member of the House (first elected in 1989), and he did not serve on either the Armed Services Committee or the Defense Appropriations subcommittee. But both members came from states with large congressional delegations, which (depending on their degree of cohesion) can offer an important source of allies on the floor and in the defense committees. For example, the House Defense Appropriations subcommittee was chaired by a Pennsylvanian, Dick Murtha, who became a powerful supporter of the V-22.

Moreover, while logrolling may have been discouraged in the past by the assumption that the fates of individual programs are unrelated, the rise in program-cutting initiatives by the administration had given logrolling new life. The behavior of the House Armed Services Committee in 1989 offers a prime example. When Cheney asked Congress that year to cut spending on the V-22, the F-14 fighter aircraft, and a number of other programs, Aspin initially supported the proposal (and, indeed, the administration's entire FY90 defense budget request) as a sound, budget-limiting initiative. But committee members opposed to the various cuts banded together and formed a coalition that defeated Aspin when he championed the administration's budget (Moore 1989; G. Wilson 1989). Aspin never again led the fight against the V-22; on the contrary, he included it in the subsequent defense budget proposals he made while chair of the Armed Services Committee.

Yet, even within state delegations, members can have reasons apart from pork for building support on behalf of a given program. Murtha was a retired Marine and a strong supporter of Marine Corps interests. And, although Secretary Cheney concluded that the V-22 should be canceled, the Marines (the intended user of the aircraft) continued to offer private, behind-the-scenes support for the program.

The policy arguments made by the Marines and their supporters on

Capitol Hill played a key role in protecting the V-22. The leaders of that fight were able to argue that, with the end of the cold war and the growing need for highly mobile forces, transport aircraft were far more important than the Bush administration had recognized. As a result, according to Weldon, "We've won the battle not because of pork, but because it has solid, deep support in Congress, and in the Pentagon from the standpoint of service leaders" (Scarborough 1991). Indeed, by making need for mobility all the more apparent, the new national security strategy may have reduced the importance of pork in shaping congressional support for the program.

Policy considerations also appear crucial in the case of sealift cargo ships for transporting tanks and other combat equipment. The Bush administration declined to include money in its proposed FY92 budget for sealift and had refused to spend funds Congress appropriated for that purpose during the previous two years. Cheney's rationale was that fast transport ships were not worth the money, in part because the United States would be able to pre-position military hardware in potential areas of conflict (Towell 1991a).

Congress rejected that position and appropriated $600 million for high-speed cargo ships designed to haul ground-based combat units to trouble spots. Some congressional districts would gain jobs from building that fleet. The appropriations bill included a provision that no more than 15 percent of the funds could be used to buy foreign-built ships (Towell 1991b, 3649). However, as with the V-22, the vast majority of legislators lacked direct constituent interests, making policy considerations more visible. Sealift advocates were able to justify their program by citing the need for greater mobility in the post–cold war era and by critiquing the assumption that the United States could predict in advance where pre-positioned arms would be needed. Again, the new national security strategy gave sealift backers a stronger policy basis upon which to argue their case. And, as with the V-22, sealift advocates were able to claim at least tacit support from military officers, as when Les Aspin quoted Gen. Norman Schwarzkopf as stating that "I've been advocating more sealift for a very, very long time" (Aspin 1991a, 3).

However, there are other grounds for rejecting the hypothesis that pork alone will drive (and distort) the congressional response to the new national security strategy. Although President Bush accused the House of parochialism in refusing to cut programs like the V-22, he also attacked Congress for refusing to spend as much as the administration requested on programs such as the B-2 bomber. If pork is as dominant a force as Bush suggested, the B-2 would have been guaranteed strong support on the Hill. It provided billions of dollars worth of jobs for constituents. Yet, as the president complained, the House voted to slash spending for the bomber. What accounts for this behavior?

Policy considerations overcame pork. With the end of the cold war, and the decline of the Soviet threat, members such as Aspin concluded that less money should be spent on Soviet-oriented programs such as the B-2. The Bush administration's budget was designed to boost the development of "cold war" items, according to Aspin; he argued that the House needed to cut such programs and fund alternatives "that could give us the right defense for the future" (Pasztor 1991b). As with the need for the V-22 and sealift programs, substantial room for disagreement remains in determining which programs should perish with the end of the cold war. These disagreements occur not only between Congress and the president but within Congress itself. Sam Nunn fought to support B-2 funding in the FY92 budget even as Aspin attempted to slash it. Thus, while policy disputes will continue to draw Congress into the defense budgeting fray, congressional preferences will be far more fragmented than would be the case if legislators were driven only by an overriding desire for pork.

Conclusion

Congress led the initial drive to formulate and implement a new overall defense policy after the collapse of the Berlin Wall. President Bush soon followed with a dramatic proposal of his own, creating a pattern of legislative-executive conflict and accommodation that continues today. The final character of America's post–cold war defense policy will not be settled for years to come. Nevertheless, the early stages of that struggle suggest some conclusions regarding when legislators will attempt to change overall policy, how Congress and the president influence each other's initiatives, and the way pork and policy concerns will determine how legislators use the budget to implement broad proposals.

The conventional wisdom that Congress ignores big-picture policy is wrong. A number of recent studies conclude that, while legislators pay considerable attention to details of defense spending (particularly when constituent jobs are at stake), their motivation to grapple with policy disputes is weaker, in part because addressing those issues rarely helps them get reelected. Yet, in 1990, legislators pushed to change policy on issues far broader than those of specific, program funding levels. The likelihood of congressional interest in an issue is not simply a function of the narrowness, or the degree of budgetary detail, of the issue at stake. But, if the scale of an issue does not determine congressional interest, what does? Under what conditions are legislators likely to seize the policy-making lead?

Congress abhors a policy vacuum. When a dramatic shift occurs in the underpinnings of U.S. policy and the president fails to offer a commensurate response, legislators will step into the breach and press their own proposals for change. The Bush administration created a policy vacuum by sticking to its FY91 request after the collapse of the Berlin Wall and by arguing (as Cheney did) that it was the worst possible time to reassess U.S. defense strategy. However, the specific reasons why Congress abhors such a vacuum also are instructive.

Bush's apparent failure to respond to the end of the cold war presented legislators with a juicy political opportunity. Despite the argument that policy issues are irrelevant to reelection concerns, members may have other political incentives to address such issues, including the desire to appear more states-manlike and to gain or preserve power within Congress. Nor are policy issues necessarily divorced from mundane political concerns. Public support for military budget cuts grew sharply with the decline of the cold war threat, giving legislators a particular incentive to attack the FY91 request and offer their own proposals for rethinking the threat, reducing overall spending levels, and changing the basic character of U.S. forces. Even the biggest of big-picture issues can become politically salient on Capitol Hill.

Congress also abhors a policy vacuum because legislators such as Con-gressman Dicks consider policy matters to be an essential part of their job. When the issues at stake are relatively narrow, as in deciding the future of naval aviation procurement, members may step into the policy-making breach because they need such guidance to make detailed, program decisions in their committee work. But larger-scale issues also can attract activism. Senator Nunn argued in early 1990 that, in the absence of adequate presidential leadership in rethinking defense requirements, his committee simply could not meet its budget authorization responsibilities, and that he and his col-leagues would have to address overall policy issues for themselves.

This suggests two criteria for judging whether Congress is likely to seize the policy-making lead. The first is how the president has dealt with an issue—in particular, whether he has allowed a policy vacuum to emerge. The second is how well an issue fits the incentives that actually exist for congres-sional policy-making. There is nothing inherent in the broader, less program-specific nature of an overall policy issue that makes it less interesting to Congress. The key is whether legislators consider an issue politically salient or essential for doing their jobs. Legislators demonstrated in 1990 that they can have both incentives to grapple with even the biggest of big-picture issues.

The ability of legislators to act on these incentives also raises some broad implications for the policy-making process. The president usually is thought to be in a better position than Congress to formulate policy initiatives. How-ever, when dramatic change occurs in the circumstances underpinning U.S. policy, as in the collapse of the cold war, Congress has organizational advan-tages in offering a quick response. While the president's budget request offers a once-a-year vehicle for proposing broad policy changes, the process by which Congress drafts its own version of the budget provides an almost continuous opportunity for new initiatives. The less bureaucratic structure of Congress also helps its members take advantage of this opportunity. For better or worse, legislators have greater freedom to propose sudden policy shifts without having to go through the formal decision clearing process that often gives executive branch suborganizations the opportunity to block (or perhaps improve) presidential initiatives.

But the president will eventually offer a proposal of his own—perhaps, as in Bush's August 1990 initiative, by skirting the usual decision-making process. Bush's initiative shrank the opportunities for congressional activism that existed earlier in the year. By embracing budget cuts, recognizing the collapse of the Soviet threat, and offering his own vision of how U.S. forces should be restructured, Bush moved to eliminate the gaps in administration policy that legislators had found so attractive. The president creates policy vacuums but he also can fill them by co-opting the basis for congressional activism. The conditions under which Congress is likely to seize the policy-making lead are at least partly under the control of the White House.

Yet, while the president can reduce the likelihood of congressional activism, doing so will not necessarily reduce the influence of Congress over policy. Congress can shape overall defense policy in a direct fashion by using the defense budget to change spending totals and restructure forces to fit revised assessments of the threat. To forestall such direct influence and regain control over policy formulation, the president can propose a policy initiative that captures and exploits the impetus for congressional action. But he does so at the price of giving Congress indirect influence over his proposals. The president can reduce the likelihood that Congress will seize the policy-making lead, yet in doing so he may simply shift the means by which legislators put their stamp on policy.

Congressional influence will be especially powerful in implementing broad defense policy changes through specific, line-item shifts in the military budget. The assumption that Congress is driven by pork incentives rests in part on a confusion between the behavior of individual members and that of Congress as a whole. The jobs created by most weapons programs are concentrated in a relatively few districts; at least in the past, most legislators have lacked a direct parochial interest in specific funding disputes. But the end of the cold war and the attendant drop in defense spending could make Congress as a whole behave in a more porcine fashion. As the president proposes drastic funding shifts to accommodate his new sense of priorities, some programs will be threatened that do provide constituent benefits in most districts. The proposed cuts in national guard and reserve forces are a case in point. For programs of direct benefit to only a few members, the growing number of such programs threatened with extinction may facilitate greater logrolling between members for their mutual protection.

Yet, the rise of pork concerns does not mean that policy concerns will become less significant in shaping congressional behavior. The leaders of the fight to save the V-22 argue that policy considerations were vital for building a winning coalition against President Bush. And, as the president proposes more sweeping changes in the U.S. force structure and defense priorities, such disputes are bound to escalate. Pork and policy are not mutually exclusive. They are closely intertwined. Both will motivate greater congressional activism on defense, and both will help determine the fate of America's military.

CHAPTER 11

Congress and Diplomacy

James M. Lindsay

Everyone agrees that Congress is more active in foreign policy today than at any time since the 1930s. Dispute arises over the impact of congressional activism. At one extreme in the debate lie the Irreconcilables, who warn that "overreaching" by an "imperial Congress" has created a "fettered presidency" (e.g., Cheney 1990a; Crovitz and Rabkin 1989; Rodman 1985; and Rostow 1989). They yearn for the good old days when the president ran the show. At the other extreme lie the Skeptics. They argue that congressional activism is more show than substance. Congress, in their view, operates on the margins of foreign policy (e.g., Destler, Gelb, and Lake 1984; Kegley and Wittkopf 1991; and Koh 1990).

The debate between the Irreconcilables and the Skeptics poses the broad question of how and to what effect Congress shapes U.S. relations with other countries. This chapter seeks to assess the impact of congressional activism by surveying the ways in which Congress, both as an institution and through the activities of its committees and members, tries to shape U.S. diplomacy. Most discussions of Congress and diplomacy lavish critical attention on efforts by legislators to conduct back-channel negotiations with foreign powers and conclude by urging more frequent consultations between the president and Congress. Yet private diplomacy is the exception rather than the rule, and presidents prefer to notify rather than consult with members of Congress. Legislators exercise more influence over diplomacy by passing legislation, by participating in international negotiations, and by mobilizing elite and public opinion.

Attention paid to the ways in which members of Congress try to influence diplomacy shows that both the Irreconcilables and the Skeptics misrepresent the impact of Congress. Irreconcilables exaggerate the extent and effect of congressional activism. Although members of Congress no longer automatically defer to the president as they did in the 1950s and 1960s, they by no means have seized control of U.S. diplomacy. The president remains the single most important actor in diplomatic matters. Skeptics, on the other hand, err by overlooking some of the tools members of Congress use to

influence diplomacy. What Skeptics tend to dismiss as mere political postur-
ing often represents concerted efforts to influence public opinion and thereby
pressure presidents to change their policies.

Any discussion of Congress's role in diplomacy inevitably raises the
normative question of what role members of Congress should play in foreign
policy. A definitive answer is hard to reach. Constitutional scholars quarrel
over the proper roles of Congress and the president. By the same token,
disagreements over what constitutes "good" policy torpedo efforts to determine whether congressional activism advances or undermines the national
interest, a concept that itself evokes no widely accepted definition. If assessments of Congress tend to vary with individual values and policy preferences,
the factual claims made by critics of Congress can be assessed. And, for the
most part, the criticisms fall short.

Legislators as Diplomats

When Edmond Genet submitted his credentials as emissary of the first French
Republic to Congress rather than to President Washington, Secretary of State
Thomas Jefferson told Genet that "the transaction of business with foreign
nations is Executive altogether. . . . Exceptions are to be strictly construed"
(quoted in J. Smith 1989, 163). Since then Jefferson's view that the president
alone has the power to negotiate with other countries has become widely
accepted. Yet Irreconcilables argue that the president's constitutional role is
being undermined by the rise of Lone Ranger diplomacy, the penchant of
some members of Congress to conduct their own foreign policy.

The most publicized recent episode of Lone Ranger diplomacy was
Speaker of the House Jim Wright's foray into negotiations on Central America (see chapter 9 for a discussion of Wright's motives). In November 1987,
the Reagan administration offered for the first time to meet with representatives of the Nicaraguan government to discuss security issues in Central
America. Speaker Wright thereupon launched his own diplomatic effort,
meeting secretly for three days with Nicaraguan President Daniel Ortega,
three members of the Contra leadership, and Nicaragua's Cardinal Miguel
Obando y Bravo. When the talks concluded, a Sandinista official said that
Wright's initiative would "leave the administration totally isolated" (quoted in
Felton 1987, 2789). Some administration officials proposed prosecuting
Wright under the Logan Act, which forbids U.S. citizens from negotiating
with a foreign power without government permission. Nothing came of this,
largely because enforcing the Logan Act would have raised a host of political
and legal difficulties.

Speaker Wright is not the only legislator to indulge in Lone Ranger
diplomacy. When the United States and Iraq disagreed over when to resume

their talks on preventing the Gulf war, Robert Dole (R-Kans.), the Senate minority leader, phoned the Iraqi ambassador to see if Baghdad would change its choice of dates (Lehman 1992, 44). Throughout the 1980s, Democrats opposed to U.S. policy toward Nicaragua held extensive discussions, both in Washington and in Managua, with officials of the Sandinista government (Cheney 1990a, 106–7; Johnston and Wines 1991). In 1979, Congressman George Hansen (R-Idaho) went to Teheran on his own to negotiate the release of American hostages. Senator Jesse Helms (R-N.C.) was accused of dispatching private emissaries to negotiate with Nicaragua and Rhodesia-Zimbabwe, and of leaking intelligence information to Chile (Cheney 1990a, 108–9; Jentleson 1990, 175–76).

The conduct of private diplomacy by members of Congress merits four comments. First, it is not a new phenomenon. During the Paris Peace conference that followed World War I, Henry Cabot Lodge (R-Mass.), chair of the Senate Foreign Relations Committee, corresponded with European leaders without informing President Wilson, and, in the 1920s, William E. Borah (R-Idaho), another chair of Foreign Relations, opened his own negotiations with the Mexican government over oil exploration in Mexico (Franck and Weisband 1979, 138; see also Holt 1933, 180). Second, neither political party can claim virtue. Both Democrats and Republicans have launched private diplomatic initiatives. Third, Lone Ranger diplomacy usually fails. As Speaker Wright discovered, most people oppose private diplomacy and the resulting public and elite criticism usually derails the initiative. Fourth, the efforts of Wright, Dole, and others stand out—indeed, they are cited time and again—because they are uncommon. Most legislators have no interest in pursuing an independent foreign policy. The reasons are straightforward: most legislators believe that the president bears the responsibility for diplomacy, they know they lack the clout needed to matter on the world stage, and they recognize that private diplomacy generally succeeds only in attracting criticism.

If Lone Ranger diplomacy is infrequent, the same cannot be said of routine, direct contacts between foreign governments and members of Congress. One important development over the past twenty years is an increased number of meetings between visiting foreign dignitaries and legislators. As Congressman Lee Hamilton (D-Ind.) once observed,

> When I first came to Washington a head of government would visit the president, the secretary of state, the World Bank, and go home. Today, it's rare for a head of state to come to Washington without meeting members of Congress. (quoted in Roberts 1985)

During the 101st Congress (1989–90), the House Foreign Affairs Committee received 132 foreign dignitaries and 34 foreign delegations, while the

Senate Foreign Relations Committee received foreign dignitaries on 80 occasions (U.S. Congress House Committee on Foreign Affairs 1990, 19; U.S. Congress Senate Committee on Foreign Relations 1991a, 158).

The flip side of congressional meetings with visiting foreign dignitaries is congressional visits abroad. Of course, congressional junkets draw ample ridicule. But, for all the jokes about trips to Bali or Cancun, congressional trips abroad usually involve legitimate business. The collapse of the Soviet bloc, for instance, triggered a rush of direct meetings between members of Congress and legislators in Eastern Europe. Senators and representatives served on international delegations overseeing parliamentary elections in Czechoslovakia, Hungary, Bulgaria, and Romania. In April 1990, the House dispatched a bipartisan task force to Eastern Europe to provide technical and procedural assistance to the newly formed legislatures. Other legislators acted on an individual basis to offer advice to their Eastern European counterparts (Patterson 1990).

Even more pervasive than congressional meetings with foreign dignitaries at home or abroad are meetings with foreign embassy personnel stationed in Washington. Before the mid-1970s most embassies conducted their business through the State Department. They rarely lobbied Congress. As legislators became more active on foreign policy, however, embassies began to lobby members of Congress. For example, New Zealand became the target of congressional legislation in 1987 after it adopted a nuclear-free weapons policy. The second secretary in the New Zealand embassy, who served as his country's day-to-day liaison with Congress, saw "the proportion of his working time usually spent on general contact work increased from forty percent to 100 percent immediately prior to the hearings, floor votes, and other legislative milestones" (Hoadley 1991, 52). The experience of the second secretary no doubt is typical. As John Tierney argues in chapter 5, embassy personnel have joined the horde of lobbyists on Capitol Hill.

Most contacts between foreign governments and members of Congress merely involve the exchange of information. Officials at both ends of Pennsylvania Avenue agree that informational exchanges are a legitimate part of Congress's work. But disagreement arises over what distinguishes legislative fact-finding from diplomatic negotiation. The line demarcating proper and improper behavior is blurred further by the fact that the executive branch encourages meetings with foreign officials when it thinks the discussions will persuade members of Congress to support its own policies.

The increase in direct contacts between Congress and foreign governments suggests a model of diplomacy different from Robert Putnam's (1988) two-level game. Putnam presents a stylized model of international bargaining in which the president links the international and domestic arenas. In his role as chief negotiator the president tries to determine the set of policies acceptable to both international and domestic actors. But, because the model presumes that legislators and foreign governments do not communicate, it suggests that the president stands to reap disproportionate gains from the negotiations. When the president determines the set of acceptable policies, he can pick the one he most prefers, even if other policies are more beneficial to both Congress and the foreign government. Likewise, if the president dislikes the policies that appeal to legislators and foreign governments, he can block an agreement.

Given the prevalence of congressional contacts with foreign governments, the assumption that only the president knows the preferences of other actors is naive, as Putnam himself recognizes (1988, 459). When Putnam's model is amended to allow for contact between a foreign government and members of Congress, the president's ability to distort bargaining outcomes in his favor disappears. If members of Congress and foreign officials know what constitutes the set of acceptable outcomes, they can push the president away from his ideal outcome and closer to their own.

Legislators as Consultants

Episodes of congressional diplomacy typically trigger a flood of proposals offering to remedy the perceived crisis in U.S. foreign policy. Many of these proposals trumpet the need to rekindle the bipartisan spirit of the pre-Vietnam years when politics stopped at the water's edge (for less idyllic recollections of executive-legislative relations in the pre-Vietnam era, see Bax 1977; McCormick and Wittkopf 1990; and Wittkopf and McCormick 1990). The route to bipartisanship is seen to lie in more consultation between the president and Congress.

Calls for more executive-legislative consultation typically evoke the early years of the cold war as a model to be emulated. The White House and leading members of Congress collaborated extensively on the United Nations Charter, the Marshall Plan, and the Atlantic Charter (Cheever and Haviland 1952, 97–142). Yet the extent of executive-legislative consultation in the late 1940s and early 1950s is exaggerated. More often than not administrations acted without consulting members of Congress. President Truman's decisions to proceed with the Truman Doctrine, to begin the Berlin airlift, and to commit U.S. troops to the defense of South Korea were made without input from members of Congress (see Robinson 1967, 44–63). As for President Eisenhower, he

> informed, rather than consulted with, congressional leaders about his major decisions: to accept a ceasefire in Korea without liberating North Korea, to stay out of Vietnam in 1954, to use the CIA to support coups in

Iran in 1953 and Guatemala in 1954, not to go to war with China over the off-shore islands (Quemoy and Matsu), not to support the Hungarian rebels in 1956 or the British/French/Israeli cabal in 1956, to force Israel to pull out of the Sinai Peninsula in 1957, to extend aid to Tito in Yugoslavia and to hold down the cost of defense. (Ambrose 1991–92, 125)

Until the late 1960s, few people complained that presidents seldom solicited congressional advice on diplomatic matters. Most members of Congress instinctively followed the president's lead. Senator Richard Russell's (D-Ga.) response to Eisenhower's decision to send two hundred military advisers to South Vietnam after the fall of Dienbienphu was typical: "I think this is the greatest mistake this country's ever made. I could not be more opposed to it . . . but if he does it I will never raise my voice" (quoted in Halberstam 1983, 181).

Russell's judgment about Vietnam proved prophetic. One of the consequences of U.S. involvement in Southeast Asia was that many legislators abandoned the belief that Congress should defer to the president on foreign policy. Members began to demand true consultation between the two branches of government. The desire for a consultative role was most evident in the passage in 1973 of the War Powers Resolution, which explicitly states that

The President in every possible instance shall consult with Congress before introducing United States Armed Forces into hostilities or into situations where imminent involvement in hostilities is clearly indicated. (quoted in J. Smith 1989, 258)

To borrow a refrain popular in the early 1970s, members of Congress wanted to be in on the takeoffs as well as the crash landings on foreign policy.

Members of Congress occasionally win a consultative role in the formulation of U.S. diplomacy. U.S. policy toward Nicaragua provides a case in point. Intent on avoiding the political battles over Nicaragua that plagued the Reagan administration, President Bush began talks with congressional leaders almost immediately upon assuming office. In March 1989 these talks yielded a bipartisan agreement on Nicaragua that included significant concessions by the administration (Felton 1989b).

Despite this success story, members of Congress find it easier to demand a consultative role than to get it. The failure is most obvious with the War Powers Resolution. Most presidents have refused to accept the resolution as constitutional let alone abide by its injunction to consult with Congress. The fundamental problem with winning a consultative role for Congress is that the ability of legislators to advise depends on the willingness of presidents to listen. As the gap between executive and legislative preferences grows—and the more important consultation becomes—presidents become less willing to solicit congressional opinion.

The evolution of Operation Desert Shield into Operation Desert Storm illustrates the conundrum. Operation Desert Shield featured substantial dialogue between the White House and Congress. To be sure, the discussions fell short of true consultation. For example, Senate majority leader George Mitchell (D-Maine) and Senate Armed Services chairman Sam Nunn (D-Ga.) learned about the decision to send U.S. troops to Saudi Arabia after the fact (Doherty 1990b). But the Bush administration went to considerable lengths to meet with members of Congress and to keep them informed about U.S. policy. In late August the president personally briefed and took questions from 170 members of Congress (Doherty 1990c).

As summer turned to fall, however, White House interest in congressional opinion faded. By October members on both sides of the aisle began to complain that they were being ignored (Doherty 1990b). Then, in early November, after Congress had recessed for the year and the mid-term congressional elections were over, President Bush announced a near doubling in the size of U.S. forces in the Gulf, a decision that shifted the troops from a defensive to an offensive military posture. In reaching his decision the president consulted with a small circle of executive branch officials; congressional leaders learned about the troop increase only minutes before the rest of the public was informed (Doherty 1990e; C. Madison 1990).

The main difference between the genesis of Desert Shield and the genesis of Desert Storm, of course, was the degree of consensus. The August dialogue between Congress and the president took place amid near unanimity on the need to deter an Iraqi invasion of Saudi Arabia. This made it relatively costless for President Bush to keep members of Congress abreast of his plans, and it left few legislators inclined to complain about deficiencies in the consultative process. But no unanimity existed on using U.S. troops to free Kuwait. Faced with potentially stiff opposition on Capitol Hill should his plans to liberate Kuwait by force become known prematurely, Bush stood to gain little by consulting with congressional leaders.

Presidents do not always decline to consult with congressional leaders. When they need congressional consent to achieve their diplomatic goals and it is questionable whether that consent will be forthcoming, presidents look more favorably on consultations. Such situations sometimes occur during the negotiation of treaties. When it was negotiating the Panama Canal treaties and the SALT II treaty, for example, the prospect of strong opposition in the Senate forced the Carter administration to solicit the views of key senators.

Another situation in which presidents feel pressure to consult with Congress occurs when a diplomatic effort depends on providing or stopping aid to another country. Take the decision by the Bush administration in 1991 to delay

$10 billion in loan guarantees to Israel. To stave off legislative efforts to end the delay, the administration turned to Patrick Leahy (D-Vt.), chair of the Senate Appropriations Subcommittee on Foreign Operations, for help in negotiating a compromise (Doherty 1992b). Even here, though, the administration's willingness to consult was bolstered by the fact that Leahy and many other legislators sympathized with the argument for withholding the loan guarantees.

Legislators as Lawmakers

The president's ability to decide with whom he will or will not consult forces members of Congress to make a choice: to accept the foreign policy choices the president makes or to act to reverse his decisions. Increasingly over the past two decades members have opted to act. One result has been a rise in the number of bills that seek to enact congressional preferences on foreign policy into law. These efforts fall into three distinct categories: substantive legislation, procedural legislation, and constraining legislation.

Substantive legislation involves bills that specify how the United States will interact with another country. Substantive legislation on diplomacy comes in several varieties. One prominent type is a bill that dictates U.S. trade relations with other countries. Thus, in 1978, Congress imposed trade sanctions on Uganda in an effort to destabilize the government of Idi Amin. In a more famous case, in 1986, Congress overrode President Reagan's veto and imposed trade sanctions on South Africa in an effort to pressure Pretoria to dismantle apartheid. Although Irreconcilables typically claim that the president is the "sole organ" of U.S. diplomacy, Congress occupies solid constitutional ground when it flexes its muscles on trade policy. The Constitution, after all, specifically directs Congress "to regulate commerce with foreign nations."

Congress also legislates substantively through its power of the purse. Foreign aid bills carry earmarks that dictate how U.S. aid can and cannot be spent. Congress can use its control of the purse strings to limit U.S. military involvement abroad. The Clark amendment, for example, barred the United States from aiding any military or paramilitary operations in Angola. The Boland amendments did much the same thing for U.S. relations with Nicaragua. Congress has even used the power of the purse to enforce U.S. treaty obligations. In 1987 and 1988, Congress inserted provisions in the defense authorization bill that, without mentioning the SALT II treaty by name, directed the president to retire submarines in a fashion that kept the United States near the treaty's limits on warheads. As with trade legislation, Congress occupies solid constitutional ground when it uses its control of the purse strings to shape U.S. diplomacy (Koh 1990, 129–30; Stith 1988, 1351–52, 1360–63).

Whereas substantive legislation affects U.S. diplomacy directly, procedural legislation does so indirectly. With procedural legislation Congress specifies the rules and procedures the administration must follow in making foreign policy. As chapter two discussed, the assumption underlying procedural legislation is that changing the policy-making process will change policy outcomes.

Examples of congressional efforts to use procedure to shape U.S. diplomacy abound. The War Powers Resolution sought to prevent another Vietnam by requiring presidents to remove U.S. troops from situations of imminent or actual hostilities if they failed to win congressional approval of the deployment within sixty days. Section 502B of the Foreign Assistance Act bars the executive branch from granting security assistance "to any country the government of which engages in a consistent pattern of gross violations of internationally recognized human rights" (quoted in Forsythe 1987, 383). To punish the Soviet Union for restricting Jewish emigration, the Jackson-Vanik amendment barred the executive branch from granting trade concessions to nonmarket countries that deny their citizens the right to emigrate.

The constitutionality of procedural legislation varies. Some is of arguable validity. The War Powers Resolution is the classic case. Likewise, when the Supreme Court ruled most legislative vetoes unconstitutional, it gutted much of the procedural legislation on foreign policy (Franck and Bob 1985; Gilmour and Craig 1984). Nonetheless, Congress clearly possesses the constitutional authority to change some aspects of executive branch decision making. Congress was fully within its rights in 1991 when it directed the State Department to create a new bureau for South Asia as part of an effort to see that U.S. diplomacy gave greater emphasis to the Indian subcontinent (Crossette 1991). Likewise, Congress is fully within its rights when it places conditions on the disbursement of foreign aid.

The third type of legislative effort that shapes U.S. diplomacy involves what may be called constraining legislation. Here Congress's actions on an issue within its constitutional purview limits the president's diplomatic options. A case in point is U.S. policy on ozone depletion. In the discussions that led up to the signing of the London Protocol in 1990, the Bush administration favored only gradual elimination of methyl chloroform. When Congress amended the Clean Air Act to require a rapid phase-out of methyl chloroform, the administration suddenly found itself in the unusual position of arguing for international regulations more lenient than those in place in the U.S. market. With its bargaining position effectively undercut, the administration agreed to an accelerated schedule for phasing out methyl chloroform (Benedick 1991, 173–74).

Constraining legislation also includes what may be called hostage taking, instances in which Congress uses legislation on one issue as a lever to pressure the president to change his foreign policy. The Scowcroft compromise, which tied MX funding to changes in the U.S. negotiating stance at the Strategic Arms Reduction Talks (START), provides a classic case of hostage taking (Drew 1983; Talbott 1984). Likewise, in 1991, the Senate Foreign Operations subcommittee rejected an administration request to give $12 billion to the International Monetary Fund (IMF). The subcommittee balked because key members believed that the Department of the Treasury and the IMF had not acted on a 1989 law demanding that the latter pay more attention to environmental issues when devising structural readjustment programs (Bradsher 1991).

As a general matter, constraining legislation does not raise constitutional problems. Congress enjoys strong constitutional authority to legislate on domestic policy and to determine how government monies are to be spent. The Constitution contains no injunction that Congress's ability to legislate and appropriate dissipates if foreign policy is affected. While one may question the prudence of specific instances of hostage taking, it generally does not raise constitutional questions. To take the examples of the MX and START, even Irreconcilables agree that "no one can dispute Congress's constitutional power to decide what weapons should be funded" (Cheney 1990a, 104).

Although legislation gives members of Congress a tool with which to influence diplomacy, it is a difficult tool to wield. Many issues lie beyond the reach of legislation: national security crises, most negotiations, and the recognition of foreign countries, to mention a few. Another problem is that legislation must win the approval of a majority of Congress. But partisan and institutional divisions mean that without consensus—and consensus is often lacking on foreign policy—Congress will not act. Legislative action is complicated further by the widely held belief that presidential leadership is essential to successful diplomacy. Electoral considerations at times reinforce the inclination to defer to the president. And, when Congress does pass legislation, the president can derail the bill with a veto. Between 1974 and 1992 Congress overrode only one foreign policy veto.

Even when members of Congress overcome the many obstacles to making law, legislation remains a clumsy instrument. When writing laws, legislators try to strike a balance between useful ambiguity and necessary precision. Both extremes create problems. As the fate of much of the legislation passed in the 1970s on human rights policy attests (Broder and Lambek 1988; Forsythe 1987, 1988), presidents can (and do) exploit ambiguity to circumvent the will of Congress. Preventing the president from exploiting ambiguous legislative language is made all the more difficult when, as often happens, Congress builds waivers into legislation in order to give presidents the flexibility they need to respond to changing events. By the same token, when Congress is precise in its legislative language it may unwisely restrict presidential discretion or it may find its legislation undercut by world events. In

1979 the House Appropriations Committee added language to the foreign aid bill barring all assistance to the Central African Empire in retaliation for the human rights abuses of Emperor Jean-Bedel Bokassa. The emperor was overthrown before the bill finished its legislative journey through Congress (Whalen 1982, 90).

If the value of legislation is undercut by the need to give the president discretion, it also is diminished by the public nature of the legislative process. This is particularly the case with legislation aimed at compelling another country to change its behavior. Diplomatic success often hinges on secrecy. The same promises and threats that work in private may fail miserably in public. When legislators responded to the invasion of Cyprus in 1974 by imposing an arms embargo on Turkey, they discovered that the move hardened rather than weakened the Turkish position (Franck and Weisband 1979, 35–45). Legislators encounter similar problems when they use procedural legislation to penalize countries with poor human rights records (Forsythe 1987, 1988; Whalen 1982, 122–26).

As chapter 2 points out, the potential for legislation to prove counterproductive often leads members to view the legislative process as a lever with which to prod the administration to do its bidding. Members hope that the executive branch will conclude that U.S. foreign policy interests will be better served if it addresses congressional concerns, and thereby defeats a legislative initiative, than if it stands firm and runs the risk that restrictive legislation will be passed. For instance, congressional threats to cut off aid to countries guilty of human rights violations have convinced the White House on several occasions to exert pressure for reforms on the countries in question (Forsythe 1987, 1988).

Legislators as Negotiators

Irreconcilables insist that the president is the sole organ of U.S. foreign policy. Although legal scholars continue to wrangle over the meaning and applicability of the sole organ doctrine, in practice presidents do not conduct negotiations in isolation. Both statutes and political pragmatism inject legislators directly into many international negotiations.

The most visible instance in which Congress has a formal role in international negotiations is trade policy. The Trade Reform Act of 1974 stipulates that five members of the Senate Finance Committee and five members of the House Ways and Means Committee be designated official advisers to trade negotiations. The congressional advisers are entitled to consult regularly with U.S. negotiators and to participate directly in trade talks. Selected congressional staff also are entitled to monitor the talks and to attend negotiating sessions. To remedy potential informational imbalances between the executive and

Congress, the act further directs the administration to keep the House and Senate "currently informed" on the status of trade talks.

Congressional negotiators played a substantive role during the Tokyo Round of the General Agreement on Tariffs and Trade. The Carter administration gave congressional delegates and their staff access to the State Department's cable traffic on the talks and several congressional negotiators became involved in the details of the negotiations (Twiggs 1987, 107). Administration officials apparently listened (Strauss 1987, vii). Congressional delegates also played a role in negotiating the U.S.-Canada Free Trade Agreement. When the talks stalled in late 1986, legislators worked to revive them (*Congressional Record* 1988b, S12783; U.S. Congress Senate Committee on Finance 1988, 5). When the negotiations faltered again in 1987, "congressional suggestions to the negotiators helped to break the impasse, and agreement [in principle] was reached" (U.S. Congress House Committee on Foreign Affairs 1989a, 102).

Congressional delegates participate in trade talks because the Constitution specifically allocates authority over trade to Congress. The fact that the allocation of constitutional powers on trade policy is atypical for foreign policy makes it hard for Congress to extend its formal involvement to other diplomatic negotiations. Yet presidents sometimes include members of Congress in international negotiations in an effort to co-opt opponents or to build support for their policies in Congress. One area in which congressional participation has become customary is the United Nations; members from both the House and the Senate sit on the annual delegations to the General Assembly as well as on delegations to various UN-sponsored conferences.

A more important instance in which members of Congress participate informally in international negotiations is at arms control talks. In the 1960s presidents ignored Congress on matters of arms control. During the SALT I negotiations in Helsinki, for example, Senator John Sherman Cooper (R-Ky.) repeatedly failed to convince the Nixon administration to include senators in the negotiating delegation (Platt 1978, 19–20). When Hugh Scott (R-Pa.), the Senate minority leader, announced that he would visit Helsinki, the delegation discussed whether to meet with him. It eventually decided to do so but agreed to tell him little of substance (Lindsay 1992–93, 614).

As congressional activism increased in the 1970s, presidents calculated that congressional participation would be necessary to win passage for any arms control treaty. The Carter administration approved the creation of a Senate SALT advisers group.

Members were permitted to attend plenary sessions of the negotiations as observers, to sit in on delegation meetings in Geneva, and even to read the joint draft text of the treaty. (Blechman 1990a, 122)

The Reagan administration initially tried to reverse the precedent set by Carter. Congressional pressure forced the administration to retreat, however, and in 1985 a Senate Arms Control Observer Group was reestablished.

In addition to the functions carried out by their predecessors, the new Senate observers were permitted to meet separately with Soviet negotiators, both to learn firsthand of Soviet positions and to express their own concerns. (Blechman 1990a, 122)

However members of Congress come to participate in international negotiations, their participation by no means guarantees that congressional preferences will be reflected in the outcome of the talks. The problem facing congressional negotiators is the same one that undercuts demands for executive-legislative consultation: presidents are free to ignore congressional advice. Many legislators complained after the U.S.-Canada Free Trade Agreement was signed that the administration had failed to consult with them during the final phase of the negotiations (Gorlin 1990, 67). While many senators praised the decision to include congressional delegates in the START talks, it is not clear that they influenced the Reagan administration's negotiating posture.

The U.S.-Canada trade talks and the arms control adviser groups show once again that legislators are most likely to influence diplomacy when the president needs Congress and many in Congress are not inclined to follow. On arms control issues, in the 1980s, the Senate was more enthusiastic about reaching an agreement than was President Reagan. As a result, the White House could afford to ignore congressional advice. Precisely the opposite occurred during the trade talks with Canada. The executive branch generated the initiative and many legislators would have been happy to see it fail. To keep it alive the Reagan administration had to agree to a series of congressional demands, including the stipulation that debate on the agreement be delayed for six months. Members wanted the delay so that they would have time to review and shape the details of the legislation implementing the provisions of the agreement (U.S. Congress Senate Committee on Finance 1988, 5–6; U.S. Congress House Committee on Foreign Affairs 1989a, 103).

Legislators as Framers of Opinion

Members of Congress also can influence diplomacy by mobilizing elite and public opinion. As the evolution of U.S. policy toward Iraqi Kurds after the Gulf war attests, what political elites and the public think about foreign policy influences the choices the president makes (see Schorr 1991). And, as chapter 2 points out, legislators influence elite and public opinion by framing issues in a way that attracts media and executive branch attention, places the issue on the agenda, and puts the administration on the defensive. To be sure, framing appeals to legislators because media coverage can enhance their electoral prospects. But framing also can place the administration in a position in which it believes it must change its policies. Framing even may affect the policies of other countries.

Sometimes framing is the work of a single legislator, usually one who occupies a key position in Congress. In 1986, Richard Lugar (R-Ind.), chair of the Foreign Relations Committee, used his appearances on Sunday morning news shows to attack the Reagan administration's support for Ferdinand Marcos (H. Smith 1988, 43–44). In 1990, Senator Nunn chaired highly publicized hearings that implicitly criticized the Bush administration's decision to use force to evict Iraq from Kuwait (Doherty 1990a; Fessler 1990a). That same year, Senator Mitchell made several speeches on the Senate floor to draw attention to the resurgence of the Khmer Rouge in Cambodia (Stanfield 1990).

A legislator does not need to chair a committee or to be the Senate majority leader to focus attention on U.S. diplomacy. In 1989, for example, the Bush administration tried to dilute the testimony a government scientist was to give before Congress on the need to combat global warming. Senator Albert Gore (D-Tenn.), a member of the Commerce, Science, and Transportation Committee, seized on the issue, playing the story to the hilt with the media. The White House suddenly found itself the focus of intense public criticism (K. Wright 1991, 30–31).

Although individual legislators at times play a crucial role in changing public and administration opinion on foreign policy, framing results more often from the actions of groups of legislators in Congress. Shortly after the massacre at Tiananmen Square, Congress and the Bush administration parted ways over how to deal with the Chinese government. Members who were angered over what they saw as a timid U.S. policy introduced bills calling for trade sanctions, gave emotional floor speeches, and met with Chinese dissidents, all in an effort to "put political pressure on the administration to take stronger stands" (Felton 1989a, 1564). Joe Moakley (D-Mass.), chair of the House Rules Committee, headed a special task force to investigate the 1989 killings of six Jesuit priests in El Salvador. Moakley's task force issued a series of reports that sparked renewed debate over U.S. policy toward El Salvador (Krauss 1991; Stanfield 1990).

Framing usually involves such relatively mundane activities as hearings, floor speeches, press conferences, and radio and television interviews. But members of Congress sometimes go to extreme (even silly) lengths to shape the climate of public opinion. Take the case in which a subsidiary of Toshiba sold sensitive technology to the Soviet Union. Washington and Tokyo initially dragged their feet on the issue. Then the matter reached Capitol Hill. On 20 June 1987, five members of Congress took sledgehammers to a Toshiba radio on the steps of the Capitol. Although the stunt was a blatant publicity ploy, the news media on both sides of the Pacific gladly went along (Warrock and Husock 1988).

Framing at times dramatically affects the substance of U.S. diplomacy. Within days after Senator Lugar publicly criticized U.S. policy toward the Philippines, President Reagan withdrew his support for Marcos. Senator Gore's media campaign forced the Bush administration to reverse itself and announce that it would sponsor an international meeting to discuss global warming (K. Wright 1991, 31). And a surge in calls for protectionist legislation usually convinces the White House to give greater emphasis to trade policy (Koh 1986; Pastor 1980).

Congressional framing also may affect the behavior of other countries. In the Toshiba case, for example, the video clip of members of Congress taking a sledgehammer to a Japanese product was played repeatedly on Japanese television. Tokyo responded by toughening its export control laws and agreeing to join the United States in a new program to develop antisubmarine warfare technology (Warrock and Husock 1988, 11–12). During Operation Desert Shield, bitter congressional criticism convinced Germany and Japan to provide financial aid to the multinational effort (Tagliabue 1990; Weisman 1990). When Congress reopened debate in 1991 on penalizing the Chinese government for its continued repression of prodemocracy demonstrators, "China agreed to join the Nuclear Non-Proliferation Treaty, and, for the first time in its history, allowed an international human rights commission to visit China" (Drinan and Kuo 1992, 39).

But congressional framing does not always have a substantive effect on policy. Foreign countries can and do dismiss the symbolic actions of Congress. And presidents sometimes respond to congressional pressure by changing the style and not the substance of policy. President Nixon reacted to opposition to the Vietnam War in part by taking the conflict underground (Schell 1975). When congressional and public criticism of U.S. policy toward El Salvador escalated in 1981, "administration officials simply stopped talking about Central America to reporters and . . . news coverage, especially on television, immediately dried up" (Hertsgaard 1989, 115). And, when President Bush came under attack in late 1991 for devoting too much attention to foreign policy, he responded by holding several highly publicized meetings with bankers, business executives, and economic advisers. The meetings were "meant more for public consumption near the start of the election campaign than as a genuine effort to bring about political changes" (Rosenbaum 1991).

Vices and Virtues

Congressional activism on diplomacy elicits considerable commentary, much of it negative. Irreconcilables claim that Congress has usurped the president's prerogatives. Eugene Rostow (1989, 7) goes so far as to argue that we are witnessing the transformation of "the President into a ceremonial figurehead graciously presiding over the activities of an omnipotent Congress." Even Skeptics seem to long for the days of bipartisanship. I. M. Destler, Les Gelb, and Anthony Lake (1984, 129) complain that Congress has made the foreign "policy debate *more* ideological and unreal." But does congressional activism actually hinder foreign policy? Does it help?

Any assessment of the vices and virtues of congressional activism is problematic. Most assessments vary with the question of whether one approves of what Congress wants to accomplish. Many of the same Irreconcilables who today denounce the "imperial Congress" applauded when conservatives on Capitol Hill obstructed Jimmy Carter's diplomatic initiatives. At the same time, no agreed-upon standard exists by which to judge whether foreign policy powers are properly allocated between Congress and the president or to measure which policies advance the "national interest." Thus, Bruce Jentleson's (1990, 184) claim that "the experiences in El Salvador and especially the Philippines should dispel the generalization that deference by Congress always is beneficial to U.S. diplomacy" might be true but it will hardly persuade those who supported the policies Ronald Reagan sought to pursue.

Without an agreed-upon standard of judgment, debates over the merits of congressional activism usually devolve into something akin to judging the merits of a flavor of ice cream—it's all a matter of taste. Yet, even without assuming a nonexistent consensus on the appropriate level of congressional activity, something can be said about the accuracy of the two major criticisms of Congress: that it meddles too much in the details of diplomacy and that it undermines the president's ability to negotiate with other countries.

Charges of micromanagement have become a standard criticism of Congress's interest in diplomacy. Upon taking office, for example, President Bush launched a campaign to reverse what he considered excessive congressional involvement in foreign policy (Fessler 1991). Observers with no institutional ax to grind worry that the foreign aid bill attracts too many amendments, that congressional reports have too many pages, and that Congress burdens the executive branch with detailed and often inconsistent advice (Crovitz 1990; Destler 1985; Jentleson 1990, 177; Owens 1990; Wiarda 1990, 219–20). Even members of Congress worry that they have gone overboard in their efforts to provide the foreign policy bureaucracy with programmatic advice (see, e.g., *Congressional Record* 1985, S 12340–41).

Complaints about congressional micromanagement have merit—legislators at times display a zest for the trivial. It does not take much effort to produce a list of congressional actions that, on the face of things at least, makes members of Congress look stupid (for just such a list, see Fessler 1991). Yet, as the Iran-Contra affair attests, members of Congress do not hold the monopoly on governmental stupidity.

A major problem with arguments about micromanagement is that many of the claims are misleading. Some commonly offered indicators of congressional activism are meaningless. Although the number of floor amendments to the foreign aid bill might interest people who value a tidy legislative process, it is hard to see why it should affect the quality of foreign policy. The same can be said for the number of pages in committee reports. Other claims about congressional activism are simply wrong. For all the complaints that Congress is placing greater and greater demands on the foreign policy bureaucracy, in several areas Congress's demands on the executive branch have fallen since the 1960s (General Accounting Office 1986).

One area in which congressional interest in the details of foreign policy has risen, an arena quite relevant to the success of U.S. diplomacy, is the budget. Again, it is easy to find budgetary changes that can be labeled trivial. Yet complaints about budgetary micromanagement typically miss two crucial points. First, Congress changes line items primarily to bring the president's budget request into line with what a majority of legislators is willing to spend (Art 1985a, 238; Lindsay 1991, 87). When the president submits politically realistic budgets, Congress makes fewer changes. Second, critics who urge members of Congress to shift their sights from budgetary details to the big picture forget that the purse strings are one of the few tools members have with which to influence diplomacy.

The other area in which congressional demands on the executive branch have increased is in the number of reports required of the foreign policy bureaucracy. But complaints about reporting requirements are overblown. The Defense Department, for example, spends $50 million per year, less than .02 percent of its budget, to comply with congressional reporting requirements and requests. This minuscule figure includes reports that virtually everyone agrees are needed, evidenced by the fact that the Defense Department has requested that some previously canceled reporting requirements be resurrected (Fessler 1991). Much the same is true at Foggy Bottom. A recent study of reporting requirements for the State Department and its affiliated agencies found that 63 percent of the reports serve a useful purpose and that another 19 percent are dead letters that place no demands on the executive branch. The cost of producing the reports is small. Nearly half "cost virtually nothing" to produce and many others "consist of information or policy analysis the administration has or needs anyway so there should be little additional cost" (U.S. Congress House Committee on Foreign Affairs 1988, 23).

The second major criticism of congressional activism is that it curtails the president's bargaining leverage and thereby hurts the national interest. Officials in the Reagan administration rallied behind the bargaining leverage argument when Democrats in Congress demanded changes in U.S. policy toward Nicaragua and in the U.S. position at the START negotiations. The bargaining leverage argument gained even greater currency during the Gulf crisis. Many commentators claimed that congressional debate over the U.S. presence in the Persian Gulf would have the perverse effect of making war more likely because it would convince the Iraqi leadership that President Bush lacked the political support needed to use military force to liberate Kuwait. Of course, the bargaining leverage argument assumes that the president's policy advances the national interest, an assumption many would dispute when the hypothetical is made concrete.

Lost amid all the complaints about members of Congress undercutting the president is the fact that the White House sometimes encourages congressional activism. When presidents want to put pressure on another country, but do not want to be seen doing so, Congress provides a convenient villain. One instance in which the administration and a member of Congress agreed to invoke a good cop–bad cop scenario was the effort in 1987 by Congressman William Broomfield (R-Mich.) to revoke New Zealand's right to buy U.S. military goods at preferential rates in retaliation for Wellington's decision to adopt a nuclear-free weapons policy. The Reagan administration already had responded to the policy by canceling U.S. security guarantees for New Zealand, and it feared that any further steps it took would be counterproductive. At a loss for an appropriate response of its own, the administration seized on the Broomfield bill. The administration not only supported the bill, it went so far as to suggest a time when the bill could be introduced so as to have maximum effect. It also asked Broomfield to remove language from the bill that would have given the president discretion in revoking the military preferences (Hoadley 1991).

Even when the White House does not want Congress's help—indeed, even if the administration bitterly opposes it—congressional activism may strengthen the president's negotiating position. Whether executive-legislative disagreement helps or hinders the president at the bargaining table depends on how the preferences of Congress and the president are distributed. When many in Congress prefer a policy that lies somewhere between what the president and a foreign country prefer, a situation that occurred with both START and Nicaragua during the Reagan years, congressional activism hurts (or at least does not help) the president's negotiating position. To the extent that foreign leaders follow and understand political divisions in Washington, they know to what extent the president faces pressure to compromise.

Whether the president compromises in these situations, however, depends on another factor, namely, how he values a compromise outcome relative to the status quo. If the president prefers the status quo to compromise, then no compromise will be forthcoming regardless of the level of congressional activism. This is what happened at the START talks during the Reagan administration. Legislators pleaded with the administration, and for a time held the MX missile program hostage, but in the end they could not force the president to bargain enthusiastically. The only exception to the general rule that Congress cannot force the president to accept a compromise are those few issues, primarily involving trade, in which Congress has constitutional authority to dictate U.S. policy.

Of course, critics worry not just that the president might concede under pressure from Capitol Hill but that legislators might prevent him from achieving his diplomatic objectives. Debate in Congress might convince foreign leaders to stand firm in the face of U.S. demands. Executive-legislative squabbling also might persuade foreign leaders that they can gain an advantage simply by waiting, that time might bring concessions.

As appealing as this logic is, it rests on the implicit assumption that foreign leaders are willing to accept the position favored by Congress. When this is the case, foreign leaders have a stake in waiting for U.S. policy to shift in the direction Congress favors. But frequently foreign leaders reject the policy positions of both the president and Congress. When this occurs, nothing that happens on Capitol Hill affects the outcome of negotiations. The Gulf war provides a textbook example. The fact that Iraq refused to capitulate to U.S. demands even after it suffered more than thirty days of heavy bombing makes it hard to sustain the argument that President Bush's attempt at coercive diplomacy would have worked if only members of Congress had been more enthusiastic in their support.

Instances in which groups in Congress want the president to compromise garner considerable media and scholarly attention. But many times members of Congress oppose compromise. This happens when members prefer an outcome more extreme than what the president prefers. In these situations congressional activism actually *strengthens* the president's bargaining position. Again, to the extent that foreign leaders follow and understand executive-legislative conflict, they know that the president's ability to compromise is limited. In turn, they know that they must be willing to compromise if an agreement is to be reached. Just such a dynamic governed the Carter administration's negotiations over the future of the Panama Canal (McDonough 1979a, 1979b). Hard-line congressional attitudes also regularly manifest themselves on trade, foreign aid, and human rights issues.

When the White House prefers the more moderate outcome, the president and Congress again play the roles of good cop and bad cop (though here the roles are not assumed by mutual consent). The danger when Congress acts as the bad cop is that this can prevent presidents from implementing policies that they think will advance the national interest. In the aftermath of the massacre at Tiananmen Square, for example, President Bush argued that the hard-line policy favored by many members of Congress would prove counter-productive in the long term. Again, one may doubt whether the president's policy made sense. But putting this complaint aside, presidents enjoy the upper hand when faced with congressional pressure to alter their policies. The widespread opposition to the Panama Canal treaties, for example, led the Carter administration to launch a nation-wide speech and media campaign that turned the tide of public and congressional opinion (McDonough 1979b, 8–11). Likewise, despite substantial criticism from Capitol Hill, President Bush resisted attempts to make major changes in his China policy.

Finally, congressional activism provides presidents with an advantage in foreign policy: a ready-made scapegoat. When presidents face pressure from members of Congress to compromise, they can blame foreign policy failures on congressional obstructionism, as Ronald Reagan frequently did. And, when substantial number of legislators hold more extreme policy views, presidents have a ready-made reason for disappointing the demands of foreign countries, even if Congress does nothing. To take just one example, presidents historically have used Congress as an excuse when they want to avoid providing U.S. aid to other countries (Siegel 1968, 35).

Conclusion

Congressional activism on foreign policy is a fact of life in the 1990s. If anything, the collapse of the Soviet Union, the intensifying economic rivalry with Europe and Japan, and the emergence of intermestic issues like global warming will encourage more congressional activism. At the same time, the pressure of long-neglected economic and social problems at home will fuel neo-isolationist sentiments, making it likely that some in Congress will try to reign in diplomatic initiatives they deem excessive.

But activism should not be confused with influence. Contrary to the apocalyptic claims of Irreconcilables, we are not witnessing an era of "foreign policy by Congress." The president (and by extension his advisers and the foreign policy bureaucracy) remain the dominant actors on foreign policy. To argue otherwise is to miss the tremendous formal and informal powers of the presidency. Presidents can veto legislation. They enjoy unparalleled access to the media and can set thereby the terms of debate. They can act in secrecy. They can take the initiative and hand Capitol Hill a fait accompli. Congress cannot begin to match these advantages.

By the same token, Skeptics err when they dismiss the effect Congress has on U.S. diplomacy. Although Congress functions as a secondary actor on foreign policy, it is an actor nonetheless. To be sure, members of Congress seldom succeed in forcing presidents to pursue policies against their will. Congressional influence is primarily negative; Congress can block presidential proposals. Failing that, it can force the president to build public support for his policies or to pay a political price for adhering to them. Nor is the braking power of Congress felt only on marginal issues. As the Reagan administration discovered with its policies toward Central America and the Philippines, Congress's influence extends to major foreign policy issues.

One consequence of congressional activism on foreign policy is conflict with the White House. The prospect of executive-legislative conflict worries many observers, some because they favor the president's policies and others because they believe that the country suffers when politics goes beyond the water's edge. The latter worry is the more troubling but, for all the concern expressed, instances in which congressional activism clearly hurts the national interest or the cause of good policy are in short supply.

The truth is that neither the president nor Congress monopolizes correct policy positions. Irreconcilables implicitly attest to this when they castigate Congress for blocking the policies of Ronald Reagan and George Bush while applauding it for obstructing the policies of Jimmy Carter. In any given situation the president and Congress both may have reasonable preferences or they both may have unreasonable preferences. Debate over which policy is correct is what, ultimately, is at stake in policy disputes. And, while observers may disagree over specific examples, in many cases the tug-of-war between Capitol Hill and the White House actually improves the content of U.S. diplomacy.

When alarms about congressional overreaching are sounded—as they invariably will be in the 1990s—it is worth remembering that conflict between the executive and the legislature is part and parcel of the American political system. As Richard Neustadt (1990, 29) notes, the Constitution provides for "separated institutions *sharing* power." As long as ideology and party divide the two ends of Pennsylvania Avenue, Congress and the president will struggle over the content of U.S. diplomacy.

Instances of conflict between the president and Congress should not be a cause for dismay. Democracies argue over the wisdom of policies. Unfortunately, the particular institutional arrangements of the American political system sometimes obscure the fact that real issues are being argued. "Politics" produces policy debates as well as other disputes. Irreconcilables and Skeptics seem to assume that politics produces *only* other—disreputable, illegitimate, and harmful—disputes. Sometimes congressional activism represents "noise" and sometimes it hurts U.S. interests. But many times it focuses on real issues and produces desirable outcomes. Congressional activism is, at its best, part of the debate on what constitutes wise diplomacy. At its worst, the president has many tools with which to outflank Congress.

CHAPTER 12

Congress and Foreign Trade Policy

Sharyn O'Halloran

For most commentators, U.S. trade policy begins and ends with the executive branch. They analyze the relation of trade policy to the president's agenda, the role of executive branch negotiators in constructing trade agreements, and trade policy as an extension of the president's overall foreign policy goals. Congress, on the other hand, is seen as playing only a minor part in shaping trade policy. Destler (1986a, 12; 1986b, 97) argues, for example, that the 1934 Reciprocal Trade Agreements Act (RTAA) marks a shift in decision-making authority away from Congress and toward the president. Extensions of the act added to the president's tariff-reduction powers and coincided with a dramatic decline in the tariff rate.

What motivated Congress to abdicate its authority? Proponents of what are sometimes referred to as presidential dominance models (Moe 1984) argue that Congress is unable to resist the demands of well-organized special interests (Destler 1986a; Goldstein 1988; Haggard 1988; Margolis 1986; Pastor 1980, 1983; A. Schlesinger 1973). The classic example of politicians being held captive by pressure groups is the 1930 Smoot-Hawley Tariff Act, in which producers' demands for protection resulted in the highest tariff levels of the twentieth century (Schattschneider 1935). To avoid disastrous political logrolls such as the Smoot-Hawley Tariff, legislators grant the president authority over trade policy-making and thereby insulate themselves from protectionist demands. The president, who has a national constituency, is less susceptible to the kind of particularism (product-specific protectionism) to which members of Congress are prone, and thus implements less protectionist trade policies than does Congress. From these delegations of authority in matters of trade, along with parallel developments in budgeting, regulatory administration, and war powers, Arthur Schlesinger (1973), Sundquist (1981), Margolis (1986), and others conclude that Congress has frittered away its constitutional authority. They contend that members of Congress are rarely active in trade policy, and that on those occasions when members are involved they are unable to alter the substance of policy.

Yet there are good theoretical and empirical reasons to believe that when Congress delegates authority to the executive it maintains considerable influence over trade policy. Recent developments in the regulatory literature that fall under the heading of the New Economics of Organizations argue that Congress is neither held captive by pressure groups nor dominated by the executive branch. Rather, the procedural arrangements that Congress designs when delegating authority play a key role in determining economic policy (McCubbins, Noll, and Weingast 1987, 1989; Moe 1984; Weingast 1984).[1]

My purpose in this chapter is to combine the logic of the New Economics of Organizations with traditional scholarship on trade policy. Similar to the conventional wisdom, I argue that Congress delegates authority to the president to overcome the dilemma it faces when passing trade legislation. But, in the spirit of the New Economics of Organizations, this delegation does not imply complete abdication. Rather, legislators design procedures by which they can limit, modify, or veto executive actions. Through these procedures, Congress can shape trade policy outcomes. For instance, one recent procedural innovation in trade policy is fast-track authority. Like many other procedural arrangements, fast-track authority empowers congressional agents in the executive branch (e.g., the U.S. trade representative) to take action on legislators' behalf, institutes a legislative veto, enfranchises new groups into the decision-making process through congressional hearings and private-sector advisory boards, and mandates an intricate web of reporting requirements. Thus, a comprehensive analysis of Congress's role in U.S. foreign trade policy must take into account not only when members of Congress delegate authority but the procedures they design to force the president to accommodate their demands.

The following section reviews the literature on trade policy formation. I present empirical evidence suggesting that congressional politics plays a larger role in regulating international trade than is generally acknowledged by presidential dominance models. The third section defines the current method for negotiating and implementing international trade agreements, namely, fast-track procedures. The fourth section examines the implementation of the U.S.-Canada Free Trade Agreement and illustrates how Congress influences policy outcomes through fast-track procedures. The final section discusses the implications of this analysis for the North American Free Trade Agreement

---

1. Unlike many other areas of foreign policy, the primacy of the legislative branch in trade policy-making is clearly defined. Article I, section 8, of the Constitution grants Congress the authority to regulate foreign commerce. In contrast, the president has no trade-specific authority and is limited to negotiating treaties subject to ratification by a two-thirds majority in the Senate.

and the ongoing Uruguay Round of the General Agreement on Tariffs and Trade (GATT).

Presidential Dominance Models

Proponents of presidential dominance models assume that Congress delegates authority to the president and then, for the most part, abdicates its control over trade policy. In pursuing foreign policy objectives, these scholars argue that the president is both willing and able to circumvent the wishes of Congress (Margolis 1986; Neustadt 1960; Robinson 1967; A. Schlesinger 1973; Sundquist 1981).

Presidential dominance models focus on the power and resources of the executive branch to initiate and enact trade policy. The president's agenda plays a central role in determining final outcomes because Congress is seen as being relatively far removed from annual decision making. Thus, presidents can forestall or prevent Congress from passing legislation that is not in line with their preferences. Legislators serve only to constrain or act as public critics of executive action. But they cannot alter the policy outcome and "they can only occasionally succeed in forcing the executive's attention on the need for change in policy, and hardly ever on developing and securing the adoption of an alternative policy on its own" (Hilsman 1958, 729–30).

A more sophisticated version of the presidential dominance model recognizes that Congress has some control over trade policy (Destler 1986a; Goldstein 1988, 191; Haggard 1988, 117; Pastor 1980). But Congress has very little desire to use it. Destler (1986b, 97) argues that Congress is the opposite of "the power-hungry force racing to protect particular industries, and that its members typically have wanted more executive branch aggressiveness on trade than have successive chief executives."

According to Pastor (1980, 191; 1983), Congress's role in making trade policy is mostly symbolic. By delegating authority to the president, legislators can shirk the blame for damaging administrative decisions while protecting their right to criticize foreign countries and the administration. Trade policy is characterized as a "cry-and-sigh" cycle (Pastor 1980). First there is a cry of protectionism when legislators introduce restrictive trade bills or amendments. A sigh of relief follows the passage of a liberal trade law, which originates with the president and benefits the economy overall. Moreover, Pastor argues that the delegation of power from Congress to the president works to the advantage of the United States because congressional committees and individual legislators are more interested in sending signals than in making policy. This decision-making process allows the United States to pursue liberal trade policies without holding members of Congress directly accountable to constituents injured by foreign imports. Legislators can thereby "claim credit" for championing the disaffected without having to deliver on their threats (Mayhew 1974).

The 1934 RTAA clearly marks a shift in power between Congress and the president regarding trade policy, as advocates of presidential dominance models claim. But it is unclear that this delegation implies the abdication of authority. Table 1 shows that, far from being disinterested observers, members of Congress continue to introduce and enact numerous trade bills. In the Ninety-fourth Congress, for example, members of the House of Representatives introduced 388 trade bills, reported 21 out of committee, and enacted 10 public laws. Further, on average, 85 percent of all international agreements and 72 percent of trade agreements are enacted through statutory authority delegated by Congress to the president (Johnson 1984; O'Halloran 1993).

Second, if the president dominates the decision-making process, then it would make little sense for Congress to pay much attention to the institutions by which trade policy is made. The history of American trade legislation reveals, however, that Congress invests an enormous amount of time and energy in defining the rules that govern executive actions. These rules include setting limits and general criteria, approving certain actions, and, as the 1988 Omnibus Trade Bill (OTB) shows, transferring authority away from presidents when they fail to respond to congressional demands (O'Halloran 1993).

TABLE 1.   Trade Bills for the House of Representatives, 90th to 98th Congresses

Congress	Total Trade Bills[a]		Total Trade Bills Reported[d]		Trade Bills that Became Law	
	Number[b]	Percent[c]	Number	Percent	Number	Percent
90 (1967–68)	1,063	5.16	24	2.25	14	58.33
92 (1971–72)	386	3.47	18	4.66	7	38.89
94 (1975–76)	388	3.45	21	5.41	10	47.61
96 (1979–80)	255	3.01	31	12.16	10	32.25
98 (1983–84)	309	4.79	19	6.15	6	31.57
Average	480.2	3.97	22.6	6.12	9.4	41.73

Sources: Coded from the *Calendars of the United States House of Representatives and History of Legislation* for the Ninetieth through the Ninety-eighth Congresses, and from the *Congressional Index*.

[a]I define trade bills as only those bills that directly affect the flow of imports and exports. The statistic does not include domestic legislation that indirectly affects imports (such as labeling requirements).

[b]The total number of bills includes all pieces of trade legislation. Some may be identical, similar, or a companion bill to another but, because there is no systematic method for eliminating possible redundancy, I include all pieces of trade legislation introduced.

[c]The percentage of all trade bills introduced is the ratio of the number of trade bills to the total number of bills introduced in the House of Representatives. The total number of bills introduced also includes similar, identical, and companion bills.

[d]This includes all trade bills reported from the House committee for consideration by the committee of the whole.

Third, standard models of congressional delegation make no allowances for partisan differences in preferences for or against protectionism. Therefore, I would expect members of the Republican party to introduce as many trade bills that become law as do members of the Democratic party. Table 2 shows, however, that on average, from the Ninetieth to the Ninety-eighth Congresses, more than 80 percent of all trade bills that became public law in the House of Representatives were introduced by a member of the majority (Democratic) party.

Similarly, if partisan effects do not influence voting patterns, a Republican should be at least as likely as a Democrat to support the policies of the president. Yet this was not the case in the passage of the OTB. The House passed the bill by a vote of 376 to 45. House Republicans voted 133 to 41 and House Democrats voted 243 to 4. In the Senate, the OTB passed by a vote of 85 to 11. Senate Republicans voted 35 to 10 and Senate Democrats voted 50 to 1. Of the Democrats, only Senator William Proxmire (D-Wis.) voted against the bill because a quota on cheese imports was not included. It would appear that congressional politics creates some partisan effects over the introduction and passage of trade legislation.

At the very least, this evidence suggests that a number of behavioral patterns are inconsistent with the hypothesis that Congress has legislated itself out of the business of making trade policy. Although Congress delegates some authority to the president, it continues to monitor the use of this authority closely and to play an active role in making trade policy. What is needed, then, is a theory of the political control of policy accomplished through, not in spite of, the delegation process. The New Economics of Organizations argues that to explain and predict policy outcomes it is necessary to pay close atten-

TABLE 2. Party and Trade Bills in the House of Representatives, 90th to 98th Congresses

Congress	Majority Party	Total Trade Bills Reported[a]	Total Bills Reported Introduced by Majority Party[b]	Total Bills that Became Law	% of Bills that Became Law Introduced by Majority Party
90 (1967–68)	Democratic	24	22	14	79
92 (1971–72)	Democratic	18	13	7	86
94 (1975–76)	Democratic	21	13	10	50
96 (1979–80)	Democratic	31	26	10	90
98 (1983–84)	Democratic	19	19	6	100

Source: Calendars of the United States House of Representatives and History of Legislation for the Ninetieth through the Ninety-eighth Congresses, and *Congressional Index.*
[a]This includes all trade bills reported from a House committee for consideration by the committee of the whole.
[b]This includes all trade bills reported out of committee the primary sponsor of which was a member of the majority party. The bill could have multiple sponsors. Cosponsors do not necessarily belong to the same party as the primary sponsor.

tion to the institutions through which policy is made. To this end, I next examine fast-track procedures for negotiating and implementing U.S. trade policy.

The Politics of Fast-Track Procedures

The 1974 Trade Reform Act expanded the institutional structure within which U.S. trade policy is made. For the first time, Congress authorized the president to enter into trade agreements meant to reduce nontariff barriers as well as tariffs. But in granting this authority Congress also established special procedures for implementing international trade agreements. The procedures have come to be known as the "fast track."

Congress adopted fast-track procedures to reduce the chance that an agreement negotiated by the president would be rejected, as happens to some treaties, or amended, as is common when Congress alone drafts the implementing legislation.[2] Once an agreement is formally submitted to Congress, debate is limited and the legislation is considered without the possibility of amendment. Pastor (1983), Destler (1986b), and Goldstein (1986) argue that, because fast-track procedures restrict Congress to an up-or-down vote, members have ceded much of their legislative authority over international trade policy to the president. As predicted by the New Economics of Organizations, however, a more thorough examination of fast-track procedures reveals that Congress retains significant control over trade policy outcomes despite the delegation of authority.

Fast-track procedures, and all procedural arrangements for that matter, serve three functions. First, they provide Congress with a veto over executive actions. Common requirements include congressional approval procedures or the possibility of a disapproval resolution.

Second, fast-track procedures provide Congress with information. Members of Congress participate directly in international negotiations and can monitor thereby the actions of the executive. This is an example of so-called police-patrol oversight, wherein members of Congress directly review and oversee the actions taken by the president or an executive agency. Congress also creates executive agents, so-called fire inspectors, such as the U.S. trade

---

2. An example of an occasion when Congress failed to enact the president's international trade agreement is the 1979 East Coast Fishing Treaty between the United States and Canada, which divided the fish and scallops in the Georges Bank area off the coast of Maine (Murray 1983, 1058). The Kennedy Round of the GATT negotiations provides an example of the conflict that can occur between Congress and the president when enacting a trade agreement. A heated debate broke out between Congress and the administration over the repeal of the American Selling Price. The end result was numerous exemptions and special provisions to compensate industries hard pressed by imports ("Pressures Mounting for Import Quota Legislation" 1968).

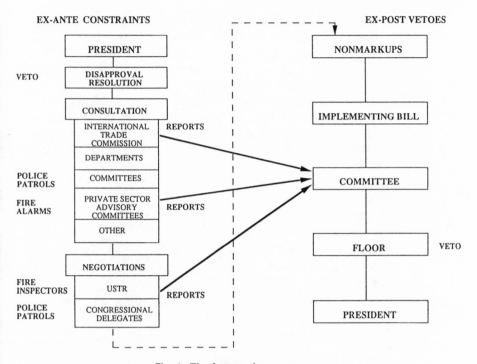

Fig. 1. The fast-track process

representative (USTR), who oversee other agencies. Further, Congress enfranchises constituents into the decision-making process so that, if the executive takes actions that are objectionable, the interest group can seek a remedy from the agency, the courts, or from Congress itself. Private sector advisory committees and public hearings serve this purpose. Such indirect monitoring is commonly known as fire-alarm oversight (McCubbins and Schwartz 1984).

Third, fast-track procedures help members of Congress define their preferred policy. They let legislators know what the president or executive agency is doing (direct and indirect oversight) and inform the president or agency, and sometimes members of Congress, about what policies are electorally acceptable. By requiring studies and reports with specified criteria, by mandating public hearings, and by enfranchising private sector advisory committees in the decision-making process, members of Congress can determine which groups will benefit from the agreement and which will be injured. Congress can thereby influence policy at many points in the negotiation and implementation of a trade agreement.

Figure 1 divides fast-track procedures into ex-ante requirements, which constrain the executive's discretionary authority before and during international negotiations, and ex-post requirements, which give Congress an opportunity to "amend" or veto the agreement. Ex-ante requirements include the initial vote over the use of fast-track procedures, congressional monitoring and advice, consultation with executive departments and private sector advisory committees, and public hearings. Ex-post requirements include "non-markup" sessions (drafting the implementing legislation) and congressional approval procedures. In this section, I describe each step in the fast-track process. My purpose is to show that Congress has considerable input in the decision-making process, much more than is recognized by cursory treatments of fast track.

Ex-ante Requirements: Constraints on Administrative Action

With implementation of the 1974 procedural reforms Congress strengthened its oversight role in the negotiation and implementation of foreign trade policy. To further safeguard producer and consumer interests, Congress created a complete prenegotiation advisory system that increased the participation of the public, members of Congress, and various government agencies in the negotiation process. It also designated the USTR as the focal point in the executive branch for carrying out trade policies.

The Disapproval Resolution

At the onset, the president faces a possible veto of the proposed fast-track procedures. Before beginning negotiations under fast-track implementing procedures, the president must notify the Senate Finance Committee and the House Ways and Means Committee. If either committee passes a resolution within sixty days disapproving the negotiations, fast-track implementing procedures do not apply. The committees determine whether traditional methods such as introducing separate implementing legislation or the treaty process are preferable to the use of fast-track approval procedures. Only agreements that members of Congress expect will benefit their constituents will be accepted. Otherwise Congress will pass a disapproval resolution. At this point Congress can force the president to make concessions such as removing certain articles from the negotiations or making the agreement contingent on other factors. Congress thereby limits not only which agreements the president can negotiate but the method by which an agreement becomes law. Further refinement of the president's initial proposal takes place through consultation with various government and private sector groups.

Consultation and Advice

Perhaps the most interesting feature of fast-track procedures is the extensive prenegotiation advisory system. Congress established an elaborate fire-alarm oversight mechanism that incorporates the private sector, government agencies, and even congressional committees in developing international trade agreements. These consultations serve two purposes. First, groups sensitive to or threatened by the proposed agreement are given an opportunity to express their concerns and seek compensation. Second, negotiators learn from the consultations which industries, if ignored, may lobby members of Congress to veto an eventual agreement. The requirements for consultation and advice are defined as follows.

In connection with any proposed trade agreement, the president must furnish the International Trade Commission (ITC) with a list of articles to be discussed during the negotiations. Within ninety days, the ITC advises the president about the probable economic effects on labor, consumers, and industries that produce like or directly competitive articles. The ITC also conducts any additional investigations requested by the president or the USTR. Further, the president consults with the agriculture, commerce, defense, interior, labor, state, and treasury departments, the USTR, and each congressional committee having jurisdiction over legislation affected by a trade agreement.

Private-sector advisory committees play a central part in the consultation stage. The Trade Reform Act established an institutional framework that gives representative elements from the private sector an opportunity to express their views to U.S. negotiators. These committees inform and advise the president about negotiating objectives and bargaining positions before he enters into an agreement, about the impact of a proposed agreement, and about other matters arising in connection with the development, implementation, and administration of U.S. trade policy. This elaborate advisory system keeps legislators informed of executive actions and lets the executive, and members of Congress, know which constituents would be adversely affected by the proposed agreement (see U.S. Congress House Committee on Ways and Means 1973, 39; U.S. Congress Senate Committee on Finance 1974, 101). Interest groups can thereby seek remuneration either through administrative procedures such as the escape clause or unfair trade practices provisions or by directly pressuring legislators for exemptions.

There are four types of private sector advisory committees. First, the Advisory Committee for Trade Policy and Negotiations is composed of forty-five members, including representatives of state and local governments, labor, industry, agriculture, small business, service industries, retailers, and consumer interests. The committee is broadly representative of the key sectors and groups in the economy. Its members are recommended by the USTR and appointed by the president for a two-year term. Second, the president can establish general policy advisory committees for industry, labor, agriculture, services, investment, defense, and other interests. Their members are appointed by the USTR in consultation with departmental secretaries. Third, the president can establish sector or functional advisory committees, which represent all industry, labor, agricultural, or service (including small business) interests affected by the agreement. Their members also are appointed by the USTR in consultation with the departmental secretaries. Fourth, the president can establish state and local government policy advisory committees, which provide advice on overall policy objectives.

To the maximum extent practicable, the USTR keeps members of the advisory committees informed before and during negotiations. Further, committee members may be designated as advisers to a negotiating delegation and participate in international meetings. However, members of the advisory committee may not speak or negotiate for the United States. In addition to the private sector and state and local government advisory committees, the president provides private organizations with another opportunity to submit trade information and policy recommendations. Before entering into negotiations, the president holds public hearings on matters relevant to the proposed trade agreement, including any article under consideration for modification and concessions that should be sought by the United States.

Negotiations

The next stage in the process is negotiation. The Trade Expansion Act of 1962 established the special representative for trade negotiations as the official who, acting for the president, represents the United States in all international trade negotiations. The explicit intention of the House Ways and Means Committee in establishing the position of trade representative was to create a "focal point in the executive branch for the responsibilities for carrying out the authorities delegated to the president by the Congress under trade agreement legislation." Additionally, the post was created to "down-play the strictly foreign policy orientation that trade agreement negotiations had been subjected to under the leadership of the Department of State" (U.S. Congress House Committee on Ways and Means 1973, 40).

The 1974 Trade Reform Act reestablished the Office of the Special Representative for Trade Negotiations as an agency in the Executive Office of the President. The Ways and Means Committee sought to

reaffirm its belief that a strong and independent office, headed by a Government official reporting directly to the President and responsible to the Congress, is the best means of assuring that in trade policy matters the United States is speaking with one strong voice on behalf of the executive branch and that positions taken accurately reflect the intent of Congress. (ibid.)

The office is headed by the USTR, who is appointed by the president with the advice and consent of the Senate.

To provide for careful and continuous congressional oversight, the 1974 Trade Reform Act allows congressional delegates, accredited as official advisers, to participate directly in international negotiations (U.S. Congress Senate Committee on Finance 1974, 113). At the beginning of each congressional session, the Speaker of the House of Representatives (upon recommendation of the chair of the Ways and Means Committee) and the president of the Senate (upon the recommendation of the chair of the Finance Committee) appoint delegates. The USTR keeps each official adviser informed of the progress of negotiations.

Reports

Reporting requirements are another form of direct oversight Congress has over the executive branch. The Advisory Committee for Trade Policy and Negotiations, each general advisory committee, and each sector or functional advisory committee meets at the conclusion of negotiations for each trade agreement and submits a report to the president, the Congress, and the USTR. The reports from the Advisory Committee for Trade Policy and Negotiations and the general advisory committees state whether, and to what extent, the agreement promotes the economic interests of the United States and achieves the principal negotiating objectives set out in the prenegotiation consultations. These reports further state whether the agreement provides for equity and reciprocity within sectors and the extent to which their advisory opinion was included in the negotiations.

In addition to the advisory committee reports, the president submits to Congress an annual report on the progress of trade agreements under negotiation and on the national trade policy agenda. The USTR consults periodically with the congressional committees regarding overall objectives and priorities, and she reports directly to the Finance and Ways and Means Committees. The secretary of the treasury and the ITC face similar reporting requirements.

Reverse Fast-Track

With the 1988 Omnibus Trade Bill, Congress added another safeguard over the president's exercise of delegated authority: the threat to repeal fast-track negotiating privileges through a "reverse fast-track." If the president fails to meet the requirements for consultation with congressional committees, and if both the House and the Senate pass a disapproval resolution within any sixty-day period, fast-track procedures for implementing an international trade agreement will be repealed, thereby terminating the negotiations. In the House, a resolution of disapproval must be introduced by the chair or the ranking minority member of the Ways and Means *or* the Rules Committee, and it must be reported by both the Ways and Means *and* the Rules Committees. In the Senate, a resolution of disapproval must be an original resolution of the Finance Committee. Congress considers these resolutions under fast-track procedures, which limit debate and prohibit amendments.

The threat of withdrawing special consideration procedures does not imply that the president will accede to all the concerns expressed by the private sector advisory committees in negotiating international trade agreements. It does, however, encourage the president to consult with members of Congress and keep them informed as to what actions are taken. The possibility that Congress will use its veto power provides a credible threat over executive actions and ensures that many of the concerns expressed during the prenegotiation stage will be reflected in the final agreement.

Ex-post Requirements: Congressional Approval Procedures

Once the president enters into a trade agreement with a foreign country or countries, the process is far from over. In many ways it has only begun. Next the agreement must be implemented by Congress.

Congressional Committees: The Nonmarkups

Before the formal introduction of a bill, Congress has one more chance to influence the outcome. In collaboration with the administration, congressional committees draft the implementing legislation. The president consults with the Ways and Means and Finance Committees thirty days before formally submitting to Congress a bill implementing an international trade agreement that changes or repeals a domestic statute. These informal consultations between the executive and the congressional committees, commonly called nonmarkup sessions, give committee members an opportunity to protect domestic industries that otherwise would be injured by more open competition. It is at this point in the implementation process that adjustment between the president and members of Congress takes place. Although technically no amendments are allowed, committee members consider the draft bill and make "recommendations" as to what changes in domestic law are required to meet the obligations of the international agreement and any additional provisions to either compensate or exempt disaffected groups. These activities perform the function of the markup sessions and conference committees in the normal legislative process. Congress thereby shapes the implementing legislation without violating its commitment not to amend the agreement once it is formally introduced.

The Implementing Bill

After entering into the agreement and consulting with the appropriate congressional committees on how to "package" the legislation, the president sends a copy of the text of the agreement to the House and the Senate. The implementing legislation includes a draft of the bill, a statement of any necessary administrative action, and a summary of the effects the agreement will have on existing legislation. The implementing bill is then introduced simultaneously in the House and the Senate by the majority and the minority leaders. Next, the Speaker of the House and the president of the Senate refer the implementing bill to the Ways and Means and Finance Committees and to other committees of either chamber with jurisdiction over the legislation affected by the agreement. If, at the end of forty-five days, the bill has not been reported, the committees are discharged automatically from further consideration of the bill.

Floor Consideration

Finally, the bill must pass by a majority vote in the House and Senate. Floor consideration is restricted and no amendments are permitted. On or before the fifteenth day after the bill is reported or discharged from committee, each chamber is required to vote on final passage of the bill. Debate in the House and Senate, which is limited to not more than twenty hours, is divided equally among proponents and opponents.

Summary

Fast-track procedures for the consideration of international trade agreements shield legislation from amendments and filibusters. These procedures allow members of Congress to overcome the dilemma they face when passing trade legislation and to obtain the collectively preferred outcome of entering into international trade agreements that promote American exports. At the same time, fast-track implementing procedures reduce the kind of uncertainty over passage that accompanies some treaties. In restricting themselves to the fast track, however, members of Congress do not just reserve for themselves the symbolic role of critic and issuer of statements, as presidential dominance models claim. At each point in the negotiation and implementation process, Congress can sway the outcome. The Ways and Means and Finance Committees can veto fast-track procedures. The USTR consults with congressional committees before and during the negotiations. Members actively participate in the negotiations. Congressional committees draft the implementing legislation. And, finally, a majority in Congress must approve the agreement. The final policy outcome is the result of each of these procedural points. The next section examines implementation of the U.S.-Canada Free Trade Agreement (FTA) and illustrates how Congress influenced its substance through fast-track procedures.

The U.S.-Canada Free Trade Agreement

The United States and Canada have the world's largest bilateral trade, totaling $166 billion in 1987. About 73 percent of Canada's total exports of merchandise and about 66 percent of its total imports are accounted for by the United States. On the other hand, the United States sells 24 percent of its merchandise exports to Canada and purchases 17 percent of its total imports from Canada. Total bilateral foreign direct investment exceeds $68 billion. The advantages of a free-trade zone are obvious.

Barriers to entering into such an agreement are evident also. The Canadian government's presence in the Canadian economy is extensive. It runs the country's major airline, the railroad, telephone services, and an oil company. Canadian tariffs on U.S. dutiable exports average 10 percent, compared to an average U.S. tariff of 3 percent on dutiable imports from Canada. On the American side of the border, there also are sources of strong opposition to the free-trade agreement. The potato farmers of Aroostook County, Maine, once "the potato capital of the world," face increased competition from imported Canadian potatoes. Washington State lumbermen complain of unfair Canadian trade practices in the form of government-subsidized stumpage fees. Truckers, oil companies, airlines, uranium miners, border television stations, gas companies, and magazine publishers all criticize Canadian trade practices (Murray 1983). This contention is further noted in the numerous unfair pricing and subsidy cases U.S. companies have filed against Canada, involving such commodities as salted codfish, raspberries, and pork products (Pattison 1991). A free-trade agreement would require major changes in domestic legislation on both sides of the border.

Nonetheless, the cornerstone of the FTA is a gradual reduction of all tariffs on bilateral trade. Tariffs on about 10 percent of all dutiable items imported from Canada—including articles such as data processing and telecommunications equipment, motorcycles, whiskey and rum, raw hides, leather, and furs—were terminated upon the implementation of the FTA. The rest of the tariffs on dutiable items are to be phased out. Tariff rates for 35 to 40 percent of all dutiable goods will be lowered over five years, with reductions of 20 percent each year. The remaining tariffs on Canadian imports will be phased out over ten years.

The FTA also reduces some nontariff barriers, liberalizes certain restrictions on investment and services, and establishes a binational system for review of national determinations on unfair pricing and subsidy practices. The FTA prohibits future Canadian and American law and regulations from discriminating against providers of services such as construction, tourism, insurance, telecommunications, wholesale and retail trade, management and other business services, and computer and some professional services. But, in seeking to open Canadian markets to U.S. exports, economic sectors such as agriculture, mining, and fishing will be injured by increased imports. Numerous provisions have been included to compensate these economic interests.

Moreover, a number of industries are exempt from tariff reductions. For example, plywood retains the existing tariff rates until a common performance standard between the two countries can be arranged. The FTA requires the president to negotiate reciprocal quotas on potatoes and voluntary export restraints on steel. Temporary duties on fruits and vegetables also have been imposed. One provision requires the president to take retaliatory measures if Canada enacts fish-landing requirements. New England sardine and herring canners, who depend upon Canadian raw fish, are thereby protected from possible Canadian export controls.

Congress incorporated numerous procedures to protect industries, including rules-of-origin requirements for duty free entry, and studies on beef, dairy, egg, and automotive products, and on numerous natural resources. These studies can be used by industries to qualify for import relief under the escape clause and unfair trade provisions.

For the most part the FTA succeeded in creating a harmonized system of customs classification and in eliminating tariffs on most product categories over ten years.[3] But with regard to nontariff barriers the results have been decidedly mixed. The agreement provides for only a few explicit regulations. It eliminates some quotas on poultry and eggs, relaxes U.S. health and safety standards on Canadian exports of pork products, and removes the duty remissions program for motor vehicle parts. But, to ensure congressional approval, many of the most contentious issues were left to be resolved either through dispute-settlement mechanisms or in future negotiations (O'Halloran and Noll 1991).

---

3. In May of 1990 the United States and Canada agreed to accelerate the elimination of tariffs on over four hundred products (U.S. Congress House 1991).

The FTA reduces minor trade irritants such as tariff barriers and relieves some of the uncertainty in dealing with domestic trade regulations. But, clearly, fewer gains have been made than were expected. To explain why the FTA took the shape it did, I next examine the negotiation and implementation of the agreement.

Negotiating the U.S.-Canada
Free Trade Agreement

On 10 December 1985, President Reagan gave formal notice to Congress of his intent to enter into negotiations leading to a bilateral free-trade agreement with Canada. The initial goal of the president was to reduce general tariff barriers and thereby open Canadian markets to U.S. exports. Reagan specifically highlighted government procurement and funding programs, air transport, energy trade, high technology goods and related services, and intellectual property rights (U.S. Executive Office of the President 1986, 1465).

To most officials of the administration, and especially to USTR Clayton Yeutter, the proposal was uncontroversial. The administration's request was almost disapproved, however. In the hearings before the Finance Committee, various senators expressed concern about the possible adverse effects of the agreement. For example, Russell Long (D-La.) protested the effects that increased Canadian imports of oil and natural gas would have on domestic industries. Max Baucus (D-Mont.) and Robert Packwood (R-Ore.) expressed concern over the lumber industry. George Mitchell (D-Maine) protested the Canadian diversion program for its potato farmers (see U.S. Congress Senate Committee on Finance 1986). The Senate Finance Committee's threat to reject the fast-track authority could have ended the negotiations. Despite the particularistic concerns expressed by some, the committee's hostility toward the proposed trade talks reflected a broader concern voiced by Senator John C. Danforth (R-Mo.) and other congressional leaders over the Reagan administration's incoherent trade policy (Tobin 1987).

On 23 April 1986, the Senate Finance Committee rejected a resolution of disapproval by a 10-10 tie. By defeating the resolution, the committee granted permission to the White House to begin trade talks with Canada under fast-track procedures (Pressman 1986). But the administration's close victory occurred only after it had made considerable concessions. For example, to win the pivotal votes of Steven Symms (R-Idaho) and Senator Packwood, President Reagan was forced to pledge to resolve the lumber dispute, a historical point of contention between the United States and Canada. The issue was resolved on 30 December 1986 when Canada imposed a 15 percent tax on exports of softwood lumber to the United States until such time that fair-pricing standards could be agreed upon (U.S. Executive Office of the President 1986, 1653; see also Pressman 1986, 906).[4]

The second step in negotiating the agreement was consultation among the administration, Congress, and representatives of various special interests. In the hearings on the U.S.-Canada Free Trade Agreement held before the Senate Finance Committee, the advisory committees expressed concern over numerous measures such as subsidies for the lumber industry, diversion programs for potato farmers, high Canadian tariffs, the treatment of foreign investment, trade in services, protection of intellectual property rights, and various forms of government assistance at both the federal and provincial level. Specific industries that opposed the agreement included New England potato farmers, and the steel, uranium, and plywood industries (see U.S. Congress Senate Committee on Finance 1986).

The administration consulted closely with the appropriate committees throughout the negotiating process and when drafting the formal language of the agreement. As evidence of congressional influence in the negotiation process, many of the concerns raised by Congress and the private sector advisory committees (such as the temporary duties on fruits and vegetables) were addressed in the agreement signed by President Reagan and Prime Minister Brian Mulroney.

**Implementing the U.S.-Canada
Free Trade Agreement**

On 2 January 1988, Prime Minister Mulroney and President Reagan signed the U.S.-Canada Free Trade Agreement. In implementing the agreement under fast-track procedures, congressional committees, in collaboration with the president, drafted the implementing legislation. Ways and Means and Finance, joined by seven other House committees and five from the Senate, had to agree on revisions in order to bring domestic legislation into conformity with the president's proposal. From February to May of 1988, the committees held public hearings, nonmarkup sessions, and a "nonconference" to reconcile the differences between the House and the Senate. Numerous provisions were introduced such as mandatory retaliation against Canadian export controls on fish, the requirement to negotiate potato import quotas, size limitations on imported crustaceans (lobsters), and aid to the uranium industry.

Senators Danforth and Baucus of the Finance Committee also introduced an amendment to the implementing bill that addressed Canadian subsidies.

---

4. The recent decision by Canada to repeal the tax on its lumber exports to the United States may ignite once again the long-standing argument between the two countries (Urquhart 1991).

The Danforth-Baucus amendment for nonferrous smelters contained three major provisions. First, the amendment defined as one of the primary negotiating objectives the elimination of subsidies. Second, it included a provision to terminate the agreement if progress was not made toward removing such unfair trade practices. And, third, it included an interim procedure to monitor Canadian subsidies and impose offsetting duties or take some other action under U.S. trade law. This measure was drafted for nonferrous metals but it could be extended to industries faced with similar difficulties such as coal. The Canadian protested the Finance Committee's recommendation because it singled them out from other countries that partake in similar trade practices. A compromise was reached and the provision was broadened to include other countries with which the United States might enter into similar agreements. The Finance Committee also pushed the administration to interpret the terms of the agreement so as to impose restrictions on Canadian wheat imports if domestic farmers were threatened (*Congressional Record* 1988b, S12789–91).

On 14 July 1988, congressional committees gave their final approval to the draft bill. Only after both the House and the Senate committees informally approved the bill did the president formally introduce the implementing legislation to Congress. In submitting the implementing bill, however, the president was not bound by the recommendations made at the nonmarkup stage. The uranium and lobster provisions were not included in the implementing legislation.[5] Although congressional consideration is limited, and no amendments are permitted, the agreement still must be approved by both chambers. Therefore, if the president does not accept the committees' recommendations, strong opposition on the House and Senate floor is likely. This was evident in the debate over the bailout proposal for the uranium industry. Senator Pete Domenici (R-N.M.) almost derailed the FTA because it exempted Canada from import restrictions on unprocessed uranium (*Congressional Record* 1988a, S1460).

On 9 August 1988, the House passed the FTA by a vote of 366 to 40. One month later, by an 83 to 9 margin, the Senate approved the implementing legislation. Finally, on 28 September 1988, President Reagan signed the bill implementing the U.S.-Canada Free Trade Agreement.

The lopsided vote in the House and Senate suggests neither indifference toward the agreement nor a situation in which members blindly followed the president's initiative. Congress devoted an enormous amount of time and attention to the trade agreement. Legislators had the opportunity to respond to

---

5. Although the uranium industry did not receive its bailout proposal, it was made eligible for special protection under the monitoring program. The lobster provision was included later in an amendment to the Magnuson Fishery Conservation Act, which limited the size of lobster imports into the United States.

constituency pressures during the negotiation and drafting process. By the time the agreement reached the House and Senate floor, only a few members voted against the legislation.

Summary

The U.S.-Canada Free Trade Agreement was designed to achieve maximum leverage for American exports. At the same time the FTA provided either protection or compensation to industries that would have difficulty competing in more open markets. These measures allowed members of Congress and the president to grant benefits to constituents who wanted improved access to foreign markets, a solution to the highly visible and politically salient problem of the mounting trade deficit, and compensation to industries adversely affected by lower tariffs. Some of these payoffs, as in the case of plywood, came as a promise to negotiate for the removal of foreign subsidies. Other payoffs came in the form of administrative protection. The FTA also contained an enormous number of exception clauses, which granted short-term protection to damaged industries: reciprocal potato quotas, voluntary export restraints for steel, fish-landing requirements, and so forth. The final outcome was a broad compromise between Congress and the president. What is important to note is that the nature of this bargain was structured by the implementing process.

Future Challenges for U.S. Trade Policy

The U.S.-Canada Free Trade Agreement illustrates what the United States may expect to achieve in future international negotiations: gains will be made on eliminating tariff barriers but the influence that fast track gives Congress makes the potential for removing nontariff barriers far more remote. By way of concluding the chapter, I apply these lessons to the proposed North American Free Trade Agreement (NAFTA) and the broader, multilateral trade negotiations held under GATT.

In the case of the North American Free Trade Agreement, it seems likely that less progress will be made toward eliminating overall trade barriers than was achieved in the U.S.-Canada FTA. One aspect that facilitated the success of the FTA with Canada was similar health and safety standards, labor laws, and environmental regulations. This is not the case with Mexico. For example, Mexico uses pesticides that are prohibited in the United States and Canada. Mexico has less stringent environmental and health and safety regulations, which has raised fears of border pollution and industry flight. Besides these differences in domestic regulations, two additional circumstances make the negotiations with Mexico and Canada uncertain.

First, protectionist pressures are rising as trade issues move to the forefront of national political debate. The United States currently faces a recession, which suggests that more industries are sensitive to import competition. The most vocal opposition to the proposed free-trade agreement comes from fruit and vegetable producers, textile and apparel manufacturers, auto suppliers, and the steel industry, all of whose products compete directly with Mexican imports. This opposition is difficult to ignore in hard economic times.

Congress has become more protectionist as well. When the House and the Senate agreed to consider the FTA under fast track, Republicans were the majority party in the Senate. This explains the strong emphasis in the U.S.-Canada agreement on western and agricultural interests whose regions are staunchly Republican. The Democrats currently command a majority in both chambers; consequently, the areas of importance now are eastern manufacturing regions and the rust belt. Traditionally Democratic constituencies in these areas (steel, textiles, manufactures, and auto producers) have voiced strong opposition to the proposed NAFTA. In the recent extension of fast-track authority, labor and environmental groups successfully lobbied Congress for amendments to the authorizing legislation. Labor won promises of retraining grants, while environmentalists received assurance that no environmental degradation would result from NAFTA. Moreover, Majority Leader Richard Gephardt (D-Mo.), who made the U.S.-Canada FTA a central issue in his unsuccessful 1988 presidential campaign, has promoted industries' positions concerning "unfair" trade practices. Even in supporting the extension of fast-track authority, he threatened that "if the administration trades away American jobs, or tolerates pollution or abuse of workers, Congress can and will amend or reject the agreement" (Cloud 1991a, 1181).

Second, institutional changes have given Congress more leverage in the negotiation process. The main procedural change since the passage of the FTA is the introduction of reverse fast-track, which allows Congress to pass a resolution repealing the use of fast-track authority. Moreover, in the recent reauthorization of fast track for the Uruguay Round of negotiations, the House passed a nonbinding resolution emphasizing that Congress could revoke fast track if the administration fails to protect U.S. workers, industries, and the environment (Cloud 1991b, 1257). These procedural changes and negotiation contingencies make the implementation of NAFTA even more precarious than was the U.S.-Canada agreement. Hence, Gephardt's threat to amend or veto the treaty may be credible.

The prospects for the current Uruguay Round are even more problematic. While the same political and economic impediments exist as were seen in the NAFTA, the GATT negotiations have additional difficulties. On the one hand, since successive agreements largely have eliminated tariff barriers between GATT signatories, the only issues left to bargain over are the more intractable, nontariff measures such as subsidies, product standards, and protection of intellectual property rights. On the other hand, whereas the scope of conflict in bilateral and regional agreements is limited, a GATT agreement requires policy coordination among many diverse nations. The GATT rounds thus face the task of negotiating agreements on difficult issues that many nations must accept simultaneously. For instance, European Community members have been extremely reluctant to surrender their agricultural subsidies. Japan is unwilling to open its domestic markets to U.S. rice exports. And the newly industrializing countries of Asia, protected by GATT rules that exempt developing countries, have refused to adhere to the codes regulating their more industrialized trading partners. In short, the debate concerning both the North American Free Trade Agreement and the Uruguay Round will not be over whether Congress approves the agreement or not. Rather, the debate will center on what concessions must be made by the president to accommodate congressional demands.

Conclusion

This chapter argues that to explain U.S. trade policy one must examine the *process* by which it is made. The question is not whether Congress or the president dominates decision making; clearly, both branches of government play an integral role in policy formation. Rather, how does Congress structure delegations of authority to retain some measure of control over policy?

Unfortunately one cannot infer back from policy outcomes to the relative influence of Congress vis-à-vis the president. If the president acts rationally, the constraints designed by Congress to limit his actions will not be used. Congressional committees will never deny him fast-track authority, reverse fast-track proceedings will never be invoked, and no agreement will be voted down. Thus, the outcomes when the president dominates the decision-making process are *observationally equivalent* to what occurs when Congress constrains the president.

The analysis presented above attempts to untangle outcomes and processes. I first enumerate the details of fast-track implementing procedures, and legislators' motives for designing them as such. I then examine the negotiation and implementation of the U.S.-Canada Free Trade Agreement and show each point in the decision-making process at which members of Congress influenced the substance of the agreement. I do not conclude that Congress dominates decision making; certainly any delegation of authority weakens members' control over the final outcome. But I do show that legislators affect policy through the procedures they design. Congress thereby can influence foreign-trade policy not *despite* delegation but *through* it.

References

Aberbach, Joel D. 1987. "The congressional committee intelligence system: Information, oversight, and change." *Congress and the Presidency* 14:51–76.

Adams, Gordon M. 1977. "Disarming the military subgovernment." *Harvard Journal on Legislation* 14:459–503.

———. 1992. *Testimony before the House Budget Committee on the direction of the defense budget and long-term defense planning.* Washington, D.C.: Defense Budget Project.

Ahrari, Mohammed E., ed. 1987. *Ethnic groups and U.S. foreign policy.* New York: Greenwood Press.

Albert, Carl. 1990. *Little giant.* Norman: Univ. of Oklahoma Press.

Albritton, Robert B., and Jarol B. Manheim. 1983. "News of Rhodesia: The impact of a public relations campaign." *Journalism Quarterly* 60:622–28.

Allison, Graham T. 1971. *Essence of decision: Explaining the Cuban missile crisis.* Boston: Little, Brown.

Almond, Gabriel A. 1950. *The American people and foreign policy.* New York: Harcourt, Brace.

Ambrose, Stephen E. 1991–92. "The presidency and foreign policy." *Foreign Affairs* 70:120–37.

Anderson, James R. 1982. "The political economy of the MX missile." Lansing: Employment Research Associates, Michigan State Univ. Typescript.

"Another day, no quorum." 1989. *Congressional Quarterly Weekly Report* 47:1338.

Apple, R. W., Jr. 1990. "Bonn and Tokyo are criticized for not bearing more of Gulf cost." *New York Times,* 13 September.

Arnold, R. Douglas. 1979. *Congress and the bureaucracy: A theory of influence.* New Haven: Yale Univ. Press.

———. 1990. *The logic of congressional action.* New Haven: Yale Univ. Press.

Art, Robert J. 1985a. "Congress and the defense budget: Enhancing policy oversight." *Political Science Quarterly* 100:227–49.

———. 1985b. "Congress and the defense budget: New procedures and old realities." In *Toward a more effective defense: Report of the Defense Organization Project,* ed. Barry M. Blechman and William J. Lynn. Cambridge, Mass.: Ballinger.

———. 1990. "From budget wars to 'real' wars: The Pentagon and biennial budgeting." In *Making defense reform work,* ed. James A. Blackwell, Jr., and Barry M. Blechman. Washington, D.C.: Brassey's U.S.

Aspin, Les. 1975. "The defense budget and foreign policy: The role of Congress." *Daedalus* 104:155–74.

————. 1991a. "An alternative approach to our national defense." House Armed Services Committee Memorandum, 12 July.

————. 1991b. *The Aspin papers: Sanctions, diplomacy, and war in the Persian Gulf.* Washington, D.C.: Center for Strategic and International Studies.

————. 1992a. *An approach to sizing American conventional forces for the post–cold war era.* House Armed Services Committee, 25 February.

————. 1992b. *National security for the 1990s: Defining a new basis for U.S. military forces.* House Armed Services Committee. 6 January.

Bard, Mitchell. 1991. *The water's edge and beyond: Defining the limits to domestic influence on United States Middle East policy.* New Brunswick, N.J.: Transactions Publishers.

Barnhart, Michael, ed. 1987. *Congress and United States foreign policy: Controlling the use of force in the nuclear age.* Albany: State Univ. of New York Press.

Barone, Michael, and Grant Ujifusa. 1987. *The almanac of American politics, 1988.* Washington, D.C.: National Journal.

Bartels, Larry M. 1991. "Constituency opinion and congressional policy making: The Reagan defense buildup." *American Political Science Review* 85:457–74.

Barth, James R., George Iden, Frank S. Russek, and Mark Wohar. 1991. "The effects of federal budget deficits on interest rates and the composition of domestic output." In *The great fiscal experiment,* ed. Rudolph Penner. Washington, D.C.: Urban Institute.

Bax, Frans R. 1977. "The legislative-executive relationship in foreign policy: New partnership or new competition?" *Orbis* 20:881–904.

Baxter, Maurice G. 1984. *One and inseparable: Daniel Webster and the Union.* Cambridge: Harvard Univ. Press.

Bedard, Paul. 1991. "Cheney adamant on cutting troops." *Washington Times,* 20 March.

Benedick, Richard Elliott. 1991. *Ozone diplomacy: New directions in safeguarding the planet.* Cambridge: Harvard Univ. Press.

Berry, Jeffrey M. 1977. *Lobbying for the people: The political behavior of public interest groups.* Princeton: Princeton Univ. Press.

Berry, John. 1989. *The ambition and the power.* New York: Viking.

Bisnow, Mark. 1990. *In the shadow of the dome: Chronicles of a Capitol Hill aide.* New York: Morrow.

Blechman, Barry M. 1990a. "The new congressional role in arms control." In *A question of balance: The president, the Congress, and foreign policy,* ed. Thomas E. Mann. Washington, D.C.: Brookings Institution.

————. 1990b. *The politics of national security: Congress and U.S. defense policy.* New York: Oxford Univ. Press.

Blumenthal, Sidney. 1991. "Claiborne Pell's twilight zone." *New Republic,* 10 June.

Boyd, Gerald M. 1986. "Bush urges restraint by Canada." *New York Times,* 13 June.

Bradsher, Keith. 1991. "Lawmakers balk on I.M.F. funds." *New York Times,* 22 July.

Brenner, Philip, and William M. LeoGrande. 1990. "Congress and Nicaragua: The limits of alternative policy-making." In *Divided democracy: Cooperation and conflict between the president and Congress,* ed. James A. Thurber. Washington, D.C.: CQ Press.

Broder, Tanya, and Bernard D. Lambek. 1988. "Military aid to Guatemala: The failure of U.S. human rights legislation." *Yale Journal of International Law* 13:111–45.

Brown, Lawrence D. 1983. *New policies, new politics: Government's response to government's growth.* Washington, D.C.: Brookings Institution.

Bullock, Charles S., III, and David W. Brady. 1983. "Party, constituency, and roll-call voting in the U.S. Senate." *Legislative Studies Quarterly* 8:29–43.

Bullock, Charles S., and John D. Sprague. 1969. "A research note on the committee reassignments of southern Democratic congressmen." *Journal of Politics* 31:483–512.

Burgin, Eileen. 1988. "Representatives' involvement in foreign policymaking: The influence of supportive constituents." Ph.D. diss., Harvard University.

———. 1991a. "Representatives' decisions on participation in foreign policy issues." *Legislative Studies Quarterly* 16:521–46.

———. 1991b. "Representatives' participation in the House: The impact of issue-related factors on foreign policy involvement." Paper presented at the annual meeting of the American Political Science Association, Washington, D.C.

———. 1993. "Congress and foreign policy: The misperceptions." In *Congress Reconsidered*, 5th ed., ed. Lawrence C. Dodd and Bruce I. Oppenheimer. Washington, D.C.: CQ Press.

Bush, George. 1990. "In defense of defense." Speech delivered in Aspen, Colorado, 2 August. Reprinted in Dick Cheney, *Report of the secretary of defense to the president and the Congress, January 1991.* Washington, D.C.: Government Printing Office.

———. 1991. *National security strategy of the United States, 1991.* Washington, D.C.: Government Printing Office.

Butterworth, Robert Lyle. 1979. "The arms control impact statement: A programmatic assessment." *Policy Studies Journal* 8:76–84.

Caldwell, Dan. 1991. *The dynamics of domestic politics and arms control: The SALT II Treaty ratification debate.* Columbia: Univ. of South Carolina Press.

Calmes, Jacqueline. 1987a. "Aspin makes comeback at Armed Services." *Congressional Quarterly Weekly Report* 45:139–42.

———. 1987b. "Aspin ousted as Armed Services chairman." *Congressional Quarterly Weekly Report* 45:83–85.

Carmines, Edward G., and James H. Kuklinski. 1990. "Incentives, opportunities, and the logic of public opinion in American political representation." In *Information and Democratic Processes*, ed. John A. Ferejohn and James H. Kuklinski. Urbana: Univ. of Illinois Press.

Carroll, Holbert N. 1966. *The House of Representatives and foreign policy*, rev. ed. Boston: Little, Brown.

Cheever, Daniel S., and H. Field Haviland, Jr. 1952. *American foreign policy and the separation of powers.* Cambridge: Harvard Univ. Press.

Cheney, Dick. 1990a. "Congressional overreaching in foreign policy." In *Foreign policy and the Constitution*, ed. Robert A. Goldwin and Robert A. Licht. Washington, D.C.: American Enterprise Institute for Public Policy Research.

———. 1990b. *Report of the secretary of defense to the president and the Congress, January 1990.* Washington, D.C.: Government Printing Office.

————. 1991. *Report of the secretary of defense to the president and the Congress, January 1991.* Washington, D.C.: Government Printing Office.

Choate, Pat. 1990. *Agents of influence.* New York: Alfred A. Knopf.

Clarke, Duncan. 1979. *Politics of arms control: The role and effectiveness of the U.S. Arms Control and Disarmament Agency.* New York: Free Press.

Clausen, Aage. 1973. *How congressmen decide.* New York: St. Martin's.

————. 1977. "The accuracy of leader perceptions of constituency views." *Legislative Studies Quarterly* 2:361–84.

Cloud, David. 1991a. "Gephardt backs fast track." *Congressional Quarterly Weekly Report* 49:1181.

————. 1991b. "Lopsided vote seen signalling win for Bush on fast track." *Congressional Quarterly Weekly Report* 49:1257–60.

Cohen, Patricia. 1985. "Fascell and the committee." *Foreign Service Journal,* January.

Cohen, Richard E. 1991. "Seeking a bigger piece of the action." *National Journal* 23:92.

Cohodas, Nadine, and Diane Granat. 1985. "House seniority system jolted: Price dumped, Aspin elected." *Congressional Quarterly Weekly Report* 43:7–9.

Collier, Ellen C. 1990. "Introduction: The role of Congress in foreign policy in 1989." In *Congress and foreign policy, 1989.* Washington, D.C.: Government Printing Office.

Congress and the nation. Vol. 4, 1981–84. 1985. Washington, D.C.: Congressional Quarterly.

Congressional Budget Office. 1988. *The economic and budget outlook.* February.

————. 1990a. *Supplemental appropriations in the 1980s.* February.

————. 1990b. *The economic and budget outlook: An update.* July.

————. 1990c. *The 1990 budget agreement: An interim assessment.* December.

————. 1991a. *The economic and budget outlook.* February.

————. 1991b. *The economic and budget outlook: An update.* August.

————. 1992a. *The economic and budget outlook: An update.* August.

————. 1992b. *The economic and budget outlook: Fiscal years 1993–1997.* January.

Congressional Quarterly Almanac 1966. 1967. Vol. 22. Washington, D.C.: Congressional Quarterly.

Congressional Quarterly Almanac 1967. 1968. Vol. 23. Washington, D.C.: Congressional Quarterly.

Congressional Quarterly Almanac 1970. 1971. Vol. 26. Washington, D.C.: Congressional Quarterly.

Congressional Quarterly Almanac 1971. 1972. Vol. 27. Washington, D.C.: Congressional Quarterly.

Congressional Quarterly Almanac 1972. 1973. Vol. 28. Washington, D.C.: Congressional Quarterly.

Congressional Quarterly Almanac 1973. 1974. Vol. 29. Washington, D.C.: Congressional Quarterly.

Congressional Quarterly Almanac 1989. 1990. Vol. 45. Washington, D.C.: Congressional Quarterly.

Congressional Quarterly Almanac 1990. 1991. Vol. 46. Washington, D.C.: Congressional Quarterly.

Congressional Record. 1985. 1 October.

——. 1988a. 23 February.

——. 1988b. 19 September.

——. 1990. 24 May.

——. 1991. 11 January.

Converse, Philip E. 1990. "Popular representation and the distribution of information." In *Information and democratic processes,* ed. John A. Ferejohn and James H. Kuklinski. Urbana: Univ. of Illinois Press.

Cook, Timothy E. 1989a. *Making laws and making news: Media strategies in the U.S. House of Representatives.* Washington, D.C.: Brookings Institution.

——. 1989b. "PR on the Hill: The evolution of congressional press operations." In *Congressional politics,* ed. Christopher J. Deering. Pacific Grove, Calif.: Brooks/Cole.

Corddry, Charles W. 1991. "Even as navy builds up its Middle East forces, a drastic build down is being eyed by planners." *Sea Power* 34:6.

Crabb, Cecil V., Jr., and Pat M. Holt. 1989. *Invitation to struggle: Congress, the president, and foreign policy.* 3d ed. Washington, D.C.: CQ Press.

——. 1992. *Invitation to struggle: Congress, the president, and foreign policy.* 4th ed. Washington, D.C.: CQ Press.

Crackel, Theodore J. 1985. "Pentagon management problems: Congress shares the blame." Heritage Foundation *Backgrounder,* no. 405, 22 January.

Crossette, Barbara. 1991. "Congress is impatient for South Asia bureau." *New York Times,* 26 December.

Crovitz, L. Gordon. 1990. "Micromanaging foreign policy." *Public Interest* 100:102–15.

Crovitz, L. Gordon, and Jeremy A. Rabkin, eds. 1989. *The fettered presidency: Legal constraints on the executive branch.* Washington, D.C.: American Enterprise Institute for Public Policy Research.

Deering, Christopher J. 1988. "Congress, the president, and military policy." *Annals of the American Academy of Political and Social Science* 499:136–47.

——. 1989. "National security policy and Congress." In *Congressional Politics,* ed. Christopher J. Deering. Pacific Grove, Calif. Brooks/Cole.

Defense Daily. 1991a. "ASW no longer navy's top priority—Garrett." 8 March.

——. 1991b. "President urges Senate support for B-2 and SDI." 10 July.

——. 1992. "Pentagon pleased with HASC mark." 15 May.

Defense Policy Panel of the House Committee on Armed Services. 1990. *The fading threat: Soviet conventional military power in decline.* Washington, D.C.: House Armed Services Committee. 9 July.

Destler, I. M. 1985. "Executive-congressional conflict in foreign policy: Explaining it, coping with it." In *Congress Reconsidered,* 3d ed., ed. Lawrence C. Dodd and Bruce I. Oppenheimer. Washington, D.C.: CQ Press.

——. 1986a. *American trade politics: System under stress.* Washington, D.C.: Institute for International Economics.

————. 1986b. *Protecting Congress or protecting trade?* Foreign Policy 62:96–107.

Destler, I. M., Leslie H. Gelb, and Anthony Lake. 1984. *Our own worst enemy: The unmaking of American foreign policy.* New York: Simon and Schuster.

Dewar, Helen. 1989. "Senate Foreign Relations panel founders." *Washington Post,* 10 October.

————. 1990. "GOP senators propose doubling Bush's defense cuts." *Washington Post,* 6 April.

Dexter, Lewis Anthony. 1969. "Congressmen and the making of military policy." In *New perspectives on the House of Representatives,* 2d ed., ed. Robert L. Peabody and Nelson W. Polsby. Chicago: Rand McNally.

Dodd, Lawrence C., and Bruce I. Oppenheimer. 1989. "Consolidating power in the House." In *Congress Reconsidered,* 4th ed., ed. Lawrence C. Dodd and Bruce I. Oppenheimer. Washington, D.C.: CQ Press.

Doherty, Carroll J. 1990a. "Administration makes its case but fails to sway skeptics." *Congressional Quarterly Weekly Report* 48:4082–85.

————. 1990b. "Consultation on the Gulf crisis is hit or miss for Congress." *Congressional Quarterly Weekly Report* 48:3440–41.

————. 1990c. "Members rally around flag as Bush solicits support." *Congressional Quarterly Weekly Report* 48:2777–78.

————. 1990d. "Slip of the pen triggers cut in discretionary programs." *Congressional Quarterly Weekly Report* 48:3888.

————. 1990e. "Uncertain Congress confronts president's Gulf strategy." *Congressional Quarterly Weekly Report* 48:3879–82.

————. 1991a. "House defeats foreign aid bill in shadow of domestic woes." *Congressional Quarterly Weekly Report* 49:3215–16.

————. 1991b. "Inquiry supporters set back in rush-to-recess chaos." *Congressional Quarterly Weekly Report* 49:3239.

————. 1992a. "House sets task force to probe arms-for-hostages." *Congressional Quarterly Weekly Report* 50:318.

————. 1992b. "Lawmakers seek political cover as Israel aid delay runs out." *Congressional Quarterly Weekly Report* 50:118–23.

————. 1992c. "Support for foreign aid wilting under glare of domestic woes." *Congressional Quarterly Weekly Report* 50:1351–57.

Drew, Elizabeth. 1983. "A political journal." *New Yorker,* 20 June.

Drinan, Robert F., S.J., and Teresa T. Kuo. 1992. "The 1991 battle for human rights in China." *Human Rights Quarterly* 14:21–42.

Edwards, George C., III. 1986. "The two presidencies: A reevaluation." *American Politics Quarterly* 14:247–63.

————. 1989. *At the margins.* New Haven: Yale Univ. Press.

Elving, Ronald D. 1990. "Trade mood turns hawkish as frustration builds." *Congressional Quarterly Weekly Report* 48:965–71.

Erskine, Hazel G. 1963. "The polls: Exposure to international information." *Public Opinion Quarterly* 27:658–62.

Eulau, Heinz, and Paul D. Karps. 1977. "The puzzle of representation: Specifying components of responsiveness." *Legislative Studies Quarterly* 2:233–54.

Evans, C. Lawrence. 1989. "Influence in congressional committees: Participation, manipulation, and anticipation." In *Congressional politics*, ed. Christopher J. Deering.

Farnsworth, Clyde H. 1990. "U.S. trade team: 'A kind of stew.'" *New York Times*, 1 December.

Farnsworth, David N. 1961. *The Senate Committee on Foreign Relations*. Urbana: Univ. of Illinois Press.

Fearon, James D. 1991. "Counterfactuals and hypothesis testing in political science." *World Politics* 43:169–95.

Felton, John. 1983. "Foreign Affairs Committee changes seen under Fascell." *Congressional Quarterly Weekly Report* 41:2622–23.

———. 1987. "Nicaragua peace process moves to Capitol Hill." *Congressional Quarterly Weekly Report* 45:2789–91.

———. 1989a. "A policy confrontation on China." *Congressional Quarterly Weekly Report* 47:1564.

———. 1989b. "Bush, Hill agree to provide Contras with new aid." *Congressional Quarterly Weekly Report* 47:655–57.

Fenno, Richard F., Jr. 1973. *Congressmen in committees*. Boston: Little, Brown.

———. 1978. *Home style: House members in their districts*. Boston: Little, Brown.

Ferejohn, John A. 1990. "Information and the electoral process." In *Information and Democratic Processes*, ed. John A. Ferejohn and James H. Kuklinski. Urbana: Univ. of Illinois Press.

Fessler, Pamela. 1990a. "Bush quiets his critics on Hill by sending Baker to Iraq." *Congressional Quarterly Weekly Report* 48:4006–8.

———. 1990b. "Do lobbying dollars shape the U.S. trade debate?" *Congressional Quarterly Weekly Report* 48:972–75.

———. 1991. "Complaints are stacking up as hill piles on reports." *Congressional Quarterly Weekly Report* 49:2562–66.

———. 1992. "With push from leadership, House OKs ex-Soviet bill." *Congressional Quarterly Weekly Report* 50:2372–73.

Finnegan, Philip. 1991. "Pentagon cancels 13 weapons." *Defense News*, 4 February.

Finney, John W. 1969. "Halt of Sentinel is traced to a ten-month-old memo." *New York Times*, 9 February.

Fiorina, Morris P. 1974. *Representatives, roll calls, and constituencies*. Lexington, Mass.: D.C. Heath.

———. 1989. *Congress: Keystone of the Washington establishment*, 2d ed. New Haven: Yale Univ. Press.

Fleisher, Richard. 1985. "Economic benefit, ideology, and Senate voting on the B-1 bomber." *American Politics Quarterly* 13:200–11.

Foley, Thomas. 1991. "Remarks of Representative Thomas Foley (D-WA), Speaker of the House of Representatives to the Brookings Institution conference." Washington, D.C. Mimeo.

Forsythe, David P. 1987. "Congress and human rights legislation in U.S. foreign policy: The fate of general legislation." *Human Rights Quarterly* 9:382–404.

————. 1988. *Human rights and U.S. foreign policy: Congress reconsidered*. Gainesville: Univ. Presses of Florida.

————. 1989. *Human rights and world politics*, 2d ed. Lincoln: Univ. of Nebraska Press.

Franck, Thomas M. 1991. "Courts and foreign policy." *Foreign Policy* 83:66–86.

Franck, Thomas M., and Clifford A. Bob. 1985. "The return of Humpty-Dumpty: Foreign relations law after the Chadha case." *American Journal of International Law* 79:912–60.

Franck, Thomas M., and Edward Weisband. 1979. *Foreign policy by Congress*. New York: Oxford Univ. Press.

Free, Lloyd A., and Hadley Cantril. 1968. *The political beliefs of Americans*. New York: Simon and Schuster.

Friedberg, Aaron L. 1991. "Is the United States capable of acting strategically?" *Washington Quarterly* 14:5–23.

Friedrich, Carl J. 1941. *Constitutional government and democracy: Theory and practice in Europe and America*, rev. ed. Boston: Little, Brown.

Frye, Alton. 1975. *A responsible Congress: The politics of national security*. New York: McGraw-Hill.

Fulbright, J. William. 1979. "The legislator as educator." *Foreign Affairs* 57:719–32.

Galey, Margaret E. 1985. "Congress, foreign policy and human rights ten years after Helsinki." *Human Rights Quarterly* 7:334–72.

Garret, Stephen A. 1978. "Eastern European ethnic groups and American foreign policy." *Political Science Quarterly* 93:301–27.

Gates, Robert M. 1987–88. "The CIA and foreign policy." *Foreign Affairs* 66:215–30.

Gellner, Charles R. 1989. "The ABM treaty reinterpretation issue in Congress 1987." In *Congress and foreign policy, 1987*, Washington, D.C.: Government Printing Office.

Gelman, Barton, and R. Jeffrey Smith. 1991. "Cheney stands by budget plan." *Washington Post*, 11 September.

General Accounting Office. 1986. *Legislative oversight: Congressional requests for information on defense activities*. GAO/NSIAD-86-65BR, February. Washington, D.C.: Government Printing Office.

————. 1991. *Defense planning and budgeting: The effect of rapid changes in the national security environment*. Washington, D.C.: General Accounting Office.

Gilmour, John B. 1990. *Reconcilable differences?* Berkeley and Los Angeles: Univ. of California Press.

Gilmour, Robert S., and Barbara Hinkson Craig. 1984. "After the congressional veto: Assessing alternatives." *Journal of Policy Analysis* 3:373–92.

Glennon, Michael. 1984. "Democrats' panel defends more for defense." *Congressional Quarterly Weekly Report* 42:729–36.

Goldberg, David Howard. 1990. *Foreign policy and ethnic interest groups*. Westport, Conn.: Greenwood.

Goldstein, Judith. 1986. "The political economy of trade: Institutions of protection." *American Political Science Review* 80:161–84.

————. 1988. "Ideas, institutions and American trade policy." In *The state and American foreign economic policy,* ed. G. John Ikenberry, David A. Lake, and Michael Mastanduno. Ithaca, N.Y.: Cornell Univ. Press.

Goldwin, Robert A., and Robert A. Licht. 1990. *The fettered presidency: Legal constraints on the executive branch.* Washington, D.C.: American Enterprise Institute for Public Policy Research.

Gordon, Bernard K. 1961. "The military budget: Congressional phase." *Journal of Politics* 23:689–710.

Gorlin, Jacques J. 1990. "Foreign trade and the Constitution." In *Foreign Policy and the Constitution,* ed. Robert A. Goldwin and Robert A. Licht. Washington, D.C.: American Enterprise Institute for Public Policy Research.

Graham, Thomas W. 1990. "American attitudes toward defense spending: Before and after the Berlin Wall." Yale University. Typescript.

Greenhouse, Linda. 1987. "A military bill like none other." *New York Times,* 13 May.

Greenwald, John. 1989. "Friend or foe?" *Time.* 24 April.

Gwertzman, Bernard. 1984. "Senator planning sweeping hearing on foreign policy." *New York Times,* 9 December.

Hager, George. 1991. "Deficit report shows no gain from pain of spending rules." *Congressional Quarterly Weekly Report* 49:1963–64.

————. 1992a. "Panetta's plan." *Congressional Quarterly Weekly Report* 50: 2159.

————. 1992b. "Rejection of walls bill spells spending squeeze at home." *Congressional Quarterly Weekly Report* 50:866–67.

Haggard, Stephan. 1988. "The institutional foundations of hegemony: Explaining the reciprocal Trade Agreements Act of 1934." In *The state and American foreign economic policy,* ed. G. John Ikenberry, David A. Lake, and Michael Mastanduno. Ithaca, N.Y.: Cornell Univ. Press.

Halberstam, David. 1983. *The best and the brightest.* New York: Penguin.

Hall, Richard L. 1987. "Participation and purpose in committee decision making." *American Political Science Review* 81:105–27.

Halperin, Morton. 1972. "The decision to deploy the ABM: Bureaucratic and domestic politics in the Johnson administration." *World Politics* 25:62–95.

————. 1974. *Bureaucratic politics and foreign policy.* Washington, D.C.: Brookings Institution.

Hamilton, Alexander. 1961. "Federalist no. 70." In Alexander Hamilton, James Madison, and John Jay, *The Federalist papers,* ed. Clinton Rossiter. New York: New American Library.

Hamilton, Lee H. 1992. "A Democrat looks at foreign policy." *Foreign Affairs* 71:32–51.

Hastedt, Glenn P. 1991. *American foreign policy: Past, present, future,* 2d ed. Englewood Cliffs, N.J.: Prentice-Hall.

Healy, Melissa. 1991. "Cheney would reduce reserve combat role." *Los Angeles Times,* 14 March.

Heginbotham, Stanley. 1984. "Congress and defense policy making: Toward realistic expectations in a system of countervailing parochialisms." In *National security affairs: The decision making process,* ed. Robert Pfalzgraff and Uri Ra'anan. Hamden, Conn.: Archon.

Helliwell, John F. 1991. "The fiscal deficit and the external deficit: Siblings but not twins." In *The Great Fiscal Experiment,* ed. Rudolph Penner. Washington, D.C.: Urban Institute.

Henderson, D. G. 1979. "The Senate Foreign Relations Committee." *Washington Quarterly* 2:3–12.

Hertsgaard, Mark. 1989. *On bended knee: The press and the Reagan presidency.* New York: Shocken.

Hilsman, Roger. 1958. "Congressional-executive relations and the foreign policy consensus." *American Political Science Review* 52:725–44.

Hoadley, Steve. 1991. "The US Congress and the New Zealand Military Preference Elimination Bill." *Political Science* 43:47–60.

Holland, Lauren H., and Robert A. Hoover. 1984. *The MX decision: A new direction in U.S. weapons procurement policy?* Boulder, Colo.: Westview.

Holt, W. Stull. 1933. *Treaties defeated by the Senate: A study of the struggle between president and Senate over the conduct of foreign relations.* Baltimore: Johns Hopkins Univ. Press.

Horowitz, Irving Louis. 1977. "Ethnic politics and U.S. foreign policy." In *Ethnicity and U.S. foreign policy,* ed. Abdul Aziz Said. New York: Praeger.

Huntington, Samuel P. 1961. *The common defense: Strategic programs in national politics.* New York: Columbia Univ. Press.

———. 1988–89. "The U.S.—Decline or renewal?" *Foreign Affairs* 67:76–96.

ICBM Associates. 1983. "Peacekeeper employment impact data (including subcontractors)." October. Washington, D.C. Typescript.

Inside the Pentagon. 1991. "Darman, Cheney may soon be at odds over defense spending cuts after war." 28 February.

Iyengar, Shanto. 1990. "Shortcuts to political knowledge: The role of selective attention and accessibility." In *Information and democratic processes,* ed. John A. Ferejohn and James H. Kuklinski. Urbana: Univ. of Illinois Press.

Jenkins, Kent, Jr. 1992. "Warner bumped from Armed Services post." *Washington Post,* 30 April.

Jentleson, Bruce W. 1990. "American diplomacy: Around the world and along Pennsylvania Avenue." In *A question of balance: The president, the Congress,Jand foreign policy,* ed. Thomas E. Mann. Washington, D.C.: Brookings Institution.

Jewell, Malcolm, and Chu Chi-Hung. 1974. "Membership movement and committee attractiveness in the U.S. House of Representatives." *American Journal of Political Science* 28:181–221.

Johnson, Loch K. 1984. *The making of international agreements: Congress confronts the executive.* New York: New York Univ. Press.

———. 1989. "Covert action and accountability: Decision-making for America's secret foreign policy." *International Studies Quarterly* 33:81–109.

Johnston, David, and Michael Wines. 1991. "Spying data on Sandinistas involved U.S. congressmen, ex-officials say." *New York Times,* 15 September.

Jones, Gordon S., and John A. Marini, eds. 1988. *The imperial Congress: Crisis in the separation of powers*. New York: Pharos.

Kaiser, Fred M. 1977a. "Structural change and policy change: The House Committee on International Relations." *Policy Studies Journal* 5:443–51.

———. 1977b. "Oversight of foreign policy: The U.S. House Committee on International Relations." *Legislative Studies Quarterly* 2:255–79.

———. 1988. "Congressional rules and conflict resolution: Access to information in the House Select Committee on Intelligence." *Congress and the Presidency* 15:49–73.

Katzmann, Robert A. 1990. "War powers: Toward a new accommodation." In *A question of balance: The president, the Congress, and foreign policy*, ed. Thomas E. Mann. Washington, D.C.: Brookings Institution.

Kegley, Charles W., and Eugene R. Wittkopf. 1991. *American foreign policy: Pattern and process*, 4th ed. New York: St. Martin's.

———. 1992. *The future of American foreign policy*. New York: St. Martin's.

Kennedy, Paul. 1987. *The rise and fall of great powers: Economic change and military conflict from 1500 to 2000*. New York: Random House.

Kingdon, John W. 1989. *Congressmen's voting decisions*, 3d ed. Ann Arbor: Univ. of Michigan Press.

Knott, Stephen. 1990. "Lifting the veil: The roots of American covert activity." Ph.D. diss., Boston College.

Koh, Harold Hongju. 1986. "Congressional controls on presidential trade policymaking after *I.N.S. v. Chadha*." *New York University Journal of International Law and Politics* 18:1191–1233.

———. 1988. "Why the president (almost) always wins in foreign affairs." *Yale Law Journal* 97:1255–342.

———. 1990. *The national security constitution: Sharing power after the Iran-Contra affair*. New Haven: Yale Univ. Press.

Kolodziej, Edward A. 1975. "Congress and foreign policy: The Nixon years." In *Congress against the president*, ed. Harvey C. Mansfield, Sr. New York: Academy of Political Science.

Kotz, Nick. 1988. *Wild blue yonder: Money, politics, and the B-1 bomber*. New York: Pantheon.

Krauss, Clifford. 1991. "Panel links chief of Salvador army to Jesuit killings." *New York Times*, 17 November.

Krehbiel, Keith. 1990. "Are congressional committees composed of preference outliers?" *American Political Science Review* 84:149–63.

LaFeber, Walter. 1972. *America, Russia, and the cold war, 1945–1971*, 2d ed. New York: John Wiley and Sons.

Lehman, John. 1992. *Making war: The 200-year-old battle between the president and Congress over how America goes to war*. New York: Charles Scribner's Sons.

LeLoup, Lance T. 1982. "After the blitz: Reagan and the U.S. congressional budget process." *Legislative Studies Quarterly* 7:321–39.

———. 1988. "From microbudgeting to macrobudgeting: Transition in theory and practice." In *New directions in budget theory*, ed. Irene Rubin. Albany: State Univ. of New York Press.

LeLoup, Lance T., Barbara Graham, and Stacey Barwick. 1987. "Deficit politics and constitutional government: The impact of Gramm-Rudman-Hollings." *Public Budgeting and Finance* 7:83–103.

Levy, Deborah M. 1987. "Advice for sale." *Foreign Policy* 67:64–86.

Lewis, Paul. 1992. "Pact on environment near, but hurdles on aid remain." *New York Times,* 12 June.

Lindsay, James M. 1987. "Congress and defense policy: 1961 to 1986." *Armed Forces and Society* 13:370–401.

———. 1990a. "Congressional oversight of the Department of Defense budget: Reconsidering the conventional wisdom." *Armed Forces and Society* 17:7–33.

———. 1990b. "Parochialism, policy and constituency constraints: Congressional voting on strategic weapon systems." *American Journal of Political Science* 34:936–60.

———. 1991. *Congress and nuclear weapons.* Baltimore: Johns Hopkins Univ. Press.

———. 1992–93. "Congress and foreign policy: Why the Hill matters." *Political Science Quarterly* 107:607–28.

Lindsay, James M., and Randall B. Ripley. 1992. "Foreign and defense policy in Congress: A research agenda for the 1990s." *Legislative Studies Quarterly* 17:417–49.

"Lobbying." 1990. *National Journal* 22:93.

Lowi, Theodore J. 1967. "Making democracy safe for the world: National politics and foreign policy." In *Domestic sources of foreign policy,* ed. James N. Rosenau. New York: Free Press.

McCormick, James M. 1985. "The changing role of the House Foreign Affairs Committee in the 1970s and 1980s." *Congress and the Presidency* 12:1-20.

McCormick, James M., and Michael Black. 1983. "Ideology and voting on the Panama Canal treaties." *Legislative Studies Quarterly* 8:45–63.

McCormick, James M., and Eugene R. Wittkopf. 1990. "Bipartisanship, partisanship, and ideology in congressional-executive foreign policy relations, 1947–1988." *Journal of Politics* 52:1077–1100.

———. 1992. "At the water's edge: The effects of party, ideology, and issues on congressional foreign policy voting, 1847–1988." *American Politics Quarterly* 20:26–53.

McCubbins, Mathew D. 1985. "Legislative design of regulatory structure." *American Journal of Political Science* 29:721–48.

McCubbins, Mathew D., Roger G. Noll, and Barry R. Weingast. 1987. "Administrative procedures as instruments of political control." *Journal of Law, Economics, and Organization* 3:243–77.

———. 1989. "Structure and process, politics and policy: Administrative arrangements and political control of agencies." *Virginia Law Review* 75:431–82.

McCubbins, Mathew D., and Thomas Schwartz. 1984. "Congressional oversight overlooked: Police patrols versus fire alarms." *American Journal of Political Science* 28:165–79.

McDonough, Mark G. 1979a. "Panama Canal treaty negotiations (A)." Case C14-79-223, Harvard University, John F. Kennedy School of Government.

———. 1979b. "Panama Canal treaty negotiations (B): Concluding a treaty." Case C14-79-224, Harvard University, John F. Kennedy School of Government.

McGrory, Mary. 1992. "Democrats' shame on Seawolf." *Washington Post*, 14 May.

McKelvey, Richard D., and Peter C. Ordeshook. 1990. "Information and elections: Retrospective voting and rational expectations." In *Information and democratic processes*, ed. John A. Ferejohn and James H. Kuklinski. Urbana: Univ. of Illinois Press.

McKenzie, Richard. 1988. "The decline of America: Myth or fact?" Formal Publication 87. St. Louis, Mo.: Center for the Study of American Business, Washington University.

McPherson, William. 1981. "Charles Percy." *Washington Post Magazine*, 25 October.

Madison, Christopher. 1987a. "Family of factions." *National Journal* 19:1271–74.

———. 1987b. "Going separate ways." *National Journal* 19:1216–18.

———. 1990. "Sideline players." *National Journal* 22:3024–26.

———. 1991a. "Follow the leader." *National Journal* 23:104.

———. 1991b. "Paper tiger." *National Journal* 23:1434–37.

———. 1991c. "Rescue mission." *National Journal* 23:1513–16.

———. 1992a. "At last, peace in El Salvador?" *National Journal* 24:185.

———. 1992b. "Awaiting a wake-up." *National Journal* 24:750–54.

———. 1992c. "A new day, maybe, for two panels." *National Journal* 24:1469.

Madison, James. 1961a. "Federalist no. 51." In Alexander Hamilton, James Madison, and John Jay, *The Federalist papers*, ed. Clinton Rossiter. New York: New American Library.

———. 1961b. "Federalist no. 58." In Alexander Hamilton, James Madison, and John Jay, *The Federalist papers*, ed. Clinton Rossiter. New York: New American Library.

Manheim, Jarol B., and Robert B. Albritton. 1984. "Changing national images: International public relations and media agenda setting." *American Political Science Review* 78:641–57.

Manley, John F. 1971. "The rise of Congress in foreign policy-making." *Annals of the American Academy of Political and Social Science* 337:60–70.

Mann, Thomas E., ed. 1990a. *A question of balance: The president, the Congress, and foreign policy.* Washington, D.C.: Brookings Institution.

———. 1990b. "Making foreign policy: President and Congress." In *A question of balance: The president, the Congress, and foreign policy*, ed. Thomas E. Mann. Washington, D.C.: Brookings Institution.

Manning, Bayless. 1977. "The Congress, the executive and intermestic affairs: Three proposals." *Foreign Affairs* 55:306–24.

Margolis, Lawrence. 1986. *Executive agreements and presidential power in foreign policy.* New York: Praeger.

Mayer, Kenneth R. 1991. *The political economy of defense contracting.* New Haven: Yale Univ. Press.

Mayhew, David R. 1974. *Congress: The electoral connection.* New Haven: Yale Univ. Press.

Mellor, Herman [pseud.]. 1990. "Congressional micromanagement: National defense." In *The imperial Congress: Crisis in the separation of powers,* ed. Gordon S. Jones and John A. Marini. New York: Pharos.

Meyer, David. 1990. *A winter of discontent: The nuclear freeze and American politics.* New York: Praeger.

Meyer, Jeffrey A. 1988. "Congressional control of foreign assistance." *Yale Journal of International Law* 13:69–110.

Miller, Warren E. 1970. "Majority rule and the representative system of government." In *Mass politics: Studies in political sociology,* ed. Erik Allardt and Stein Rokkan. New York: Free Press.

Miller, Warren E., and Donald E. Stokes. 1963. "Constituency influence in Congress." *American Political Science Review* 57:45–56.

Mitchell, George. 1991. "No: China hasn't earned it." *Washington Post National Weekly Edition,* 10–16 June.

Moe, Ronald C., and Steven C. Teel. 1971. "Congress as policy-maker: A necessary reappraisal." In *Congress and the president,* ed. Ronald C. Moe. New York: Goodyear.

Moe, Terry M. 1984. "The new economics of organization." *American Journal of Political Science* 28:739–77.

Moore, Molly. 1989. "Cheney, Aspin rebuffed on 2 projects." *Washington Post,* 29 June.

———. 1990. "Aspin: Weapons too costly to be bargaining chips." *Washington Post,* 7 February.

Morrison, David C. 1990. "Defense contractors trying to hold on." *National Journal* 22:885–89.

———. 1991a. "Another czar bows out." *National Journal* 23:43.

———. 1991b. "Sam Nunn, Inc." *National Journal* 23:1483–86.

———. 1992. "Sharing command." *National Journal* 24:1394–98.

Moynihan, Daniel Patrick. 1988. "Debunking the myth of decline." *New York Times Magazine,* 19 June.

Munger, Michael C. 1988. "Allocation of desirable committee assignments: Extended queues versus committee expansion." *American Journal of Political Science* 32:317–44.

Murray, Allan. 1983. "Trade-conscious Congress embroils itself in complexities of U.S.-Canada Relations." *Congressional Quarterly Weekly Report* 41:1058.

Neustadt, Richard E. 1960. *Presidential power: The politics of leadership.* New York: Wiley Science Editions.

———. 1990. *Presidential power and the modern presidents: The politics of leadership from Roosevelt to Reagan.* New York: Free Press.

Nivola, Pietro S. 1990. "Trade policy: Refereeing the playing field." In *A question of balance: The president, the Congress, and foreign policy,* ed. Thomas E. Mann. Washington, D.C.: Brookings Institution.

Noble, Claire E. 1990. "Ideology and the foreign policy committees, 1977–1988." Paper presented at the annual meetings of the Southern Political Science Association, Atlanta, Georgia.

———. 1991. "Committee chairs of the foreign policy committees, 1977–1988."

Paper presented at the annual meetings of the Midwest Political Science Association, Chicago, Illinois.

Nowels, Larry Q. 1989. "The foreign affairs funding debate in 1987." In *Congress and foreign policy, 1987.* Washington, D.C.: Government Printing Office.

Nowels, Larry Q., and Ellen C. Collier. 1992. "Foreign policy budget: Priorities for the 102d Congress." *CRS Issue Brief,* 26 May.

Nunn, Sam. 1990a. "A new military strategy." In *Congressional Record,* 19 April, S4449–4445.

———. 1990b. "Defense budget blanks." In *Congressional Record,* 22 March, S2965–2970.

———. 1990c. "The changed threat environment of the 1990's." In *Congressional Record,* 29 March, S3444–51.

Nye, Joseph S., Jr. 1990. "The misleading metaphor of decline." *Atlantic Monthly,* March.

Office of Management and Budget. 1991. *Mid-session review of the budget.* 15 July. Washington, D.C.: Government Printing Office.

Office of Technology Assessment. 1988. *Paying the bill: Manufacturing and America's trade deficit.* OTA-ITE-390, June. Washington, D.C.: Government Printing Office.

Ogene, F., Chidozie. 1983. *Interest groups and the shaping of foreign policy: Four case studies of United States African policy.* New York: St. Martin's.

O'Halloran, Sharyn. 1990. "Congress, the president, and U.S. trade policy: Process and policy." Paper presented at the annual meetings of the American Political Science Association, Washington, D.C.

———. 1993. *Politics, process, and American trade policy.* Ann Arbor: Univ. of Michigan Press.

O'Halloran, Sharyn, and Roger G. Noll. 1991. "Institutions as congressional commitments: International trade policy in the postwar liberal era." Paper presented at the Social Science Research Council Conference on Congress and Foreign Policy, Stanford University.

Olson, Mancur. 1982. *The rise and decline of nations.* New Haven: Yale Univ. Press.

Omnibus Budget Reconciliation Act. 1990. Public Law 101–508, 5 November. Washington, D.C.: Government Printing Office.

Ornstein, Norman. 1984. "Interest groups, Congress, and American foreign policy." In *American foreign policy in an uncertain world,* ed. David P. Forsythe. Lincoln: Univ. of Nebraska Press.

Ornstein, Norman J., and David W. Rohde. 1977. "Shifting forces, changing rules and political outcomes: The impact of congressional change on four House committees." In *New perspectives on the House of Representatives,* ed. Robert L. Peabody and Nelson W. Polsby. Chicago: Rand-McNally.

Ortmayer, Louis L. 1990. "The political economy of national security: The FSX agreement." Paper presented at the annual meetings of the International Studies Association/South, Raleigh, North Carolina.

Overby, L. Marvin. 1991. "Assessing constituency influence: Congressional voting on the nuclear freeze, 1982–83." *Legislative Studies Quarterly* 16:297–312.

Owens, Mackubin Thomas. 1990. "Micromanaging the defense budget." *Public Interest* 100:131–46.

Palazzolo, Dan. 1989. "The Speaker's relationship with the House Budget Committee." Paper presented at the annual meetings of the Midwest Political Science Association, Chicago, Illinois.

Parry, R. 1985. "Defense PAC money skyrockets." *Washington Post*, 1 April.

Passell, Peter. 1990. "America's position in the economic race: What the numbers show and conceal." *New York Times*, 4 March.

Pastor, Robert A. 1980. *Congress and the politics of U.S. foreign economic policy, 1929–1976*. Berkeley and Los Angeles: Univ. of California Press.

———. 1983. "Cry-and-sigh syndrome: Congress and trade policy." In *Making economic policy in Congress*, ed. Allen Schick. Washington, D.C.: American Enterprise Institute for Public Policy Research.

Pasztor, Andy. 1990. "Pentagon shields long-range spending plans as big guns in Congress aim at defense budget." *Wall Street Journal*, 23 March.

———. 1991a. "Mismanagement, budget cuts, doubts over role have navy sailing against the wind in Congress." *Wall Street Journal*, 4 June.

———. 1991b. "Some Gulf war weapons are targeted for deep cuts." *Wall Street Journal*, 5 February.

Patterson, Samuel C. 1990. "Congress and the emerging legislatures in new democracies." Paper presented at the Conference on Congress and Foreign and Defense Policy Challenges, Ohio State University.

Pattison, Joseph. 1991. *Antidumping and countervailing duty laws*. New York: Clark Boardman.

Penner, Rudolph G., and Alan J. Abramson. 1988. *Broken purse strings: Congressional budgeting, 1974–88*. Washington, D.C.: Urban Institute.

Peterson, Mark A. 1990. *Legislating together: The White House and Capitol Hill from Eisenhower to Reagan*. Cambridge: Harvard Univ. Press.

Pianin, Eric. 1992. "Senate rejects bid to cut military budget below Bush proposal." *Washington Post*, 10 April.

Platt, Alan. 1978. *The U.S. Senate and strategic arms policy. 1969–1977*. Boulder, Colo.: Westview.

———. 1982. "The politics of arms control and the strategic balance." In *Rethinking the U.S. strategic posture*, ed. Barry M. Blechman. Cambridge, Mass.: Ballinger.

Pocalyko, Michael W. 1992. "Riding on the storm: The influence of war on strategy." In *Reconstituting America's defense: The new U.S. national security strategy*, ed. James J. Tritten and Paul N. Stockton. New York: Praeger.

Poole, Keith T. 1988. "Recent developments in analytical models of voting in the U.S. Congress." *Legislative Studies Quarterly* 13:117–33.

Povich, Elaine S. 1991. "Congress to probe charges of 1980 deal on hostages." *Chicago Tribune*, 6 August.

Powell, Colin L. 1990. *Remarks to the Armed Forces Communications and Electronics Association*. Washington, D.C.: Department of Defense.

Pressman, Steven. 1983. "Congress harks to the home folks: Summertime, and the living is easier around Capitol Hill, but lobbyists never let up." *Congressional Quarterly Weekly Report* 41:1720–22.

———. 1984. "The lobbying: A hard fight by both sides." *Congressional Quarterly Weekly Report* 42:1156.

———. 1986. "Larger issues almost derail Canada trade talks." *Congressional Quarterly Weekly Report* 44:905–6.

"Pressures mounting for import quota legislation." 1968. *Congressional Quarterly Weekly Report* 24:155–60.

Purvis, Hoyt, and Steven J. Baker, eds. 1984. *Legislating foreign policy.* Boulder, Colo.: Westview.

Putnam, Robert D. 1988. "Diplomacy and domestic politics: The logic of two-level games." *International Organization* 42:427–60.

Rasky, Susan. 1990a. "Democrats shift on military cutbacks." *New York Times,* 15 March.

———. 1990b. "Senator to seek big military cuts." *New York Times,* 8 March.

———. 1990c. "Two unlikely voices that find harmony on the defense budget." *New York Times,* 2 May.

Ray, Bruce A. 1982. "Committee attractiveness in the U.S. House, 1963–1981." *American Journal of Political Science* 26:609–13.

Reiselbach, Leroy. 1986. *Congressional reform.* Washington, D.C.: CQ Press.

Ripley, Randall B., and Grace A. Franklin. 1991. *Congress, the bureaucracy, and public policy,* 5th ed. Pacific Grove, Calif.: Brooks/Cole.

Roberts, Steven V. 1985. "Foreign policy: Lot of table thumping going on." *New York Times,* 29 May.

Robinson, James A. 1967. *Congress and foreign policy-making: A study in legislative influence and initiative,* rev. ed. Homewood, Ill.: Dorsey.

Rockman, Bert A. 1987. "Mobilizing political support for U.S. national security." *Armed Forces and Society* 14:17–41.

Rodman, Peter W. 1985. "The imperial Congress." *National Interest* 1:26–35.

Rohde, David. 1988. "Variations in partisanship in the House of Representatives." Paper presented at the annual meeting of the American Political Science Association, Washington, D.C.

Rosenbaum, David E. 1991. "Talk about tax breaks is . . . just talk." *New York Times,* 22 October.

Rostow, Eugene V. 1989. *President, prime minister, or constitutional monarch?* McNair Papers, no. 3. Washington, D.C.: National Defense Univ.

Rourke, John. 1983. *Congress and the presidency in U.S. foreign policymaking: A study of interaction and influence, 1945–1982.* Boulder, Colo.: Westview.

Rubin, Barry. 1978. "The media and the neutron warhead." *Washington Review of Strategic and International Studies* 1:90–94.

Russett, Bruce M. 1970. *What price vigilance? The burdens of national defense.* New Haven: Yale Univ. Press.

Said, Abdul Aziz, ed. 1977. *Ethnicity and U.S. foreign policy.* New York: Praeger.

Scarborough, Rowan. 1991. "Cheney can't ground Osprey." *Washington Times,* 24 May.

322   References

Schattschneider, E. E. 1935. *Politics, pressures, and the tariff.* Hamden, Conn.: Archon.
———. 1961. *The semisovereign people.* New York: Holt, Rinehart.
Schell, Jonathan. 1975. *The time of illusion.* New York: Vintage.
Schick, Allen. 1977. *Congressional control of expenditures.* Report prepared for the House Committee on the Budget, 95th Cong., 1st sess. Committee Print 1.
———. 1990. *The capacity to budget.* Washington, D.C.: Urban Institute.
Schilling, Warner R. 1962. "The politics of national defense: Fiscal 1950." In *Strategy, politics, and defense budgets,* ed. Warner Schilling, Paul Y. Hammond, and Glenn H. Snyder. New York: Columbia Univ. Press.
Schlesinger, Arthur M. 1973. *The imperial presidency.* Boston: Houghton Mifflin.
Schlesinger, James R. 1988. "Debunking the myth of decline." *New York Times Magazine,* 19 June.
Schlozman, Kay, and John Tierney. 1986. *Organized interests and American democracy.* New York: Harper and Row.
Schmitt, Eric. 1991a. "Focus of clash on military budget is how to reduce reserve forces." *New York Times,* 26 May.
———. 1991b. "House votes military budget, cutting arms programs." *New York Times,* 23 May.
———. 1991c. "Pentagon making a list of choices for spending cuts." *New York Times,* 24 November.
———. 1992a. "Military planning deep budget cuts." *New York Times,* 30 August.
———. 1992b. "Pentagon offers some deep cuts but stops there." *New York Times,* 30 January.
Schorr, Daniel. 1991. "Ten days that shook the White House." *Columbia Journalism Review,* July–August.
Shapiro, Catherine, David Brady, Richard Brody, and John Ferejohn. 1990. "Linking constituency opinion and Senate voting scores: A hybrid explanation." *Legislative Studies Quarterly* 15:599–621.
Sia, Richard. 1991. "Plan to cut guard, reserves gives Pentagon political trouble." *Baltimore Sun,* 27 May.
Siegel, Richard L. 1968. *Evaluating the results of foreign policy: Soviet and American efforts in India.* Monograph Series in World Affairs, vol. 6, Monograph No. 4.
Simon, Rita. 1974. *Public opinion in America, 1936–1970.* Chicago: Rand-McNally.
Sinclair, Barbara. 1982. *Congressional realignment.* Austin: Univ. of Texas Press.
———. 1983. *Majority leadership in the U.S. House.* Baltimore: Johns Hopkins Univ. Press.
———. 1989a. "House majority party leadership in the late 1980s." In *Congress reconsidered,* 4th ed., ed. Lawrence Dodd and Bruce Oppenheimer. Washington, D.C.: Congressional Quarterly Press.
———. 1989b. *Transformation of the U.S. Senate.* Baltimore: Johns Hopkins Univ. Press.
———. 1991. "Strong party leadership in a weak party era: The evolution of party leadership in the modern House." In *The atomistic Congress,* ed. Ronald Peters and Allen Hertzke. Armonk, N.Y.: M. E. Sharpe.

————. 1992. "House majority party leadership in an era of legislative constraint." In *The post-reform Congress,* ed. Roger Davidson. New York: St. Martin's.

Smist, Frank J. 1990. *Congress oversees the United States intelligence community, 1947–1989.* Knoxville: Univ. of Tennessee Press.

Smith, Hedrick. 1988. *The power game: How Washington works.* New York: Random House.

Smith, Jean E. 1989. *The Constitution and American foreign policy.* St. Paul, Minn.: West.

Smith, Louis. 1951. *American democracy and military power: A study of civil control of the military power in the United States.* Chicago: Univ. of Chicago Press.

Smith, Steven S. 1989a. *Call to order: Floor politics in the House and Senate.* Washington, D.C.: Brookings Institution.

————. 1989b. "Taking it to the floor." In *Congress reconsidered,* 4th ed., ed. Lawrence C. Dodd and Bruce I. Oppenheimer. Washington, D.C.: CQ Press.

Smith, Steven S., and Christopher J. Deering. 1984. *Committees in Congress.* Washington, D.C.: CQ Press.

————. 1990. *Committees in Congress,* 2d ed. Washington, D.C.: CQ Press.

Smyrl, Marc E. 1988. *Conflict or codetermination? Congress, the president, and the power to make war.* Cambridge, Mass.: Ballinger.

Stanfield, Rochelle L. 1990. "Floating power centers." *National Journal* 22:2915–19.

————. 1991. "Weighing arms sales for Saudis." *National Journal* 23:79–80.

Steinbruner, John. 1974. *The cybernetic theory of decision: New dimensions of political analysis.* Princeton: Princeton Univ. Press.

Stimson, James A. 1990. "A macro theory of information flow." In *Information and democratic processes,* ed. John A. Ferejohn and James H. Kuklinski. Urbana: Univ. of Illinois Press.

Stith, Kate. 1988. "Congress' power of the purse." *Yale Law Journal* 97:1343–96.

Stockman, David A. 1986. *The triumph of politics: Why the Reagan revolution failed.* New York: Harper and Row.

Stokes, Bruce. 1989. "Beat 'em or join 'em." *National Journal* 21:459–64.

Strauss, Robert. 1987. "Foreword." In Joan E. Twiggs, *The Tokyo round of multilateral trade negotiations: A case study in building domestic support for diplomacy.* Lanham, Md.: Univ. Press of America.

Stritch, Andrew J. 1991. "State autonomy and societal pressure: The steel industry and U.S. import policy." *Administration and Society* 23:288–309.

Sundquist, James L. 1981. *The decline and resurgence of Congress.* Washington, D.C.: Brookings Institution.

Tagliabue, John. 1990. "Kohl vows to widen role in Gulf effort." *New York Times,* 14 September.

Talbott, Strobe. 1984. *Deadly gambits.* New York: Alfred A. Knopf.

Tierney, John T. 1987. "Organized interests in health politics and policymaking." *Medical Care Review* 44:89–118.

Tivnan, Edward. 1988. *The lobby: Jewish political power and American foreign policy.* New York: Simon and Schuster.

Tobin, Glenn. 1987. "US-Canada free trade negotiations: Gaining approval to proceed (B)." Case C16-87-786.0, Harvard University, John F. Kennedy School of Government.

Tolchin, Martin. 1991. "Senator who hunted bank scandal is watching doubters take his path." *New York Times,* 29 July.

Tolchin, Martin, and Susan Tolchin. 1987. *Buying into America: How foreign money is changing the face of our nation.* New York: Times Books.

Towell, Pat. 1985. "Aspin: A coalition-builder at Armed Services." *Congressional Quarterly Weekly Report* 43:99–102.

————. 1990. "Aspin moves to avoid reruns of his political missteps." *Congressional Quarterly Weekly Report* 48:1141–45.

————. 1991a. "House defense funding bill keeps cuts in SDI and B-2." *Congressional Quarterly Weekly Report* 49:1518–22.

————. 1991b. "New wars and cold wars reflected in budget." *Congressional Quarterly Weekly Report* 49:3645–49.

Towle, Michael D. 1991. "Pentagon sends $200 million for V-22 Osprey." *Fort Worth Star-Telegram,* 27 April.

Treverton, Gregory. 1990. "Intelligence: Welcome to the American government." In *A question of balance: The president, the Congress, and foreign policy,* ed. Thomas E. Mann. Washington, D.C.: Brookings Institution.

Tritten, James J. 1992. "The new national security strategy and base force." In *Reconstituting America's defense: The new U.S. national security strategy,* ed. James J. Tritten and Paul N. Stockton. New York: Praeger.

Twiggs, Joan E. 1987. *The Tokyo round of multilateral trade negotiations: A case study in building domestic support for diplomacy.* Lanham, Md.: Univ. Press of America.

Twight, Charlotte. 1989. "Institutional underpinnings of parochialism: The case of military base closures." *Cato Journal* 9:73–105.

————. 1990. "DoD attempts to close military bases: The political economy of congressional resistance." In *Arms, politics, and the economy: Historical and contemporary perspectives,* ed. Robert Higgs. New York: Holmes and Meier.

Tyler, Patrick E. 1990. "Webster sees no reversal of Soviet threat." *Washington Post,* 2 March.

————. 1991. "Brookings study seeks military spending cuts." *New York Times,* 24 September.

————. 1992. "Top congressman seeks deeper cuts in military budget." *New York Times,* 23 February.

U.S. Congress. 1991. *Budget process law annotated.* Washington, D.C.: Government Printing Office.

U.S. Congress. House. 1991. *United States–Canada Free-Trade Agreement biennial report.* Washington, D.C.: Government Printing Office.

U.S. Congress. House. Commission on Administrative Review (Obey Commission). 1977. *Final report.* 95th Cong., 1st sess., H. Doc. 272.

U.S. Congress. House. Committee on Foreign Affairs. 1971. *Rules of the Committee on Foreign Affairs.* Washington, D.C.: Government Printing Office.

————. 1973. *Rules of the Committee on Foreign Affairs.* Washington, D.C.: Government Printing Office.

————. 1985. *Survey of activities, 98th Congress.* Washington, D.C.: Government Printing Office.

————. 1988. *Required reports to Congress on foreign policy.* Washington, D.C.: Government Printing Office.

————. 1989a. *Congress and foreign policy, 1988.* Washington, D.C.: Government Printing Office.

————. 1989b. *Report of the task force on foreign assistance.* Washington, D.C.: Government Printing Office.

————. 1990. *Historical review of 95th–101st Congresses: Distinguished visitors and delegations received.* Washington, D.C.: Government Printing Office.

————. 1991. *Rules of the Committee on Foreign Affairs.* Washington, D.C.: Government Printing Office.

U.S. Congress. House. Committee on Ways and Means. 1973. *Report on the Trade Reform Act of 1974 to accompany H.R. 10710.* 93d Cong., 1st sess., H. Rept. 571.

U.S. Congress. Joint Committee on Printing. 1991. *1991–92 congressional directory.* Washington, D.C.: Government Printing Office.

U.S. Congress. Senate. Committee on Finance. 1974. *Trade Reform Act of 1974.* 93d Cong., 2d sess., S. Rept. 1298.

————. 1986. *Proposed negotiations of the United States–Canada Free-Trade Agreement.* 99th Cong., 2d sess., S. Hrg. 743.

————. 1988. *Approving and implementing the United States–Canada Free-Trade Agreement.* 100th Cong., 2d sess., S. Rept. 509.

U.S. Congress. Senate. Committee on Foreign Relations. 1986. *170th anniversary, 1816–1986.* Washington, D.C.: Government Printing Office.

————. 1991a. *Legislative activities report of the Committee on Foreign Relations.* 102d Cong., 1st sess., S. Rept. 30.

————. 1991b. *Rules of the Committee on Foreign Relations.* Washington, D.C.: Government Printing Office.

U.S. Executive Office of the President. 1986. *Public papers of the president of the United States: The administration of Ronald Reagan.* Washington, D.C.: Government Printing Office.

Urquhart, John. 1991. "Canada to end lumber pact with US: 1980s' trade dispute may be rekindled." *Wall Street Journal,* 14 September.

Uslaner, Eric. 1991. "A Tower of Babel on foreign policy?" In *Interest group politics,* 3d ed., ed. Allan J. Cigler and Burdett A. Loomis. Washington, D.C.: CQ Press.

VanDoren, Peter M. 1990. "Can we learn the causes of congressional decisions from roll-call data?" *Legislative Studies Quarterly* 15:311–40.

Vogler, David J., and Sidney R. Waldman. 1985. *Congress and democracy.* Washington, D.C.: CQ Press.

Waller, Douglas. 1987. *Congress and the nuclear freeze: An inside look at the politics of a mass movement.* Amherst: Univ. of Massachusetts Press.

Warrock, Anna M., and Howard Husock. 1988. "Taking Toshiba public." Case C15-88-858.0, Harvard University, John F. Kennedy School of Government.

Watanabe, Paul Y. 1984. *Ethnic groups, Congress, and American foreign policy.* Westport, Conn.: Greenwood.

Weingast, Barry R. 1984. "The Congressional bureaucratic system: A principle-agent perspective." *Public Choice* 41:147–91.

Weisman, Steven R. 1990. "Japan defends aid in Mideast effort." *New York Times,* 15 September.

Weissberg, Robert. 1979. "Assessing legislator-constituency policy agreement." *Legislative Studies Quarterly* 4:605–22.

Whalen, Charles, Jr. 1982. *The House and foreign policy: The irony of reform.* Chapel Hill: Univ. of North Carolina Press.

White, Leonard D. 1948. *The Federalists: A study in administrative history.* New York: Macmillan.

Whittle, Richard. 1981. "Foreign Relations Committee searches for renewed glory." *Congressional Quarterly Weekly Report* 39:477–79.

Wiarda, Howard J. 1990. *Foreign policy without illusion: How foreign policy-making works and fails to work in the United States.* Glenview, Ill.: Scott, Foresman/Little, Brown.

Wildavsky, Aaron. 1966. "The two presidencies." *Trans-Action* 4:7–14.

Wilson, George C. 1989. "Aspin, contractors trying to save defense budget." *Washington Post,* 15 June.

Wilson, James Q. 1973. *Political organizations.* New York: Basic Books.

Wines, Michael. 1992. "Bush and Rio." *New York Times,* 11 June.

Wittkopf, Eugene R., and James M. McCormick. 1990. "The cold war consensus: Did it exist?" *Polity* 22:627–53.

Woodward, Bob. 1987. *Veil: The secret wars of the CIA, 1981–1987.* New York: Simon and Schuster.

Wright, Gerald C., Jr. 1978. "Candidates' policy positions and voting in U.S. congressional elections." *Legislative Studies Quarterly* 3:445–64.

———. 1989. "Policy voting in the U.S. Senate: Who is represented?" *Legislative Studies Quarterly* 14:465–86.

Wright, Karen. 1991. "Heating the global warming debate." *New York Times Magazine,* 3 February.

Yanarella, Ernest J. 1977. *The missile defense controversy: Strategy, technology, and politics, 1955–1972.* Lexington: Univ. of Kentucky Press.

Yoffie, David B. 1989. "American trade policy: An obsolete bargain?" In *Can the government govern?,* ed. John E. Chubb and Paul E. Peterson. Washington, D.C.: Brookings Institution.

Contributors

James M. Lindsay is Associate Professor of Political Science at the University of Iowa.

Randall B. Ripley is Professor of Political Science and Dean of the College of Social and Behavioral Sciences at Ohio State University.

Lance T. LeLoup is Director of the Public Policy Research Centers and Professor of Political Science at the University of Missouri—St. Louis.

Eileen Burgin is Assistant Professor of Political Science at the University of Vermont.

John T. Tierney is Professor of Political Science at Boston College.

James M. McCormick is Professor of Political Science at Iowa State University.

Christopher J. Deering is Associate Professor of Political Science and Associate Dean of Arts and Sciences at George Washington University.

Joseph White is a Research Associate in the Governmental Studies program at the Brookings Institution.

Barbara Sinclair is Professor of Political Science at the University of California—Riverside.

Paul N. Stockton is Assistant Professor of National Security Affairs at the Naval Postgraduate School in Monterey, California.

Sharyn O'Halloran is Assistant Professor of Public Affairs and Political Science in the School of International and Public Affairs at Columbia University.

Index